STORYTELLING IN NORTHERN ZAMBIA

Man playing the *banjo*, Kaputa (northern Zambia), 1976. Photo by Robert Cancel

World Oral Literature Series: Volume 3

Storytelling in Northern Zambia:
Theory, Method, Practice and Other Necessary Fictions

Robert Cancel

http://www.openbookpublishers.com

© 2013 Robert Cancel. Foreword © 2013 Mark Turin.

This book is licensed under a Creative Commons Attribution 3.0 Unported license (CC-BY 3.0). This license allows you to share, copy, distribute and transmit the work; to adapt the work and to make commercial use of the work providing attribution is made the respective authors (but not in any way that suggests that they endorse you or your use of the work). Further details available at http://creativecommons.org/licenses/by/3.0/

Attribution should include the following information:
   Cancel, Robert. *Storytelling in Northern Zambia: Theory, Method, Practice and Other Necessary Fictions*. Cambridge, UK: Open Book Publishers, 2013.

This is the third volume in the World Oral Literature Series, published in association with the World Oral Literature Project.

   World Oral Literature Series: ISSN: 2050-7933

Digital material and resources associated with this volume are hosted by the World Oral Literature Project (http://www.oralliterature.org/collections/rcancel001.html) and Open Book Publishers (http://www.openbookpublishers.com/isbn/9781909254596).

   ISBN Hardback: 978-1-909254-60-2
   ISBN Paperback: 978-1-909254-59-6
   ISBN Digital (PDF): 978-1-909254-61-9
   ISBN Digital ebook (epub): 978-1-909254-62-6
   ISBN Digital ebook (mobi): 978-1-909254-63-3
   DOI: 10.11647/OBP.0033

Cover image: Mr. Chishele Chuulu explains the meaning of some royal implements at the court of Tabwa Chief Kaputa (1983). Photo by Robert Cancel.

All paper used by Open Book Publishers is SFI (Sustainable Forestry Initiative), and PEFC (Programme for the Endorsement of Forest Certification Schemes) Certified.

Printed in the United Kingdom and United States by Lightning Source for Open Book Publishers (Cambridge, UK).

*For Margaret and Avelino Cancel, Helen and Jack Finnigan,
Paul Nsama, Anna Chilombo, Viv Shone, Stanley Kalumba,
Booker Kapapula, Paul Chisakula, William Musonda and Rabbon Chola*

Ancestors all.

Contents

Audio-Visual Resources		ix
Acknowledgements		xiii
Foreword		xvii
Mark Turin		
I.	Writing Oral Narrative: The Role and Description of Self in Recording Living Traditions	1
II.	The Tabwa Context: Mature Shifting of Frames and Adolescent Assertion	31
III.	Chiefs, Tricksters and Christians: Bemba Tales and Lessons	75
IV.	Bisa Storytelling: The Politics of Hunting, Beer-Drinks, and Elvis	123
V.	Telling Tales While Keeping Secrets: Two Lunda Storytelling Sessions	165
VI.	Stories on Demand: A Performance Session Among the Bwile	211
VII.	Conclusion: Lessons from Frozen Moments	247
Works cited		261
Index		271

Audio-Visual Resources

This book draws upon the digital archive of videos and audio recordings collected by Robert Cancel during his research trips to Zambia during 1988-1989 and 2005. Recordings of thirty-nine of the oral narratives transcribed in this book are freely available on-line. In order to access these recordings you can follow the links given below and at the bottom of the relevant pages. Alternatively, you can scan the QR code which appears alongside each story. If you are reading this book in a digital format you may need to enlarge the QR code in order to scan it.

Tabwa Storytelling 1 (120 MB)
    http://dx.doi.org/10.11647/OBP.0033.02/Tabwa1   45

Tabwa Storytelling 2 (162 MB)
    http://dx.doi.org/10.11647/OBP.0033.02/Tabwa2   47

Tabwa Storytelling 3 (184 MB)
    http://dx.doi.org/10.11647/OBP.0033.02/Tabwa3   61

Tabwa Storytelling 4 (39.4 MB)
    http://dx.doi.org/10.11647/OBP.0033.02/Tabwa4   67

Bemba Storytelling 1 (48.9 MB)
    http://dx.doi.org/10.11647/OBP.0033.03/Bemba1   77

Bemba Storytelling 2 (71.7 MB)
    http://dx.doi.org/10.11647/OBP.0033.03/Bemba2   80

Bemba Storytelling 3 (52.6 MB)
    http://dx.doi.org/10.11647/OBP.0033.03/Bemba3   84

Bemba Storytelling 4 (61.8 MB)
    http://dx.doi.org/10.11647/OBP.0033.03/Bemba4   88

Bemba Storytelling 5 (42.6 MB)
    http://dx.doi.org/10.11647/OBP.0033.03/Bemba5   93
Bemba Storytelling 6 (91.2 MB)
    http://dx.doi.org/10.11647/OBP.0033.03/Bemba6   96
Bemba Storytelling 7 (133 MB)
    http://dx.doi.org/10.11647/OBP.0033.03/Bemba7   102
Bemba Storytelling 8 (108 MB)
    http://dx.doi.org/10.11647/OBP.0033.03/Bemba8   111
Bemba Storytelling 9 (153 MB)
    http://dx.doi.org/10.11647/OBP.0033.03/Bemba9   114
Bisa Storytelling 1 (162 MB)
    http://dx.doi.org/10.11647/OBP.0033.04/Bisa1   130
Bisa Storytelling 2 (68.4 MB)
    http://dx.doi.org/10.11647/OBP.0033.04/Bisa2   136
Bisa Storytelling 3 (49.9 MB)
    http://dx.doi.org/10.11647/OBP.0033.04/Bisa3   140
Bisa Storytelling 4 (84.6 MB)
    http://dx.doi.org/10.11647/OBP.0033.04/Bisa4   144
Bisa Storytelling 5 (148 MB)
    http://dx.doi.org/10.11647/OBP.0033.04/Bisa5   147
Bisa Storytelling 6 (86.4 MB)
    http://dx.doi.org/10.11647/OBP.0033.04/Bisa6   152
Bisa Storytelling 7 (27.9 MB)
    http://dx.doi.org/10.11647/OBP.0033.04/Bisa7   156
Lunda Storytelling 1 and 2 (110 MB)
    http://dx.doi.org/10.11647/OBP.0033.05/Lunda1   168
Lunda Storytelling 3 (121 MB)
    http://dx.doi.org/10.11647/OBP.0033.05/Lunda3   171
Lunda Storytelling 4 (30 MB)
    http://dx.doi.org/10.11647/OBP.0033.05/Lunda4   174
Lunda Storytelling 5 (87.6 MB)
    http://dx.doi.org/10.11647/OBP.0033.05/Lunda5   176
Lunda Storytelling 6 (65.9 MB)
    http://dx.doi.org/10.11647/OBP.0033.05/Lunda6   178

Lunda Storytelling 7 (252 MB)	
http://dx.doi.org/10.11647/OBP.0033.05/Lunda7	182
Lunda Storytelling 8 (37 MB)	
http://dx.doi.org/10.11647/OBP.0033.05/Lunda8	192
Lunda Storytelling 9 (43.5 MB)	
http://dx.doi.org/10.11647/OBP.0033.05/Lunda9	194
Lunda Storytelling 10 (26.5 MB)	
http://dx.doi.org/10.11647/OBP.0033.05/Lunda10	196
Lunda Storytelling 11 (146 MB)	
http://dx.doi.org/10.11647/OBP.0033.05/Lunda11	198
Lunda Storytelling 12 (33.8 MB)	
http://dx.doi.org/10.11647/OBP.0033.05/Lunda12	201
Lunda Storytelling 13 (119 MB)	
http://dx.doi.org/10.11647/OBP.0033.05/Lunda13	202
Bwile Storytelling 1 (100 MB)	
http://dx.doi.org/10.11647/OBP.0033.06/Bwile1	214
Bwile Storytelling 2 (37 MB)	
http://dx.doi.org/10.11647/OBP.0033.06/Bwile2	217
Bwile Storytelling 3 (205 MB)	
http://dx.doi.org/10.11647/OBP.0033.06/Bwile3	218
Bwile Storytelling 4 (121 MB)	
http://dx.doi.org/10.11647/OBP.0033.06/Bwile4	224
Bwile Storytelling 5 (125 MB)	
http://dx.doi.org/10.11647/OBP.0033.06/Bwile5	228
Bwile Storytelling 6 (143 MB)	
http://dx.doi.org/10.11647/OBP.0033.06/Bwile6	233

For additional resources, and for information on downloading a QR code scanner, visit our web-site: http://www.openbookpublishers.com/product/137

Acknowledgements

This has been a project of such long duration that it is difficult to properly recall and identify all the people who have in some way contributed to its realization. Obviously, most heartfelt gratitude goes to the many performers who gave their time and considerable talents to the narratives discussed in this book. Many of them have since died and I can only hope that they are represented here in ways that both accurately reflect their performances and honor their memory.

People who have provided aid and comfort in Zambia are, again, too numerous to realistically list here. Among the Tabwa people, Chiefs Mukupa Katandula, Nsama and Kaputa all graciously supported my efforts and granted me access to their respective territories. Local friends and contacts included Paul Nsama, Rabbon Chola, Jameson Mpundu, and William Musonda. Work among the Bemba was greatly facilitated by Paramount Chief Chitimukulu Mutale Chitapankwa, Stephen Komakoma and Father Michel Genelot. At Ilondola in 2005, a small group of Catholic priests and brothers of the Missionaries of Africa (formerly the White Fathers) provided a great deal of assistance to me during my stay at the Bemba language center, as did my tutor Evans Bwalya. Collection and the ongoing analysis of material from the Bisa in Nabwalya was made possible by Stuart Marks and Kangwa Samson. My work in the village of Puta among the Bwile was facilitated directly by Chief Puta Kasoma and, many years later, by the current Chief Puta and his two councilors, T.D. Koti and Ferry Chansa. In the Lunda region, two, then, graduate students, Anthony Kafimbwa and Samuel Ng'andwe provided valuable introductions to local verbal artists, while in 2005 Job Kachingwe aided in providing background on the performers and interpreting themes of the narratives collected in 1989.

Zambian friends and colleagues at the University of Zambia have provided logistical, intellectual and moral support for this project.

Old friends Professor Mwelwa Musambachime, his wife Phoebe, Dr. Moses Musonda and Dr. Mwesa Mapoma were invaluable in sharing their knowledge of the Bemba-speaking societies covered in this work. Colleagues and some students in the Department of Literature and Languages at UNZA provided a sounding board for my ideas and were also supportive of my teaching efforts during the 1988–89 academic year. Administrators at UNZA and the Institute for African Studies, including Professor Robert Serpell, Dr. Steven P.C. Moyo, Dr. Jacob Mwanza and Mrs. Ilse Mwanza continually provided material and intellectual support to this project. While numerous Zambian colleagues contributed to the transcription, translation and analytical efforts of this study, special thanks are due to Mr. Dickson Chishimba Nkosha who very quickly meshed his translation skills with my own style so that he seamlessly worked over and improved my initial efforts as well as transcribing and translating a few narrative texts on his own. Here in San Diego, our great friend Mrs. Josephine Mabula Huckabay supplied a convenient and always sensitive source of transcription and translation assistance for a number of narrative performances. In Lusaka, Dr. Joseph Mwenya Mwansa, newly returned from his doctoral studies abroad, made some last revisions on one or two narrative translations that I had been trying to finish.

Sincere appreciation must be expressed for the institutional and financial assistance that made the project possible. CIES Fulbright provided a lecturing/research award for the 1988–89 year in which these performances were collected. US Embassy staff in Lusaka were supportive in many ways, and these included T.J. Dowling and Ambassador Jeffrey Davidow. The University of Zambia provided housing and official affiliation status to ease our time in and out of Lusaka. The University of California, San Diego has generously supported this project with a number of research and equipment grants over the last twenty years. Specifically, the Dean of Arts and Humanities, Stanley Chodorow and the former Provost of Muir College John Stewart, provided funds to purchase a vehicle in 1988. Cecil Lytle, former Provost of Thurgood Marshall College more than once contributed financially to stages of this research. The UCSD Department of Literature has been steady in its financial support, including equipment, travel funds and regularly granting leave and sabbatical time to sustain my research. Moreover, the UCSD Geisel Library has nearly completed the digitalization of over thirty years of my Zambian research material (audio, video, text and slides) and the physical archiving of the original data. Special thanks must go to library staffers Vickie O'Riordon, Larry Andrews, Reid Otsuji and Cathy Li. The UCSD Media Center has always been ready to assist me in technical matters and former Director Sherman George and engineers Jim Smith and Bill Campagna have been particularly supportive of my work.

Our three month stay in Kasama in Northern Province in 1989 would not have been nearly so comfortable or successful without the unstinting hospitality of Viv and Brigitte Shone. In Mansa, Booker Kapapula and his family gave their time and hospitality to me and my family over many years. Numerous school teachers and head masters assisted us with accommodation during short stays at Mukupa Katandula, Mbereshi, and Kasongole. Four different groups of Dutch medical volunteers living in Kaputa graciously provided accommodation on numerous occasions. Officers of the government Fisheries helped us with housing and transportation in Nsama, Sumbu and Mukupa Katandula.

Colleagues who have read and offered suggestions on early drafts of this project include David Westley, Allen Roberts and, especially, Kenneth Harrow, Stuart Marks and Stephen Belcher. At Open Book Publishers, Alessandra Tosi has been unstinting in her enthusiasm and support for completion of the manuscript. Similarly, Mark Turin at the World Oral Literature Project generously encouraged me and facilitated the use of their site to make available the initial video recordings of the narrative performances examined in this study. Finally, my work and life overall have been sustained and enriched by my wife Donna Cancel and our sons and their families.

Foreword

Mark Turin

It is surprisingly difficult to tell a good story about storytelling. It is harder still to make the storytellers themselves come alive, helping their in situ oral performances flourish in text on a printed page. Robert Cancel achieves both of these goals, and more still. Storytelling in Northern Zambia is a masterful book in which Cancel grapples with collection, representation and fieldwork ethics, and a work that showcases the agency of his interlocutors.

At the centre of the monograph are the performers of specific oral narratives. Through a powerful repositioning that highlights the agency of these narrators, the author acknowledges common pitfalls when writing about fieldwork: "the more I wrote and translated, the more obscure the conditions of research and the contexts of the performances became."

Through such reclamation, Cancel brings the documentary moment of gathering to the fore—'capture', as he calls it. Performance and collection become rooted in actual historical moments, replete with agendas, attitudes, histories and doubts. But just as Cancel 'captures' Zambian worlds on his recording device and through his writing, he too has been captured by the performers for their own ends. This re-capture is not cause for concern, but rather a first step in the rebalancing of traditionally lopsided power relationships. "Capture, if we are doing what we should be doing, is inevitable," Cancel concludes.

Throughout the book, the author reflects with candour on his own position in the text and context. "My role," Cancel suggests, "was primarily as an instigator, secondarily as a recorder." At points he even portrays himself as "a simple functionary [...] there to record whatever people chose to do." Ever cautious and tentative in his own analysis, and mindful of "assertive interpretations based on incomplete or superficial data [that] only risk instances of essentialism," Cancel is insightful and compassionate throughout.

The author describes the subtitle of his book as ironic—Theory, Method, Practice and Other Necessary Fictions—but it underlies a more serious point. Our scholarly frames of reference and our work practices need to be communicated transparently, both so that the voices of our research partners can be heard and to allow our colleagues and students to know more about the techniques of our work. Invoking anthropologist Michael Jackson, Cancel describes his study as one that emphasises storytelling over stories, with a focus on the "social process rather than the narrative activity" itself. In keeping with the shifting analytical frames he consistently employs, Cancel adds that he has also "kept the tales themselves in close focus, since these are indeed the products created by the storytellers."

Cancel has crafted a sophisticated narrative about narration without lapsing into simply descriptivism or journalistic asides. His lasting lesson to the reader is "that people are not necessarily their performed stories—though in many ways they are "performing" themselves—and their lives do not begin and end when I arrive then leave." Storytelling in Northern Zambia is a singular achievement, laying bare the complex realities of fieldwork. It is an excellent addition to the World Oral Literature Series with our committed partners at Open Book.

New Haven, Connecticut
May 2013

I. Writing Oral Narrative: The Role of Description and Self in Recording Living Traditions

> Lukhero's essay forcefully raises the question of the extent to which ethnographers, and in particular indigenous ethnographers, can gain access to the sentiments of the people they study without being captured by them. This empirical question is perhaps not as important as the disciplinary query: should the committed ethnographer solicit capture or try to avoid it?
>
> J.A. Barnes, 1999/2000, cited in Schumaker, p. 259

At around the time I was finishing a monograph on the fictional oral narratives of the Tabwa people of Zambia, a number of doubts and questions that had been only touched on in that project reemerged to occupy my thinking.[1] At the base of these preoccupations was the problem of ethnographic authority as it has been debated over the last three or four decades. Questions of power, neocolonialism, inscription, and effacement—in the poststructuralist sense—forced me to reconsider the confusing and ambiguous experience of field research and the ways we represent it to others.[2] In particular, how can we preserve or at least frame the agency of the performers who contribute their artistry and self-assertion to our

---

1 See Cancel 1989.
2 As Jackson notes, it is important to "throw light on the anthropological project, for in both cases [of the dialectic between private and public performance] an interplay is implied between authorship and authority, and the knower and the known." (Jackson 2006, p. 292).

DOI: 10.11647/OBP.0033.01

work? In a related disciplinary question, I was not willing to carry out a purely "literary" analysis that considered mostly formal and thematic elements while playing down the living context of the storytelling sessions I had recorded. Yet, again coming back to the contextual or ethnographic dimension of the research, it was difficult to gauge exactly how much truly accurate information I could provide to the overall analysis.[3]

I will interrogate some ideas in the ongoing ethnographic/critical debate, and then suggest some strategies of description that will lead to a clearer, if not necessarily a deeper, understanding of the collection of story-performances in my fieldwork and, in particular, the narratives contained in the chapters that follow. There are many ways to go at the dynamics of living performances and these cross a number of scholarly disciplines. No one approach is entirely satisfying and any combination of methods can be both convincing and raise questions about their efficacy at the same time. I will selectively employ methods that grow out of ethnography, folklore, performance studies, literary studies and discourse analysis; ultimately using one or a combination of these as dictated by the specific situations of performance context. If there is a central concern in this project, it is to represent the storytellers who provided me material in as honest and evocative a manner as possible. "Analysis" will grow out of this concern and always return to the living situations and contexts of the field work's recordings.

Ethnographic Authority and Power

For over thirty years anthropologists, partly drawing on postcolonial and poststructuralist discourses, have been conducting a fairly radical reexamination of fieldwork and the ways it is transformed for publication. The scholars involved in this discussion are numerous, but we can profitably look at one of the more interesting discussions focusing on the historicizing of ethnographic theory and method. One of the earlier primary spurs of this discussion is Bronislaw Malinowski's field diary, published posthumously in 1967.[4] It is a fascinating work. The reader is exposed to the heretofore

---

3 Johannes Fabian identifies my concerns and intentions by wryly positing the scholarly genre of "the second book" wherein the researcher "having already fulfilled the academic obligation to publish his or her dissertation research in monograph form, now feels compelled (and free) to reflect on what that project was really about." (2008, p. 136)
4 Malinowski 1967.

rare personal field insights of a seminal figure in ethnographic research. The loneliness, isolation, and periodic outbursts of xenophobia of the individual working in an alien culture are not only very human responses to the situation but also engender an intense familiarity for many who have worked in similar circumstances.

Moreover, we have evidence that Malinowski was aided by the conditions that promote the kind of research and scholarship that James Clifford, in his study of the work of Marcel Griaule, calls "ethnographic liberalism."[5] This process is framed by underlying colonial, religious or political power that allows the foreigner to move pretty much unimpeded through the area of study, empowered by the same forces that keep the local people under foreign or at least distant hegemony. From this rather privileged position, the ethnographer will often speak out against the oppressiveness of the colonial/national power structure that seeks to entrap, debilitate, or deculturate local societies. The ethnographer sees his or her efforts as something opposed, or at least not connected, to elements of that imposed hegemony. "We" — and I mean this is what I thought in 1976 — are living with the local people and recording their culture in order that they have representation on the national and international level. Claims are often made for getting to "know" the other in unprecedented and unique depth through the tried and true forms of participant observation. The form of this representation will, naturally, be our unbiased, positive reporting of these ancient traditions and intricate art forms.[6]

---

5   See Clifford 1983, p. 142. This insightful and thorough reading of Griaule's work sets it into a clear historical frame. Part of the study considers another French anthropologist, Griaule's contemporary and colleague, Michel Leiris, whose approach tended to move away from Griaule's certainty to throwing doubt on the concept of truly knowing another culture. "Griaule's energetic confidence in cultural representation could not be farther from Leiris' tortured, lucid uncertainty. The two positions mark off the predicament of a post-colonial ethnography. Some authorizing fiction of "authentic encounter," in Geertz's phrase seems a prerequisite for intensive research. But initiatory claims to speak as a knowledgeable insider revealing essential cultural truths are no longer credible." (p. 152)

6   When I was writing my dissertation on Tabwa oral narratives, I was both brought up short and also inspired by Ngugi wa Thiong'o's opening observations in his literary study *Homecoming: Essays on African and Caribbean Literature and Politics*. In his Author's Note, Ngugi warned against what Jomo Kenyatta had described as "professional friends and interpreters of the African...[who] have the arrogance of assuming they have more and closer natural ties to Africa than have Africans in the West Indies and in America. It is such people who acquire a most proprietorial air when talking of the part of Africa they have happened to visit; they carve a personal sphere of influence and champion the most reactionary and most separatist cause of whichever group among whom they happen to live. They are again the most vehement in pointing out the unique intelligence,

The intervening years have seen a revision in my thinking, as not only humanistic but also social science writings have come to be seen as so many historically situated texts; texts that have specific points of view and particular ways of presenting material knowledge.[7] Questions of self and other, subject and object have been incorporated with historical perspectives that allow us to see such writing in context, as texts within larger frameworks and discourses. These concerns allow anthropologists, for example, to critically evaluate their methods and theories in a reflexive manner. History, language, power and empowerment are forces that suffuse ethnography of all types, despite particular methodological differences. One fascinating frame for these explorations is the first volume of the series "The History of Anthropology," entitled *Observers Observed: Essays on Ethnographic Fieldwork*, edited by George W. Stocking, Jr. (1983). Almost every chapter resounds with revealing information about famous fieldworkers—Franz Boas, Griaule and Malinowski, for example—and their projects, often using original field notes or early publications supplemented by the historical and contextual commentary of current critical scholarship. What I see, more than anything else, is the essentially literary core of the original writing. As Geertz and Clifford both suggest, we are actually reading/writing elaborated fictions, fictions that are, to be sure, new and eclectic in their generic make-up, but fictions, "not necessarily falsehoods," nonetheless. And, as Geertz emphasized, these are necessary fictions, for how else can we propose to do the near-impossible and write in any substantial way about cultures that are not our own?[8]

Troubled by just such concerns, anthropologist Michael Jackson followed two major monographs on the Kuranko people of Sierra Leone with a book he designates "an ethnographic novel," *Barawa and the Ways Birds Fly in the Sky* (Jackson 1986). Jackson, elsewhere, says of the book that it was "a point of no return, and of disenchantment. It ends at the edge of the sea: an ethnographer, unsure of his direction and identity, walking along the tide-line, looking down at a film of water that reflects 'pale grey

---

amiability and quick wit of their adopted areas and groups." (Ngugi wa Thiong'o 1972, p. xviii)

7 An important contribution to this reevaluation is Clifford and Marcus 1986.
8 Clifford, in his 1983 piece on Marcel Giraule, cites Geertz's 1968 essay on "Thinking as a moral act...": "Usually the sense of being members, however temporarily, insecurely and incompletely, of a single moral community, can be maintained even in the face of the wider social realities which press in at almost every moment to deny it. It is this fiction—fiction not falsehood—that lies at the very heart of successful anthropological field research..." (Geertz 1968, p. 154)

clouds in a cocoa-coloured sky.'" (Jackson 1989, p. 1) In this extraordinary experiment, Jackson is able to say and do things that cross literary/disciplinary boundaries. He is able to act as an historian collating and telescoping details of the African and European explorer past, as well as weaving in family histories of his Kuranko associates to evoke the history and culture of a specific region and people. Further, he places himself in the narrative in both the third and first person, including elements of fieldwork in their profound lunacy as well as moments of gratifying insight and beauty, the various situations whereby the ethnographer is both the used and the user. His ethnographer—himself—ends the book with what most honest researchers experience, a combination of accomplishment and questions, of connectedness to local friends and a realization that those friends comprise only a small part of a much larger, more complex reality. Whose side are we on? Who has "captured" us? What is the significance of such designations?

Jackson has authored at least three sets of essays that explore these questions in a more scholarly framework. While I cannot say I enjoyed these latter observations as much as the ethnographic novel, these at least have the advantage of spelling out his concerns in a prescriptive and thereby more replicable, theoretical manner. In *Paths Toward a Clearing* he describes and employs the elements of the book's subtitle: *Radical Empiricism and Ethnographic Inquiry* (1989). In most of the essays, the author explores various levels and entities of Kuranko society using both written and observed sources. He does not hesitate to use personal, what we might call subjective, evidence to make his points, as he employs a good deal of biographical and autobiographical material. The result is a picture of a living and breathing society, one that is every bit as knowable and confusing as our own. One of the more interesting ideas Jackson puts forth is the efficacy of an existential model for understanding Kuranko social and self-images. Jackson is less concerned with proving one idea over another than emphasizing the plural and pluralistic qualities of Kuranko society, and how these extend into what had hitherto been considered static and proven social "facts." It is also a welcome departure from older models of dominant or unyielding "tradition," built on narrow notions of ritual, religion and kinship. He takes these ideas further in *Existential Anthropology: Events, Exigencies and Effects* (2005), wherein he asserts, beyond the Sartrean notion

> ...so often associated with existentialism, that our humanity consists in our individual will-to-be, a striving for self-realisation or authenticity, for most human action is less a product of intellectual deliberation and conscious

choice than a matter of continual, intuitive, and opportunistic changes of course—a 'cybernetic' switching between alternatives that promise more or less satisfactory solutions to the ever-changing situations at hand. (p. xii)

Jackson focuses on notions of intersubjectivity and reciprocity to guide his analyses of cultural and social behaviors in a number of societies and, by definition, the terms tend toward an analytical approach that utilizes continual shifting and recontextualizing of primary data.

I would further go along with another of Jackson's assessments (1989) that seeing ethnography as only an elaborate literary genre tends to place too narrow an emphasis on the discipline as art form rather than social science.[9] It is much more helpful to consider a balance of approaches that places the elements of ethnographer, "other," location, and time into a flexible frame. Such a frame would allow for provisional statements of analogy as well as the understanding that such comparisons and contrasts are often based on frozen moments in time that reflect certain ideas, perhaps certain individuals, and not necessarily entire societies or "realities." Geertz locates two opposed but complementary approaches to ethnographic research, grounded in the kinds of writing that present the findings of the anthropologists Claude Lévi-Strauss and Malinowski. Lévi-Strauss has always had a strong inclination to look beyond surface, or even below underlying, cultural data to deeper systemic interpretations of human social order: "… Lévi-Strauss argues that the sort of immediate, in person 'being there' one associates with the bulk of recent American and British anthropology is essentially impossible: it is either outright fraud or fatuous self-deception" (Geertz 1988, p. 46). The other side of this assertion is that "being there" does engender positive, accurate interactions of observation, participation and, significantly, exchange and dialogue.

---

9 Burawoy 2003 probably states an extreme version of the critique of Geertz's reflexive/discourse approach, "In his hands ethnography becomes a mesmeric play of texts upon texts, narratives within narratives. By the end of its cultural turn, anthropology has lost its distinctive identity, having decentered its techniques of field work, sacrificed the idea of intensively studying a 'site,' abandoned its theoretical traditions, and forsaken its pursuit of causal explanation. Theory and history evaporate in a welter of discourse. Anyone with literary ambition can now assume the anthropological mantle, making the disrupted discipline vulnerable to cavalier invasion by natives and imposters. Once a social science, anthropology aspires to become an appendage of the humanities." (p. 674)

Africans "Write Back"

> Next day the anthropologist began taking down the words of informants sent by Saif....Shrobenius's head teemed with ideas. Reeling off spirituality by the yard, the men paced the courtyard with anxious, knit brows....Saif made up stories and the interpreter translated, Madoubo repeated in French, refining the subtleties to the delight of Shrobenius, that human crayfish afflicted with a groping mania for resuscitating an African universe — cultural autonomy, he called it — which had lost all living reality; dressed with the flashy elegance of a colonial on holiday, a great laughter, he was determined to find metaphysical meaning in everything, even in the shape of the palaver tree under which notables met to chat....African life, he held, was pure art, intense religious symbolism, and a civilization once grandiose — but alas a victim of the white man's vicissitudes. (Ouologuem 1971, pp. 87–88)[10]

Another important perspective is provided by some African scholars and artists on the findings of western anthropologists regarding African culture. Years before Geertz, Clifford and others began the deconstruction of heretofore standard ethnographic writing practice, Horace Miner published a satirical, though straight-faced essay in *American Anthropologist*, titled "Body Rituals Among the Nacerima" (1956). It is a classic cautionary piece on the power that vocabulary and frames of reference, i.e. discourse, can have on descriptions of other cultures. The above quote from Yambo Ouologuem's provocative novel *Bound to Violence* [*Le devoir de violence*], moves the focus beyond skeptical views of dominant discourses to the other side, the manipulation of ethnographic "data" by the local colonial subjects. That the process can work both ways must be, by this point in time, an accepted truism. It is also clear that African intellectuals have long been aware of the many ways their societies have been written by outside explorers, colonial officers, missionaries, social scientists, creative writers and, more recently, aid workers. Even people I encountered in rural villages were self-conscious, at least initially, about how photos I took of them might be received and interpreted by residents of *"Bulaya,"* the generic word for Europe and other lands of white people.

Ouologuem's book spans a long period, but the section I cited is set in the early 1900s, when the German anthropologist Fritz Shrobenius — a thinly veiled caricature of Leo Frobenius — arrives in the West African land of Nakem and begins to buy up "authentic" artifacts of local culture

---

10   Originally, *Le devoir de violence*, Yambo Ouologuem (Paris: Editions du Seuil, 1968), p. 102.

and aggressively elicit information about that society. While Ouologuem's intent here is wicked satire, there is also the irony that underlies it, which is that European ethnographic studies would serve as a source of information on "real" African culture for some of the brilliant black intellectuals who, in 1930s France, originated the revolutionary cultural movement called Négritude. Among others in that group, Léopold Sédar Senghor, the Senegalese poet and nationalist, used the images of African art found in Parisian museums and discourses of traditional cultures found in works of European social science to reconstruct an African past that he and his colleagues felt they had been denied by the deculturation processes of the colonizing mission.

In the mid 1930s, Kenyan nationalist and student, Johnstone Kamau, read anthropology at the London School of Economics under Malinowski. In 1938 he published his revised thesis as *Facing Mount Kenya*, under his new name, Jomo Kenyatta. Clearly, taking control of the ethnographic discourse of the time, forming the images of his own people, the Gikuyu, as he himself deemed proper, was an important step in Kenyatta's nationalist project. This kind of "writing back,"[11] would spur a new vision that was promulgated by postcolonial authors such as Chinua Achebe. In what many feel to be the seminal novel of modern anglophone African literature, Achebe brings the tragic story of the Igbo warrior Okonkwo to a bitter and ironic conclusion by switching narrative voice and point of view to the local British District Commissioner. In two paragraphs Achebe evokes a chilling and ominous premonition, whereby the D.C. seeks to encapsulate the epic story of this "native's" death into a single paragraph for the ethnography/administrative handbook he is writing, titled: *The Pacification of the Primitive Tribes of the Lower Niger*.[12] Reclaiming an authoritative voice in self-representation, then, remains an ongoing project for African writers and scholars.

In Zambia, in the Luapula Valley, Ian Cunnison's historical and ethnographic texts have been used to valorize local customs and political practices. More significantly, one of Cunnison's research assistants, Chileya J. Chiwale, went on to conduct his own research in Lunda culture and history, especially in the collection and analysis of praise poetry. Building on an earlier history produced by a committee of elders, under the auspices of the Lunda king, Mwata Kazembe XIV, and French Catholic

---

11 See Ashcroft, Griffiths and Tiffin 1989.
12 Achebe 1959.

Missionary Fr. Edouard Lebrecque,[13] Chiwale and Mwata Kazembe Munona Chinyanta XVIII collaborated on a study of Lunda customs and, in particular, the annual kingship festival, the Mutomboko.[14] Another long term research assistant at the Rhodes-Livingstone Institute—later changed to the Institute for African Studies—Matshakaza Blackson Lukhero, built on earlier work by European researchers and wrote studies of his own people, the Ngoni of Zambia. Like Chiwale, Lukhero had a hand in reviving and codifying an annual kingship rite, the Nc'wala.[15] In all these cases, local people have found textual models to either validate or rewrite for their own purposes. Zambian scholars have consciously set out to conduct their own forms of fieldwork and evaluations of older studies.[16] The work of all non-local, and even indigenous, scholars needs to be open to similar revision and reclamation, especially as it applies to such linguistically dense representations as oral literary traditions. Clearly, whatever I write about Bemba-language oral performances is in many ways preliminary, even considering the substantial degree of collaboration that I've sought in the process of transcription, translation and interpretation.[17]

---

13   See Kazembe and Labrecque 1951.
14   See Chinyanta and Chiwale 1989.
15   See Lukhero 1993.
16   An excellent example of local African scholars revising work done earlier by Europeans is Chipungu, ed., 1992. Zambian anthropologist Owen Sichone evocatively states one of the reasons for him choosing to become an anthropologist was his "dissatisfaction with the accounts of Zambian life that I read in the classic literature and a desire to rework them from a Zambian perspective." (Sichone 2001, p. 371)
17   Numerous African universities contain departments of Anthropology or Sociology staffed by western-trained anthropologists. There is no shortage of monographs and articles by African ethnographers. The point I want to make is that ethnographic discourse is contentious and the scope and intent of even indigenous scholars vary widely. Sichone notes, "Many African scholars dislike anthropology intensely. I have frequently heard many political scientists and economists insult each other by referring to aspects of their work as 'anthropological'. The tarnished reputation of the discipline is blamed on anthropology having participated in the imperial strategy of divide and rule. But was anthropology the handmaiden of imperialism in a way that geology, cartography and land surveying were not?" (Sichone 2001, p. 370) Some well known ethnographic monographs by African scholars include: Francis Mading Deng, *The Dinka of the Sudan* (1972); A.B.C. Ocholla-Ayayo, *Traditional Ideology and Ethics Among the Southern Luo* (1976); Philip O. Nsugbe, *Ohaffia: A Matrilineal Ibo People* (1974), etc. Bernard M. Magubane offers a well-known set of critiques of colonial social science practices and alternative African scholarly approaches that have been collected in a set of essays (2000).

Researching Oral Traditions (1976–77)

> Fieldwork, then, is a process of intersubjective construction of liminal modes of communication. Intersubjective means literally more than one subject, but being situated neither quite here nor quite there, the subjects involved do not share a common set of assumptions, experiences, or traditions. Their construction is a public process. ...That the communication was often painstaking and partial is an equally important theme. It is the dialectic between these poles, ever repeated, never quite the same, which constitutes fieldwork. (Rabinow 1977, p. 155)

When I began conducting research in Zambia in 1976, I was only vaguely aware of the unusually rich tradition of ethnographic and sociological studies in what used to be called Northern Rhodesia. While the history of this research is well documented, I want to briefly describe the framework of scholarship that evolved and how I came to interact with it. Although Zambia is not the only former colony to be well represented by a large corpus of ethnographic and historical social research, the creation of a formal institution for these endeavors suggests a deep commitment to such efforts by the colonial power. The Rhodes-Livingstone Institute came into being in the late 1930s. It both grew out of and was spurred on by the efforts of pioneering ethnographers such as Godfrey Wilson, Audrey Richards and Max Gluckman.[18] Following the Institute's establishment, a most impressive coterie of researchers would eventually produce numerous ground-breaking studies, creating a nearly unprecedented body of data and methodological practices, modeled on what was broadly identified as "British functionalism," that would serve future scholars in that and other regions of ethnographic endeavor.

Links to seminal thinkers of British social anthropology were prevalent among these scholars, many of whom were students of Malinowski and/ or A.R. Radcliffe-Brown. By the late 1940s, a strong link between the Institute and Manchester University grew into a continuous reciprocal flow of scholars and publishing opportunities. Some of the most influential and highly regarded book-length studies of the time appeared under the Manchester University Press/Rhodes-Livingstone Institute imprimatur, for this reason the authors of these monographs are collectively known as the "Mancester School". At independence, the name was changed from Rhodes-Livingstone to the Institute for African Studies, linked to the new University of Zambia. From its inception, directors of the Institute were

---

18 See Schumaker 2001.

themselves respected researchers who enabled affiliates in their projects, perpetuating a tradition of thorough and careful fieldwork. Consequently, there was a near industrial amount of scholarly production coming from the IAS in the 1950s through the early 1970s.[19]

From December 1975 until March 1977 I conducted research and field work in Zambia under the auspices of the Institute for African Studies. My initial exposure to the Institute was as a resident research affiliate, expected to take part in the intellectual and quotidian life at that location and on the campus of the University. Armed with a good deal of archival work, personal contacts, written government permission and ten weeks of intensive language study my wife and I began almost ten months of field work in three Tabwa villages. We were sanctioned by the government and university, and this allowed me to secure the help and cooperation of local government workers at schools, health clinics, fisheries, courts, game control, and agricultural stations. However, once "officially" situated, the work began with no guarantees that local people would help us in our endeavors to record storytelling traditions. In fact, it seemed most people were suspicious of us, not because of political relations with South Africa or Rhodesia,[20] but simply because we were strangers and did not fit the usual conceptions of what white people might be doing in the area. We were not missionaries, doctors or technical advisors. We did not have children, so some neighbors were not even convinced that we were really married; some thought we were brother and sister. Paul Rabinow discusses a similar situation in his memoir *Reflections on Fieldwork in Morocco* (1977):

> In fact, I was forcing my way into the village through my official connections. That was the only way that it could be done. Informing the officials had been

---

19 Moreover, the seminal early studies have led to a more recent secondary wave of revisionary work, treating the same areas and people that some of the more famous the Institute researchers had written about. For example, Audrey Richards' *Land, Labour and Diet: An Economic Study of the Bemba Tribe* (1939) has been revisited and recontextualized in Moore and Vaughan's *Cutting Down Trees: Gender, Nutrition and Agriculture in the Northern Province of Zambia, 1890–1990* (1994). Similar revision has been conducted on William Watson's socio-economic study *Tribal Cohesion in a Money Economy: A Study of the Mambwe People of Zambia* (1958) by Johan Pottier in *Migrants No More: Settlement and Survival in Mambwe Villages, Zambia* (1988).

20 From the end of the 1960s to the late 1980s, Zambia was frequently under a state of emergency because of its involvement as a "Frontline State" in the wars of liberation in Rhodesia (Zimbabwe), Southwest Africa (Namibia), Angola, Mozambique and, finally, South Africa. Security concerns often focused on foreigners, especially whites, who stood out so obviously. See Molteno 1979 for what was at the time a common opinion of the US role in the region and the suspicions brought to bear on foreign, especially American, academics and researchers.

unavoidable, but their approval had made the affair a dangerous one from the villagers' perspective. To think that these rural countrymen should have accepted my proposal at face value and graciously granted it in the spirit of mutual respect between cultures is absurd. Why, the villagers asked, should a rich American want to move into a poor rural village and live by himself in a mud house when he could be living in a villa in Sefrou? Why us? Why get ourselves into a situation where the government holds us jointly responsible for this stranger? What's in it for us? The risks are all too evident. (pp. 77–78)

Our initial contacts and early friends and neighbors were educated Zambians of one type or another: the local school teachers, the local health clinic workers, people who worked for the government fisheries, the court clerk, and the Rural Council postman. All spoke at least some English and all had some prior experience with "Europeans." Because these people, often not from this particular area or not even native speakers, all spoke Bemba with much greater facility than either my wife or I, they served as initial bridges to the local people. They provided introductions or explained our presence there. In fact, the original idea of settling in Mukupa Katandula came from a Scots Catholic White Father who worked in the district. He felt the village was the most remote of the three Tabwa chiefs' courts and therefore was, by his thinking and mine at the time, more "traditional." It was also his early intervention that spurred the village authorities to approve our stay and help to find us a government house that was at the time unoccupied.

My first efforts to tape record storytellers were characterized by uneven and at times inadequate language skills. As I struggled to transcribe the material, I began enlisting the help of several local schoolboys. They became another inroad to village residents. After a while, for their own reasons, people decided to get involved with our efforts to record stories, and I had a fairly steady stream of storytellers to work with. We established a method of compensation that involved the giving of gifts over time, rather than a simple "payment" for stories told. Although I still felt deep down, in retrospect quite naively, that the stories should be freely provided in the spirit of scholarly cooperation, the preservation of vital traditions, and the avoidance of commercialization or commodification of these verbal arts, it became clear that the exchange of gifts or services was one of the most common ways to establish relationships between people. In fact, what I was doing was forming ties that, over the years, have proven to be both personally gratifying and professionally invaluable.

As the year progressed, and we moved to the two other main villages of the Tabwa chiefs, Kaputa and Nsama, our language skills improved dramatically and we were able to conduct everyday interactions much more effectively. The initial uncertainty and self-consciousness over being the center of attention wherever we walked, of being stared at constantly, of frustrations over not understanding what people were saying or knowing how to express ourselves had faded into a more comfortable and secure situation. We progressively came to know and interact with our neighbors and get involved in various everyday activities and special occasions. Later, my wife and I ended up spending almost two months in the Northern Province capital, Kasama, where I did translation work with two students from Malole's St. Francis Secondary School. After another month or so in Lusaka, we returned to the US where the task of writing the dissertation would be completed.

In all this time, I never questioned the notion itself of my presence among the Tabwa. Trained in a renowned area studies program and rigorous academic department, using a half-century of ethnographers, folklorists and literary scholars as my model, and sanctioned, as it were, by Zambian church and state, I simply went in and did my research, initiated some marvelous friendships, enjoyed the company of a host of different nationalities and social strata, and went home. As with many scholars, the period of reflection really began when writing up my data and trying to transcribe and translate the stories I'd collected. The more I wrote and translated the more obscure the conditions of research and the contexts of the performances became. I was literally textualizing living events, distilling story texts, and isolating moments out of a continuum, and this was somehow depleting the richness of my experiences and the complex interactions that surrounded these sessions.

Though I found ways to incorporate more and more of these elements into what eventually became my first monograph, I became increasingly uncomfortable with the use of an ethnographic frame in my writing and with the necessity to take charge of all these cultural elements and order them for my readers. Nowhere in this writing, for example, is there a sense that Zambia was undergoing many changes as we sat in villages and recorded stories. That our neighbors were also undergoing changes was not evident in the way I wrote about them. I remember being most obviously struck by this notion in 1988, when I realized that my closest friend among the Tabwa, a man very near to my age, was himself undergoing fundamental upheavals in his life that I'd never expected. A devout Jehovah's Witness, with a close relationship to his family and a propensity for industrious, back-breaking labor in farming, salt-making and fishing, my friend revealed to me in 1988 that he had divorced his wife and gone to work for the government cooperative union. This also meant that he had to leave the Watchtower movement that prohibited involvement in secular government activities. Somehow I'd set him into a static, rather romanticized image that depended on all these socially defining elements and was rather shocked, perhaps even disillusioned, that he'd taken such a different course in his life. Why had I so easily framed him in such a position, somehow immune from the possibility of personal change?[21] This eventually brought me back to the problem of representation in my writing and thinking.

Locating a Discipline/Method

There is, moreover, a hazy boundary between the study of oral narrative performance and what might strictly be termed ethnographic research. The former is in some ways harder to pin down than the latter. In my initial work, I did not ignore individuals or their social contexts, indeed that kind of information was important in locating them and their storytelling efforts within Tabwa society. However, the premise then and now is that their creations rely upon aesthetic form and a cultural knowledge of narrative conventions and imagery. The way the narratives worked involved the manipulation of a very old system of discourse, image and structure to create seemingly fresh, new narrative experiences. Ethnography, if it takes up storytelling performance at all, often focuses on the social over the aesthetic, looking for what the tales or performances say about the society. Geertz may see the Balinese cockfight as a kind of art form, but his concern is what it says about the Balinese.[22] Even discourse analysis kinds of approaches often lose the art — at the same time claiming to be identifying aesthetics — in favor of evaluating performances in frames of linguistic competence or the jockeying for power in social relationships.[23]

---

21 Jackson makes a similar point when he says, "Clearly, therefore, it would be a mistake to reduce any person to some abiding essence or self that remains constant throughout an entire lifetime, or to reduce a human life to the general conditions that define his class, her culture, or his credo. Even to speak of variations on a theme is a misnomer, for any one moment every variation is in effect experienced as a theme." (Jackson 2006, p. 294)
22 See Geertz 1973.
23 These approaches are grounded in the work of Roman Jakobson, but more readily in the pioneering work in language and ethnography of Dell Hymes (1964, 1974, 1996). Important studies in this vein include Bauman 1986; Labov 1972; Scollon and Scollon 1979; Shuman 1986 and 2005; Tannen 1982.

In any event, although my work certainly crosses disciplinary boundaries, in the end I am not an ethnographer. I don't focus on the same concerns and do not try to build models that broadly explain cultural behavior. This, therefore, might be the boundary between ethnographic and oral tradition scholarship that keeps me mostly on one side rather than the other. My observations are more likely to look at behavior or intent only in specific situations without drawing wider conclusions, except for the instances where overlap with other examples seems obvious and suggests recurring patterns. Moreover, my aesthetic evaluation of a performance is drawn from the combination of story elements and the storyteller's skills in conveying that narrative vision to an audience.

In a very real sense, then, one concern I had about this study is identifying my object of investigation; narrative "text" and/or performer and/or context. The question was simplified in 1988–89 by going to places where I knew virtually no one and ended up with a pretty clear object of study: video records of the performances, memory, some field notes and whatever other printed or oral data I could apply to the events and their various texts. Consequently, this could not approach the deeply interactive research explored in Tedlock's marvelous evocation of a spectrum of earlier studies that attempted real dialogical engagement.[24] His citing of an ethnographer/local subject interaction from Dwyer (1982) suggests the ongoing and shifting paradox of trying to represent such interactions.

> Dwyer: And what do you think that I think about you? What might I say to myself about you?
>
> Faqir Muhammad: You're the one who understands that. Why, am I going to enter into your head? (p. 285)

Titon (2003) describes a related consideration when it comes to discussing living performances, which is the unavoidable textualization that scholarship entails.

> A deeper dilemma turns on the practice of performance analysis, for insofar as analysis constitutes its object, it is forced to remove performance from living processes and treat it as a text. This dilemma appears to be inherent in our scholarly procedures, not only because we write our scholarship as text but because analysis and interpretation are directed at objects, and if a text is anything that can be interpreted, then there is no interpretation without text. And so even when performance theory has driven folkloristic analysis,

---

[24] Tedlock 1995.

transcribed texts remain in our work, embedded now in new interpretive contexts. (p. 78)

This challenge is at the base of how we choose to examine story performances and will constitute, along with the ongoing questions of reflexivity, authority and local individual assertion, the methodological discourse of this study.

This current project explores ways to consider narrative performances, and to concentrate on representing these performances and how I gathered them, entailing what is often referred to as "the vagaries of fieldwork," among other concerns. Moreover, because what I recorded in 1988–89 was shaped by whatever the performers wished to give—or, more accurately, "sell"—me, the material I will consider here is a generic mix of mostly "fictional" narratives, proverbs, heroic praises, some history, and some explorations of topics people felt were of significance. Though the recordings and transcriptions form objects of analysis, "texts," they will be only part of a wider examination of the situations and contexts of the performance events themselves. As an example of how I focus on these various events, I will describe the conditions of recording the efforts of a particular group of Bemba performers, and suggest how these can be used to evaluate the material. The goal of such a discussion is to open the examination to factors of performance context and ethnographic immediacy, thereby keeping the performance and collection in an actual historical moment.

My initial example is taken from research carried out during the 1988–89 academic year. I was teaching at the University of Zambia on a Fulbright award and conducting research in urban and rural Zambia. This period followed two intensive returns to the Tabwa area, for six months in 1983 and three months in 1985, to collect more narratives and information for my first monograph. My research goal in 1988–89 was to record material from all the Bemba-speaking groups of Northern and Luapula Provinces. The task was much greater than I could realistically accomplish during university holidays and the ten weeks of spring term that I was given leave, but I did manage to visit and record performers from five ethnic groups; securing a somewhat representative sampling from each. The nature of the work militated against my method of long-term collection and analysis among the Tabwa people. Rather than live in close proximity to and interact daily with neighbors I came to know fairly well, I was forced to depend on very brief concentrated visits with a variety of people. My entrée into these different communities was, similarly, of a varied nature. For example,

I visited the village of the Bemba Paramount Chief Chitimukulu armed with a letter of introduction from the Chief himself. What hopefully is clear from the following description is that I was working with people who did not know me, or even of me, but who were willing to help on a friend-of-a-friend basis. On more practical terms, this meant an early and concerted necessity for negotiating the appropriate compensation for people's time and help. In the Tabwa area, my credit, in a manner of speaking, was good. This meant that I could stop and record or discuss material almost anywhere I'd been earlier without prior consultation about money or gifts. It was generally known that at some point I would compensate people who assisted me. Working in new areas required that we set the exact conditions of compensation. For a Bemba royal bard, this meant agreeing to a set price for the entire session beforehand. For some Lunda storytellers it meant establishing an arbitrary but strictly adhered to three-story minimum for a specific payment. How did this affect the performance events? We can examine this question with evidence from the following performance session.

Chitimukulu is the Paramount Chief of the Bemba, one of Zambia's largest ethnic groups. He was also, in 1989, a Member of the Central Committee, one of the more prominent non-elected government posts in the country. I had first met Mr. L.M. Ng'andu, whose royal title was Chitimukulu 36, Mutale Chitapankwa II, in a rather remote village while he was visiting his constituents prior to national elections, and he encouraged me to drop by and see him.[25] Some five months later, I did, in fact, visit his office in Kasama, and he gave me a letter of introduction and names of people to see in the area around his home. He added what at the time seemed a curious caveat, saying he wasn't sure anyone would pay attention to the note but that I should try in any case. When, accompanied by my eight year-old son Daniel, I later visited the chief's village these comments became clearer to me. Near to Chitimukulu's capital, I recruited a teacher at Malole's St. Francis Secondary School, Mr. S.M. Kalunga, who had kindly agreed to help with introductions. We tried to see several people whose names were provided by Chief Chitimukulu but were mostly unsuccessful in finding anyone at home. However, at the local courthouse, we met two men whose names had been on the list and arranged a visit for the next day.

---

25 See my chapter on Bisa storytelling for a more detailed description of my first interactions with Chitimukulu.

When we returned to the courthouse at around 2:30 PM there was no one around. We inquired as to where everyone had gone and ended up at the nearby home of the "headman" of that section of the village.[26] There was a group of some twenty men and women drinking *katubi* inside the house. This beer is generally made from finger millet and is distinctive for the frothy, thick residue that floats on its surface. It is therefore sipped through a straw that is forced down through the surface layer to the warm liquid at the bottom. Daniel and I drew a good deal of attention as we sat down on small stools against one of the walls. However, things loosened up noticeably after I tasted the *katubi* and pronounced it to be of high quality. [*Ee, ciisuma.* (Yes, it's good.)] Then I drew some laughs when I responded to exhortations to have some more by saying "*Saana.*" [That's plenty.] Mr. Kalunga and I reminded the men of our agreement of the previous day, and we were invited outside to discuss the matter. The local court magistrate and the headman eventually emerged and spoke to us about our desire to record oral traditions. Supplementing the note from the Paramount Chief, I tried to validate my status by stressing my identity as a university lecturer on research assignment, brandishing a dog-eared copy of my UMI bound dissertation. At around this time, a short, compactly built man who was probably in his late 50s walked up and started shouting rapid-fire words at me. I recognized the style as *imishikakulo*, or Bemba praise poetry. I found the experience uncomfortable since, from a Western perspective, that tone of voice is culturally a sign of anger or insulting language and it was aggressively spewing from someone I'd never met. Further, the Bemba words themselves are often archaic or at least heavily allusive, so I felt the disadvantage of understanding almost nothing of what was being said. After a minute, the man spoke with the court magistrate and made it clear that he would not perform without first settling the payment of compensation. I said I'd pay after seeing what was performed, but he would have none of it. Down deep, the fellow really put me off and I didn't care if he performed or not, but people around him seemed to be taking his side, so I eventually settled on paying a set sum, roughly twelve

---

26 The term "headman" is mostly a carryover from the colonial era, but it remains the most common gloss of the Bemba language title "*mwine mushi*," "owner of the village." Essentially, headmen are lineage leaders whose relatives and non-blood constituents live under his authority in a section of a larger village. His duties include acting as an intermediary to the chief, settling disputes as an initial local court of appeal, before the matter needs to be brought to the chief or civil authority, and involvement in daily arrangements concerning labor, land, familial duties and so forth.

or fifteen dollars, to the court magistrate who would then portion it out at the end of the session. When we came to an agreement I placed a bench next to the courthouse and set my camera on a tripod.

The first performer, with an audience of around twenty people, was the magistrate, Mr. Chituloshi. He discoursed on the importance of heeding wisdom provided by one's society, illustrating it with the tale of how a grasshopper outwits a hornbill trying to eat him. He then explained the tale by coming back to the significance of group knowledge and values. His delivery was slow and emphatic. The audience was polite but did not really seem to be engaged by the tale. I replayed the audiotape for all to hear and then recorded the second performer, Mr. Bernard Chitompwe, the headman. After a brief introduction, Mr. Chitompwe launched into several elaborate praises, employing the same style that the earlier man used to welcome me. This same man responded to the praises with a shouted word *"pama"* [Go on! Right on!] This performance caused a bit more of a stir among the audience, which now numbered around forty people. During these performances, my son sat next to or near Mr. Kalunga. After the two performances, Daniel took to moving around a bit, returning to his seat only when groups of children or adults surrounded him, staring in curiosity or trying to engage him in conversation. This interest in the strangers waned as the performances heated up. The third person to perform was the man who had greeted me, Mr. Ng'ongo Yuba, who also introduced himself as Kangwa Kabunda, a royal bard, or *ing'omba*. He performed with a young man who played a single-headed drum, while he himself played a double-headed drum that hung from his neck and shoulder by a thin rope. Mr. Yuba introduced himself and his accompanist in elaborate terms, then proceeded to play the drum vigorously, as women in the audience began to ululate. When he stopped playing Mr. Yuba sang a different kind of praise song called *ing'omba* or drum poetry.[27] Yuba's performance of this genre consisted of taking a deep breath and singing loudly and rapidly, bending at the waist as he expended the air in his lungs. He then rose up straight as he inhaled deeply and did the same thing for the next set of verses. During one of these renditions, as the drumming

---

27 Both the style of poetry and its practitioner are called *ing'omba*. The bards often play the two-headed drum called *ishingilili*, that incorporates both a "male" (high) and "female" (low) set of tones. Mr. Yuba was accompanied by a young man playing a smaller, cylindrical drum called *"sensele"*. See Mapoma 1974, on Bemba royal bards and their instruments.

intervened between instances of singing, an older woman, also in her 50s, joined him rather spontaneously, to sing harmony to the poetry and dance to the drumming. By now, there were over one hundred people in the audience. Most of them responded to the performers by laughing in a delighted way, ululating, or making encouraging exclamations like *Pama!* or *Eeya!* When the performers stopped, I replayed the entire session on my video monitor. This caused more excitement. Mr. Chitompwe sang more *imishikakulo*, and Mr. Yuba performed more *ing'omba*, with his, now two, accompanists.

By this time, people had pretty much turned all of their attention to Mr. Yuba's efforts. The audience swelled to nearly two hundred participants. It seemed to me that I'd become a simple functionary at this point, there to record whatever people chose to do. After each playback, the performers seemed to try to outdo their earlier efforts. A man came to tell me that the women insisted on singing some of *their* songs. So we moved to the rear of the courthouse, where the crowd was not yet packed, and I recorded singing, drumming and dancing that became more and more controlled by the women. They did not like the drumbeat set down by Mr. Yuba's accompanist, so a woman took over that drum. Then, during the performance of a song, one young woman spontaneously jumped into the central clearing and began to dance as the song came to an abrupt close. She was embarrassed by the action and fled back into the crowd. Soon thereafter, however, women encouraged her to return, and she and a much older woman, easily in her mid 60s, danced together to another song. This performance intensified the already strong level of audience response and participation, as evidenced by the almost complete involvement of all present. By the time the last performance began, with a woman dancing at the center of attention, there was almost no distinction, almost no space, between performers and audience. In fact, performers, spectators, camera and cameraman were all but enveloped in one rhythmically moving mass.

It was by now nearing sunset and we had been at it for almost four hours. We prepared to take our leave by packing up and thanking our hosts and performers. As the crowd dispersed, Mr. Yuba insisted we return to record some *really* good material and visit him at his home where he would have the time, space and control to perform his specialties. Mr. Kalunga, Daniel and I mounted our vehicle and drove back to Malole then continued on to Kasama.

Though a broad, formal study of this session would obviously focus on the verbal texts of material created by Mr. Yuba and the other performers, it is also clear that the event itself makes an interesting subject for analysis. Even when considering the taped material, it is important to take into account the dynamics of large gatherings, and my use of video and audio playback, as well as my presence as both an economic and archival source.

So, an analysis of the material collected at this session—besides a thorough consideration of the verbal texts of story, praise, dance and song—would include a description of the factors that led to and surrounded the various performances. It is important to note the history or lack thereof of my relationship to the people performing and reacting as an audience. They were not familiar with me or my work. The performances formed the core of activity and attention to such an extent that people virtually forgot the camera, my presence and the notion of compensation and were carried along by the competitive and expressive energies of the session.[28] The material itself would require detailed work with previous studies and local experts in these genres, since much of it was fairly esoteric and particular to the things that constitute the repertoire of a royal bard and to the themes and images, mostly from initiation songs, that the women wanted preserved.

My role here was primarily as an instigator, secondarily as a recorder. Understanding these conditions help me to evaluate what I have elsewhere called the performance context of any tale or session.[29] This data can be important for understanding elements of style or intent on the part of a performer, as well as framing types of audience response, or lack thereof. Do people perform more energetically when they are being paid? I would say this was not a significant factor for at least the women participants, as was evidenced by the spontaneous performances that evolved from the otherwise elicited recording session. Further, realistically, I doubt that the men who initially negotiated their own compensation were about to share any of it with the virtually amorphous group of women. It is also worth looking deeper into the manner in which women participated in then took over the session, beginning with the first woman who danced with Mr. Yuba and including the many women who drummed, sang and danced. If nothing else, it is clear that the first woman broke into an initially

---

28 See Schechner 2003, for a wide-ranging discussion of the many elements and types of performances.
29 See Cancel 1989 and 1988–89.

male event, and that the other women eventually formed a communal rather than individual expressive performance entity.[30]

We are really looking at considering the historical moment of collection and performance as it pertains to the collector and his or her collaborators, as well as what the situation was politically and socially in that area at that time. What I mean is that Zambia in 1988–89 was experiencing economic and political instability that led not only to the prices set for performances but also the attitude of the performers towards any particular researcher. While we did not know it then, due to broad national dissatisfaction and unrest, the long-standing government of President Kaunda was only little over a year from being voted out of office in the first multiparty elections in decades. In my case, I was aided immeasurably by introductions from local people, but this still did not place me in the same circumstance that held sway when working among the more familiar Tabwa. Also, my status as a university lecturer was ambiguous. It helped me receive official sanction to conduct research, but, because the university was experiencing unrest among the students and faculty due to financial and curricular issues, it made me a bit suspect in the rural areas as well. Ordinary people often had little sympathy for what they perceived, and relatively speaking not entirely incorrectly, to be privileged students and faculty trying to get more for themselves at the expense of taxpayers and government. Moreover, depending on the area visited, the people's feelings about the government varied dramatically. Even armed with a letter from the Bemba Paramount Chief, I still had to negotiate and scuffle for the performances I eventually recorded. This said something about chiefly and governmental power and its influence when the chief/government official was not around.[31] Ultimately for a lot of the performers in this study, cash or in-kind payments were the deciding factors, while in some other cases, as with the women at Chitimukulu's capital, I sensed a clear, overriding concern for expressing and preserving ideas for posterity.

---

30 I will examine concerns of gender in performance in some of the chapters that follow, but clearly in this session there was a sense that women wanted to express themselves as a group in the material being recorded.
31 It became clear to me some time after the recording session that this particular Chitimukulu was not as popular as some of his predecessors, in part because he sought to change some of the older, traditional ways of doing things. In 1994, when I returned to the area, I visited Chitimukulu Mutale Chitapankwa at his *musumba*, or palace, and he provided me with a long autobiographical account that I videotaped. In it, he talked about some of the traditions of the kingship he'd been seeking to change.

An analysis of the performances described above would also take advantage of the curious aftereffects evidenced by my presenting Chitimukulu with an audiocassette of the event. While in his Kasama office, he listened to one of Mr. Yuba's songs and told me it was "not correct" in some of its historical assertions. I thought little of this until five years later when I visited the Chief at his court and he summoned Mr. Yuba to our meeting. The man had changed dramatically, looking rather unkempt and haggard, acting very submissive in the Chief's presence, and reacting to my greetings very solicitously. Chitimukulu had earlier told me that Mr. Yuba had fallen on bad times, as some people in the village had been accusing him of witchcraft. During our meeting the Chief demanded that he produce a more accurate version of the song he'd performed earlier, but he responded by saying he could not remember which song he'd been singing and would have to see or hear the performance so that he could make his revisions. This incident says a lot about the significance of royal praises and the concerns nobles might exhibit over how they or their ancestors are portrayed.[32] Clearly, Chitimukulu had a sense of how my recordings might present him or Bemba history to a wider academic or public audience. A thorough analysis of the earlier performance, with detailed knowledge of the often allusive imagery of royal praise poetry would combine with this latter epilogue to provide a richer understanding of the roles played by bards and their art at the court and in the wider society.

In each location I stopped to do research, slightly different conditions were in effect. Among the Bemba of Chief Nkula, I was sanctioned by a Catholic missionary, which gave me easy and effective access to the people living around the Ilondola mission. On the other hand, people did not perform tales that were at all ribald. In fact, one man performed a fascinating tale that he explained as being about the Catholic Church, with one of the wiser characters representing the Pope. Among the Bwile of Luapula Province, I was aided by the fact that Chief Puta was enthused with my project and called a meeting of a number of his headmen and councilors, some thirty or so men. He led off with a brief historical narrative then a shorter reminiscence, then around five of his colleagues followed with a series of fictional tales. My visit to the Bisa in the Munyamadzi

---

32 A similar occurrence can be examined in some detail regarding historical information imparted in a narrative by the Bwile Chief Puta in 1989 and how this was received and then modified by his successor during a visit in 2005. The original performance is referred to below and presented in more detail in Chapter V on Bwile oral performance.

Corridor was facilitated by an American researcher who had, at that time, been living and working off and on with that group for over twenty years. Two Zambian graduate students I'd been working with at UNZA provided initial entrée into two Lunda villages for recording sessions. Again, while it is speculative to discuss the motives of the people who allow me to record their material, I'd reiterate one obvious and sensible conclusion is that most do it for the compensation, a compensation that takes the form of cash, goods, fulfilling obligations and/or garnering attention. However, there is another factor to consider and that is why do some performers turn in outstanding efforts and others seem to be going through minimal motions? Here I believe that an alternate motivation is a combination of pride and interest in the project. Older people often want to see the material preserved, while many younger people mostly relish holding the stage and having the opportunity to show off.[33]

Reflexively, there are at least two concerns I have in my descriptive, not entirely "analytical," writing. The first is that I try to honestly present myself as a player in the ongoing event. The second is that I avoid the temptation to become the star player in that event, writing others rather than simply acknowledging our several texts and trying to work within and, perhaps more significantly, between them.[34] So, to this end, I include both photos of the performers and a subtitled DVD record of the performances so that, limited as this technical framing of the sessions might be, the video record can at least give the narrators a greater presence in this discussion. If nothing else, these video records and my descriptions will provide a more direct representation and, therefore, some form of agency to the performers included here. Moreover, the lesson that has been forming in my mind over the years pertains to the fact that people are not necessarily their performed stories—though in many ways they

---

[33] West 2007, discussing his relationship with his local subjects among the Muedan people of Mozambique, makes an important point about how one of the elders he worked with "'saw in me a kindred characteristic,' I believe, because he knew, that in my writings, I would attempt to produce of the Muedan world an order of my own description— because he appreciated that such interpretive visions *of* the world necessarily constitute a means of leverage *on* the world." (p. 81)

[34] A good examination of texts by writers from the colonized world satirizing the notion of anthropologists as heroes, is Graham Huggan's essay "Anthropologists and Other Frauds." (1994) He examines Ouologuem's novel as well as works by Alejo Carpentier (1999), considering Claude Lévi-Strauss, and Albert Wendt (1999), rethinking the impact of Margaret Mead in Samoa. Jackson 1989, also notes that we can "no longer assume that *our* texts have some kind of epistemological superiority over *theirs*." (p. 168)

are "performing" themselves—and their lives do not begin and end when I arrive then leave. We need to see ethnographic data in the form of recorded observed activities, in my case story performances, as limited, in some cases misleading, information. I was reminded of this fact a couple of years ago, when my friend and colleague, who had been my host in 1989 at the Bisa village of Nabwalya, sent some photos from that visit. One of the shots was of the recording session at the place where people had gathered to harvest their sorghum crop. In the photo, the perspective was from the back of a performer, framing my son Daniel, a friend named Marie who'd accompanied us, and me sitting on stools or chairs in front of someone's house, with the video camera on a tripod and many audience members around us. At the time I saw this snapshot I'd been studying the video record of this session for nearly fourteen years, but had forgotten many of the details revealed by this photo. Seeing what the performers were seeing altered my perspective of what was encompassed by the overall tone and experience of that recording effort.

We can discover behavior or attitudes that might help us to understand pieces of people's lives and perceptions, but at the same time we need to carefully set these against the mountain of social and cultural relationships that are beneath the surface of not only our but our subjects' recognition. Ultimately, I want to represent the oral traditional performances of Bemba-speaking people within a writing style that moves from close reflexive observation and the careful recording of details to the recognition that true and thorough analysis and interpretation is often limited and, indeed, limiting in its need for absolute or unifying conclusions.[35] I believe it is the rare researcher, particularly someone who is not a member of the society being studied, who can truly attain a deep knowledge of that culture.[36] Most

---

35 Jackson 2006, notes some of the limits of both reflexivity and trying to take the stated views of others at face value when he says "we can neither assess the truth of our understanding *representationally*—in terms of its fidelity to the espoused views and observed practices of others—nor *confessionally*—as a disclosure of our own ulterior motives and unconscious desires." (p. 293)

36 Some examples of what appear to be in depth insights and near total immersion in African societies include Stoller's intimate study of the Songhay (1989), and, in an amazing longitudinal study, Colson and Scudder's reporting on the Gwembe Tonga (1958, 1971, 1988). Griaule's unprecedented work with Ogotemmeli (1965) purports to reveal some fascinating details of the Dogon way of life and cosmology, though how this was gathered and written, and how that framed the information, remains a matter of scholarly debate (see, for example, Clifford 1983). A last example is Stuart Marks's long term study of the Valley Bisa of Zambia and their interrelationships with their environment and the practice of hunting. (See Chapter IV below and, Marks 1979, 1984, 2005, 2008, etc.).

important in this anthology are the narrative performances themselves, since these are what the storytellers chose to present and shape for their audiences, and for my camera.[37] Most of what I provide to these efforts is meant to contextualize and describe them as accurately as I can.

Bemba-speaking Groups

The five ethnic groups represented in this project all fall under the linguistic range of the language spoken by the largest of the groups, the Bemba of Zambia's Northern Province. Linked historically by a common migration from what is today the Democratic Republic of the Congo, the Bemba, Bisa, Bwile, Lunda, and Tabwa all trace their origins, or at least the origins of their chieftaincies, to the Luba people. There are, therefore, strong linguistic and cultural links between numerous Zambian and Congolese societies. Matrilineal systems of descent are a common bond, as are, for the most part, economic practices, kingship and clan structures. In Zambia, or rather its earlier incarnation as Northern Rhodesia, the British colonial government and various Christian missionary groups, especially the Roman Catholics, early on chose a dialect of the language spoken by the Bemba people as the standard for education, evangelization, electronic media and official communication in this region of the colony/country. This led to numerous publications, initially and most significantly translations of the Bible, that reified the Bemba language over the other languages/dialects spoken by the related ethnic groups in the region. At times, the numerous other groups found it convenient to identify themselves with the larger, more influential Bemba polity, and at other times they felt it important to assert their own ethnic identities.[38]

While there are at least a dozen groups that identify themselves as related to the Bemba but constituting separate entities, it would be another kind of project to closely investigate and try to define how each group determines this difference.[39] Certainly, in the instances that I've recorded

---

37 A good overview of approaches to African oral literature, past and present, is provided by Finnegan 1992 and 1997; and Okpewho 1992.
38 See Cancel 2006, on how claiming Bemba identity has vacillated over time for some segments of the Lunda population.
39 Crehan 1997, for example, examines historically how the Kaonde of northwestern Zambia underwent a series of classifications under British rule that had profound effects on their socio-economic lives. A broader study of how colonial rule first imposed certain notions of identity on indigenous peoples then how these identities persisted in fundamental ways is edited by Leroy Vail (1989).

oral history or had access to published and unpublished studies, it is clear that each society has its own story of how it came to the place where it now lives. While the Lunda and Bemba, for example, both claim they originated from a place known as Kola, among the Luba in the Congo, and followed the same physical route into Zambia, historical studies suggest that the migration might not have taken place at the same time or along the same route for each group.[40] Their respective oral histories, and the scholarly studies that built on these and other types of documented evidence, point to the evolution of several kinds of political states and systems of royal succession that are also unique to each entity. Royal lineage, for example, is not reckoned in the same way between the Bemba and Lunda and succession is figured in dramatically different fashion. Similarly, the Bwile and Tabwa have differing stories of how they came to be. In the case of the Bwile, I recorded a brief account about their arrival in the place they now live and how a historical/mythological offence by a "captain" of an early Lunda king resulted in land being ceded to the Bwile in compensation.[41] Elsewhere, I've documented the origins and migration of the Tabwa, again from Kola but on a different path than that taken by the Bemba and Lunda.[42] The Bisa of the Luangwa Valley share their ethnicity with the Bisa who live near Lake Bangweulu, on the boundary of Luapula and Northern Provinces. While these historical accounts are significant in explaining how foreign kingship systems came to dominate the original inhabitants of these regions, it is difficult to point to these narratives as the central formative elements in ethnic identities. My intention, therefore, was to collect narratives from as many Bemba-speaking groups as I could, in order to consider a comparison of their stories, themes, performance techniques, etc. In fact, these fictional and non-fictional stories have suggested mostly a good deal of cultural overlap between the groups, certainly as it pertains to common plots, images, tropes and styles of performance. If any dimension can be more profitably explored to gauge ethnic identity among these groups, it is probably their relative levels of economic practices, prosperity, prospects and opportunities. The northern Zambia region has had a complex history of conquest and migration followed by British colonial rule then the post-independence national government that has strongly influenced

---

40   See A. Roberts 1973, and Cunnison 1959 and 1961.
41   See Chapter V on Bwile performance.
42   See my 1981 PhD dissertation, "Inshimi Structure and Theme: The Tabwa Oral Narrative Tradition."

how groups see and define themselves. These subjectivities and group claims of identity remain, at least for some groups, in an ongoing state of flux. Benedict Anderson's seminal notion of "imagined communities"[43] is a simple yet not unreasonable way to view how ethnicity is figured for at least a number of the smaller groups. Shifts in notions and assertions of group identity have been reflected in contemporary Zambia by the relatively recent proliferation of annual traditional festivals and rites.[44]

Following Up Original Visits

An added dimension to the study is material I collected in a follow-up visit sixteen years after the fact. Zambia had undergone some intensive changes since 1988–89. The current ruling party, the Movement for Multiparty Democracy (MMD), is the one that unseated President Kaunda in 1991. The former socialist economy had been liberalized, along with those of many other countries in the third world following the fall of the Soviet Union. Former parastatal organizations and businesses had been privatized, with all the familiar concomitant consequences: a huge rise in unemployment, the weakening of social welfare institutions such as health care, education and housing, and a dramatic shift in the way business was conducted. Subsidies for crucial foods, such as the staple maize "mealie meal" flour [*mukaiwa* (Bemba)], were done away with. The currency was allowed to "float" at its actual value. In the short term these economic measures, mandated by the International Monetary Fund and the World Bank, took a severe toll on the Zambian population. Based on visits in 2003 and 2005, I also saw evidence of how desperation breeds innovation and industriousness. This was obvious in my travels in the Luapula and Northern Provinces, where many young people were now running businesses such as private transport of goods and people, in the form of mini-buses or cargo lorries, and starting up shops that catered to technical or business needs, in the form of internet cafes and office services. With the sudden availability of many imported goods, young entrepreneurs were building and stocking dry goods stores or restaurants with an eye towards attracting customers to more aesthetically pleasing venues. The national demographic was definitely getting younger, due in large part to

---

43 Anderson 1991.
44 Cancel 2006, alludes to this phenomenon when discussing the Lunda annual kinship festival, the Mutomboko.

the dropping of the average life expectancy to around thirty-seven years of age, a continually rising birth rate, and the tragic thinning of the sexually active population by the HIV/AIDS pandemic. In the case of education, the government had loosened bureaucratic restrictions on fund-raising and local control. Parents and teachers had more of a say as to where national monies, meager as they were, would be spent. This local empowerment, a consequence of seriously depleted public coffers, could be seen in many local government institutions. I can't guess what all this means for the future, only that it has resulted in notable economic and social changes, diminishing the importance of the extended family as people often cannot afford to care for their relatives, especially surviving kin of AIDS victims, and increasing instances of individual assertion and innovation. That all this is accompanied by deep poverty, chronic unemployment and desperation in what is considered one of the world's poorest countries, only adds to the complex mix of extant conditions characterizing Zambia today.

In 2005, armed with photos of each performer, printed transcripts of their narratives, and DVD recordings of the performances I attempted to retrace my steps and find out a bit more about the storytellers. Having gotten to know them only on video for many years, my intention was simply to discover or augment biographical information about each performer, to properly credit them for their efforts and give readers, and myself, a chance to "know" them better. Since I was not able logistically, to spend the time in any one place required to truly chart the lay of the land, the data I collected was ultimately fragmentary and often raised more questions about these performers than it really answered. Moreover, of the thirty narrators included in this study, nineteen, possibly twenty, had died by the time I'd returned to seek them out. Of the ten who were still alive, I could not reach the area where five still lived, and though I reached the village of another narrator, she was not immediately available. I actually had a chance to speak to only two of the remaining ten performers. Yet this reflects the nature of the entire study, given that I did not in 1988–89, and could not in 2005, spend the time to get to know the people and the places as well as I'd consider sufficient for a proper exploration of the interpersonal and socio-cultural milieu in which they lived. The more recent experience elicited a strange feeling of nostalgia and loss, directed at people I'd only gotten to know on videotape. Having gathered the information, however, I include it in the form of footnotes and postscripts to most sessions in order to add more depth to my initial observations and to aid in forming an overview of the project's results.

Method and Focus of Chapters

In the chapters that follow, I will employ several methods to evaluate performances and the verbal texts of the various narratives collected from, in order of appearance, people who ethnically identify as Tabwa, Bemba, Bisa, Lunda and Bwile. Detailed observation, similar to what Geertz refers to as "thick description," will be my central method. This includes information about how the recording sessions were arranged, the immediate contexts of performers and audience, details on compensation for the work and description of performance techniques that include use of voice, gesture and mime. I will include information about the particular ethnic groups being recorded and socio-historical information pertaining to the time of the performances as necessary and/or available, though this will not in most cases be a vital part of analytical assertions. I identify and sometimes evoke the traditional context of fictional narratives, based on the broader formal characteristics and conventions of story-construction and thematic focus. This will be based on my earlier work on Tabwa narrative and, obviously, on a much broader body of published and unpublished studies of oral traditions in and outside of Africa. Every chapter will have a different focus, based on the amount of cultural and personal information I was able to bring to bear on each performance session. In the next chapter, considering the productions of two Tabwa performers, I will provide a more detailed frame for the analysis of the performances that comprise this study.

II. The Tabwa Context: Mature Shifting of Frames and Adolescent Assertion

Umusha afwa ne fyebo mu kanwa [A slave dies with words in his mouth]
(Stanley Kalumba 1989)

Accepted African oral literature scholarship, under normal circumstances, harbors a built-in mechanism to silence the African voices. By concomitantly reducing African oral performance to writing, and their performers to the role of "informant," the collectors/editors, with the best of intentions, promote themselves to the status of the heroic midwife of an exercise in literary parturition for the international, mostly non-African, gaze. (Olabiyi Yai 1999, p. 5)

Folklorists, after all, did fieldwork; and in an academic world grown sensitive to power relationships and exploitation of the marginalized groups folklorists traditionally studied, the image of the folklorist as collector, strip-mining folklore while traveling and surveying the field, was not a pleasant prospect." (Titon 2003, p. 82)

As we continue to look for ways to adequately represent performance art forms, several dialectical arguments recur in scholarship that will shape the theoretical basis of this discussion. One debate focuses on the ethnographic process itself. How much can scholars, particularly foreign scholars, learn about a society's artistically created self-images?[45] How do

---

45 The preceding chapter discusses these concerns in some detail. Beninois scholar Olabiyi Babalola Yai (1999), cited in the epigraph to this chapter, in an insightful evaluation of Frances and Melville Herskovits's well known study of Dahomean oral narrative tradition, finds numerous faults with western scholarship's approaches to African verbal arts.

DOI: 10.11647/OBP.0033.02

we collect and evaluate the data? How much weight do we give explanation and commentary of local people and how much do we apply our own perceptions of context and intention in devising theoretical frames for the material? Another side of the same relationship treats the question of compensation and cooperation. Is simply paying a performer for his or her efforts enough to justify what we do with the material? Do, or should, scholars discuss these arrangements and negotiations?[46] Finally, can we create opportunities for the experienced and empathetic researcher to incorporate the voice or personality of the artist and his or her milieu in the way we write about the event? I will first discuss some of these issues, then describe two Tabwa performance events and their contexts, and conclude by reviewing the methodology my description employed.

The performance and appreciation of oral art forms is a multi-layered experience for even the simplest manifestations. There is a lifetime of knowledge and interaction involved in recognizing allusions, assertions, or even deliberate obfuscation. This complexity extends from the pliability of language, to the uses of subtle gesture, and to the mundane knowledge of the performer's relationship to the audience. Even the indigenous researcher needs to take various levels of interactions and links into account when evaluating what his or her participation in these activities means for the resulting scholarly description. So we begin by acknowledging the difficulty, if not the impossibility, of completely describing and evaluating these performances.

To this end, we need to balance the desire for analysis and explanation— which in some ways might reiterate colonial practice, or *praxis*—and the desire to let the performers and audience speak for themselves, by either limiting intrusive commentary and "simply" presenting the performance or by taking the performer's retrospective explanations as the true analysis. A great deal depends on how we move between these two approaches, since the former opens the material to certain critical frames and the latter more closely approximates the immediacy and self-contained nature of living performance.

---

46 While the concerns are mostly legally-based and often pertain more to medical experimentation than to the social sciences and humanities, it is significant that most US universities require the vetting of research involving "human subjects," and stipulate the careful documentation of "permission" agreements between researchers and their subjects/targets. It is an acknowledgment that more and more people cooperating in all manner of research endeavors are either recognizing their positions as actors in this process or having that recognition drawn for them in a legalistic manner.

II. The Tabwa Context: Mature Shifting of Frames and Adolescent Assertion 33

Folklorist Linda Dégh recognizes the vital role of performers in the externalizing of ancient images and plots in storytelling, claiming that in "no other form of folk poetry does personality play such an important role as the folktale." (Dégh 1995, p. 38) She goes on to suggest that "[f]actual knowledge, creative imagination, the gift of formulating and structuring the intricate web of episodes into an enrapturing story, and sensitivity to adapt to audience expectation are the abilities that qualify the narrator to fulfill the mission of entertaining." (pp. 38–39) Dégh, finally, sets out a program of study that ideally treats the living role of storytellers within the wider oral tradition of a society.

> We need more thorough and detailed analytical characterization on the basis of the total corpus of tales individuals possess. We also need to know how these individuals acquired their tales, and how they shape and formulate and perform their texts under the influence of personal motivations and social situations....To study personal creativity of storytellers may enlighten us not only about how personal variants originate but also what function the tales can fill in the life of the person. (p. 39)

For the most part, this study will at best approach but not truly fulfill the goals and methodological steps she proposes. The nature of the brief visits that characterize most collection sessions in this project militates against the depth Dégh proposes. The dimensions, then, that will be considered will mostly frame and explore the immediacy of the performance situation and the conditions that spawned them while, when possible, using a broader sense of narrative repertoire in descriptive and analytical remarks.

Hence, I want to emphasize the importance of setting the context of a performance within the wider frames of the researcher's project. The outside observer did not materialize out of nowhere then disappear in a wisp of smoke when the event ended—though in the case of most of the sessions described below, this is more or less what happened. Our presence at these events is often the excuse or impetus for the occasions themselves.[47] Our various techniques of soliciting material are important to what we get back. So before the performance and its evaluation, we ought to set a broader context, the ethnographic deal-making involved in

---

47 In one of the earlier accounts of this relationship, Haring 1972, asserts that researchers, just by their presence, influence what they collect from their sources. "The interviewer—anthropologist, historian, literary critic, folklorist—is inescapably a participant, not an observer, in an aesthetic transaction." (p. 387)

most research efforts.⁴⁸ This is a basic responsibility for all researchers if we hope to open up the process to demystification and acknowledge the impossibility of totally objective recording.

This brings me to the question of voice and how we employ it in our scholarship. The balancing act between methods becomes a juggling act for the writer, as we try to avoid being transformed into either "mere essayists or stenographers" (Snow and Morrill 1993). At the same time we are revealing the mundane machinations of our efforts to gather data, we must use what we know, or think we know, to supply texture and understanding to the performance event. As we keep admitting that we were there and influenced—and were influenced by—at least some of what happened, we must keep describing away, as accurately and dynamically as possible, creating space for the reader to appreciate some of the event's intricacies and the performer's self-assertions. One way we do this in our writing is by moving from the "objective" third person descriptive voice to the first person questioning voice, and back again, as often as the shift is necessary to underscore relevant ideas and processes.⁴⁹ We also need to refer to the people we work with by their names and fill in what we know about them, their lives, personalities, and performance styles. As often as possible, we must cite the performers or audience as commentators on the event or on its participants. Then we need to add dimension to those remarks by looking at them contextually. If "authority" is ultimately less shared than it is unfixed, this resulting lack of synthesis is in some ways the best result we or, certainly in this instance, I can hope for.

Representational options can be weighed by considering two particularly dense and detailed studies of oral narrative performances. The first is a well-known work by Richard and Sally Price, providing a thorough account of oral performance in a Surinam community in *Two Evenings in Saramaka* (1991). The second is a more recent book by Annekie Joubert on two South African societies' performance events, *The Power of Performance: Linking Past and Present in Hananwa and Lobedu Oral Literature* (2004). The former is a product of years of research and deep cultural knowledge of Saramaka society, using many personal details about performers and their lives and

---

48 See Deborah Kapchan citing Joni Jones's humorous, reflexive "performance" text, wherein she asks "was I really making friends, or was I making deals?/laughs How about this for my next article!" (Kapchan 2003, p. 129)
49 Titon 2003, p. 85, provides a good summary of the usual ethnographic text, as it begins with a first person kind of immediacy and reflexive frame and then soon devolves into the third person voice that characterizes most ethnographic observation and analysis.

even providing transcriptions of the music that accompanied song lyrics and photos of the participants. The latter is a similarly dense evocation of performances that spends a lot more time on the smaller details of the events, including descriptions of body movements, non-verbal techniques of gesture and mime, parallel English translations with original language texts, and a lot of theoretical and technical framing of what is presented. There is also a DVD video record of the performances that accompanies the book. While the Prices' work reads more like literature, moving almost viscerally into the experiences of the two nights, Joubert's text is more directly, self-consciously "scholarly" in its intentions and presentation. The first smoothly takes us along for the ride, while the second keeps stopping to look very carefully at almost every imaginable angle of examination. The feeling one gets in comparing the two approaches is of gazing at an impressionist painting from a certain distance and seeing the seamless evocation of colors and shapes, versus looking at the same painting close up and studying the textures of brush strokes. Both methods are valid, but they reveal their subjects in strikingly different ways. While I simply do not have the depth of knowledge, information and, indeed, the inclination to replicate the Saramaka study, I do prefer its overall tone and approach and choose it as a guide in what I do with the Bemba-language performances in this current project.

Taking Geertz's notion of thick description even further, and aware of the postmodern and postcolonial scholarly wariness of "writing" other cultures, Titon proposes a style of scholarly, ethnographic writing he calls:

> ...'knowing texts.' By a knowing text I mean a text that a reader will find to be self-knowing (reflexive), aware of the basis for limits of its knowledge-claims (authority). I mean a text skillfully crafted, particularly in terms of point of view, to establish an intersubjective relation among author, text, the 'characters' (persons represented in the text), and reader. I mean a text written to take full advantage of the techniques available to authors. (2003, p. 82)

A study of North African oral traditions is particularly strong in asserting the repositioning of views by both the scholar/writer and the performers. In *Romancing the Real*, Sabra J. Webber investigates the genre of *hikayat*, practiced by the people of Kelibia in the Cap Bon on Al Wata Al Gibly region of Tunisia. The *hikayat* is a form that combines a content of "real" or personal histories with the conventions of storytelling performance. This means that Webber can work within a frame of the stories being asserted as true events, which in turn allows her a wide scope to illustrate how the immediate world and the history of place and individuals come to the fore in these traditionally structured tales. They are seen as highly individualistic at the same time as being representative of the lives of people in this small town. Webber succeeds in emphasizing the active and transformative role this type of storytelling plays in the community. Rather than simply dredging up and fixing archaic or conservative imagery, the performers show themselves to be aware and part of the historical and creative processes of their town, region, nation, and world. Mostly, they live in the present, not timeless or unfixed ethnographic neutrality. Webber recognizes that "all culture, including cultural history, derives from social negotiation, my interest is in understanding something of a Kelibian artistic perspective on the past, present and future." (p. 11) As a result of her moving in and out of the stories while employing the words of speakers, Webber balances what the storytellers have to say with her own soundings of the local society and its wide network of associations. She resists the notion of closure at almost every juncture. Webber's work is particularly suited to evaluating a genre of personal assertive storytelling. Beyond "narrating the self," these performances touch many nodes of the wider society.[50]

Though the Tabwa of Zambia tell similar stories about their lives, I want to focus in this chapter on the fictional genres of narrative. Without spending a lot of time looking at the stories as allegorical or symbolic constructs, I choose to examine the way in which two performers used the occasion to boost their status or self-image in front of particular audiences. To do this, I will situate the performances, talk about the tales' traditional contexts—or, their relationship to other stories in the Tabwa repertoire—then point out their immediate application to the performance context. In the case of Tabwa storytellers, where I am more familiar with their repertoire of tales and images, raising elements of a traditional context and even comparing versions of the same story told by a single performer are analytical stances I can more confidently assert. This will firm up some of the methods applied to performances in the chapters that follow.

Performance Studies encompasses a broad approach to numerous genres, enactments and expressions. It grows out of a number of disciplines and frames. One main assertion is that performance is usually marked off, or contextually framed apart, from ordinary life. (Goffman 1974; Hymes 1975; Bauman 1977; Schechner 2003) This is clear in the genres of fictional storytelling or simply speaking on important topics

---

50 For an extensive, thorough study of personal narrative and its vital links to several social science and humanities fields of research, see Ochs and Capps 1996.

II. The Tabwa Context: Mature Shifting of Frames and Adolescent Assertion 37

while employing narrative-performance conventions. What seems just as important as acknowledging the characteristics of performed narrative is also the complex relationship between speakers and audiences, between performance and social reality. Kapchan cites Keeler on this relationship in a clear and informative manner.

> 'An art form,' he asserts, 'provides us indigenously generated representations of people's lives while still constituting a part of those lives. Both observed and lived, and so both a representation of social life and an instance of it, a performance provides a commentary upon interaction and yet also exemplifies it' [Keeler 1987: 262]. Implicit in Keeler's astute rendering of the art form's double function is the observation that performance is not only a specular event but a way of inhabiting the world. (2003, p. 131)

When we consider a performance session, and all the factors that brought it into being, there will always be the two areas of analysis that relate the efforts of performers and audience in their creation of artifice and the actual time and place of the event that emerges from its social context. As Kapchan reiterates:

> Performances are cultural enactments ... they appeal to all our senses, recalling us not only to our bodies and selves, not only to the subjectivities of others, but to the perpetual task of limit making, where we balance on the edge of the imaginary and the real. It is the task of performance to pivot on this border and to pluck the tense string of differences between the two realms, sending sound waves out in all directions. (p. 137)

So when we consider any of the performances examined below, we can acknowledge the deep complexity of any such expression while also look to identifying as many of the immediate and wider connotations of the specific event/enactment as possible.

Even the scholarly notions of "performance" are complex, nuanced and at times debatable. McKenzie does a good job of synthesizing some core ideas contributed by Schechner and Turner to the, paradoxically stated, centrality of liminality in understanding performance. As McKenzie notes, liminality is "a crucial concept for the theorizing of the politics of performance: as a mode of embodied activity that transgresses, resists, or challenges social structures." (1989, p. 218) This formative concept for the discipline will be "troubled" as McKenzie puts it, by the work of Judith Butler, who is mostly concerned with the performance of gender as seen partly through the lens of "existential phenomenology" and partly through proposing a view counter to the transgressive in performance, "a dominant and punitive form of power, one that both generates and constrains human subjects.... She theorizes the transgressivity and the normativity of performance genres." (pp. 220–221)[51] While it is difficult to reduce Butler's wide-ranging scholarship to any one or two key ideas, the point that I want to emphasize is the importance of viewing the complex nature of "performance," both the embodied and discursive types, as contextually framed and flexible enough to be used in various, sometimes diametrically opposed, modes. In particular, when we consider storytelling or narrative performance, we need to acknowledge the embodied qualities of performance while also focusing on its discursive dimensions. The intentions of performers or the outcomes/themes of their efforts must also be seen in their shifting frameworks, whether transgressive, normative or even a combination of the two.

Several schools of thought exist concerning the ways that members of oral societies remember the material they use in their performances. One of the most obvious practitioners this question applies to is the oral historian, who must produce on demand kingship lists or detailed chronicles of events or actors in those events.[52] While there is no doubt that memory is a primary factor in this activity, it must also be noted that historical events have a way of coming together in ways that make them easier to remember or reconstitute than details of imaginative oral narratives, even as they tend to employ similar tropes, actions and frames of the fictional tales. Further, the oral historian, as usually a paid practitioner, is particularly sensitive to shaping the material for his or her audience according to the conditions prevailing at the time of the telling or performance. This means that even historical narration is subject to selective "editing" by performers, based on the context of their recitations. Although few scholars still believe that performers of oral narrative fiction simply memorize their material, there remains a debate over whether these narrators exercise complete latitude

---

51 McKenzie selects four of Butler's publications from 1990 to 1993, to make his argument, but her two book-length studies contain the main themes he is focusing on.

52 It is worth looking at Okpewho's work in oral epic and oral traditions when considering the role of the oral historian. In particular, look at *The Epic in Africa* (1979) and "Rethinking Myth," (1980) where questions of fact, fancy and intent are considered in revealing ways. Vansina's seminal *Kingdoms of the Savanna* (1966) and *Oral History as Tradition* (1985) form, for many scholars, the basis for analyses of African oral historical traditions. It is significant to note that in the latter study, a reworking of his earlier *De la tradition orale* (1961), Vansina acknowledges the important role played by performance in oral history as well as admitting the virtually inevitable prevalence of imagination and performance context over historical "accuracy."

in the construction of their tales or are constrained by a fairly rigid notion of what their particular story ought to be.

Scholars taking formalist approaches to oral narrative believe that the performers have a sense of construction that allows them to alter tales as they desire, for example, selecting one ending for a tale on one occasion and another at a different time while employing the same frames.[53] Other scholars postulate a more rigid sense of story and plot, suggesting that narrators are more bound to repeat their narratives in the same way at each telling.[54] The question is important because it first of all effects the way we try to view the meaning of these stories. If they are simply repeated at every telling using the same details and structures we can hypothesize a more generic, complete meaning for the stories; that the teller uses an entire story in the way a proverb is used to point to a particular meaning or moral. If there is deliberate manipulation of the details between renditions of a tale by the same performers, the implication is that there is a subtlety, a shading of meaning within the workings of the stories that suggests a more intricate system of argument, or play, than is stipulated in the earlier model.[55] For over a century, folklorists simply assumed that unlettered peasants could not remember the details of what was a single or correct version of certain stories. The assumption was that an *ur-* or original version existed somewhere at the point of the tale's creation, followed thereon by a diffusion of that tale over space and time.[56]

My immediate intention here is to compare two versions of the same story told by the same person six years apart. Since there was little opportunity

---

53 Dègh makes reference to this earlier in this chapter. Scheub 1975, with his "cueing and scanning" assertion, works at one end of this spectrum of thought. He suggests that at times some storytellers begin their tales without knowing exactly what they will include or how the adventure will end.
54 This may pertain to notions of genre in some studies. See Ben-Amos's remarks in his introduction to Lindfors's collection of articles on African folklore (1977). One sense that Ben-Amos has of the storytelling process is fairly Proppian in nature. He gives the example of a Yoruba performer who explains how he would tell the researcher's biography by following a fairly straightforward structural/plot formulation to illustrate salient personal events and development.
55 I've taken this argument to more depth in looking at how Zambian radio and media might be able to employ oral narratives and their various versions to shape nationalist, socially engaged themes and messages. (Cancel 1986)
56 Diffusion theory has been pretty much refuted by one of its former proponents, Stith Thompson. But the adjacent activity, the collection and categorization of motifs and tale types, continues. In the last twenty years, the combination of this procedure with a formal, structural model has yielded some interesting results. See Haring's Malagasy index published in 1982.

to examine the data at the time of recording, I will be proceeding by violating a central tenet of this kind of investigation; in fact, this is the case with virtually all the performances I examine in this study. I have not been able to question the storyteller regarding the differences between the two versions. Any conclusions, therefore, developed in this discussion must be seen as tentative and circumstantial. Moreover, my comments as teller will in a sense play or even prey on the silence of the other teller, living some nine thousand miles out of earshot and unable to react to my observations.[57] While his interpretations would certainly bring welcome dimensions to our consideration of the tales, we would also have to factor in the performer's memory of what he intended at the time of the recording and what he wanted me to believe or take away from those earlier efforts.

Three dimensions of investigating oral narratives, set out in an earlier study, are the verbal text, the traditional context, and the performance context (Cancel 1989). The verbal text is the record of what the storyteller actually said.[58] The traditional context is the store of images, structures and possible plots contained in the memories of the members of the society, somewhat akin to what traditional folklorists refer to as *märchenstock*. The formal underpinnings of any narrative are found in the wider traditional context. These and images, actions and relationships are all drawn from this common pool and create both familiarity and expectations from an

---

57 In fact, when I visited Zambia in the summer of 2003, I learned that Stanley Kalumba had passed away four years earlier. He was not the first of those who had contributed material to this study to die before I had a chance for a return visit.

58 There are more than a few choices of how to write or render an oral text on the page. The format I've chosen reflects a literary prose genre framework, representing the narratives as a string of discrete sentences organized into paragraphs. I also make several concessions to the oral nature of the narration by including false starts, repeated words, employing non-standard punctuation and including explanatory, sometimes of only inferred assertions, material in brackets. Another common approach is to write the narrative in lines of text that look more like poetry, usually reflecting pauses in the performers' speech. (See Tedlock 1977; Seitel 1980; Okpewho 1990) Since, in this particular study, I am including the video record of the actual performances, I will leave it up to the reader/viewer as to how the verbal text can best be typographically visualized. Clearly, another historical problem in this kind of rendering has more to do with editorial choices made by the collectors or scholars who bring the performances to print. Here, all manner of ideological and self-serving intentions were indulged in the way tales were collected, transcribed, translated and edited, reflecting the desires and erroneous assumptions of early explorers, colonial administrators, missionaries and scholars. Yai 1999, takes Herskovits and Herskovits to task for some of these reasons, Clifford 1983, details the intricate and, some would argue, distorting methods by which Griaule rendered the narration of Oggotemeli. Scheub 1971, treats these problems more systematically in a historical context.

audience at any performance. These expectations are often controlled, channeled by a narrator to shape the performance experience.[59]

Any story-performance, therefore, will invariably be measured against the audience's memory of earlier performances and themes. By comparing the verbal text with the traditional context we can note the differences between versions of the same plot and similar or even very different tales existing in oral memory or, in my case, the body of recorded narratives. What I mean by this is that I can only judge the tradition and its context by the tales I have recorded and understood, and by examining other collections of story texts from this region. This means, as a serious limitation, that I am evaluating the tales based on knowledge gleaned by recording over 1300 performed narratives, but having selected, transcribed, translated, and/or considered only around 140 tales. The performance context comprises the non-verbal storytelling techniques[60] of the narrator as well as the various conditions of the performance occasion: characteristics of the performer, composition of audience, comments from the audience, time of day, tales that preceded the narrative in the session, storyteller's relationship to the collector, etc.

Numerous ongoing discussions between scholars persist, pertaining to how performance is to be evaluated. Barber and Farais sum up much of the debate that my own project grows out of:

> On the one hand, literary critics and folklorists have taken up a stance which combines a limited contextualization (the emphasis being on 'performance' and the immediate conditions of performance) with a formalist analysis of texts (with emphasis on the incidence of wordplay, repetition and other literary devices): thus ignoring by and large what the texts actually *say*. Historians, on the other hand, seem increasingly to be regarding oral texts either as raw material which, subject to a certain amount of processing, will yield historical information; or as the unmediated voice of an alien past. (Barber and Farais 1989, p. 1)

---

59 The formal methodology that I will often employ in this project is more clearly set out in my earlier monograph (1989). It is the basis from which I will evaluate the verbal text/traditional context elements in the narratives that follow.

60 The numerous techniques of performance include voice, personal style, strategies of giving form to imagery and themes, and gesture. While most of what I do with these elements in this project is descriptive, there is obviously a large body of literature spawned from disciplinary approaches such as folklore and performance studies. When it comes to close study of living performance, the emerging work on gesture in African storytelling will become an important dimension in describing the links between words and physical act. See Klassen 2004, 1999, Eastman and Omar 1985, Creider 1997, 1986, and Olofson 1974.

Considering the scenario they lay out, it should be clear that my emphasis is on the combination of formal and performance/contextual analysis. In fact, this approach does consider the "historicity" of performance in its immediacy, its relationship to the event of performance itself. Ideally, as Barber and Farais suggest, "what seem[s] to be required [is] an approach that acknowledge[s] simultaneously the historicity and the textuality of oral texts, that combined a sociology with a poetics of oral literature" (1989, p. 1). As I keep emphasizing, the current study is based on incomplete knowledge and will not meet an absolute standard set by a number of disciplinary approaches. Moreover, by introducing the question of ethnographic authority and the problem of writing other cultures, I am challenging even the modest observations and conclusions that are elicited by the performances under consideration. In other words, my analytical writing looks to avoid the pitfalls of eternally reflexive Derridian spirals of meaning and doubt[61] while skirting the assured and absolute terms of the well-wrought ethnographic text that supposes some kind of accurate closure in rendering performances and their meanings.

It should be emphasized at this early point that among the Tabwa of Zambia, and all the groups recorded for this study, storytelling events vary in their occasions and locations. Most instances take place in the well-known domestic space of the household verandah or around an evening fire outdoors. Usually family members and sometimes friends pass the time after the evening meal with ordinary talk and gossip which often evolves into more formal storytelling endeavors. In many cases, stories are told by elders to children as a form of entertainment and instruction; something to wind down their day and lull them to sleep. It is not unusual for the stories to take on a more mature bent of theme and complexity when the children have gone off to sleep and the remaining adults shape their performances for an older audience. The themes and allusions of these tales can be drawn from broad social and cultural concerns, but these can also hone in on local relationships between people and be used allusively for direct commentary on events and situations well known to the audience.[62] Men often defer

---

61 One of the best discussions of writing and scholarly authority is Derrida's 1978 "Structure, Sign, and Play in the Discourse of the Human Sciences."
62 See Cancel 1989, pp. 55–84, for a more thorough discussion of performance contexts and quotidian instances of storytelling. Cosentino 1982 spends a good amount of time on considering local allusions in themes and images of stories told by the Mende of Sierra Leone. Jackson 1982, 2006, focuses on the interactions of various performers and their stories in single performance sessions.

to women when it comes to performing narratives in intimate, familial settings, since storytelling is often seen as something for children. There are, however, some men who relish the opportunities storytelling offers and enjoy showcasing their considerable skills in performance. Gender particularly comes to the fore when narratives, for whatever reasons, are performed in a more public space or occasion, where men tend to dominate. These occasions can be common rites such as weddings, funerals, church services, or rites associated with the beginning of planting, hunting or fishing seasons or the harvesting of crops. It is not unusual for storytelling, both fictional and anecdotal, to break out during labor, such as fishing or farming, and these narratives are most obviously marked by the distinctive verbal rhythms of performance and devices of speech to induce and prolong audience interaction.[63] From a practical scholarly perspective, my efforts to gather and record this material, especially in areas where I was not well known, were framed by gender concerns that mostly limited my pool of possible performers to men. Socially, it was almost impossible for a man, particularly a stranger, to engage only women performers in a recording session. As I describe the various conditions of performance in this study, these frames and contexts should be kept in mind.

Kaputa[64]

In June of 1989, at Kaputa, the rural capital of Zambia's northernmost district, I was escorted towards the place where I was staying by Mr. Stanley Kalumba. It was around 5:30 PM, and the sun was low on the horizon, elongating our shadows as we walked the red dusty road past the police station and government staff houses. We had been discussing a proverb in the story he had just told me when Mr. Kalumba suddenly stopped and said something to the effect of "Have I told you this one before?" In fact he had, six years earlier, and I said as much. He seemed apologetic but

---

63 Unlike other African societies who at least claimed prohibitions against telling stories during daylight hours or while performing labor, I was not able to ascertain similar strictures among the Bemba-speaking peoples with whom I worked. I have, recently found evidence of these sayings/strictures among the Bemba.

64 My 1989 monograph on Tabwa storytelling contains some information on this ethnic group, their physical environment and history. A more systematic and detailed account of Zambian Tabwa culture and history can be found in my doctoral dissertation (1981). Since the Tabwa also stretch across the border into the Democratic Republic of the Congo, a lot of scholarship exists by Belgians, missionaries, Congolese scholars and, in particular, Allen F. Roberts (1980, 1984, 1996, 2000).

I assured him I enjoyed the tale very much, both times. Of course, even at the time I'd heard the story earlier in the afternoon, my mind turned to the possibilities of a comparative study of the two versions.[65]

So we will deal with at least two tales and two tellers. Mr. Kalumba is the first teller, a Tabwa man who had over a period of six years been kind enough to perform a number of stories for me to record on video and audiocassette. The second teller is me, who, due to the particular circumstances of my work, will provide not only my story—my analysis—but also Mr. Kalumba's, through transcription, translation and commentary. That I feel this is a less than ideal situation is hopefully apparent in the words and framing employed to situate this discussion. Theoretical discourses running side by side in this analysis treat the question of oral narrative composition and performer control of this performance, as well as the choices made in representing and writing it. While the former is the focus of my discussion, the latter is critically—in several senses of the term—linked to how we come to understand the storytelling process, the shaping of identity and the world in speech. Whose speech? Whose identity? are questions I put forth now to qualify most of what will follow.

In 1983, when we first met at his home in the village of Nsama, Stanley Kalumba was fifty-eight years old. He was a slim, soft-spoken man, with a shaved head. His performance style was direct and low-key, with fluid hand and arm-movements as he gestured to places where action took place or imitated the various characters in his narratives. When I recorded him again in 1989, he looked very much the same, if a bit grayer, and was living at Kaputa. It is helpful to consider both versions of the story, back-to-back, beginning with the 1983 performance at Nsama.

---

65 There have been few instances where I was able to record storytellers performing the same story more than once. One notable example was a long narrative by Tabwa performer Chola Chilengwe at Mukupa Katandula village in 1976, whereby I recorded the first version then days later a friend coincidentally recorded a second rendering by Mr. Chilengwe at a beer drink. Among the Wolof of the Gambia, Emil Magel (1984) recorded two versions of a story he titled "Hyena Wrestles a Konderong," by the same performer (pp. 138–143).

Tabwa Storytelling 1 by Stanley Kalumba*

Stanley
Kalumba: I am Stanley Kalumba.

Robert
Cancel: Stanley Kalumba?

SK: Yes.

RC: Yes. Begin.

SK: It was said, there was a little thing. A lion lived with how many wives? [Holds up two fingers] Two. And his children. Then this Kalulu [the Tabwa trickster hare] had no clothes at all, because he had no cloth. He was naked. Now he told his wife, "My wife, we will surely be wealthy soon." She said, "No, I doubt that." He said, "Oh? Fine. Just wait and see." So Kalulu set out and walked into the bush. He found the lion and his children there. The father had gone to prepare the fields for planting [*citemene*]. Kalulu said, "You children, are you there?" They said "*Mukwai?*" "When your father returns, tell him 'Your un…uncle said he wants you to make him a bark cloth by tomorrow. If you don't make him a bark cloth, you will be like the bush buck with one year to live.'" He then went away. When the lion returned there, the children told him, "Father!" "*Mukwai?*" "A person came and said, 'My nephew must make me a bark cloth by tomorrow. If he does not make the bark cloth, he will be like the bushbuck with one year to live.'" "So who is this 'uncle' of mine? In this land I've defeated all the animals. I'm a lion. I'm strong and devour animals. You…you see, no…none can surpass my power in the land." They said, "Fine." He did not worry. Another morning, he cut down a tree and began to pound bark cloth. Ka-Ka-Ka-Ka-Ka-Ka-Kka-Ka. He pounded, he finished. He draped it over a tree stump. He went off to garden. So Kalulu returned again in the morning. "You children! Has he finished the cloth today?" "No *mukwai*, it's done." "Fine when he arrives tell him his uncle thanks him very much." The bark cloth, he carried off. So when the lion returned from the task, he found the bark cloth was not there. He questioned his children. They said, "Yes, he's already taken it. He told us to tell his 'nephew' that it was he who took it." "Agh. What kind of 'uncle' is this?" So the lion made a proclamation throughout the entire country. He said, "All animals must gather so that I can come see that 'uncle' of mine who had me make the bark cloth."

* All the teller's photos in this book are taken from videos shot by the author. To watch the video of this story follow this link: http://dx.doi.org/10.11647/OBP.0033.02/Tabwa1

Then Kalulu who had fooled him heard this news on Saturday. "As of today, we will go there to gather to find the one who ordered the lion to make the bark cloth." Then all the animals set out: hartebeest, the duiker, and the...the...what-do-you-call-it...the elephant, and the buffalo. All of them went there to the lion. Now as they walked on the path, truly, Kalulu appeared, saying to himself, "Truly we are called because this bark cloth, it's the problem." Then he called the bushbuck over, he said, "My friend, Bushbuck." He said, "*Mukwai?*" "Come closer here." He said, "Boi, I'm giving you this bark cloth. Go and wear it, because you can't go to the palace naked. If you arrive naked, they'll drive you away. Wear this cloth to the palace." So *mukwai*, the bushbuck said, "*Mukwai*, I thank you *mukwai*." [Claps his hands to show his gratitude] He donned the cloth and went on.

They all arrived and sat down. The lion rose and roared. "Truly *mukwai*, I've called you all here because I want to know this 'uncle' who sent me to make bark cloth. In this land there is no animal that surpasses me in strength. I have the strongest teeth, the strongest claws. All these things I have. Now here I want to see that 'uncle' who had me pound bark cloth. So I want, right here, him to be shown to me." So they said, "Very well my lord. We thank you, your majesty. 'We draw your firewood and water!'" [Claps hands as he speaks words of lion's subjects to emphasize their obeisance] So *mukwai*, they gathered right there. Little Kalulu rose, "My uncle, truly, I think we should waste no more time, no. The...the one who wears the bark cloth, your majesty, that you made, is this one!" [Points in front of him to indicate the bushbuck] They pointed at the bushbuck next to Kalulu. So *mukwai*, he tried to rise and speak in their midst. They all said, "Shh! You! Quiet! 'A slave dies with words in his mouth' you." So *mukwai*, right there, the lion said, "Cut this one up. So it's this one who said to me 'you...you are my nephew!' Am I your nephew, you, bushbuck?? You are a very stupid person!" So here, th... they...rose and grabbed the bushbuck. So *mukwai*, they rose up, and took the bushbuck. He said, "No! The one who gave me this bark cloth was Kalulu!" "Tch! Shut up, you! 'A slave dies with words in his mouth.'" So *mukwai*, what became of the bushbuck? They whipped the bushbuck. He just died. So, then the bushbuck died from Kalulu's tricks. Then, Kalulu, he survived. But Bushbuck, they killed him.

RC: Yes.

SK: Yes. They killed him. This is why they killed the bushbuck, because he could not speak cleverly. Kalulu fooled him by giving him the bark cloth, while he remained free. That's it *mukwai*.

Here is the 1989 version of the narrative Mr. Kalumba performed at Kaputa:

Tabwa Storytelling 2
by Stanley Kalumba, 1989*

Robert Cancel:	Give me your name, then begin. [Mr. Kalumba takes time to adjust his chair and get into a comfortable position amidst a group of children and adults.]
Audience Member:	Sit down. [Spoken, I think, to someone in the audience.]
RC:	Your name? Bring (us) your name.
SK:	I am Stanley Kalumba.
RC:	Begin *mukwai*.
SK:	Yes. There was a little thing. The lion lived with his wife in a hut[66]...the lion. So then over there, as they lived, little Kalulu appeared. He went and found the lion's children at the hut. In the village...the owner [the lion] had already gone...to cut brush (before planting time).[67] At that time when he returned, he came and found this message from his children, "Truly father, right here there came a person. That one said, 'When your father comes he must try to pound bark cloth. If he doesn't make bark cloth he will be like the male bushbuck who had only one year (to live).'"[68] So the lion wondered, "Ah! Truly, in this country...I have the strongest claws and teeth. But this person who came here, what sort is he?" They said, "Truly *mukwai*, we don't know him at all from the village, father." He said, "O.K., fine." He went.

---

66 I use the word "hut" to translate *"mutanda"* which is a rough shelter, often used as a temporary lodging when hunting or farming far from home. I use the word house or home to gloss the word *ng'anda*, which is a permanent structure, one's main residence.

67 The principle form of agriculture in Northern Province is still the system of "slash and burn," whereby dried brush and trees are cut down and burned just prior to the rainy season. The ashes, washed into the ground act as fertilizer for the crops. The Bemba/Tabwa word for this type of agriculture is *citemene*, and used as a specific verb it means to cut the brush and or trees.

68 The phrase is a proverb that is usually employed as a threat. The speaker warns the listener that if he or she does not do as he or she is told, there will be painful physical consequences, a beating or something unpleasant. The proverb is spoken here as: *Nga taasalile cilundu, ninshi ni nkulungwe aali umwaka umo.* [Literally, "If he does not pound bark cloth it is like the male bushbuck with one year."] The word for a male bushbuck is *nkulungwe*, while the generic term for a bushbuck is *cisongo*. It is the latter word that is used to refer to the character in the story; though it seems less than coincidental that the core proverbial saying is about a bushbuck.

* To watch a video of this story follow this link: http://dx.doi.org/10.11647/OBP.0033.02/Tabwa2

Another morning, early, the lion went to cut brush. Again, he (Kalulu) returned. "*Odi*, over here!" "Enter *mukwai*." "So, have you told your father, that is, have you seen him about making the cloth? Tell him that it's your uncle who wants this very nice bark cloth, so that he makes it." He said, "Yes, that's truly what we told him but he didn't understand. He said, 'No, I don't know this person.'" He said, "Go tell him, say, 'It's your uncle who directs you to make the bark cloth. You must make it.'" The children said, "Yes *mukwai*." So their father returned in the evening from cutting brush. "Father." "Yes?" "Right here, there came a person who brought these words, as he did yesterday." He said, "Fine, my children, let me make the cloth." So that lion got a...a...what-do-you-call-it...the material to make bark cloth. He pounded. He pounded. Nko, nko, nko, nko, nko, nko, nko. He praised himself. He said, "Let's make it, so that you can wear it...

Arriving Speaker:	"How are you *mukwai*?" [A man has just arrived at the site of the performance and, obviously intoxicated, is trying, I think, to get my (the most obvious stranger) attention. Mr. Kalumba continues with his story while an audience member tries to quiet or chase the newcomer off.]
SK:	"Let me make it for the chief's wife..."
Audience Member:	"Go away. He's telling a story."
SK:	"The chief's wife is none other than the buttocks..."[69]
AS:	"How is your work going?"
Audience Member:	[Same audience member who had earlier admonished the man said something inaudible on my tape but which was obviously intended to make the speaker be quiet.]
SK:	"Our buttocks." He said, "I'm tired, like a bark cloth maker pounding in an ant's stomach. A stomach is filled with mysteries."[70] So that lion finished the cloth. He put it down. He said, "This person who wants the cloth will come and get it."

That morning the lion went to cut brush. So he (Kalulu) arrived soon after. Kalulu said, "Bark cloth?!" They said, "Yes *mukwai*, it's over there on the tree stump." So, the children went. They went and got it. They gave it to him. Upon the lion's return, in the evening, he came

---

69 Here Mr. Kalumba is probably using a euphemism for nakedness. The cloth is meant to clothe the buttocks of the chief's wife, referring, I think, to the grandeur of the cloth he is making, which is fit for even a queen.

70 Here it seems the lion is praising his own skills for their delicacy, since pounding the stomach of an ant from within, without injuring the ant, suggests a high degree of competence with the pounding mallet.

and asked, "What about the bark cloth?" "So *mukwai*, he's already come and taken it, your uncle. He said, 'Fine, since if he'd refused to make a nice cloth he would have been like the male bushbuck with one year to live. But now this is fine.'" So that lion thought, "Well, here in this country there is no one as strong as I, stronger than all the big animals, including elephants, and all the rest. I've defeated them by my strength, my strong teeth and claws. So let me call all the animals so that we see this uncle who made me make the bark cloth." So, then he made a decree, he said, "So my friends, in a week every animal must gather here at my place. I will come and see the uncle who had me pound bark cloth."

So then the day that followed, all the animals just gathered, all of them: Kalulu, the duiker, just all of them, and the bushbuck (as well). Kalulu was one who was very clever, he set out during that week. When that time came near, he knew...he said, "Truly, if I arrive at the lion's place wearing this cloth, I Kalulu, they will kill me." So then he saw the bushbuck and said, "Grandfather, come here." So he called him, "What is it *mukwai*?" "You...you see, listen well grandfather, you will shame us if you go there naked. Put on this cloth. I myself can go just like this because it is at my uncle's place. I can go without problems. You put on this bark cloth father to conceal your nakedness." "Yes *mukwai*, thank you *mukwai*." So that bushbuck had the bark cloth, he wore it.

Then when they arrived there, they gathered at the lion's place. They gathered in a group. Right there, all of them: the elephant, all the animals...the buffalo, roan antelope, hartebeest, they all gathered. So, the lion came out from his home. He said, "Truly, this summons was for all my friends, all you animals. I want to know who set me up, saying 'if he doesn't make the bark cloth, he will be like the bushbuck with a year to live.'" So, there the bushbuck had wrapped the bark cloth all around himself. So Kalulu sat far away. Then all the animals said, "Your highness, we gather your firewood and water." So then, "We will see him *mukwai*, the one wearing the bark cloth sent our chief to make cloth." So they came, they saw the bushbuck, they said, "You! Stand up!" So he stood up, he was sitting there, nearby. So that lion then said, "So really, you are in this gathering. This person, so it's this one who sent me to pound bark cloth, who threatened me by saying, 'If he doesn't make the cloth he will be like the bushbuck with a year to live.'" One said, "Yes *mukwai*, it's this very one."

So the bushbuck said (to himself), "Truly, that's how people die. What can I do? Perhaps I can be clever. (then aloud) Though it is true *mukwai*, your majesty, that they say a slave dies with his words in his mouth, let me explain the situation..." Kalulu stood up over there...and said, "You, shut up! Stop it. It's you who...who sent the chief to pound cloth. So the one who you point at is whom? Who pounded the cloth? It's you who wanted the bark cloth. It's you who wanted the bark cloth!" So then, right there, the lion said, "Fine. You, my people, this person must die because I have the greatest strength of all the animals in the bush. I have...

Audience
Member: "Mmm hmmm." [Assenting sound.]

SK: "I have strong teeth and claws. So this one who threatened me, the bushbuck who said, 'If he doesn't make the bark cloth he will be like the bushbuck with a year to live,' kill him!" He said, "No *mukwai*! It's Kalulu who gave it to me..." "You, stop it! I didn't give it to him. He's just lying." They grabbed the bushbuck and killed him.

So *mukwai*, that's my *mulumbe* about the lion.

Several elements of the 1983 version bear mention. The story begins with a near destitute Kalulu declaring he will find wealth, while his wife refuses to believe him. Kalulu visits the lion's home once before and once after the bark cloth is made. The first time he uses a threat and a self-inflating title, as the lion's maternal uncle—which is a father-like kinship position—in order to get the bark cloth. The lion simply makes the cloth and soon thereafter the hare claims it. The hare explains to the bushbuck that he must wear a cloth as proper protocol for visiting the lion's place. Kalulu is the first to point to the bushbuck wearing the cloth, and the antelope is not given a chance to speak, silenced by a proverb. The story's end is focused on the bushbuck's lack of clever speech, as opposed to the hare's ingenious ploy.

Thematically, the tale is on one level a typical trickster story, in which the diminutive hare is able to dupe the lion into making him a garment. Similarly, Kalulu escapes punishment by fooling the dim-witted bushbuck. The pattern is a familiar one in trickster tales from all over Africa and, in particular, the lion and bushbuck as dupes for Kalulu are featured in numerous Tabwa stories as well as those of other Bemba-speaking peoples.[71] Cleverness and clever speech are the traits that are revered in this tale, a reflection of the position speech and discourse hold in society. Further, speech is able to overcome both physical and social limitations, as the hare not only deceives

---

71 Kalulu is found in stories beyond the Bemba-speaking area. Among the Nyanja/Cewa-speaking groups of Zambia and Malawi, Kalulu is also a central, trickster figure. Moving east and north, Swahili and neighboring groups feature a trickster hare in their narratives called Sungura.

II. The Tabwa Context: Mature Shifting of Frames and Adolescent Assertion 51

a powerful animal but also a chief, creating for himself the identity of that leader's "uncle." Looking a bit closer but again staying within the obvious realm of the trickster tale, we can see a commentary about power and equity. The lion as king is shown to be an improper leader, not able to catch the hare early on in his activities, then believing the trumped up evidence against the bushbuck. Since Tabwa chiefs are more likely skilled mediators than divinely empowered rulers, this kind of commentary relates to the fallibility of the leaders and their susceptibility to flattery and superficial evidence.[72] Not hearing the bushbuck's side of the story was another error of judgment that "speaks" badly for the lion's leadership skills.

Three sayings play a role in both versions. The first is the not so veiled threat "*Ninshi ninkulungwe yali umwaka umo,*" [(He will be) like the bushbuck with only a year to live]. Kalulu uses it and the lion cubs repeat it to their father. Another saying refers to the fate of slaves "*Umusha afwa ne fyebo mu kanwa,*" [A slave dies with (his words) in his mouth]. This is twice addressed to the bushbuck to squelch his attempts to defend himself. Finally, the people address a saying to the lion that is a praise for chiefs, "*Mwansabamba, twatasha, kanabesa, kalungu wewe nkuni na menshi,*" [Chief, we thank you, your highness, we gather your firewood and water]. The saying places the chief above his subjects and reiterates their respect by emphasizing the common tasks they perform out of a sense of duty.

The sayings are obviously used outside of the narrative context, with everyday references, but here they form a kind of model for their appropriate application. Mr. Kalumba used them judiciously in a story that focused more on the events than the meanings of the proverbs, though clearly they are woven into the fabric of the tale's connotations. What happens to Kalulu and bushbuck are the important elements of the narrative as it is presented here. In the second version of this tale, the function of the proverbs is altered slightly.

In the 1989 version, Stanley Kalumba changed the narrative in a few significant ways. He does not mention wives, for either the lion or Kalulu. The lion is mentioned at the tale's start then Kalulu simply shows up while he is at his farm. Where Kalulu interacts with the cubs only twice in the first version, here he visits them three times. The dialogue is repeated to the lion by the cubs more often here than in the first version. In fact, the cubs describe Kalulu's first visit to the homestead after the fact, instead of Mr. Kalumba, as

---

72   See Cancel 1989, pp. 156–158, 172–174, 200–201.

narrator, directly detailing the actual visit. At almost every repetition or visit the saying that contains a threat, about the bushbuck with one year to live, is uttered. It is this saying, more than the claim that his "uncle" demanded a bark cloth, that most annoys the lion. In this version we have a more detailed scene in which the lion makes the bark cloth while he praises himself, using a euphemism for clothing that refers to its function as covering the buttocks of the chief's wife, and says the skills needed to pound the cloth are as subtle as pounding the inside of an ant's stomach. The hare lets the animals discover the bark cloth-clad bushbuck rather than pointing him out himself, though he does speak out when the antelope tries to explain himself, reiterating the evidence and urging swift action. At one point, Mr. Kalumba voices the bushbuck's thoughts, as he sees the danger of his situation and tries to find a way out of it, "*Kwena ifyo baafwa na naafwa pano pantu. Bushe, kwena, ndecita shani? Kana na ine kancite amano.*" ["Truly, this is how people get killed, I'll get killed right here. What will I do? Let me try a trick."] Here the acuity of the hare is highlighted against the bushbuck's ill-fated effort at cleverness. But, as in the first version, his efforts are shouted down and he is killed. A final difference between versions is that in this latter rendering there is no explanation at the end of the narrative.

While the plot of this tale is essentially identical to the earlier version, the differences in detail are important. The lack of wives for the characters reduces the competitive, domestic exchange that initially motivated the hare to engage the lion. Further, without stating that Kalulu is impoverished, Mr. Kalumba keeps this condition from contributing to the motivation. If these details are assumed to exist in the traditional context, the memories of audience members, then Mr. Kalumba is possibly depending on the situation as being understood in the second version, part of what an audience brings to a performance. He might also be intentionally blunting those details to give the Hare's actions a more aggressive, self-serving tone. The focus on the bushbuck proverb is much stronger here, and seems to be a major source of the lion's anger. The proverbial emphasis becomes, because of its repetition, an important constituent of the tale's theme. Here, more than in the earlier version, the fit between saying and bushbuck as dupe of the hare becomes stronger. The saying is therefore emphasized because of the predicament of the antelope and the fact that it specifically refers to this species of animal.[73]

---

73 The tie between story and proverb is not uncommon in Tabwa tales. There are two proverbs associated with the tale of the monitor lizard in the tree: one about the lizard's talkativeness and the other about the necessity to be near someone when explaining

Moreover, the proverbial core of the tale seems to be reflected in the differences between the original and second performance contexts. The first telling, in 1983, was in the late afternoon outside of Mr. Kalumba's house at Nsama. The audience was small, made up of three adults and around ten children. It was the first tale I collected from him and the first time I ever used a video camera to record a performance. He did not use proverbs in a repetitive way and was also careful to explain the tale's meaning at the end. In part, the presence of children would explain his strategy of obviously highlighting meaning, a strategy termed "external" by Labov (1972), and in equal or greater part my own presence would stimulate this approach. Mr. Kalumba did not know me and wanted to make his meaning clear to a stranger who most likely had a poor command of the language and who may not have heard similar tales. He could not, in short, assume knowledge of the traditional context on my part. That he cared about teaching me with his tales became evident on other occasions, where he would tell stories with dilemma endings and try to elicit explanations from me—mostly, I'm embarrassed to say, to mixed results.[74]

This observation underscores the different strategy in the second version, performed in 1989 at Kaputa. Mr. Kalumba had moved to a much larger village, in his capacity as a Rural Council mailman. When he told this story again, again in later afternoon, he lived in closer proximity to neighbors, and a sizeable audience of adults and children quickly gathered when I arrived with my equipment. While I did not take a specific count, there were at least fifteen to twenty adults and as many children. Mr. Kalumba clearly was aware of the large group, and even pushed on at one point in the performance when a drunken man joined the throng and tried to hold a conversation with me while the other audience members urged the latecomer to be quiet or leave. At this juncture, Mr. Kalumba was describing the scene where the lion was pounding bark cloth and praising himself. The new arrival interrupted the lines about the chief's wife's

---

    something. (Cancel 1989) In an initial translation of the first bushbuck version, one that I used on a subtitled videotape, I was unaware of the proverb being used and instead misread the phrase by improperly breaking up the noun *nkulungwe* [a male bushbuck] into a verbal construct having to do with being hunted. Therefore, though my translation "I will hunt you down" was semantically incorrect, the sense of a threat against the lion conveyed essentially the same idea. In a recent translation of the second version, also subtitled on videotape, I used the literal proverb without explanation so that, as in the performance, the context of the situation points to the saying's meaning.

74 Mr. Kalumba's approach to stories and, in particular, my presence as researcher is detailed in my Tabwa monograph. (1989, pp. 80–81)

buttocks which, it seemed to me, caused him to cut the reference short and move on to the allusion to the fine craftsmanship involved in pounding an ant's stomach. Overall, the video record of this performance confirms that he was speaking in a faster, louder, more intense manner to the larger audience than he had in the 1983 session, where he had been more relaxed in his style of presentation.

This later version was more rooted in metaphorical or allusive depth of language than the earlier one. It was aimed at the large adult audience and, I'd like to think, at the ostensibly more experienced and knowledgeable researcher. The "internal" (Labov 1972) strategy of not explaining the tale at the end also supports this interpretation of the performance context.

At this point, I want to continue my tale in a slightly different vein. Using a literary appropriation as a starting point, we can see the tale as a compact model of the ethnographic, interpretive "mission."[75] In the tale I am telling, the scholar plays the role of trickster, the one who controls not only events but language in his account. The actual storyteller becomes a character in the wider academic epic, someone whose real power is akin to that of the bushbuck in the Tabwa tale. Whether I act responsibly or not, Mr. Kalumba's words are here represented through a cultural filter, broader than a linguistic translation. The lion or chief can be seen as the audience of my scholarly efforts, susceptible to the information and shadings of meaning that I provide. As reliable as I intend to be, we will have this problem in perpetuity. The reader accepts or finds fault with the story, but the bushbuck will often be silenced or have his words misconstrued because Kalulu remains the orchestrator of the event, the manipulator of data and situation.

The Tabwa audience rarely feels pity for the bushbuck, since he has little to recommend him. Wit and the ability to manipulate language are traits of both the storyteller and the trickster. In many ways, they are parallel beings, for each seeks to better his or her position within the context of action and discourse. This is an understandably ambiguous position, since at times craft and craftiness will win out over "truth" and

---

[75] See Kapchan's comparison of performance with the "enterprise" of ethnography. (Kapchan 2003, p. 136) A more provocative evocation of the ethnographic process is detailed by West 2007, where he compares the ethnographer and his or her writing with forms of sorcery. Toon van Meijl suggests that in order for an ethnographer to successfully work between the demands of the scholarly process and the real political and social goals/needs of the people being studied, the social scientist would do well to take on the mantle of the "divine trickster." (2005) This also goes back to the question that opened this study about whether or not a researcher allows him or herself to be "captured" by the people with whom he or she works.

innocence. I as interpreter must acknowledge this ambiguous role and continue to pursue the tale because its telling is important to me and my intentions. What I can do is to make this clear and try to keep the dialectics of interpretation, ignorance, and mystery at least at the edges, if not at the forefront, of my writing.

If I were to include Stanley Kalumba as an active participant in this kind of writing, the text would be to an obvious degree more "accurate," more "honest." But the process is never completely finished, since it spirals back to my mediation and his intentions. This kind of storytelling is not unlike the Tabwa tradition, since it is always apparent in the living event that the storyteller arrives and leaves with a personality and intention that drives and frames the images, words, and gestures of the performance. We do well, as "readers" of such performances, to follow the example of the storytelling audience. In this way, we can appreciate the few instances when the trickster is duped and the bushbuck, or some other victim, gets his or her revenge.[76]

Let me end my tale by suggesting several possible conclusions. On the one hand, we can see that Mr. Kalumba stayed close to the same plot and events in both versions of the story. This suggests that he did not take large scale or dramatic liberties with the narrative. On the other hand, the changes he did make seemed significant and point to some of the ways he can shift meaning and depth of language within the same plot. I assert here the importance of performance context as an influence on these different versions. A third point is that he may simply have forgotten some of the finer differences between the versions, focusing only on what he felt were the important details of the core story and adding a few new images in the latter version.[77] Whichever interpretation may or may not be accurate, they all feed into the text of my tale and conform to the discourse that I use to frame these observations.

The other teller, who has his own reasons for placing himself or rather his desires into his tale, is obviously Stanley Kalumba. Mr. Kalumba was never a passive object of my scholarly efforts. In fact, he controlled our interactions over the first six years I knew him.[78] We conducted these

---

76 See the narrative by Mr. Henry Chakobe, where the bushbuck eventually gets the better of Kalulu, in Chapter III, on Bemba storytelling.
77 A Lunda performer, Mr. Idon Pandwe, told another version of this tale and, assuming a culture region overlap, its details can be weighed against Mr. Kalumba's narratives (see Chapter V).
78 Echoing Haring 1972, Bauman emphasizes the potential and real instances of performers or subjects of research controlling aspects of their encounters with

interactions in Bemba, which narrowed the range of our conversations and my ability to delve into his narratives or personal history. He did let me know that he'd spent many years working in the urban Copperbelt area of Zambia, and that he became a Rural Council postman after he retired.[79] In 1989 I was stunned to find out, sometime after the performance discussed above, that he had a more than functional command of English. He revealed this ability in a conversation we'd been having where I agreed to bring him a small radio when I next visited and, as I walked away, he called after me in English, "You won't forget, will you?" This made me remember the several occasions where I'd strained to find the proper words to ask questions or to understand his explanation of a particularly obscure story and its symbolic elements, and how a few English words might have significantly eased the laborious process.

However, Stanley Kalumba is represented here by the kind of silence some scholars, including some ethnographers, depend on to put forth their theories and interpretations.[80] Since I cannot sit down with him again and discuss my perceptions of his tales and his own recollections and motivations, this analysis remains a contingent framework of observations and propositions. Unless we can speak, write, hear, or read, both our tales in their several dimensions and interrelationships—and this will not happen—the analysis of the story of Kalulu, the lion and bushbuck remains in that unsettled realm of stories about stories, tales told by one teller about another one, based on well-intentioned but none-the-less, inevitably, open-ended scholarship. At the least, and as is the case with all the performance

---

researchers, in part to question what he calls "poststructuralist" scholars' concerns with the power relationships in these interactions. (2004, pp. 157–162) I will return to this situation in the concluding chapter, but also note that West 2008, pp. 80–85 focuses on the same concerns.

79 Stanley Kalumba followed a common pattern of rural-urban migration at that time, which mostly entailed men moving to the copper mines and their surrounding cities for wage labor. Strong ties would be kept with their home areas and relatives in the form of regular visits and money sent back to help with local finances. After putting in enough years to draw a pension, the men would move back to the rural areas, build themselves houses, and retire to take part in the local economy in the form of farming, fishing or related activities. See Watson 1958, for a more detailed description of this practice in the wider rural social life of the Mambwe of northern Zambia. Mr. Laudon Ndalazi, a Bisa storyteller featured in Chapter IV, also followed this employment pattern of migration and retirement back to his rural home. Two other performers in this study, Mr. Henry Chakobe and Mr. Stephen Chipalo, were retired school teachers living in the village around Ilondola Mission (Chapter III).

80 Sichone states his concern in blunt terms, "Ethnographers capture by description…and to be translated is as humiliating as to be colonized." (2001, p. 371)

records in this study, I am pleased to bring Mr. Kalumba's efforts and image into the wider scholarly purview, preserving in somewhat inadequate fashion his talents and public persona.

Postscript

In October 2005, Kaputa District, where I'd recorded Mr. Kalumba, was in the midst of a slight economic upswing after a decade of dramatic decline. In the twenty-nine years since I first lived there, the district has experienced two economic booms and two downturns. Most of this had to do with the availability of fish from Lake Mweru Wantipa. The lake was a plentiful source in 1976, but the roads leading into and out of the district were in very bad condition, no more than dirt tracks running down a very steep and long escarpment as one traveled north from the town of Mporokoso towards the lake. The road coming from the west, from Mununga in Luapula Province, was not much better. The government and foreign aid agencies managed to upgrade the roads that ran into the district and around the lake by late 1984. At that point, commercial traffic, bringing goods into the area and taking fish out, had rapid and consistent access. Public transportation in the form of regularly running buses moved people to and from the district. Shops in numerous villages sprang up and there were opportunities of various types associated with fishing and related economies. By the mid nineties, however, after local fisherman consistently ignored laws providing for fallow periods where fish were supposed to spawn and have time to maintain their population, the output of the lake dropped precipitously.[81] The lake was more or less fished out by the turn of the millennium. The government, as a consequence of both lack of funds to maintain infrastructure and the diminishing status of the district as an economic resource, failed to keep up the quality of roads in the area. This steady decline of infrastructure led to a paucity of public transportation. Even the fish lorries that had provided transport in the days of very bad roads rarely made the arduous trips to the lake.

In 2005, while the roads were almost as bad as pre-1976 standards, there was a slight economic recovery underway. Partly, the district government had turned toward Luapula Province to the west, instead of the more distant provincial capital at Kasama, for their links to most national and

---

81 For a detailed description of how nearby Lake Mweru was similarly "fished-out," see Gordon 2006.

provincial offices, due in large part to the fact that the roads in that direction were of better quality. Secondly, the presence of government offices at Kaputa spurred construction of a large electricity generating station that supplied the central village where civil servants lived and worked. In particular, the power lines fed a large police barracks and housing area that accommodated a substantial force that patrolled the nearby Congo border and dealt with smuggling and other concerns. A satellite telephone LAN link followed, providing communications for the government offices and any local residents who could afford the cost of installation. Thirdly, and perhaps most significantly, due in part to the military conflict in Congo, numerous Congolese merchants and entrepreneurs brought their skills over the border to form the backbone for a large market in Kaputa that served the civil servants and locals, spurring more traffic, despite the bad roads, for commerce in the town and surrounding areas. By 2005, when I arrived to conduct follow-up research for this project, there were more shops than ever before, and more goods available than I could have imagined. Due also to the unrest in Congo, there was a large garrison of Zambian soldiers based near the post office and just a mile or two from the border. Their presence constituted another set of consumers for goods and food in the town.

For all the material, or at least commercial, progress at Kaputa, regular transport was still at a premium. This made it very difficult to travel to Chishela, on the shore of Lake Mweru Wantipa, where Stanley Kalumba had moved before he passed away. For the years I'd know him, I knew relatively little about him. I arranged for a friend, a local Zambian Catholic priest, to ask around at Chishela when he made his next visit. Two months after I returned to the US, my friend sent a brief note with the sketchy outlines of Mr. Kalumba's life. Stanley Kalumba was born in Kashela Village in 1925 and took up a job on the Copperbelt as a Council messenger. He retired from that position and returned to Kaputa District, first living at Nsama and working as a Rural Council mailman in the early 1980s. He finished his time as a mailman in Kaputa, from 1984 to 1993, when he moved to Chishela. He died there in 1999 at seventy-four years of age.

Mukupa Katandula: A *Balumendo* Story

I recorded a very different Tabwa story-performance in 1988 at Mukupa Katandula. Because the performer was a young man, in his early twenties, I want to preface my analysis by introducing a theme of youthful assertion,

II. The Tabwa Context: Mature Shifting of Frames and Adolescent Assertion 59

and its prevalence in African societies, that has steadily increased and come to the fore in the early Twenty-first Century.

> In its cultural and political visions, the nationalist project sought to do two things: to maintain the frontier between elders and juniors that characterized traditional African values, and to put young people at the center of plans for economic development and national liberation. (Diouf 2003, pp. 3–4)

> The failures of nationalist economic, cultural, and political models had particularly dreadful effects on young people. As national models of economic development proved inadequate or irrelevant, so did customary rites of socialization through work or education. Requiring extensive investments of money and time, these activities and preparatory stages no longer inspired young people, who preferred risk and immediate profit. (Diouf, p. 4)

Reflecting on this rise of youthful participation in many key activities of Zambia's rural areas reminded me of an encounter with a young man at Mukupa Katandula back in 1983. I'd been a couple of days videotaping storytelling performances and was sitting, in the early evening, outside the home of some old friends. A clearly intoxicated young man made it a point to meander over after he spotted me during his unsteady progress along the dusty village street. It is almost axiomatic, when it comes to being a visiting researcher, that the consumption of alcohol often dispels inhibitions and some people under the influence decide it is a good time to approach the foreigner in their midst. I might add that this works both ways, with researchers, after some convivial imbibing, sometimes with mixed results, crossing lines that are more rigidly maintained under ordinary circumstances. While he was addressing the three or four of us seated around a small fire, he targeted me in particular because he spoke in English. Looking back at my sketchy field notes, I guess it did not seem all that funny at the time:

> In the meantime, a very drunk young man named David (Chalwe?) came over. He was extremely obnoxious, especially to me, in English even! He kept talking about Samuel Doe of Liberia being Africa's youngest head of state, taking power at age 28.[82] It had been a long time since I'd wanted to jump up and punch someone out, but he was bringing me close. However, things cooled down, especially with dinner, and he kept inviting us over to his house. (Cancel, field notes, 1983)

---

82 Strictly speaking, Doe was twenty-nine or thirty when he came to power in 1980. He actually changed his birth year from 1951 to 1950, in order to meet an age minimum when he ran for the presidency in an election that took place some time after his military take-over.

Years later, I honestly can't recall what it was that had gotten me so angry, but it was probably the intensity of his youthful insolence and my own fatigue, looking only to relax inconspicuously with some friends over a meal after a strenuous couple of days of work. In any event, that same evening, my traveling companion and old friend Rabbon Chola and I found ourselves laughing about the fervent way David Chalwe kept referring to Doe's age and implying that the time was near when the continent's elders would give way to youthful leaders who really knew what to do.[83] In many ways, this attitude is echoed in the posturing and assertiveness of many young men, who must claim social status at an age when it is not accorded them in the traditional scheme of things. Moreover, as the recent history of the continent illustrates, in the form of sectarian wars, fought in part by child soldiers, and dramatic demographic shifts due to forced migrations and diseases such as HIV/AIDS, the current realities of Africa, and in particular Zambia, suggest the growing prevalence and influence of youth in the economic and social future, though not necessarily the future as envisioned by leaders of the early nationalist period.[84]

The 1988 performance I recorded can be seen as an example of this kind of adolescent assertion that has since, in many ways, come to fruition in contemporary Zambia. Some residents used to joke that the village of Mukupa Katandula is so far removed from any main line of transport that even the chief moved away—which, in the late 1980s, he did, for this and other reasons not germane to the current discussion. My son Michael and I had arrived in the late afternoon and sought lodging at the Mukupa Katandula Primary School. We were allowed to put our sleeping gear in one of the school offices, and were hosted by a couple of the teachers, in particular the headmaster, Mr. Kancule. The next morning, I had walked to a part of the village near the clinic to visit an old friend whom we have known since 1976. Falace Mwenya was a

---

83 Having seen a virulent civil war tear apart Sierra Leone, Michael Jackson, with strong research and personal links to that nation, has spent a lot of time thinking about the causes of such violence and the seemingly easy militarization of young men. Among his several conclusions is a notion of reciprocity and its denial, at least in the minds of those who feel insulted and deprived of their rightful share of social and economic benefits. (2004; 2005, p. 36)
84 In Chapter IV, focusing on performance sessions among the Bisa, I discuss game management policies that had repercussions for the older social order, essentially bringing to prominence young men over elders and tradtions.

woman of singular personal strength and good-humored aggressiveness. She had six children by at least four men and to my knowledge had never formally married or lived with any of them for an extended period. She supported her family by farming, brewing an especially popular sweet beer called *susuta*, and baking and selling bread and sweet donut-like pastries called *ifitumbuwa*.

After I videotaped her at home, sending a greeting to my wife, three young men came by her house as I sat waiting for Falace to prepare a meal. They asked to tell a story. Having nothing better to do, I agreed to pay for some more of the home made distilled liquor (called *kacasu* or *kancina*) they'd been drinking, set up my camera on Falace's verandah, and proceeded to tape the efforts of a young man named Chipioka Patrick. Mr. Patrick and his friends were roughly between the ages of 18 and 24, a bit drunk, having a good time, and displaying the attitude of assertiveness and bravado that seems common among adolescents everywhere.

Mr. Patrick was dressed in a thin red nylon jacket, zipped up to his chest, with a high, "Nehru" style collar, and dark trousers. He was in his late teens or early twenties and employed a storytelling style that was humorous, detailed, and hyperbolic. He wanted to make his companions laugh at the events and thematic dimensions of the tale. Quick to focus on scenes that successfully elicited laughter, he chose to repeat phrases or descriptions that worked well for him. Possibly due to drink, he was a bit bleary-eyed and deliberate in his delivery, but was nonetheless tuned into the shaping of an entertaining tale.

Tabwa Storytelling 3
Chipioka Patrick*

Chipioka Patrick:	There was a little thing. People lived in a big village, just as we are living. There was a person, his name is Biti Mupalume [Biti the Great]…
Robert Cancel:	Wait, let me…[Pause while I change batteries in my audiocassette recorder] OK, OK, let's continue.
CP:	That boy, that one, was a school-going child. [As for] his learning, he had reached grade seven.

* To watch a video of this story follow this link: http://dx.doi.org/10.11647/OBP.0033.02/Tabwa3

RC: Uh huhn.

CP: He was learning. He was learning. However, in his work in school, he liked to play football [soccer/"*bola*"].[85] He was working. He was working, just like that, playing football a lot. Wherever he was called, he was **number one** in playing football. One day they called him, to say, that he should come to play football, to come to Mporokoso. That's how he left to go to Mporokoso there. When he went there he went and played football, he was the one who was winning **numer one**...football.

One day which did not eat a thing [i.e. one day], this chief, Chitimukulu, sent people to say that "The one who will come here to Kasama, who will beat eleven people, will marry...my child. I don't want my child, the one who will say that, the one who will marry my child, just this one I have given birth to, her name is Kasuba. If he beats eleven people, then he marries my child."

Then Biti came to hear, to say "OK," there in Kaputa where he was staying. "What should I do?" Biti, when he heard that said, "There in Kasama, there is a person, how many? One. The child of the chief, the one they were saying that...they should marry her. Even me, then I [will] go there to throw myself there [i.e. participate in the competition]." Biti started off his journey to go and reach Kasama...humn...in Mporokoso." When he arrived in Mporokoso, his father had given him money amounting to six thousand kwacha. He finished, he even drank it...he finished beer, all of it, iffwmm [wipes hand across mouth as he utters ideophone to indicate totally or completely]. He squandered [the money]. He returned again to Kaputa. His father then told him, saying "My child, there where I gave you money to use to go and marry the child of Chitimukulu, the money, where have you taken it?" He said, "Father, my money, I finished it in Mporokoso." Again, they came to give him three thousand and said, "Go and use it to marry."

Again, he started off on his journey to go and reach Kasama. He went and found, certainly in Kasama, his friend, the one he used to play football with all the other players. "How is it boy, Biti?" "How is it boy, Biti?" He said, "No, I am just fine." Then *mukwai*, right there, Biti...ah...that friend of his, he found there, told him, saying, "What about the child of Chitimukulu, where does she sleep?" He said, "She sleeps there." He said, "Now boy,

---

85 Mr. Patrick uses several terms or phrases for soccer or playing soccer. An older form he begins with is "*ukuteya umupila*," where *–teya* is basically the verb "to play," and *umupila* is the word for ball, but also for a rubber tire. He also says "*-teya bola*," which uses the English borrowing for "ball." He uses, a few times later in the story, the more common verb for playing soccer, which drops *–teya* in favor of verbalizing the word for ball into "*ukubola*," often used to say, for example, "*nalabola*," "I'm about to play soccer."

II. The Tabwa Context: Mature Shifting of Frames and Adolescent Assertion   63

you even want to go and see the child of Chitimukulu?" He said, "Yes, me, I want to see her." He said, "Now how can you go there on your own, to a place which is under lock and key there?" He said, "Yes, me I want to reach there in the house." He said, "No, boy, it will not work."

RC: Uhm hhn.

CP: He said, "No, me, just show me the house. If you show me, I will go and reach there." Then they showed the young man the house, and he went and reached where? There inside the house, there. He even entered using medicine [magic].

RC: Uhn huhn.

CP: He even entered the house right in there. He even began talking to that very woman, Mary, the child of Chitimukulu.

RC: Is it not Kasuba? The name…?

CP: The name?

RC: Mary?

CP: It's Mary Kasuba.

RC: Oh.

CP: Yes *mukwai*, yes.

RC: I understand.

CP: Yes *mukwai*, yes. Then he discussed with the woman in there. "You, woman, you are the one I have followed here to Kasama. You also know this news." She said, "OK, even me, you are the man I have been waiting for."

Then that woman, he did what? He made her pregnant…by…by Biti. That woman, when she became pregnant in there, then she did what? She even gave birth. Then her father, Chitimukulu, did not know anything [enough] to say that, "My child has what? A pregnancy in there?" Then she gave birth to twins, how many? [Holds up two fingers.]

RC: Two.

CP: Two, yes. One day the father said, "Oh. Who will do what, [for] my child, he who will beat [my] eleven players, a person, how many? [Holds up one finger.] One, then he'll do what? He marries my child."

Biti did what? He went to hmm…there to the palace. He went to pay a fee [for a wife]. And to do what? He [Chitimukulu] said, "No, me I don't want fees. I want someone who will play with eleven players, and even beat these people." Biti went in there inside and showed them, he said, "On Friday, it is the day of playing football." He even began to play…when they arrived there, to say, "Now, this is the day of playing."

At fourteen hours [2 PM] they started playing football, with eleven people. He himself was alone. He didn't have any goalkeeper, he himself was just alone. They even began playing football, they even began playing. Biti, when he moved with the ball, the whole ground [implying the spectators' cheers] echoed shouts, saying "Biti! Biti!" The whole ground echoed shouts, saying "Biti!" All the people who sat around the sides of the field, they began shouting, saying, "Biti!" "Mupalume!" All those who shouted said, "Biti!" "Mupalume!" The football boots [cleats] he was wearing, both were writing [leaving impressions in the dirt of the field] everywhere he was walking, they were writing, saying "Biti" "Mupalume." Everywhere [on] the jersey he was wearing it was written, "Biti Mupalume." Now the ground which was shouting praises, saying "Biti," it stopped, just saying "Mupalume." It was just shouting praises, saying "Mupalume." [The audience, Mr. Patrick's friends, are laughing hard at these images.] Now, from there, all of them, when Biti Mupalume carried the [the ball], carrying it, saying "Football." When he carried, a woman there was saying, "Biti." When he kicked the ball hard at the goal post, a woman, if she tried to catch the ball, the leg…the arms, both of them, would break." If he tells, to say, "He kicks the ball hard," a woman, if she says "Let me ward it off," her arms can break…both [of them]. Then Biti, even he, these people… these who were eleven, he himself alone beat the women…yes…goals. Then they gave Biti that woman, telling him, saying, "Now this woman, we are going to give you, she is a child of Chitimukulu."

Now the following day, it was on Saturday, saying, "Now we are about to give you that woman." Then when it was daytime in the morning, Chitimukulu said, "Go now and fetch the woman from where she stays." They went and found that woman whom they went to get, she even had given birth to twins, how many?

RC: Two.

CP: Two. Then women, these children, they were both girls. In the places they were walking, in those places, were imprints saying Biti Mupalume, Biti Mupalume, Biti Mupalume. Now Biti, he has not come alone himself. The father said, saying, "We want the person who has given this woman, Mary Kasuba, the pregnancy and begotten thereby twin girls." Then this Biti, where he remained, they had gathered the whole ground in the whole chiefdom, in there where they had gathered them to tell [them], saying "We want to tell, we wish to know the father of the child. Who is the one?" Both these children failed to point at any man as their father. They came to point at Biti when he came later on, to come and point, saying, "The father is this one." Chitimukulu gave him the chiefdom, and guess what? He should even become ruler of the chiefdom.

And the little thing, me, this is where I end. My [dear] Mr. Cancel, I am Tiko Veranda. I end here. Chipioka Patrick.

RC: Yes.

In itself, the basic plot of the story recalls several other tales found among the Tabwa, Bemba and Lamba people, according to documented examples. The Tabwa have a version where the local chief demands the capture of a troublesome monitor lizard from a very tall tree. Most fail, but one clever young man uses the trick of feeding a dog and goat improper foods, causing the intrusive lizard to keep trying to correct him and eventually coming down the tree to be better heard and eventually captured.[86] The hero is rewarded with the chief's beautiful daughter, Kasuba (Sun). Most versions of the narrative contain a proverb about education, *Mulangilishi wa muntu, aalaapalama* [To teach someone something, one must draw near], which is usually how the hero induces the lizard to come down the tree. Among the Bemba, there is a related proverb that says *Abalya imbulu baalaapalamana* [Those who eat the monitor lizard are always close together]. It suggests the importance of unity, but also the drawing together of people who do something unusual or even prohibited. One Tabwa version I recorded includes an image not found in the others, whereby the young hero sneaks a peak into the small house where the chief's daughter is secluded, in order to decide if his efforts to capture the lizard would be worth the trouble.[87] Conversely, there are a number of other similar narratives that espouse the value of elders. Usually, an arrogant chief has the younger generation kill off their parents so that he alone will rule over them. Inevitably, some disaster befalls the community and the wisdom of elders is missing. One young man has hidden his parents or father, refusing the order to kill them, and it is he who provides the answer to the problem. In one Lamba story, an ogre has eaten everyone and everything in the village, and the young man's father uses the trick of feeding a goat and dog improper foods in order to lure it from a chasm. (Doke 1976, pp. 150–153) Clearly, an ongoing tension and debate exists between these sets of stories over which age group is best suited to steer the course of the society.[88]

These are only a few elements of the tale's traditional context. I want to play them against Mr. Patrick's performance. He first of all localizes and names his hero, Biti Mupalume, a praise name: "Biti the great." Interestingly, since Patrick lives in Mukupa Katandula, he locates Biti in Kaputa which, in relative terms, is a much larger, even somewhat cosmopolitan place. He also contemporizes him by using soccer as the venue for the test to

---

86 See, for example, Cancel 1989, pp. 35–36, 38–39.
87 Unpublished, Chongo Alison, 1983, Kaputa.
88 See related version where a snake wraps itself around the arrogant chief's neck and an elder must provide the solution to the problem. (Cancel 1989, pp. 43–44, and Lunda version of this tale told by Mr. Idon Pandwe, in Chapter IV, on Lunda storytelling.)

win the beautiful heroine. By identifying the chief as Chitimukulu, he increases the status of the contest and its prize, as well as playing upon a historical competitiveness that long ago was an actual militant adversarial relationship between the Tabwa and Bemba.[89] Mr. Patrick also complicates the basic movement to resolution, or the winning of the contest, by taking the image of looking at the chief's daughter further, actually having the hero sleep with her and produce twins.

Looking closer at the stylistic inventiveness of the narrative, the soccer imagery is not unprecedented in tales collected from this region. There is a soccer-playing scene in a tale collected from the Lamba people in the 1920s (Doke 1976, pp. 70–75). I found a similar image in a Tabwa tale told by an elderly woman, Mrs. March Mulenga, in 1976 (Cancel 1989, pp. 113–118). What Chipioka Patrick contributes to the other images, and I do not know if these are his innovations or gleaned from other performers, is a hyperbolic sense of detail and the grandeur of Biti's prowess and celebrity. For example, Biti borrows money, K6,000, [back in 1988, the Zambian kwacha was worth around sixteen to the dollar] from his father to pay for the journey to Chitimukulu's. Instead, Biti travels only as far as Mporokoso, some 70 miles away, where he proceeds to spend the entire sum on beer and partying. He returns home to borrow another K3,000 to actually complete the trip. During the football match, his football boots [soccer cleats] stamp his name on the dirt field, one word on each sole. His soccer jersey has "Biti Mupalume" written all over it, a marvelous rural version of product branding, that also replicates the practice of professional soccer teams using advertising on their jerseys. Later on in the tale, he takes this already striking image and uses it to add to Biti's renown, when the twin daughters also walk along verbally echoing the visual impressions in the dust that spell out Biti's name. When he plays against the chief's team, the spectators chant his name in call and response fashion, "Biti!" "Mupalume!" He scores his goals by kicking the ball so powerfully that he breaks the hands of several goalkeepers who, for some reason, are women. Fame, fortune, sexuality, prodigious procreation, and the arrogance that frames them all are qualities in the hero played up by the performer.

There are more stylistic innovations, but let's stop here and look again at the performance context. Chipioka Patrick is around the age of his tale's

---

89 David Livingstone passed through the Tabwa area of Chief Nsama during his last journey and reported on a war between the Tabwa and the Bemba (Livingstone 1874). For more details and references see A. Roberts 1973.

protagonist. Fame and fortune come to the hero despite, or because of, his aggressive self-serving behavior and his initially impoverished conditions. By drinking, bragging, carelessly spending his father's money, engaging in premarital sex, and potentially antagonizing one of the most powerful chiefs in Zambia, Biti Mupalume successfully pits his youthful bravado and skill in soccer against the forces of authority and community. The image of the teenager as trickster, in the African sense of the term, comes to mind as an apt metaphor to describe these protagonists. It was clear during the performance that Mr. Patrick and his friends thoroughly enjoyed and identified with the imagery of Biti's cockiness and triumphs. In fact, the tale falls under a type of story I earlier identified as commonly told by adolescents amongst each other. I termed the tales *"balumendo,"* or young men's, stories (Cancel 1989). These tales uniformly question older authority and support the impetuousness, impatience, and brashness of young heroic characters. Their heroes regularly flaunt proper behavior to assert their desires for fame and wealth. Some tales borrow images from books and films, such as James Bond and car chases. One tale even detailed the successful robbery of the Bank of England by some daring young tunnellers. We can in many ways see these performances as wish fulfillment or the transformation of the relative social powerlessness of adolescence into the assertion of agency and desire over conventional norms of behavior and the wisdom of age.[90]

In an effort to continue his dominance of the performance situation, Chipioka Patrick commenced to tell a story with a conundrum ending.

Tabwa Storytelling 4
by Chipioka Patrick*

Robert
Cancel: Let's begin.

Chipioka   Me, I was a bachelor; I did not have any wife at all. Now, when
Patrick: I expected to tell, saying, "O.K. let me go and look for a woman to marry," I found her. When I married my wife, that one expected

---

[90] There are numerous studies, mostly from social science perspectives, on adolescent creative assertion, particularly in the form of oral narrative. See, for example, Lightfoot 1997; Shuman 1986; and Wilson 1997. It is certainly not a stretch to relate these contexts of adolescent assertion to the "Hip-Hop Culture" that emerged out of the difficult socio-economic conditions of New York City's South Bronx in the late 1970s and early 1980s, and that has grown to be a world-wide economic and cultural phenomenon. See Rose 1994.

* To watch a video of this story follow this link: http://dx.doi.org/10.11647/OBP.0033.02/Tabwa4

that my wife will conceive. Now my wife, as we continued living together, she did not conceive at all. My mother-in-law who did not...the one we stayed with, she was the one who conceived. She had no husband; she was the one who became pregnant, my mother-in-law. And then my mother-in-law, she had the pregnancy, the pregnancy began growing, but the mother who bore me also was the one who gave birth to this child. Now what does this mean? Me, I end here.

RC: Uh hmn. Can you explain to me? Explain this to me.

Audience: To explain...[laughing]

CP: I had told you to say, me, I will not explain, unless...the *mulumbe* demands money.

RC: Ooh.

CP: Yes.

Audience: Those who want it explained should pay.

RC: Me? I can buy you more beer?

CP: Yes, unless they pay me...This *mulumbe* is very difficult. This *mulumbe*, if it was explicitly stated, many of you would understand it.

RC: I am saying, I could buy you [more] beer.

CP: Yes, unless you follow me to our place, that's when I would explain a lot.

Audience: To explain this, unless you are how many people? Even just two. Because as things are now, there are [too] many people [around]. He cannot explain.

RC: Ohh.

Audience: It does not need to be known to many people.

RC: Oh. Now...ah...what can I do?

CP: Yes.

RC: What can I do?

CP: You just come to our place there, tomorrow.

RC: Ohh. Tomorrow?

CP: Yes, in the morning.

RC: Yes, I will come there. O.K. It's alright.

CP: O.K. I am happy.

The answer to this kind of conundrum may have been obvious to the audience members, but I hadn't heard this particular set up before. Chipioka Patrick refused to provide the answer, despite my offer of buying another bottle of *kancina*, because he wanted me to return the next day in order to "buy" the answer. Here the sense of manipulation and control was extended from simply holding the stage in performance and carefully coloring the story's images to influencing my own presence, movement, and resources of time and money. The notion that the tale could not be explained in mixed company might have had something to do with Falace's presence, nearby if not at the session. The answer might have had something to do with a male view of marriage or even of in-law prohibitions, but nothing was specified. After the performance, we adjourned to Falace's home for a meal she'd prepared, no longer touching on the narratives at all. My discussion of the conundrum, similarly, ends here, since circumstances did not allow me to visit Mr. Patrick the next day. In fact, looking back at my field notes, I saw that I was not as interested in the performance as I would later come to be, dedicating only a few lines to the occasion, while focusing more on my time with Falace:

> A drunken young man had me buy him some kancina then told a wonderfully cock-eyed story of a chief giving his daughter to the best soccer player. I got tired of his trying to extort everything I owned out of me, but then we went inside and had some good fresh fish and mukaiwa bwali [maize inshima or "pap"] at Falace's. She told me she had ulcers and had been at Mporokoso hospital last year. They recommended she eat things like milk and rice. But both are pretty much in short supply. (Cancel, field notes, 16 January, 1989)

Over the years, however, the performance and performer took on much more significance for the reasons I've been propounding above.

In a historical and cultural context, these *balumendo* [young men's] tales seem a common phenomenon in the life of the society. Several older men have commented to me in conversation that they too, when younger, would create and/or repeat these kinds of tales. When they became adults and responsible men in the culture, they grew interested in preserving the older, more "important" stories they'd learned or heard when growing up. Seen in this way, the *balumendo* performances were a natural part of coming of age within the traditional society, challenging the limiting of youthful status and influence. Seen, however, as a harbinger of the consequences of globalization in the economic and cultural spheres, the tales also mark a point of transition to a new world of youthful assertion in a fading nationalist project. Chipioka Patrick told his story in an era of a failing socialist government. It seemed clear, especially for young people living in a seemingly backwater place like Mukupa Katandula, that progress in a modernist sense was not easily attainable, if at all. He is willing and able to create his own venue or space for success through narrative and interaction with a videocamera-wielding visitor who can provide a modest form of money, fame and/or immortality in the electronically captured performance. If Chipioka Patrick's generation was suspicious of the tiresome nationalist rhetoric and practice of the Kaunda government in 1989, it is logical to conjecture an even higher level of disenchantment and creative assertion in the globalized realties of the Twenty-first Century. Young men tend not to be seen, or see themselves, as biding time before entering into a successful adult stage of life. Being an adult no longer assures economic or social success or security. As Diouf points out,

> In many ways, young Africans can be seen as searching for a narrative that provides a territory for the free play of their imagination. As J.D.Y. Peel observes, "Narrative empowers because it enables its possessor to integrate his memories, experiences and aspirations in a schema" (1995: 587). Looking beyond national borders, young people appropriate new technologies (digital and audiovisual) in such a way as to recreate the dynamics of the oral and the spectacular, along with the literary and iconographic imagination. (Diouf 2003, p. 6)

In retrospect, we can see that the performers Stanley Kalumba and Chipioka Patrick comprise generational counterpoints in their subject matter and approaches to their narratives. Mr. Kalumba focused on the older elements of his tale, adding few if any contemporary touches. His dependence on proverbs and the essential nature of the trickster hare forms the core of his performance. Humor and message were borne by the audience's experience of other trickster stories and of versions of the same tale he told. Kalulu and the other animals followed their age-old script in a way that entertained and underscored the hare's cleverness and the deeper notion of eloquence, in both its positive and negative manifestations. Chipioka Patrick's performance was steeped in a contemporary version of modernity and fame, linking the desires and talents of youth to older plot structures of tasks being set by chiefs or fathers for suitors to win their daughters. The story had elements of quick fortune, quick sex, and physical prowess leading to fame. In the end, Biti Mupalume, perhaps Mr. Patrick's aesthetic doppelganger, is less the clever trickster of the oral tradition than the youthful pícaro of Spanish Golden Age literature, someone responding to real world conditions and hardships. Both performers embody the opposite ends of a spectrum that captures the possibilities and functions of their oral narrative system.

I want to end my own story by returning to the question of method. For reasons of space and focus, I have not exhausted all the information from the traditional and performance contexts that was available. However, even what was presented here suggests that we can highlight the personality and individual content and stylistic characteristics of the performers while using our own knowledge and experiences to flesh out description and push it in the direction of analysis. I must, in all honesty, continually cast doubt on my own observations by pointing to the insufficient facts and the unavoidable over-prevalence of personal impressions I read into these performance events. As much depth and dimension as I can add to situate the performance and its components will always balance against the inadequacy of scholarly methods of representation and the question of ethnographic authority, a question, ultimately, of power. Language is power and social power is augmented by discourse, personal and systemic. As Stanley Kalumba noted in the epigraph to this chapter, the powerless are rarely accorded a stage on which to speak.

Postscript

I learned little about Chipioka Patrick when I visited Mukupa Katandula for only a day and a half in 2005, accompanying my Catholic priest friend on some church business. For all the pessimism I'd felt over the last two decades, Mukupa Katandula had become a more vibrant village, with a refurbished and well-staffed primary school and a new health clinic. A major change was that hand-powered pumps now dotted the village in various neighborhoods and provided clean water for the residents. For many years, contractors, local and foreign, had failed at digging bore holes into usable water strata in most of Kaputa District. The area is geologically undergirded by volcanic fissures containing sulfuric water that bubbles up in places in the form of hot springs. This is the basic resource for the arduous but relatively lucrative practice of processing salt out of the briny water that flows out of the springs in the rainy season and inundates the surrounding grounds or pans. The sulfuric liquid is undrinkable and water had to be obtained from Lake Mweru Wantipa, its tributaries or shallow water holes. In the case of Mukupa Katandula, people had to walk up to two miles to draw water that was not particularly potable but was nonetheless used for drinking, washing, cooking, etc. The water pumps had definitely changed life for the better, improving health and reducing labor, as was affirmed by some of the old friends I saw during our brief visit.

I heard first that Falace Mwenya had died a few years earlier. My friends who gave me this news seemed less than empathetic regarding Falace's passing. I think she was considered by many of the village's "proper" women to be a little too loose and independent. Then when I asked about him, I was told Mr. Patrick was alive and still in Mukupa Katandula. Later on, I realized there'd been a misunderstanding, since his father had the same name. When I met briefly with Mr. Patrick's sister, she confirmed that the young man I recorded had died six years earlier. He was born around 1963 and lived most of his life at Mukupa Katandula. At the time we met and I recorded him, Chipioka Patrick was nearly twenty-five years old. He later married, had a child and moved away. It was unclear when or where, but it sounded like he lived somewhere in the eastern part of Northern Province, since his sister told me he'd been going to the hospital there, at Chinsali, after he became ill. The nature of the illness was not clear to me from her explanation, only that it left his legs paralyzed at a late stage in the disease. He died at age thirty-six, in 1999, coincidentally, the same year that Mr. Kalumba passed away. His wife and daughter now live in the city of Kabwe, just north of Zambia's capital, Lusaka.

Mr. Patrick led rather a short life—though, sadly, not far off from the thirty-seven year average life-span of Zambians [reckoned in 2005 by several world health organizations]—and if the main character of his story Biti Mupalume is an actual reflection of how he felt about that life, we could use the old sixties maxim of "live hard, die young and leave a good looking corpse" to encapsulate his youthful fatalism and view of grabbing some wealth and fame wherever the opportunity presented itself. In any event, this example of identity-creation reflects the wider trend by adolescent storytellers, especially young men, who I've seen in many performance sessions. Suspended in the liminal areas between adult achievement and adolescent dependency and powerlessness, these performers use the occasion of holding the stage at storytelling sessions and fashioning images of themselves within and without the narratives that stress personal power and prowess as well as social status.

In fact, in a wider sense, these possibilities have been more and more realized in the new liberalized Zambian, and world, economy. Even upcountry, it was clear that many young men were involved in the transport, fishing and agricultural economies. The ones I'd met were different from earlier entrepreneurs. They were focused, sober and often religious—usually fundamentalist Christian—in their outlooks. They saved money, grew their enterprises, and kept relatives who might conceivably drain their resources, at arm's length. Clearly, as it always does, and for better or worse, "tradition" as it pertained to kinship and generational status was in a phase of change and evolution.[91] So in some ways, Chipioka Patrick has the last word here as he did in our encounter. He still owns the answer to the conundrum I was unable to buy.

---

91 Stuart Marks's latest research on the Bisa of the Luwangwa Valley has noted a similar shift in the relative influence of elders and young men in recent times, due in large part to game management schemes and the rise of evangelical Christian practices. See Chapter IV on Bisa storytelling.

III. Chiefs, Tricksters and Catholics: Bemba Tales and Orations

Katongo Soolo:	Who is lisping out words? Don't you realize it is the teeth which make people speak properly?
Audience member:	What do you want to speak with? And you even have teeth, those are your health.
KS:	*Mukwai*, unless the tongue is touching the teeth you can't...
Audience:	Yes, we have all grown old, all the teeth are gone.

(Performance by Mr. Katongo Soolo at Malole, 1989)

The focus of this chapter is three performance-recording sessions in two locations in the home region of the Bemba. Each session has its own set of contextual conditions and developments and the performers are mostly elders. Not surprisingly, a characteristic common to most of the sessions is didacticism, tied into the promulgation of wisdom and correct action growing out of tradition and experience. The narrative-performances were mostly of the fictional type, mostly *imilumbe* (tales without songs) with only one *lushimi* (a tale that contains a song). One session also included praise poetry and straightforward expository oration on matters of social concern. This same session evidenced an easy movement between these genres as well as a free mixing between men and women when it came to performance and commentary.

The Bemba are the largest and most influential of the ethnic groups living in Zambia's Northern Province. Historically, they dominated the region in a powerful and militaristic manner, known more for their raiding of neighbors and hegemonic assertion than for any particular economic pursuit, such as farming, hunting, or fishing. They have a rich and well-documented oral history, illustrating how they migrated into Zambia from the Luba kingdom in the Congo, then expanded in a way that brought most neighboring chiefdoms under their political domination. Not surprisingly, the various ethnic groups involved in these interactions all have their own versions of how they relate to the Bemba and these often do not coincide exactly with the details of the Bemba oral traditions.

The Bemba are among the most "studied" of Zambia's groups, with a significant body of excellent scholarship documenting various levels of their cultural and economic history.[92] Though I had for years lived and worked at least on the edges of the Bemba area, I'd rarely attempted to record their oral traditions. During my broader research swing through Northern Province in April through June 1989, one of my goals was to gather stories at villages of the three senior Bemba chiefs: Chitimukulu, Mwamba, and Nkula. The Bemba Paramount Chief, Chitimukulu (Mutale 30 Chitapankwa II), Mr. L.M. Ng'andu the Member of the Central Committee for Northern Province, met with me at his provincial office in Kasama and recommended that I see several elders in his village, providing me with a rather elaborate letter of introduction.

Malole

Research at Chitimukulus was done in conjunction with my stay at Malole, a neighboring village and the site of St. Francis Secondary School. My son Daniel and I began by visiting St. Francis' headmaster, who introduced us to one of his teachers, Mr. S.M. Kalunga, who agreed to chaperone us around. We stopped in to see Fele, who was headman of the village nearest the school and was a member of the council of elders [*bacilolo*] who advised the Chitimukulu. Mr. Ng'andu had, in fact, included his name on the list of people I should contact. He turned out to be a gregarious man who remembered my old graduate school colleague, a Catholic nun working on her doctorate in African Languages and Literature, who had researched in the area nearly fifteen years earlier.[93] He agreed to summon some people

---

92 Among many resources, see Richards 1939; A. Roberts 1973; and Moore and Vaughan 1994.
93 Mary Frost collected hundreds of Bemba narratives and included some twenty or thirty in her dissertation. At the time of her efforts at Malole, a different man held the headman title of Fele. Frost concentrated her collecting efforts in or near villages of the three senior Bemba chiefs, at Malole, Ilondola and Mulobula. (1978)

together for the next morning so that I could record them. A bit later we traveled to the village of Chitimukulu and, stopping at the local courthouse, we were able to set up a time to come and record on the afternoon of the next day.

Later, in the afternoon, as we walked near Fele's village, I was trying to locate an elder whose name had been mentioned as a man who told good stories. Mr. Dismas Kampamba, who seemed to be in his mid or late sixties, had just returned from his farm in the bush and appeared to be rather tired. He wore work clothes, which included old patched trousers, a tan colored crocheted cap, a tan overall jacket and a brown short-sleeved buttoned cotton shirt with a collar. As we sat outside his verandah talking, he also recalled working with my old classmate, and this served as a good initial introduction for me. I showed him a brief video of a talking-drum performance by the Lunda bard, Mano, recorded months earlier in Mbereshi. This seemed to interest him enough to agree to tell us a story.

Bemba Storytelling 1
by Mr. Dismas Kampamba*

Robert Cancel:	Begin *mukwai*.
Dismas Kampamba:	A person had stayed; when he stayed, this is a *mulumbe*, it is a *mulumbe* with a parable. When he stayed, he had stayed like that. He had even borne children, how many?
RC:	[I responded to four fingers held up by Mr. Kampamba by erroneously saying] Three...
DK:	Four. And then he stayed, he even went and built temporary shelters in the bush. When he went and built there in the bush, his name was Fipindulule [one who influences or changes things or direction of things]. Then he went with his children, then he told his children and said, "My children, what you should be doing is that when the honeyguide [bird] comes, that one which leads you to the honey, you follow this side. That one that...that goes to the east. The one that goes to the west, don't dare to go there." And then there they stayed. Whichever went to the east, the children

* To watch a video of this story follow this link: http://dx.doi.org/10.11647/OBP.0033.03/Bemba1

followed, they removed honey from the beehive and brought it. Whichever went to the east, they went and got the honey and brought it.

Then one day the children said, "Let's go there...where the honeyguide is signaling, to the west." They followed it. They even found a very, very big tree. And then that tree, that one, his friend said, "What are we going to do?" The other one said, "We shall fell it," he even struck it with an axe. As he struck it with an axe like that, the thing that was there came out, Kashimweshimwe [an ogre]. When it came out, Kashimweshimwe, that one, said, "Who are you?" Said...they said, "I am the child of Fipindulule." It said, "You change things then so that we can see." He said, "If my father was here he would have changed things." Kashimweshimwe took these children, it swallowed them.

In the morning, their father and...he came back also from where he had gone into the bush alone. He came, he did what? He came and found the children were not there. "Oh these children! Perhaps they have gone to the west there." He did not bother. He slept. In the morning the honeyguide signaled his wife towards the western direction, she followed...

Audience: His wife?

DK: His wife. She went and even found an axe where it had stood like that. She, too, struck (the tree) with an axe. The ogre came out and said, "Who are you?" She said, "I am...am...am the wife of Fipindulule." It said, "You change (the direction of) things so that we see." She said, "If my husband was here, he would have changed things." It swallowed her.

And then there he stayed. He came back from where he had gone, Fipindulule. When he came and found that person, his wife, was not there, in the morning he dressed up, he even dressed up. He even took a very big belt and fastened it round his waist, it was made of leather. Then he started going, he started going. He himself just went straight there because he knew the place. And so he found axes, the axe, he struck the tree with it. Kashimweshimwe came out and said, "Who are you?" He said, "I am Fipindulule." It said, "You change things so that we see." He tied it, he tied a very big belt round it, mfya! Mpaa! [sound of very tight grip] He fastened it tightly. Kashimweshimwe cried out, saying, "Grandfather, let go of me, I beg for mercy. Grandfather, let go of me, I beg for mercy." And finally he managed to throw it onto the ground, then uhnn! He killed it, the ogre. When he killed it like that, he said, "What shall I do? My wife and the children? All right."

He went to a black ant. The black ant there told him and said, "Grandfather, go and heat a potsherd then rub it on top of the ogre's stomach." So, truly, he went and did just that, he heated a postsherd and rubbed it on its stomach. Kwaa! And then his children started coming out and people whom it had swallowed, all of them, came out. When all of them finished coming out, that man, Fipindulule now built a village. He now became the chief of the village. There was a little *mulumbe*, it ends.

RC: Very good, *mukwai*.

Before a small audience of a few children and a young mother with a baby in a sling, Mr. Kampamba told the story while seated on the small verandah that wound round his home, leaning back with his hands resting between his slightly open thighs. He mostly used his left hand to gesture, point, and indicate action, space and direction in the narrative. He also at times mimed actions, such as when characters used the axe or when the ogre, Kashimweshimwe, grabbed and devoured various victims. Twice Mr. Kampamba used a common gesture, tapping the palm of his right hand over the thumb and index finger side of his left fist, when indicating how tight Fipindulule tied the belt round his waist, then again to show how tightly he bound up the ogre. He also moved his right hand over his stomach, from top to bottom, to act out the drawing of the potsherd across the belly of the ogre. He then used both hands; spread at the bottom of his abdomen, to indicate how Kashimweshimwe was split open and all the people emerged.

Thematically, the narrative seemed less a cautionary tale than one about the extraordinary abilities of Fipindulule, whose very name is descriptive in the form of a praise epithet. While it is clear that the wife and children disobeyed the interdiction not to follow the honeyguide in a westward direction, there is never any admonishment of these indiscretions and the victims are in fact restored to life at the story's end. Rather, the narrative's events serve to create an expectation, based on the repetition of interactions with the ogre, with first the children then the wife claiming that Fipindulule would show his powers if present and Kashimweshimwe taunting them by saying, "…change things so that we can see." After he shows his power, Fipindulule also shows his wisdom by seeking out the advice of the lowly black ant. The image of cutting open the stomach of an ogre or monster is pan-traditional in this region, found in tales from the Lamba and Tabwa, among others.[94] Like many heroes of oral narratives who become leaders,

---

94 See Cancel, 1989, comparison of Lamba and Tabwa tales. Indeed, the motif is common throughout southern Africa, as evidenced in older collections such as Callaway 1868,

he possesses both destructive and restorative powers. After resurrecting the people in the ogre's stomach, he becomes their chief in a new village.[95]

The young mother carrying a baby in a sling, who'd witnessed Mr. Kampamba's performance, offered to tell a story as well. She only gave her first name, Elizabeth. She was probably in her late teens, rather tall, with very close-cropped hair. Elizabeth wore a maroon, multi-colored *citenge* around her waist, over a light blue patterned, short-sleeved dress. Taking Mr. Kampamba's place on the verandah of his house, she arranged her sleeping baby in her lap, still in the sling, and began her narrative. Generically, the tale is a *lushimi*, a narrative that contains a song.[96]

Bemba Storytelling 2 by Elizabeth*

Robert Cancel:	We can begin... uh...give me your name. [By now there were around ten adults, mostly women, witnessing the performance. This made for a rather noisy atmosphere and I had a hard time initially hearing Elizabeth's responses. She was also a bit shy at first, looking down, and speaking softly.]
Elizabeth:	Elizabeth.
RC:	Again...a...again.

---

reprinted 1970; and Theal 1970.
95 See my discussion of heroic power combined with wisdom as they pertain to a set of Tabwa narratives. (Cancel 1989, pp. 129–158)
96 Folklorists often use the term *"cantefable"* to describe this genre. Bauman treats the intersection of genres in verbal art in some detail in several studies. (Briggs and Bauman 1992; Bauman 2004) Sub-Saharan African oral narratives so often contain songs, sayings or chants, that the mixing of genres is almost definitive. Throughout this study, I've tried to use the local terms for genres and approximate their English and scholarly equivalents. Ruth Finnegan, after surveying all manner of terminology for oral narrative traditions and pointing to various scholarly disciplines says, I think quite sensibly, "None of the terminologies or approaches can be applied in any mechanical way to the African forms analyzed and celebrated in this volume. The final choice must be for individual scholars, weighing up the costs and benefits in the light of particular genres, settings, questions, or theoretical aims, while at the same time, recognizing the complexity of the subject matter that is too dynamic, subtle and multifaceted for single-line dogmatic reductionism." (2004, p. 313)

* To watch a video of this story follow this link: http://dx.doi.org/10.11647/OBP.0033.03/Bemba2

E: Elizabeth.

RC: Oh, It's all right. Let's go on.

E: There is a thing [Elizabeth was speaking very softly, and some women in the audience encouraged, or maybe admonished, her to speak up]... there is a thing. People had stayed. There was even a person, one. He had married women, there was Ntoole (meaning: Let me pick up) and Mweo (Life) and then Nunde (Let me stick or put pieces together). Then that young man was a very skilled hunter. Then he had told his wives to say, "Wherever I go, if I do not return, you should follow me." And those women, they had understood. They had all set out to go and live at a small village. And then the young man did just like that, he started off, he went hunting. Right there when he went hunting, he went and died. And then those women...they...they tried to follow where he went. They, the women, found their husband had died. And then their friend began to say, "Yah! And so our husband has died, what shall we say?"

Ntoole began, she said, "Begin to pick up my friend, you gather the bones (and put them in one place)." And so their friend started the song and said:
    Let me pick up, let me pick up, yes let me pick up.
    Let me pick up, let me pick up, yes let me pick up.
    Let me pick up my husband,
    Let me pick up, yes let me pick up.
    Let me pick up my husband,
    Let me pick up, yes let me pick up.
Nunde also began:
    Let me join, let me join, yes let me join.
    Let me join, let me join, yes let me join.
    Let me join for my husband,
    Let me join, yes let me join.
    Let me just join my husband,
    Let me join, yes let me join.
Mweo began:
    Life, life yes life.
    Let me put back, let me put back, yes let me put back.
    Let me just put back my husband's life,
    Yes let me put back.

And certainly *mukwai*, the husband rose, he rose and they started going to the village. They had put his pieces together. And again, just like that on another day, just like that, on another day, just like that. And then on the following day, they refused Mweo *ubwali*, she just went on becoming thinner and thinner. And their husband started off, he went right there to hunt. Again, he went and died. Mweo also, that one, where she had remained she also died.

And then those two said, "Let that good-for-nothing woman die." They said, "We don't care about her." They said, "As if she is the one who ever does the work; in fact we are the ones who just do the work." She said, "Without us she...she would not have been doing anything. We shall go and do the work, we are going to try even to breathe in life itself, he is going to rise." And so, they set out, they went and arrived where their husband was. Then Ntoole started:

> Let me pick up, let me pick up, yes let me pick up.
> Let me pick up, let me pick up, yes let me pick up.
> Let me pick up my husband,
> Let me pick up, yes let me pick up.
> Let me pick up my husband,
> Let me pick up, yes let me pick up.

Nunde also began:

> Let me join, let me join, yes let me join.
> Let me join, let me join, yes let me join.
> Let me just join my husband,
> Let me join, yes let me join.
> Let me just join my husband,
> Let me join, yes let me join.

Her friend said, "Yah, no my friend, since we have finished, what shall we do? Now life, how shall we blow it in, since Mweo is not there?" She said, "Yah, we are going to try." She said, "Let's both begin, we try."

> Let me put back, let me put back, yes let me put back.
> Let me put back, let me put back, yes let me put back.
> My husband's life,
> Let me put back, yes let me put back.
> Let me just put back my husband's life,
> Yes let me put back.

However, it couldn't work. Until they just took that corpse then they carried and took it to the village, they even found that Mweo had died; they then carried the two corpses and then went and buried (them). There was a little tale, it ends.

RC: Very good *mukwai*.

Elizabeth employed an understated performance style, possibly due to being somewhat inhibited by the video camera and the audience. She used her left hand to partially support her baby in her lap and kept her right hand resting on her right thigh and knee during most of the performance. Often, she rhythmically picked at the cloth of her *citenge* while telling the story. She also used the same hand to subtly gesture and keep time during the singing of the songs. Her main departure from this posture and set of movements was when the baby began to fret and she shifted it in the sling and drew her left breast from the dress to nurse the child. At that point, her left forearm supported the baby and she moved to the story's end with her right hand holding onto the index finger of her left hand as the right forearm helped to secure the nursing infant.

Elizabeth's performance followed Mr. Kampamba's narrative about how a harmonious family, with only one wife/mother, is serially eaten by a monster then saved by their powerful husband/father. There is a shift in family structure and outcome in her story. Thematically, the tale focuses on both the strength and precarious nature of an initially harmonious polygamous family, endangered by the always looming threats of jealousy and pettiness in such households. Each of the three wives have names that reflect their talents, and these talents must be used together in order to resurrect their hunter husband and, by extension, form an effective and creative family. Little is known of the husband, or even how he meets his death in the bush. It is the wives who are the center of the narrative, first emphasizing their life-giving skills, then pointing to the divisive tendencies that bring disaster to their family. Each of the wives' songs stresses their life-affirming abilities, and when the third song (the song of the wife named "Life") is missing from the second instance of trying to resurrect the husband, it is clear that enmity between wives has broken up the family in an irreversible way. To emphasize this sad situation, the remaining two wives try twice to bring their husband back by singing their individual songs, pointing to the glaring absence of the third wife, Mweo. As in Mr. Kampamba's story, the action is focused by repeating a similar action; in this case a successful then an unsuccessful attempt to resurrect the husband. Like the previous story, a character that travels out from the homestead leaves instructions or orders for those at home to obey. Where in the first narrative, the orders are disobeyed, in Elizabeth's tale, they are followed. What brings disjunction or trouble is the way the co-wives treat each other. The husband's well-being, therefore, becomes a metaphor or marker for harmonious marital relations in the polygamous home, while his death signals the disjunction and negative consequences brought on by jealousy and selfishness.

The narrative is performed by a young nursing mother and witnessed by older women. It has an interesting resonance for the audience, though I did not ascertain Elizabeth's actual marital status and whether or not she was part of a polygamous household.[97] It is not uncommon, however, for the youngest co-wives, who are often the most attractive and fertile, to be disparaged by older co-wives for being inexperienced or lazy. Whether or

---

97 I recorded one more performance at this session, by a young boy who had witnessed the earlier two. While the narrative was of some interest, I'm opting not to include performances by children in the present study.

not there was an actual personal reference involved in the tale, it did connote common social tensions that must be negotiated if households are to remain harmonious and productive. On taking my leave, I paid Mr. Kampamba a bit of money (around two or three US dollars) for his efforts, with the understanding, made in front of everyone, that he'd share some of it with Elizabeth. We returned to the mission for a meal and to spend the night.

The next day we passed by Mr. Kalunga's home to pick him up then made the very short drive to Fele's place. We arrived at around 9 AM, and found that he had gathered five or six elders next to his verandah. There were a handful of children present as well. Fele described my work to the group and I played back Mr. Kampamba's performance on the video monitor so that people could see what I was doing. I also assured everyone that I wanted to record whatever kinds of stories or commentaries they cared to offer. I had set up one of Fele's wooden chairs in front of his verandah, partly in the shade and partly in the morning sun, allowing performers to choose between warm and cool. My small television monitor and some other gear were set up on a table on the verandah. Some of the performers opted to lean or rest an arm on the table as they spoke.

A woman named Elizabeth Chama was the first to speak. I'd estimate her age as over seventy. Her eyes appeared to have fairly advanced cataracts. Ms. Chama wore a light green kerchief tied behind her head, possibly indicating that she belonged to some kind of Catholic women's group. Her red blouse had very short sleeves, just covering her shoulders, and she began the performance wearing a tan loose-fitting jacket, which she removed near the end. Her *citenge* was cream colored with green flowers printed on the cloth. Ms. Chama had long, wrinkled, very slim arms and large hands, reflecting her advanced age. She chose to discuss traditional forms of honoring the chief, explaining three ways in which the chief was praised by panegyric poetry, and how these forms are adapted to the Catholic mass and beliefs.

Bemba Storytelling 3 by Elizabeth Chama

Robert Cancel:	Before you begin, give me your name…name.
Elizabeth Chama:	Elizabeth.
RC:	Yes, Eli…OK
Audience (Fele):	You should say "Elizabeth Chama."

* To watch a video of this story follow this link: http://dx.doi.org/10.11647/OBP.0033.03/Bemba3

EC:	Elizabeth Chama.
RC:	Yes, *mukwai*, begin.
EC:	Let me begin with a jesting oration [praise poetry] used in church; the one…the one used to eulogize chiefs.
Audience (Fele):	Anyone, even the oration used to eulogize chiefs, you can begin with that one.
EC:	That is so! They traveled, the tall one and the other one; especially covering a long distance. The brave, fearless ones, when we find them we become submissive to them [i.e. we talk to them very meekly]. One open rest-hut has its own limitations. The chief's food [*ubwali*] is eaten by the wise ones. The ones who grab their own things while their attention is called elsewhere; the first ones to arrive receive the best gifts, certainly, they receive the best gifts. The people of Chief Ntalasha [Chitimukulu] deliver. The chief's councilor humbles himself. The child who experiences difficulties even in the presence of his father. He is a servant; he is a humble, poor servant. Chief Ntalasha [Chitimukulu] and Sampa and Chikwanda have left us in misery. We are in abject poverty.
RC:	Uhmn, it is alright *mukwai*; now is it…is this Bemba [as opposed to an older form, possibly of Luba origin]:
Audience:	It is Bemba, yes.
Audience (Fele):	Yes, those are compliments or praises [i.e. *Indyombo*]; let her sing the praises of the chief, the chief's compliments.
RC:	Oh.
Audience:	Or, we can listen. Let's listen.
	[I then played the audiocassette of Ms. Chama's remarks, while the video camera kept recording, and everyone listened closely to them.]
Audience (Fele):	Start again.
EC:	They traveled, the tall one and the other one; especially covering a long distance. When they find the chief seated [i.e. resting]; now when they greet him, they say "*Bendele umutali no wanu*." This is how they greet the chief, saying, "Greetings to you, your Royal Highness Chief Chitimukulu." They say, "When we find the chief, because he is a brave, fearless person [implying a difficult man] we must speak to him meekly; we cannot be insolent to him or disagree with him." When you find the chief and you treat him with a lot of respect—to be given food by the chief you have to speak, you have to speak meekly because some people are too proud, when they go to the chief they do not humble themselves. The chief's food is certainly eaten by the wise ones. The one who grabs their things while their attention is called elsewhere, you grab from all those who arrive first. This means, "Those who grab things have grabbed the chieftainship of the land."

RC:	Hmm.
EC:	Therefore, you should be careful. You should not be frustrating things.
Audience:	You should even ululate, you say…alalalalalala!
EC:	When they lift bread [during Communion], the oration [praises] of Jesus, when they lift bread we clap our hands [claps hands] then we clap. At this time they lift bread. When they lift cups of wine we ululate, we say, "Ulululu."
Audience (Fele):	Even clapping, you clap! [ululates a bit]. And then God the Almighty, the King, the wealthy one, His Majesty, God Almighty the wealthy one, the overseer, creator of everything. When he comes, He who is the owner of heaven and earth. When He comes, He who rose from the dead, the truthful one who never lies; we praise you, we thank you, God Almighty.
Audience (Fele):	…and so you should have ululated again.
EC:	No, we ululate once.

Elizabeth Chama sat quite straight in the wooden chair as she performed, using her hands minimally to describe things. She began by first informing Fele, who was seated on her right, what she intended to do, then went on with her recitation of the praises or epithets. Because the audience was aware that her words were being recorded, one member asked that her initial set of praises be replayed. After listening to her remarks, Ms. Chama slightly altered some of the allusions and added some explanatory comments. As with other examples of this genre I'd witnessed, the vocabulary was highly allusive and dense with esoteric words and phrases. The explanation, therefore, was meant less for the audience than for my own understanding. This attitude of didacticism pervaded the entire session. Moreover, this first performance set another interesting pattern for the ones that were to follow. Clearly, Ms. Chama wanted to share what she felt was an important traditional activity and how it had been merged with contemporary Christian practice; we were sitting, after all, less than half a mile from a Catholic mission and church. Catholicism, historically, has been very strong in this immediate area.[98] Further, being a white man

---

98 The story of how Catholicism came to this part of Zambia and to the Bemba in particular is well known locally and is tied into the broader history of the colonial era in Zambia. The "White Father" missionary Bishop Dupont arrived in the northernmost region of Northern Rhodesia in the late Nineteenth Century by way of the Tanganyika colony.

who clearly had links to the Catholic missionaries in the area, people often assumed I was interested in religious ideas or forms of worship. A direct link was made between these kinds of chiefly praises and their use in Catholic rites, explaining that even the very common practice of ululation, mostly by women, was incorporated into the Mass. The audience also felt comfortable with commenting on and augmenting her oration. While Ms. Chama spoke, there were times when she stopped for long periods, either waiting for me to comment or for some reaction from her cohorts. Since I found it difficult to follow a lot of the specialized vocabulary and deep allusions of the praises, I left it up to the audience to move the performance on or to decide when it was over. This approach elicited commentaries during virtually every performance, particularly from Fele, who continually spurred further discussion of various topics raised by the performers. At one point in his commentary, echoing the form of the traditional panegyric, Fele set out a string of praises for God: "…the Almighty, the King, the wealthy one, His Majesty, God Almighty the wealthy one, the overseer, creator of everything. When he comes, He who is the owner of heaven and earth. When He comes, He who rose from the dead, the truthful one who never lies; we praise you, we thank you, God Almighty."

The mixing of genres here is notable and not the only time it happened in this session. There is a good deal of what Bauman calls "decontextualization," (2004), or removing oral texts from their previous and more common uses, as not only royal panegyric but also citations from parts of the Catholic Mass are combined in this exposition. In its use by Ms. Chama, the material is clearly "recontextualized" for the purposes of the recording session. That there are intertextual and generic manipulations and associations brought to bear seems clear. One intention of the narrator is to educate me on these important esoteric praises, as well as reveal their recontextualization, or

---

Eventually he won the trust of the powerful Bemba Chief Mwamba who, on his death bed, ceded the regency of his chiefship to Dupont, in hopes of fending off incursions of the neighboring Ngoni, slave traders, and the British government. This led to a strong and long-lasting relationship between the Bemba people and the Catholic Church. See A. Roberts 1973 and B. Garvey 1994. The evangelical efforts of Christians in this part of Zambia entail a long and complicated history. In the area near Chief Nkula's village, Lubwa, there was a direct competition that at times bordered on violence between Catholic and Church of Scotland missionaries. This is in part covered in Oger 1991 and in Roberts (ibid.) and Garvey (ibid.). Comaroff and Comaroff 1991, especially pp. 252–308, produced a wide-ranging study of evangelical efforts in southern Africa at the advent of colonial expansion, and many of the dynamics they identify can be found to some degree in the Bemba and neighboring territories.

in another sense their appropriation, in the context of Catholic religious ceremonies. The other important dimension of this performance is the near antiphonal commentary of Fele, which continues in varying degrees in the other performances of this session. When he asks that the tape of the initial panegyric be replayed, it also serves as an opportunity for Ms. Chama to sharpen her initial allusions and interpretations when she comments on her first set of remarks.

Ms. Chama was followed by Mr. Peter Mutale, another elder around seventy years-old. He sat in the same chair, and wore a long, oversized tan rain coat that he kept tightly wrapped around him to ward off the morning chill. On his head, he wore a brim-less multi-colored cloth cap of green and black, that resembled what, in older American parlance, used to be called a "beanie." Mostly, he kept his hands in his lap, moving them a bit to make his points and, occasionally, bending a bit lower and using them to indicate places or actions, and at times crossing his arms as he spoke. He preferred to look right or left to indicate which animals were speaking or where the father of the roan antelope stood in relation to the others. Mr. Mutale related what he called a *lushimi*, but the fact that it did not include a song and required an explanation at the end suggests it was actually a *mulumbe*.[99]

Bemba Storytelling 4 by Peter Mutale*

Robert
Cancel: You can begin *mukwai*.

Audience: You say…

RC: Begin *mukwai*.

Audience: I am Mutale.

Peter
Mutale: They say to begin, with what?

---

99 See Cancel 1989, on definitions of two fictional narrative genres found in Bemba-speaking groups, but more specifically among the Tabwa. Basically, a *mulumbe* does not contain a song and a *lushimi* does. During my four weeks at Ilondola in 2005, brushing up on my Bemba language skills, it became clear to me that the people living in the Bemba heartland tend to have a broader view of the stories called *inshimi*, associating them more commonly with didactic storytelling, often adapted to the type found in church preaching orations. It may have to do with a fairly literal application with the root verb for storytelling, *-shimika*.

* To watch a video of this story follow this link: http://dx.doi.org/10.11647/OBP.0033.03/Bemba4

Audience:	Yes, you should say, "I am so and so, the one who will tell this story [*ulushimi*]. I am Peter Mutale.
RC:	Yes *mukwai*.
PM:	The story I am going to narrate, I say there was a little thing, as it started. There were problems in the world. Lions arose in the country. They caught all the people and even the animals. Then the animal which remained, which animal is that? It is the roan antelope with its child and wife. Three. When they started off, they ran away; now there where they used to stay, now they went and climbed the mountain. Then he reached the top of the mountain, and there was water there. Then he told his child, he said, "My child, do not dare to go to the bottom of this mountain [i.e. descend the mountain], where we came from. If you have ears to hear with, listen to this advice: you should just be eating right here on top of the mountain when we go out looking for food." And then, certainly for two days he stayed and said, "Let me observe my parents' advice." However, on the third day the roan antelope's child left the top of the mountain when his mother and father had gone away. He went to the foot of the mountain, there in...the plain. Then he began to eat, to eat... The lion's child was also looking in that direction where the roan antelope's child was. When he saw him, they began playing on the plain. They played and played and played. Roan antelope's child said, "Uhm uhm, as for me, the sun is about to set." He knew that, "my mother is about to come." Then the lion also said...then lion's child, when he went to his father, he said, "Oh father, where I went I made friends with someone who has white spots around the mouth and had horns." "Didn't it look like something we can eat?" He replied, "It did, we can go...we can go and eat." He even said, "It is all right; so we shall go with you tomorrow."

They set off one morning. When they reached the place, his father remained behind creeping along [i.e. stalking game]. His child quickly met his friend; because they were playing he could not delay. They were playing right there. His father was just creeping along. Hmm! He caught the child of the lio...the child of the roan antelope. That antelope which was caught, said...said...said... [the lion said] "I feel thirsty...my child, what is it?"

Kalulu came. They said, "Kalulu, guard this animal for us, as we go to the river to drink water." Certainly, they went to the river to drink water. Kalulu even took both ears [of the young antelope] and did what? Cut them; he even removed them. When the lion came back, he looked, "Aah! This animal, it had ears, doesn't it really have ears?" Kalulu said, "Inquire about this from its father at the mountain." Then lion called loudly, "Roan antelope! Roan antelope!" "Hello!" responded the roan antelope. "Does your child have ears?" His father refused, he said, "No, if he had ears he would have been able to listen." Kalulu said, "Have you heard? You have heard, am I lying to you? Well ask again." Again Lion called loudly, "Roan antelope! Does your child have ears?" Roan antelope said, "He has no ears. If he had ears he would have been able to listen." Right there and then again...again, Lion even carried roan antelope's child, and did what? He took him to his house where they went to eat. Therefore, as things could be, this is how the whole episode ended. If he had ears, he would have been able to listen.

Audience: These are the children who do not listen.

RC: Ehn!

Audience: I said these are the children who do not listen, they just know... [lots of laughter from children in audience].

Audience (Fele): Say, that is certainly the case, they are helping you, that any parable [*mulumbe*] if...if you narrate it like that...

Audience (Women): Yes, you interpret it.

Audience (Fele): Teaching comes about through interpretation. You say according to the way you put it, as Mrs. Chitupa (audience member) said, you say the moral lesson in this parable is that most of us do not take advice [i.e. we do not listen to what other people say].

RC: Oh yes.

Audience (Fele): That is why we many times get into trouble [another voice obscures some of his words]...If we paid attention to what the elders said, or if we obeyed the rules, we would not get into trouble...You see, nowadays, when you tell boys and girls, you say, "You youngsters look after yourselves properly," they do not want to listen to your advice. They say, "For us it is Zambia, for us it is Zambia." They further say, "What you are saying is old fashioned." "What about this reckless immorality?" They say, "For us it is Zambia." But the following day he/she contracts this disease they call AIDS for which there is no cure. His/Her end is to do what? To go into the ground! Just as roan antelope taught his child, he said, "Do not graze at the foot of the mountain because you will get into trouble." Therefore, even nowadays...

Audience: There are such people...

Audience (Fele):	There are many people who do not want to obey the general rules and regulations spelt out by you [the] elders [or adults]; you who began seeing things a long time ago. Therefore, this gets them into trouble. And some of them lose life.
Audience (Woman):	These things are uncouth [or barbaric]. They say, "Those things are uncouth, one should not pay attention to them."
Audience (Fele):	They say that's paganism but they are getting themselves into trouble, now again, the ones who claim to believe in God, they do not do the right things at all.
Audience (Group):	Uhunn.
Audience (Woman):	When you have your fill [i.e. when you have eaten enough food] you come to bother me as if you are the one who begat me.
Audience (Fele):	You say…you should say, "This is where my narrative ends."
PM:	This is where I end *mukwai*, my narrative ends here.
Audience:	Oh yes…because it [referring to red light on video camera] flashes repeatedly.
Audience:	Aren't you feeling the heat from the sun…can't you move into the shade? [Addressed to me]
RC:	I should switch it off, shouldn't I?

When audience members call on Mr. Mutale to interpret the tale, he hesitates, and others jump in, at least in part to attempt to educate me, the stranger, and possibly the children in the audience, on the importance of tales that elicit wisdom by interpretation and discussion. The commentaries that emerge concern young people who do not listen to elders. Fele says of the tale, "Teaching comes about through interpretation…the moral of the lesson in this story is that most of us do not take advice." The conversation and commentaries move back and forth between people, adding their own slant to the theme, including how young people disregard traditions and rites. More than once in this performance session, participants cite the callous ignorance of young people, who answer calls for proper behavior by evoking "Zambia" as a marker for nationhood, modernity and secular beliefs. Mostly, Mr. Mutale listened to the interpretations of his colleagues, particularly Fele's remarks, at times nodding in agreement or supplying a supportive grunt or sound. That the old narrative is applied to contemporary times is not surprising, though associating it with the specific problem of HIV/AIDS and promiscuity is notable for how relatively early this comes (1989) in the identification, or acknowledgment, of the disease as a social problem in Zambia. On the prompting of Fele, Mr. Mutale finally concludes the performance by applying the formulaic ending that signifies he's finished the story.

It is notable that Kalulu, the trickster hare, takes a rather minor role in this tale. Usually the center of action and attention, the hare in this instance uses his wits in order to emphasize the lesson of the narrative. When he cuts off the young antelope's ears, he spurs the lion to question its father up on the mountain. The father's answer is comical but instructive, as he asserts that his child, at least figuratively, has no ears. As is sometimes, and not very often, the case, Kalulu is a supporting player in this story, serving mainly to underline the key themes and make the antelope see how he erred by not listening to his parents. Formally, the theme is emphasized by twice repeating the scene where the young antelope plays with the young lion. Besides showing how the antelope is foolishly moving towards his fate, there is an implicit comparison between the young lion who listens to its father and the young roan that does not. Kalulu also spurs repetition when he encourages the older lion to twice question the elder antelope on whether or not his child has ears. Below I'll return to Kalulu and how he is employed in somewhat atypical ways in other performances.

A woman named Densa Kangwa, who I'd guess was in her early fifties and probably the youngest performer in the session, then proceeded to take up the same theme of young people no longer knowing much of the older ways and ideas. She wore a brown and white head-tie, with the ends knotted near the top of her head, and a wide v-necked, white short-sleeved dress that was covered from the waist down with a multi-colored *citenge*. Unlike the other speakers, Ms. Kangwa leaned back in a casual manner of repose as she spoke. She eventually sat straighter and put her hands in her lap, mostly keeping them folded, lifting both as she occasionally emphasized a point. As she got into her discourse she became more demonstrative, using her separated hands to emphasize ideas as she responded to comments by the audience, even acting out a few elements, such as wrapping a baby in a cloth. The non-fiction narrative was clearly a straightforward exposition of real concerns in the village.

Bemba Storytelling 5 by Densa Kangwa*

Robert Cancel: Let's go, *mukwai*.

Densa Kangwa: Me, the one who will start talking, I am Densa Kangwa of Fele's village.

Audience (Woman): Give way [move] friends so that I can pass.

RC: What?

DK: Our observation is that the biggest problem among our own children is disobedience; their failure to follow Bemba traditions or customs. As for us, we followed traditions or customs but nowadays, these children we have don't observe the traditions at all. Because when you begin explaining to him/her, saying, "Young one, listen to the way we used to spend time with elders at the *nsaka*."[100] They used to tell us: "Child, listen, the way the world is…" we used to listen to them carefully. But nowadays, these modern children, you cannot tell them anything; they retort: "That is paganism, as for us we are Zambians."

But this very Zambia, I don't know are the people found in it today different from those who were there in the past? I can see that they are descendants of our ancestors. But nowadays these very children we have begotten, they are a very big problem. Now, we do not know how we shall teach them. They have rebelled against us, and what has contributed to their rebellion is these things which have been brought, things like films [i.e. cinema]. These are the things that have made children rebel against their parents. Because after they have watched these films, when you tell them about our old traditions they refuse and say, "Don't waste our time, we are even going away."

As for us, certainly, we used to listen to this kind of advice; that's why we grew up and are able to beget children, people…people of

---

100 Used in this context, *nsaka* indicates both the common structure that is often found in someone's yard but also, in this case, a larger version in public space in the village. It is often simply constructed of four or five wood poles, supporting a conical thatched roof. Stools, benches or chairs comprise the furniture, and it is a place where people relax out of the heat of the sun. The term is also used here to refer to its institutional purpose, which is not only a place for elders to gather and talk, but also a place where young people were expected to sit and listen.

* To watch a video of this story follow this link: http://dx.doi.org/10.11647/OBP.0033.03/Bemba5

	our own image, we have even grown old. If the same old traditions are emphasized or brought back, children will be brought up well, but I doubt if this will happen. *Mukwai*, this is where I end.
RC:	Yes.
Audience (Woman):	How can they be brought up well when you accept and look after the children they beget outside wedlock? It is you, their mothers, to blame; if you disdained their illegitimate children, as our ancestors used to, such things would not be there; they would stop. But you even carry their babies on your backs. There is no disapproval, so even the remaining ones [those who have not yet involved themselves in this kind of mischief] hmm! [They follow suit]
Audience:	Yes, certainly, what has been said is true; we are the ones who are receiving, because whenever she brings money you receive it. When she conceives you cannot send her away from home. You just begin saying, "No, no, the child, the child…" As soon as she gives birth, you will be the first person to surrender your wrapping cloth [*citenge*], saying, "You wrap your baby in it, the child should not complain." Even next time she will bring another baby. However, if we were acting decisively, as soon as she conceives we say, "Leave this house to go live with the man who has made you pregnant." You chase her from home; they would be avoiding such mischief.
Audience:	That would have put things straight.
RC:	Now what should we do?
DK:	*Mukwai*?
RC:	What should we do?
DK:	If we could start chasing them when they conceive. You chase her from home, you say, "Go to the person who made you pregnant." Things would be straightened up.
RC:	Yes *mukwai*.
DK:	However, if she conceives and when she delivers a baby, you take your wrapping cloth, which you are wearing, you quickly wrap the baby in it, you receive the baby, you have encouraged your child to misbehave. Even next time she will bring another baby. And then you break your back tilling the land [trying to fend for the baby], you don't even know the father of those children [your daughter is bringing].
Audience:	That is true.

An initial emphasis in Ms. Kangwa's commentary is the importance of traditions, especially as practiced at the *nsaka*. There are several dimensions to this notion of the *nsaka* as an actual place or location and as a concept. What she meant, I think, is that in times past children often sat in the shade of these shelters with elders and listened to their conversations and the posing and settling of difficult social and legal situations.[101] In this manner they learned the ways to understand and order their society. Today, with formal schools and other pastimes, the young people no longer take part in this important way of learning. There is, obviously, a general allusion to what seem to be the very common conflicts between generations in this and neighboring societies. On a broader level, the *nsaka* is the concept of wisdom and its exchange in a communal way. Moreover, these commentaries are infused with a general disdain for certain elements of modernity, such as urban/rural migration and the resulting non-traditional sexual relationships between men and women that often result in unmarried pregnancies and leaving children to be raised by relatives in the villages. At the same time, evident in the other performances in this session, Christianity and its concepts seem to fit more seamlessly into what is usually thought of as older tradition. Ms. Kangwa's concluding remarks are rather poignant in the way she describes how a maternal instinct overrides what should be the practical response to unmarried pregnancies. She uses the image of how a woman would take the *citenge* wrap from her own waist in order to swaddle her daughter's new born. Further, the same woman would carry out "back-breaking" cultivation in order to feed that child.

Mr. Katongo Soolo, probably in his seventies, began his performance by giving examples of some royal praises. A tall, slim man, he wore a white crocheted cap, possibly originally meant for a woman, with a loose-fitting tan tunic that had sleeves down to his elbows, and a light green pair of trousers. His face was lined and he had a short, Charlie Chaplin-like mustache and rather intense eyes. He began with his hands clasped between his knees, then abruptly stood as he recited the beginning of his praise, then sat down as he continued it. When he began his narrative he clapped his hands together to indicate the change in genre/tone, then

---

101   In this respect, the *nsaka* tradition is very similar to what the Tswana call *kgotla*. See Shapera 1953 and Landau 1995. Landau's study particularly deals with changes wrought on traditional systems of thought and power by colonial and Christian-evangelizing incursions. Rather than simply making a dichotomy between tradition and modernity, the study looks at the complexities of how these forces interacted in differing ways in a Botswana society. In a Tabwa narrative, a father says of his young son who just rescued his sister from evil lion-man husbands, "That is the meaning of the thing they say, 'A small man in the house is good. It is that young man who always sits at the ready'." (Cancel 1989, p. 103)

became a bit more animated with his hands and arms, pointing out spaces and actions. They were, initially, repetitive and symmetrical, as he described the human's and then the lion's actions.

Bemba Storytelling 6 by Katongo Soolo*

Robert Cancel: Begin, *mukwai*. Give me your name.

Audience: Your name.

Katongo Soolo: I am Katongo Soolo…

Audience: Begin speaking, won't you?

KS: In order to show respect to every elderly person, they used to call him, saying, "Let's listen to Chitimukulu." So that everyone knows that the person being addressed is so and so, in…in olden days [begins to shout a praise in a loud, rapid delivery…takes some audience members by surprise] "Parent of Kalumbu Kayombe whose name is as famous as a beautiful horned animal! Even the bed is too small for you. The bed is small, which is from afar; you, who are…[has a coughing spell for a few minutes]…the keeper who knows no segregation; looking after women is a laborious task just like conquering an illness.

Audience: How many have you taken? [Refers to number of wives he has.] [Has another long coughing spell, while audience remarks about his coughing and praise singing efforts. Eventually, he begins a story.]

Audience: Oh! Now the youngsters have moved the thing [so and so] [a child has accidentally bumped the camera while carrying something], don't take it nearer to the machine [video camera] there…you put it on the other side.

Audience (Woman): [Referring to Mr. Soolo's coughing spell.] Well, that's what happens when you try to speak loudly if your voice is hoarse, you can cough like, like the roan antelope.

Audience: Like a bushbuck [laughs].

KS: Bushbuck.

Audience (Fele): You say you can cough like a bushbuck.

Audience: Hmm! Surely, if you have a voice you should be speaking in a low tone.

Audience: We have given an opening [for him to speak].

* To watch a video of this story follow this link: http://dx.doi.org/10.11647/OBP.0033.03/Bemba6

Audience (Woman):	Well, he has something, now he has choked.
Audience:	Oh!
Audience (Woman):	He who has swallowed meat sauce. [Possibly a reference to a proverb?]
Audience:	Oh!
Audience (Woman):	He will visit. [Answer to or second part of the proverb?]
KS:	He will visit. (?)
Audience:	Yes!
Audience:	You have untied it…[Referring to correctly applying the proverb?]
KS:	Looking after women is a laborious task. It is like conquering a severe illness.
Audience:	Don't men also have the same problem!
KS:	Well, this is a word of praise to the chief, praising any wealthy person who regularly supplies you with food, he who is respected. It [the words of praise] says, well this person is a revered man; he is a lion. This means you regard him with a lot of respect, so you give him this kind of praise. He, too, acknowledges. If you err in presenting your praise, you are pronounced guilty. If he is listening attentively, the honorable chief, where he is sitting and is convinced that these people are praising the chief…this is where we temporarily end.

[Sits up abruptly and claps his hands together] A little thing was said [formulaic story opening, marks shift in genre], a long long time ago, it was time to start cutting trees in order to prepare gardens. "Tomorrow we shall go and start cutting trees." Lion was also planning, saying, "Tomorrow we shall start cutting trees to prepare our garden." They even found a big forest that stretched over a big area. A human being swung his axe and said, "I will be cutting trees here." Lion also came [from his home]. He, too, swung his axe there and said, "I will be cutting trees here."

The human being used to come and clear his area while Lion also came and cleared his area. The human being cleared his area, Lion also cleared his area. It was time to drag the branches and pile them up in thick layers. Lion's wife [performer, given the parallel actions he is developing, probably meant to say "The man's wife"] used to drag the branches and piled them up; when she left, Lion's children also gathered and…and did the same. They did this until all the branches were gathered, and they were burnt.

Lion also came and burnt the remaining part of the piled up thick layers of branches. The whole place was thoroughly prepared. It was time to sow the seed. The human beings came to sow but the field was too big for them to finish. Lion also came in the morn… at night. They, too, sowed the seed and finished the whole field. Millet sprouted up. The human being said, "Now we should go and construct temporary huts near the garden so that we could scare away birds that may want to eat our millet." The man came to cut poles near the garden. Lion, the great one, also took…he, too, came in the evening to cut poles.

Lion…the human being said, "Today I will shift to my temporary hut near the garden." The man [the Lion?] also said, "Even me, today I will shift." His friend said, "But who is building this other house here?" The other one also said, "Who is building this other house here? We shall see them." The day of shifting…just found [them] in the garden there…"What! So it is Lion who comes to work in my field here?" The human being also said, "So it is Lion…" Hmm! The human being left; he went to consult the giant black ant… to divine what had happened. He said, "Listen my lord…my lord, what I have. As soon as I shifted to the forest here, the Lion also moved to the same place." [Aside to audience] "I am lisping out my words because there are no teeth here. Look." [Laughter]

Audience: Continue! Continue!

KS: Then *mukwai*, then Lion the great also came and said, "So it is a human being?" That human being also said, "So it is a lion?" He went to consult a diviner. He went to consult a diviner who said, "Ah, my friend, since you have come to divine what has happened, you go and see the Hornbill; invite him and say, 'You should come and see things which are at home,' while the lion is away."

Early in the morning, Hornbill arrived and said…His beak was even aglow; it was extremely red! He went straight to Lion and said, "Give me some water, if there isn't…what, yes, as you see me here, I am the one who has finished killing all the people in the world. [The beak looks as if it's been saturated in blood.] If you stop your children from fetching me water, you will be in big trouble. I have killed all the people in the world; I have finished all of them; you are the only one left in the entire world." And then Lion prepared himself and said, "Hmm! For me to survive I should start talking to my children, one at a time." He sent one child to the river and said, "Go and draw some water but when you get there don't come back, go and never come back." That's how the child went forever. He sent another child who, also, went forever. He sent another who didn't return as well. Even his wife left in the same way. He, too, as a father said, "Oh dear. It has taken my children such a long time without coming back. Even my wife, let me just follow and check what's happening." So even the father followed. He (Hornbill) saw all of them go to the river and he followed them. "With my beak" he said, "I am the one who has finished killing [all] the people in the world."

Then, Lion there and then finally ran away from the man's garden. The garden was finally owned by the man alone, and Lion did... he even deserted the place. Who is lisping out words? Don't you realize it is the teeth which make people speak properly? [Laughter]

Audience (Woman): What do you want to speak with? And you even have teeth, those are your health.

KS: *Mukwai*, unless the tongue is touching the teeth you can't...

Audience (Same woman): Yes, we have grown old, [all] the teeth are gone.

KS: Now there are no teeth.

Audience: Oh dear! This is the problem with the young ones; they do not pay attention to what is being said.

Audience (Same woman): Yes, they [teeth] have dispersed; they have gone back where they came from...

Audience (Man): Continue narrating *mukwai*.

KS: It is over *mukwai*.

Audience: Is that the end?

KS: Hmmm.

Audience: Explain the meaning.

KS: Even nowadays such things are here in Malole. Some people would find where their friend has cleared trees [in preparation for planting a garden]; they, too, start making a garden there. The following morning his friend is cultivating here [there]. He who is strong as the human being or man [in the story] even encroaches upon his friend's field. After three days, the one who is more aggressive outwits his friend and says, "You have encroached upon my field, you have encroached upon my field."

Therefore, *mukwai*, this is where it ends; it is difficult to predict what is going to happen. I am a farmer.

RC: That's it *mukwai*. Well done *mukwai*.

Audience: You have finished...you have ended.

[[KS: That is a chief. That is to say, now we have reached a very important/rich person...oh!]][102]

---

102 Mr. Soolo did not explain this last remark. He seemed to be using a stock phrase or saying to mark the ending of the discussion, but no one responded to it and I haven't been able to find a clear explanation from colleagues who've viewed the video recording.

Mr. Soolo's initial efforts at praise poetry were interrupted for some minutes by a very deep and persistent cough. I could not tell if this was caused by a dry throat, a cold or something more debilitating and long-lasting. As he paused to catch his breath and clear his throat, audience members at first speculated as to the cause of his coughing, and then jokingly related the noise he was making to that of the roan antelope, then to the bushbuck. They also raised an image of swallowing meat sauce, as part of a proverbial expression that predicts someone will soon visit, having to do with posing then explaining a story or proverb, concluding that "*Wakakula...*" ("You have untied [literal]/solved it...") When he was able to speak again, Mr. Soolo explained the praises he'd recited initially, then said, "...this is where we temporarily end." He then goes on to tell the story of the lion, farmer and hornbill, regarding a potential land dispute.

Audience members, further, asked him to explain the narrative and he said that "Even nowadays such things are around here in Malole... Therefore *mukwai*, this is where it ends; it is difficult to predict what is going to happen. I am a farmer." Mr. Soolo's tale focuses on the theme of people trying to take what is not theirs. While the lion is in some respects mimicking or duplicating the farmer's efforts, the man understands that when the crops come the lion will use his physical advantage to take everything for himself.[103] By following the proper procedures of consulting a diviner,[104] then asking help from the Hornbill, the human is able to drive out his lion competitor and reap the fruits of his own labors. At least part of the imagery portraying the Hornbill relates to similar actions in the traditional context whereby smaller animals use their fearsome voices or forms of trickery to defeat larger, deadly animals.[105] Mr. Soolo relates the

---

103 The question of a potentially deadly lion following or mirroring a human's action is found in several variations in a number of Tabwa stories. In most of them the lion proves to be a well-meaning benefactor (Cancel 1989, pp. 129–160). In a Bwile tale in Chapter VI of this book, the lion turns out to be much more hostile. A wider spectrum of narrative images speculates on the wisdom or folly of trusting animals to assist humans in their tasks or predicaments in tales.
104 Consulting an ant as a diviner is found in a Tabwa narrative about a lion-man husband who keeps devouring the children he has with his human wife (Cancel 1989), as well as in a narrative from the Lamba collection by C.M. Doke, wherein an arrogant chief has all the elders killed then is himself endangered by an ogre who only an elder can outwit. In fact, the character is utilized in the tale about Fipindulule, told by Mr. Kampamba earlier in this chapter.
105 A Bisa narrative in Chapter IV reveals how a small animal scares off a lion threatening a human family using only its voice. This version is told by George Mwampatisha at

narrative to actual situations that he, as a farmer, has witnessed in his home area of Malole. These conflicts could involve land disputes or even simply taking crops from someone else's plot.[106]

A humorous and rather telling set of audience interactions play out around the narrative and its theme. Initially, as Mr. Soolo was wracked by a coughing spell, his cohort spent time good-naturedly speculating on what was causing the coughs and how he should more properly modulate his voice in order to avoid this reaction. Further, they joked about how his coughs sounded like the calls of first the roan antelope then the bushbuck. Half way through his tale, Mr. Soolo notes how he has begun to lisp because he has no upper teeth. Women in the audience egg him on, saying things like, "Yes, we have grown old, [all] teeth are gone," or "Yes, they have dispersed, they have gone back where they came from..." which seems to allude to the absence of teeth in infants when they are born. As most of the session suggested, audience members were of the same age group and felt comfortable joking with and insulting one another. No longer of an age where sexual tension or socio-economic competition came between them, they exhibited an easy camaraderie that comes with growing old together. This comfort level did not keep one woman from questioning Mr. Soolo about some of his statements regarding women, though, again, the exchange was friendly.

Much of their concern was directed at the younger generation, which did not, in their view, adhere to the wisdom of elders and traditions. While comments on the relationship between old age, the lack of teeth and the ability to speak properly were being exchanged, one audience member injected the somewhat anomalous observation, "Oh dear! This is the problem with the young ones; they do not pay attention to what is being said." Even one of Mr. Soolo's earlier observations regarding praise poetry alluded to the importance of eloquence and paying proper respect to authority when he notes, "If you err in presenting your praise, you are pronounced guilty. If he is listening attentively, the honorable chief, where he is sitting, and is convinced that these people are praising

---

Nabwalya, while another is told fourteen years later by Kangwa Samson as a way to give a better sense of what he thought the correct version of the narrative *should* have been, in 2005.

106 The latter situation is portrayed in a different and complex manner in a Lunda tale performed by Ms. Emeliya Muleya in Chapter V. The stealing of neighbors' crops, depicted in a humorous vein, is often a subject of trickster tales in many African traditions.

the chief..."[107] Words and respect are venerated even to the point of danger if one falters in the quality of how one addresses someone of high status. So, although his narrative was directed at a more common problem of land use and access, Mr. Soolo's performance was framed by these broader concerns of unity, humor, eloquence and correct behavior that permeated the overall session.

Finally, Fele, whose actual name is Stephen Komakoma, discoursed at length on Bemba history and other matters. He was most likely in his mid or late sixties, still strongly though slimly built, with close-cropped grey hair. He wore a loose, light grey, short-sleeved buttoned shirt with a collar and black trousers. Fele rested his left elbow on the table that held the video monitor and kept both his hands on his thighs as he spoke and, mostly, used subtle gestures, barely lifting his hands, to make his points. He seemed comfortable with speaking publicly about matters of cultural significance.

Bemba Storytelling 7 by Stephen Komakoma*

Robert
Cancel: Let's begin.

Stephen
Komakoma: I am Masaku. My names are Stephen Komakoma. I am the one who has succeeded Fulendiko Kafula here in Malole. I am a councilor and friend of Chief Chitimukulu. I work with the Chief in the highest council or court at the royal palace. I just want to say a few things about the way of life among the Bemba people, our group, starting from the way we used to live a long time ago [or, in the past].

---

107   Interestingly, the problem of improper, inaccurate, or disrespectful praises was raised by Chitimukulu in Chapter I, as he listened to the tape of Ng'ongo Yuba's performance. He felt compelled, even years later, to try to have the bard rectify this problem. Similarly, when Chief Puta watched the video of the performance of his predecessor, he was moved to have his advisors come in to record an addendum or correction to the earlier narrative. In the pan-traditional narrative context there are often chiefs portrayed in various tales who do not exhibit much wisdom in understanding the cases being brought before them. An obvious example is the Kalulu tale performed by Mr. Stanley Kalumba in the previous chapter, where the trickster manipulates the chief/lion into first making the bark cloth garment then pronouncing a rash and unfair judgment on the bushbuck.

* To watch a video of this story follow this link: http://dx.doi.org/10.11647/OBP.0033.03/Bemba7

III. Chiefs, Tricksters and Catholics: Bemba Tales and Orations 103

The Bemba people, as you might know and have heard and read from books, [that] the Bemba people are not original inhabitants of this country, Zambia. This people came from a country of…which used to be called Congo, or let's say these days it is called Zaire.[108] It is a group that broke away from the Luba people, even these who came here were being referred to as the Luba people. The chiefs who are well known are very many. I will mention their names towards the end. When they arrived in this country they found people of different ethnicities, but they defeated them and drove them out of this land. They gained control of this land and became famous as the Bemba people. I am just summarizing, eh…it is not my intention to say everything about the life of the Bemba people, not at all.

I just want to pick a few points. The Bemba's way of life, they used to live in ordinary villages and the chiefs' villages. And these villages, just as they look nowadays, after they had built the village they used to live in harmony as a family. However, there were some problems that used to disturb their harmony. There was danger of wild animals, lions and others. These things hindered their development because many times they failed to go out to work [in the fields]. They were afraid of these animals. There were other things which disturbed their stay; these tribal wars. In these wars, they often fought with the groups they found in this land. Therefore, their story was not peaceful. There were other people who came from far away countries, as you have heard of the Ngoni people. They came from the country called…South Africa. They conquered many lands and finally entered the country…of Zambia. Even there they defeated some peoples. However, they often struggled with the Bemba because they were equally strong. The Bemba were aggressive, and the Ngoni were also aggressive.

Lions and wars were not the only things which made life difficult for the people; not at all. Locusts used to give people a lot of problems. Therefore, whatever people wanted to do in terms of development, these three things I have mentioned frustrated their progress. According to the way they lived, they were ruled by chiefs. The Bemba land was divided into different parts. The biggest part was controlled by Chitimukulu. The other part was under Chief Mwamba, while the other was controlled by Chief Nkula. Other areas were controlled by their sons.[109] For example, Makasa's area, Munkonge's chiefdom, Chief Mporokoso's area, and… and…other smaller chiefs who were below their sons. Therefore, all these chiefs ruled people who belonged to one group called "Bemba." In their running of their affairs they worked together; they were not leaving things

---

108 The name has reverted to (the Democratic Republic of) Congo since this session was taped.
109 "Sons" is used here in a positional manner, since succession of Bemba chiefs is, strictly speaking, through nephews, sons of the chiefs' sisters. Actual succession is obviously more complicated in actuality than this matrilineal model suggests.

in the hands of one chief, so that he could do everything alone, not at all. They used to help each other. They were united just like this that you are nowadays calling "Humanism."[110] Even in the past, they had their own humanism.

For example, in the village, as I was narrating, they used to have the *nsaka*, as things are nowadays there are schools or welfare halls where people meet to discuss issues and do certain things. At the *nsaka* people learned a lot or gained a lot of knowledge that they imparted to others who did not have this knowledge. It was also at the *nsaka*, as I heard Mrs. Chitupa say something about bringing about development such as farming, that they used to plan things, saying, "Friends, how shall we work this year? In which area shall we work?" Counseling of certain people who didn't know certain things was done at the *nsaka*; as you can see nowadays that's why some people are ignorant of a number of things [because there are no regular gatherings at the *nsaka*]. Some people cannot even make axe or hoe handles; others cannot even…make a basket; others don't know how to make winnowing baskets. In the past we used to have people at the *nsaka* who knew how to make such things. These were the ones who used to teach their friends such skills. Even nowadays, inhabitants of this place [the Bemba area] want to revive those good old practices because people used to learn a lot of things at the *nsaka*, just as they are learning things from welfare societies or schools or any other place where people gather. That's the same way the *nsaka* used to work. Even organization used to start from *nsaka*. "Friends, you have seen the way we are living here…at this village. Calamities are befalling us every now and then. There are fierce animals—lions and all the other things. What shall we do?"

Other messages would come. "Ah friends, have you heard the message from the chief's palace? We are being warned thus: 'You people of village so and so, take care. Yes, there are rumors that the Ngoni or enemies will attack us in this land.'" People used to get all this information from the *nsaka*. Therefore, this "Humanism" which has been taught to us by the party and its government, that this is what we should follow but it hasn't worked the way it used to work in the past. In the kind of humanism that was practiced at the *nsaka*, there was mercy—helping those who were not fortunate enough to get their basic needs. Those who were at the *nsaka* consulted and planned how to help such needy persons. Although there were many obstacles that hindered development and generally made people's lives unpleasant, there were certain things that they did very well.

---

110 Humanism is the term given to the political philosophy originated, espoused and applied by Zambia's first president, Kenneth D. Kaunda. It put forth a program that was ostensibly a combination of western capitalism and African socialism. Over the years, in effect, it took on the trappings of socialism that had evolved in many third world nations.

I can give one example of these things. They had started mining although they were not digging very deep. They were just scooping out soil from the anthills or near the river. This is what they used to call iron ore. It was right there at the *nsaka* where the blacksmiths were also found, let me say, those people who were very skilled workmen. Those very skilled workmen could scoop out soil from an anthill to build a very big smelting furnace. These are the things that are nowadays called "smelters." These are used in smelting ... eh, that soil so that it is heated to extract the things they want. When they melt, slag goes this way, that waste matter goes this way. Then the metal, which is called iron ore or the real metal remains. This is what they would take. After doing such things, they used to teach each other at the *nsaka*; that's where blacksmiths, who could process these things, were. These were usually very few [in number]. It was at the *nsaka* that people learned different ways of making garments to wear. Some were wearing hides of sheep, wild animals; others were wearing bark cloths which even today... [Videotape ends here, rest of narrative is recorded on an audiotape of the session.]

Mr. Komakoma began by sketching out the migration of the Bemba from the Congo into what is now Zambia, and describing their militaristic conquest of new lands and peoples. He talks about how lion attacks, ongoing wars, and even locusts regularly plagued the efforts of people to live and work peacefully. These problems were addressed by the cooperation of the numerous Bemba chiefs and their constituents. Here Fele refers to the older practices resembling what was at the time of the performance the national philosophy known as "Humanism," something vaguely akin to but never as celebrated as Julius Nyerere's Tanzanian "Ujamaa." From this contemporary analogy, he moves back to the concept of the *nsaka* and, although he had initially stated he only had a few remarks with which to conclude the session, he produced the longest of the orations, covering many topics. He enumerates and describes the many instances whereby this central meeting space served as a site of educating young people, communicating urgent news, learning various skills and crafts. There is a brief but thorough description of how people use the soil from anthills to construct traditional ovens to smelt iron. Most of his remarks add more details to the viability of that traditional place of wisdom, and he returns more than once to the secular modernity of the younger generation.

One interesting dimension of his performance was that he was rarely interrupted, even by a sound of ascent, such as "Uh huh," or "Yes." In many ways, he was summarizing a lot of what had been said thematically during the session, as well as asserting his role as village headman, owner of the house we were at, the convener of the session, and the main discussant during each performance. In a sense, Mr. Komakoma speaks as a rural "company man," asserting both the importance of Bemba traditions and church, lauding the powers of Bemba chiefs and the nation's philosophy and practices.

I had been playing back the audio after each person's efforts, so they were quite aware of what I was recording and what they sounded like. It was overall a very hospitable situation. Living in Malole and a few miles from the compound of the Paramount Chief, they'd all had a fair amount of contact with European missionaries, teachers, aid workers and some researchers as well. They did not appear to find my presence all that unusual and seemed to be quite at ease. Comparatively speaking, this particular session both paralleled and differed from others I'd recorded among other Bemba-speaking groups, particularly those involving elders. Perhaps the most dramatic difference was the continual interaction between performers and audience and the ways in which the themes of different oral genres were intertwined: praise poetry, fictional oral narrative, historical descriptions, proverbs, humorous verbal sparring, and outright didactic exposition. The themes of wisdom, respect, piety, power, cooperation, education, sexuality, and generational contestation interwove liberally and produced a dense insight into the ways people gave artistic and verbal form to the things that concerned them. It was particularly instructive for me at that point in the research, because it was a reminder of the broad canvas that an oral tradition occupies, and how generic categories are constantly tested, redefined or completely ignored in favor of the ongoing communicative experience, manipulated in performance, especially by elders.[111]

Although he initially refused to take payment, I convinced Fele to accept a small amount of money [around $8] to compensate people for their time. We returned to the secondary school for some lunch then drove out to Chitimukulu's village at around 1:45 PM, arriving around 2:10. I've described this occasion in some detail in the first chapter of this study. We ended our session shortly before sunset, amidst the

---

111   See Briggs and Bauman 1992 on genre in oral traditions. Their notion of intertextuality and power are apposite for the discussion of how people mix and cross generic boundaries in order to strengthen their arguments or make broader statements or connections in their discourses.

rather chaotic energy of that increasingly spontaneous gathering. After promising to send photos of the event, Daniel and I dropped Mr. Kalunga at his home then drove back to Kasama. While the long recording session at Chitimukulu's was decidedly different from the earlier two, involving as it did a preponderance of music, dance and praise singing, it also exhibited the ways in which performance can be both emergent and transcendent. At the same time that men were putting forward their individual performance personas, women demanded a share of the stage and expressed their own, more communal, selves. This competitive relationship differed markedly from the more relaxed and shared atmosphere at Fele's compound. Gendered elements of performance, of presence and power, will be further considered in the next chapter on Lunda performance.

Postscript

In late October 2005 I made a brief return to the Malole area and, in particular, to Fele's village. It had been difficult to get there, spending five hours in Kasama waiting for a minibus to fill up before we could leave for the forty minute trip to Malole. Once at the village, I had to ask help from a schoolboy to take me to Fele's village, where I met the successor to Stephen Komakoma. Though polite and hospitable, the new Fele evidenced little interest in my project and less in my intention to find or find out about the people who'd performed stories for me in 1989. With the help of the schoolboy, I tried to track down the family of Dismas Kampamba, but no one was home. In fact, there was a funeral in a distant part of Malole that had drawn most people. In over three decades of rural research, I'd learned that one of the best reasons to spend a good amount of time in any one place was to account for the very common occurrence of funerals and the responsibility felt by local residents to attend these rites. A half-day visit to Malole was clearly not going to be sufficient to locate the performers, or their families, that I was looking for. Eventually, we were able to find the home of Ms. Densa Kangwa, and she was sitting outside on her verandah scraping the husks off of large cassava tubers. Dressed in older working clothes and headscarf, Ms. Kangwa had clearly aged since my first visit, having become noticeably thinner and greyer. After an initial introduction and reminder of when I'd come and of our recording session, Ms. Kangwa smiled and seemed delighted to see me again, even remembering that I'd come that time with my young son.

We sat in front of her small home and chatted a bit then I set up my DVD player on a small table so that she could see the stories that were told at Malole in 1989.

While her memory was quite good, she could supply only a few details on the performers, most of who had since died. Ms. Kangwa clearly enjoyed seeing the performances again, noting the importance of the themes explored at Fele's session. She had been born in 1938, which made her around fifty-one at our original session and near sixty-seven in 2005. She'd had ten children, and nine were still living. Of the performers we were watching, she could only recall that Elizabeth Chama was in her eighties when she died. Peter Mutale, she said, was also known as Telensa Shula, and had died in 1995. Fele, Stephen Komakoma, was nearly ninety years old when he passed away in 1995. She also recognized the young Elizabeth, who'd told a story after Mr. Kampamba, as Bana Chinondo, mother of Chinondo. While Bana Chinondo was away at that moment, her adolescent son, Chinondo, soon arrived in time to see his mother telling a story while holding and nursing him on her knee. Ms. Kangwa spoke to the two young men sitting on her verandah in order to enlist their help to later on distribute the photos and transcriptions of the tales I'd brought to the appropriate relatives of the performers.

One notable event that occurred as we sat and watched the performances was the arrival of three young women, none of whom seemed older than sixteen years old. Two had babies on their backs or hips and they wandered over in a very proprietary and somewhat aggressive manner, demanding to know who I was and what was going on. Ms. Kangwa explained my presence, at the same time she indicated that she was performing on the video at that particular moment. The young women watched for a while, feigning the kind of disinterest that seems universal for adolescents, taking cassava from Ms. Kangwa's stack, even though she asked them not to, and biting off and chewing the raw pieces. One of the young women kept looking me up and down while she alternately ate cassava and picked her teeth with a piece of straw. They eventually tired of standing there watching us do nothing, laughed at me and then sauntered away. I think I was the only one to notice the irony of the themes of the performances preserved by the DVD video—about how young people no longer paid attention, how girls bore children for their parents to raise, or how the young no longer spent time learning at the *nsaka*—and the current behavior of these young women.

I took some photos of Ms. Kangwa, after she'd gone into her home to change into a newer dress and headscarf, and promised to send them as soon as I could. I also gave her the equivalent of $5 as compensation for her time. It was nearing 5 PM and I was going to have to find a ride back to Kasama before it got dark or try to secure a place to spend the night at Malole, possibly at St. Francis Secondary School. So I took my leave. This was the last stop in my two-month stay in Northern Province trying to find more contextual information on the sessions and performers from my 1988–89 visits. The researcher in me wanted to spend more time in Malole to track down additional data on the lives of these narrators, while the practical side realized that spending the night would have entailed a lot more work for perhaps meager results. The practical and world-weary side won out, not the first time this happened during my 2005 time in the north. I then walked to the road and waited almost an hour before the first vehicle going west passed by. The car contained four union organizers, returning from a meeting with school teachers in a nearby town. After some interesting conversation on the ride to Kasama, they dropped me near some shops, where I could walk back to the rest house where I was staying.

Ilondola

My efforts to record stories at or near Chief Nkula's village in 1989 pretty much typified the things that come up in field research. Initially, I'd hoped to find Father Louis Oger at Ilondola mission and secure his cooperation in my recording plans. Originally from France, Fr. Oger had lived and worked in Zambia for many years and had written articles on Bemba language, history and culture.[112] He was one of the chief organizers and teachers at the Bemba language school based at Ilondola. Fr. Oger also has authored many of the language study texts published by the White Fathers for use by students in these courses. As my son Michael and I drove out of Chinsali, on the road to Ilondola, we met a Toyota pickup truck going the other way. Inside were two white men who looked like Catholic priests—after a while it really isn't too difficult to identify them, especially knowing that Toyota pickups were often the vehicle of

---

112 Fr. Oger has written a detailed history of the establishment of the Catholic mission at Ilondola in 1934 (1991). See also Garvey 1994.

choice for the White Fathers in Zambia. We waved them down as we came abreast of their truck and indeed it turned out to be Fr. Oger. He was on his way to Lwitikila Secondary School at Mpika, around 60 or so miles away, to watch Pope John Paul II's visit to Zambia on television. While I was disappointed, he encouraged me to go on to the mission and seek the help of Fr. Michel Genelot, or "Father Mike."

We pushed on, stopping on the way at the village of Chief Nkula. This area of Zambia has an important history in the nationalist struggle. Near Nkula's is the Prostestant mission at Lubwa, where the nation's first president, Kenneth D. Kaunda, was raised by his cleric parents.[113] Years after independence, it was also the initial site of the Zambian government's dispute with the charismatic religious leader Alice Lenshina.[114] In any event, we were led to Nkula's by a couple of local men we'd picked up along the road. The chief was out, but several young women explained that he'd return that evening. I left one of my several official letters of introduction and said we'd come by the next day. We drove on to Ilondola and found Father Genelot outside the church. He was most cordial and agreed to show me around the village and introduce us to some potential storytellers.

Father Genelot was soon to leave Zambia for a post in Canada, where one of the White Fathers' headquarters is located. He was interested in our work, and we shared stories of people we knew in common. We first visited the home of a man known as a fine storyteller, but the 87 year-old had left for his gardens and would be spending a few nights at his *mutanda* or temporary bush shelter. We moved on to find Mr. Stephen Chipalo at home. He was a retired schoolteacher who currently worked as a teacher for the mission's language courses. He was very hospitable and spoke Bemba, at least to me, in a very clear and deliberate way. It was apparent that students would benefit from this kind of articulation and enunciation of the language. We made arrangements for me to

---

113   Much has been written about and by Zambia's first head of state. Several informative works include Hall 1973 and Kaunda 1963.
114   Lenshina's Lumpa Church rose in the mid-1950s as a charismatic movement that was thought to threaten government power in the area. For a discussion of her influence and the complex confrontation between her Lumpa movement and the national government see A. Roberts 1972 and 1973, and a more recent study by van Binsbergen 1981. Only recently, ca. 2006, have a good number of the church's adherents returned to Zambia from exile in the Congo. Gordon 2008, has written the most recent historical evaluation of this seminal period in Zambia.

return in the morning to record some stories. We walked on to another man's house. Mr. Makombe was quite old, one of the oldest converts who actually traveled to Ilondola with the first Catholic missionaries (Oger 1991). I arranged to come for him in the morning and take him to Mr. Chipalo's house for a recording session. By this time it was getting dark, so we returned to the mission to settle in for the night, observing the pleasant rituals of a meal with Father Mike and more conversation about his twenty-two years in Zambia and some of the people we both knew.

At around 7:20 AM, I drove over to pick up Mr. Makombe at his home and we arrived at Mr. Chipalo's at around 7:40. Also attending the session was Mr. Chakobe, the headman of a nearby section of the village. The first story was told by our host, Mr. Chipalo.[115]

Bemba Storytelling 8
by Stephen Chanda Chipalo*

Robert Cancel:	Have you prepared? OK, can you mention your name?
Henry Chakobe:	Your name.
RC:	That's it.
Stephen Chipalo:	First? On...before?
RC:	Yes *mukwai*.
SC:	I, the one who is about to start speaking, am Stephen Chanda Chipalo.
RC:	Uhn hum. You can begin *mukwai*.
SC:	There goes the *mulumbe*; there was a very big stone in the bush. And that big stone stood forever. In the bush there was a small animal, a lemur [*canga*]. This lemur used to leap in the tree. He used to jump in a tree [from branch to branch]. All the other animals saw how

---

115 Stephen Chanda Chipalo was born around 1926 and died in July 2001 at the age of 75. His home is less than half a mile from Ilondola mission. I visited his widow, Mrs. Sarafina Chipalo in September 2005. She told me they'd married around 1941 and had fifteen children, eight of whom were still alive. Mr. Chipalo had taught at around five primary schools and retired in 1974. He'd been an elder in the local Catholic church; at different times holding the positions of church council chairman and also the council's bursar.

* To watch a video of this story follow this link: http://dx.doi.org/10.11647/OBP.0033.03/Bemba8

the lemur used to play in the tree. One day the lemur fell on a big stone. He fell on the stone and died. All the other animals sat still and said, "What's the matter?!" They began arguing. One animal said, "Me, even if I fell on a stone I could not die at all." The elephant, the buffalo, the roan antelope, the lion, the small antelope [Sharpe's steenbok], the duiker… Then one day the elephant was taking a stroll. It stumbled against something. It fell on…it fell near the stone, it hit its head against the…the stone. It even died. The buffalo and other animals said, "Oh dear! This is beyond comprehension! No, me I can't die at all. Even if I fall onto the stone I can't die."

Then one day the buffalo also set out, it was taking a stroll, it hit its foot against a stone, hit its head against a stone; it even died. The hippopotamus said, "You young ones, the way you walk is childish, you walk like a young boy." Then the hippo also took a stroll; it took a stroll. Within a short time it also stumbled, it also hit its head against the stone and died. The duiker said, "Poor fellows! Perhaps these fellows have met this fate because they are heavy." Because the duiker is quick, it hopped about. It hopped about. It also stumbled; it hit against the stone. Then it also died.

Kalulu [the hare] said, "You hopeless animals, you all lack wisdom! Why do you jump about like this, you just crawl, the giant elephants just crawl? Even the hippo also crawls, Mr. Duiker was also crawling. How foolish! This is the way I, the hare, do things." It began hopping about, it hopped about, it hopped about. Well! Poor thing, it jumped high and hit against the stone, mpaa! And then the hare's head was what?…was cut off.

How terrible! All the animals were gripped by fear. However, there were some which were not scared at all. They went round the stone, but they were afraid of hitting against the stone. Some of them said, "We shouldn't be afraid. Let us just hit ourselves against this very stone."

Therefore, this *mulumbe* means that…I will explain. The king who came from heaven is Christ, Jesus Christ. He came to this earth and taught us, and suffered for us. When he finished his work, as he was about to return to his father, he gathered his workers. Then he said to Simon, "Now you are not Simon at all. Your name is Peter, you are the stone. You are the foundation on which I will build my church, which will go…which will stand forever." Therefore, the name Peter is "the rock." And the one who has taken Peter's place especially at this time is Pope John Paul the Second. Therefore, he, too, has ascended to the place of the Disciples of Christ. Even Pope John Paul is the rock. Therefore, this rock is the Catholic Church. The Catholic Church will never break at all. Therefore, every person should get closer to the rock so that they may find salvation. If we human beings do not draw closer, if we do not hide in the everlasting rock, we will not find salvation. This is the end of this *mulumbe*.

RC: Very good *mukwai*.

Stephen Chipalo was at that time in his mid sixties, though he looked to be much younger. He was slim and held himself quite erect, sitting or standing. He wore a thin black turtle neck sweater and dark trousers, both of which accentuated his thin frame. As he began the performance, he had his arms crossed with his hands rubbing his elbows. He kept his arms crossed for the first part of the story, slowly and subtly rocking back and forth, and using his head to nod and sway in accentuating his words. At the point where the hippo dies in the narrative, he moved his hands between his legs, forearms resting on his thighs. His main gesture, aside from the continued rocking and use of his head to make his points, was to use his hands to imitate the prancing of the duiker, as described by Kalulu, and Kalulu's own prancing over the rock. Then he leaned back and interlaced his fingers over his right knee for most of the remainder of the narrative. Overall, his voice and inflections, along with the rocking of body and head, carried most of the performance's non-verbal techniques, giving form to the words of the narrative. Speaking clearly, almost deliberately, Mr. Chipalo first depicted the tale's events then explained them carefully at the end.

There seems little coincidence that the narrative had a Christian, indeed a Catholic, thematic thrust. Living virtually in the shadow of the venerable mission and church at Ilondola, and engaged as a teacher at the Language Center, Mr. Chipalo emphasized the power of the rock in the story as standing for St. Peter, the first in a line of popes that ended, at that time, in John Paul II, who happened to be visiting Zambia on that same day. It is interesting to note that Kalulu, as was the case in a Bemba narrative performed at Malole by Peter Mutale, plays a relatively small role in this *mulumbe*. While expectations may have been raised when the trickster hare appeared in the narrative, these were quickly channeled to the overall pattern of animals declaring they would overcome the deadly power of the rock, only to immediately fall victim to it. Mr. Chipalo reveals that even the clever Kalulu cannot stand before the power of the church. This tale may easily have been the kind of story told as a homily during Mass, by a priest or a lay lector.

When Mr. Chakobe took his turn at performance, he turned out to be one of the most animated and engaging storytellers I'd recorded in a long time.

Bemba Storytelling 9 by Mr. Henry Chakobe*

Robert Cancel: All right *mukwai*.

Henry Chakobe: I, the one who will be speaking this time, am Henry Chakobe. My home is right here at Ilondola. In fact, I am the village headman. The cleverness of the roan antelope, its burden is on the back. [proverb]

A little thing was said. Kalulu and Bushbuck lived in temporary huts [*mitanda*] in the gardens. They liked each other very much. They used to eat together, even sleeping, they used to sleep in the same house. One day they went...Kalulu took a stroll in the bush. He found the *musongwa*[116] tree that was heavy with ripe *nsongwa* fruit. However, the *musongwa* tree was very tall. Kalulu could not climb this *musongwa* at all. Then he thought, "What shall I do?" He said, "I will go and get my friend Bushbuck. He himself [Bushbuck] will be able to climb this *musongwa*." He returned home and told Bushbuck. He said, "My friend, where I went I saw a *musongwa* tree that was bearing the fruit very well. However, it is very tall. Since it is night time now, we shall go together tomorrow so that we go and eat the fruit because there is famine in this land." Bushbuck was very happy. And so, they almost failed to fall into deep sleep because of the excitement and anxiety. Very early in the morning they set out. Kalulu led the way to the *musongwa* tree. Then he...they arrived. He said, "See my friend?" As could be expected, Bushbuck was so happy that he started salivating. He enquired, "Who will climb this fruit tree my friend?" Kalulu said, "Well, you are the one who will climb it my friend."

Bushbuck certainly got hold of the tree and climbed. As he got up into the tree, Kalulu decided to leave. He said, "My friend, I will be

---

116 The *musongwa* tree bears the *lusongwa* fruit, identified in the dictionary and by local people as the "Cape Gooseberry." While this fruit seems mostly to grow in shrubs rather than trees, the narrative clearly locates the fruit atop a very tall tree.

* To watch a video of this story follow this link: http://dx.doi.org/10.11647/OBP.0033.03/Bemba9

back soon, I am going somewhere." He stood and left. As he hid behind some objects, he saw Bushbuck shaking the *nsongwa* fruit. He shook the branches, he shook, he shook; the fruit fell down in big quantities. Finally he saw that they were plenty. Hare took his skin...he removed it from his body. He just remained exposed flesh, red! He set out, he began going [back]. Then he stood under the *musongwa* tree and looked up. He said, "You fellow, who is shaking off my *nsongwa* fruit, who are you?" As Bushbuck was up in the tree, he looked down, he saw the...hare who looked red! And then *mukwai*, he said, "Come down. Who told you to climb this tree?" "Well *mukwai*, it is Kalulu who brought me." He was saying this because he didn't know that he was actually talking to Kalulu. Bushbuck quickly tumbled down from the tree, pulululululu. As soon as he tumbled down the tree, Kalulu began beating him with a whip, lopoo! lopoo! Bushbuck cried a lot and ran away.

Hare remained there and at the *nsongwa* fruit. He ate and ate until he had his fill. He even carried a few *nsongwa*. He started going to the temporary huts. He found his friend Bushbuck and said, "Oh! My friend, when I returned from where I had gone I found you were not there. Where did you go?" Bushbuck said, "Can you see how swollen I am? Something red came, it beat me thoroughly." "Why didn't you call me?" said Kalulu. Bushbuck said, "Certainly my friend, I called for help from you." Kalulu even gave him some of the few *nsongwa* fruit he had carried. Bushbuck ate but he did not eat enough, he didn't have his fill at all.

The following morning again Kalulu said, "Let's go. Today I will keep an eye on the thing that beat you." Again Bushbuck climbed the tree. Hare said, "Just go up, I am watching." He looked all around; he looked sideways. He said, "My friend, I have a stomach ache, I will be back soon." Again he went to the same place. He did the same thing; he removed his skin exposing his flesh, red! Again he came back. He found Bushbuck in the tree. He said, "You! You have again come back here today after that beating I gave you yesterday? You are a very stubborn person? Even today you have come back here!" "Well *mukwai*, even today it is Kalulu who led me to this place, even today it is Kalulu..." He said, "Come down, today you will take me where Kalulu is." Bushbuck replied, "*Mukwai*, today he went in the same direction." Kalulu answered, "You just come down." Just as Bushbuck was coming down, Kalulu began as he did previously; he began beating him, "Oh dear!" Bushbuck jumped down and ran away very quickly. He reached the huts. He sat down and thought, he said, "Oh no!" His friend Kalulu, there he came, he ate the *nsongwa* fruit. He ate a lot of them; he was satiated. Again he carried a few. "My friend, what demon has entered you, are you mad?" Bushbuck said, "My friend, even today come and see what this thing has done to me. It has beaten me a lot, come and see. Look! I am swollen, even in my eyes, see?" "Oh! I even came with…I…I even have…a knobkerrie [fighting stick]. I said that today we will kill this thing." Then that was all. He said, "Oh, it's all right." Therefore, my friend, let's go there again tomorrow." But Bushbuck began thinking, he said, "How strange. Huhm. Tch. This friend of mine is not a good person at all."

The following morning, they went back to the *musongwa* again. Let me say they continued going there a number of times like that. Then that morning they went; Bushbuck climbed the *musongwa* tree. Hare said, "Excuse me for a moment." Bushbuck also kept an eye on him as he went and stood somewhere. Hare removed his skin in the same way he used to do it; he removed it and put it somewhere. He came back red, carrying whipping sticks. "Who told you to climb this tree?" "Well my friend, well…!" As his friend was beating him with whips, Bushbuck ran away, but he went straight to the spot where Kalulu had left his skin. And he found the skin Kalulu had left. Bushbuck…ahn [slaps hands]! He snatched it with his mouth; he carried it with his teeth. He quickly ran away. Kalulu saw that and said, "Heh! He's taken away my skin. My friend! My friend!" Bushbuck kept on running. Kalulu followed him, "My friend! My friend! I beseech you!" This was to no avail. Bushbuck just continued running. Now Kalulu became dry, his body became dry, he was dry. Even grass hurt him. And then Kalulu failed to run; he ran briefly… he fell down, mpaa! He even died.

Therefore, deceit is not good because if you are cunning in dealing with your friend, he, too, will deal cunningly with you. These things are seen even nowadays in this world. This is my *mulumbe mukwai*, this is where I end. [claps and wipes hands].

Mr. Chakobe[117] was a heavy-set man, with a friendly and humorous bent in his performance style. His head was balding and round, matched by his stocky body. He wore a long-sleeved, brown knit shirt, with a thick white stripe and smaller black and brown stripes encircling him around the chest, with all its three buttons fastened. His humorous story about the trickster

---

117 Henry Chakobe was around 67 years old when he performed the tale included in this collection. He was born in 1922 around the village of Chief Nkula. He did his primary schooling at Ilondola and ended his teacher training at the college at Malole. He basically taught in many of the primary schools in the Chinsali area, most of which were parochial schools, and most of these Catholic. He married Sarafina Puta the same year he began his teaching career, 1945. Soon after he retired in 1975, he became the headman of the village sector that is still known by his surname, Chakobe.

hare Kalulu included his acting out of various roles and generally causing his audience to laugh, at times uncontrollably. His technique and energy were notable for successfully engaging the audience. He began the narrative a bit stiffly, with his hands in his lap, like Mr. Chipalo before him, rocking back and forth a bit with his head nodding to emphasize his words. As he warmed to his task, Mr. Chakobe began to gesture, take on different voices and more directly delineate the narrative's actions. His first clear gestures helped him describe the way the bushbuck was shaking the tree so that the *nsongwa* dropped to the ground. Each time he used the ideophone "*Cee!*" to emphasize how red Kalulu had become, he also marked it with his hands, briefly spread apart and dipping down once as if making a parenthesis around the red character. When depicting the conversation between the red Kalulu and the bushbuck in the tree, Mr. Chakobe alternately looked up then down, depending on the point of view of the character who was speaking. The most laughs were elicited from the audience when he mimed the creature whipping the bushbuck mercilessly, a stereotypical gesture of whipping his hand and arm down from way up and behind the head and snapping his fingers at the point of impact. The children especially, but also Mr. Chipalo himself, spent a lot of the performance tittering or laughing out loud.

The narrative has an interesting thematic focus. Whereas Kalulu most often wins out over his adversaries, large and small, friend or foe, there certainly are tales in which he falls victim to his own greed or excess. Mr. Chakobe prefaces the tale with a saying, "The cleverness of the roan antelope, its burden is on its back." [*Ubucenjeshi bwa mpelembe, icifulukutu cili pa numa*]. The "burden" refers to the hump on the roan's back, which is thought to be the site of the antelope's intelligence. The saying is a warning against being "too" clever. This story will thereby bear out the truth of the saying. The proverb also echoes the theme of Peter Mutale's narrative, earlier in this chapter, about the ears of the roan antelope and its warning about not following good advice. While most Kalulu stories are enjoyed for his humorous flaunting of most rules of decency and decorum, as well as exercising his almost unrivaled wit, this tale combines the delight of these traits while at the same time bringing Kalulu to ground for his greediness and cruelty. When the bushbuck finally catches on to his friend's machinations, he manages to have the last laugh by running off with Kalulu's skin, leaving him to die a rather unpleasant death. Mr. Chakobe ends the performance by saying, "Therefore, deceit is not good because if you are cunning in dealing with your friend, he, too, will deal cunningly with you.

These things are seen even nowadays in this world." The tale becomes a moral or cautionary lesson, and this is congruent with Mr. Chipalo's story that preceded it. There too, Kalulu was an actor that in the end succumbed to the greater power of the Catholic faith. In Mr. Chakobe's tale, trickery and greediness are marked as unworthy traits, in spite of the delightful humor to be enjoyed in the story. Again, in the shadow of Ilondola Mission, the erstwhile headman of a village sector and noted member of the church is trying to focus the story he provides a stranger on what is at least in part a Christian message.

Finally, Mr. Makombe performed several praise songs, *imishikakulo*. After we chatted for a while, I paid the three men around five dollars, took some photos, and arranged to send them through Fr. Oger. We took our leave, also, of Fr. Genelot and headed for Nkula's village. We arrived to find that the Chief had come and gone, leaving word for us to return on Friday or Sunday, possibly utilizing a strategy or ploy chiefs have employed to put off unwanted visitors since the days of the early exploration of Africa by Europe. In any event, we had to push on to Mpika that day, so we left the area without recording at the *musumba*, the chief's home or village.

Poscript:

I spent most of September of 2005 living at Ilondola mission, doing some advanced Bemba study at the Language Center. The mission was still run by White Fathers, whose order is officially known as Missionaries of Africa. I lived in a small room in the complex, along with two other students who were in the midst of taking the standard three-month beginning course. It was overall a very positive experience, with a lot of time spent speaking Bemba with the priests and mission staff as well as taking long walks through the village with one of my fellow students. Moreover, my Bemba tutor, Evans Bwalya, and I had a chance to watch all of my DVD recordings of the performances that are the focus of this study, and discuss obscure or fine points of both content and storyteller styles. During this period, I was able to arrange to visit with the families of two of the men who'd performed narratives for me in 1989, Mr. Chipalo and Mr. Chakobe. Most of the biographical information I've included in footnotes here was gathered at that time. How I gathered the information is worth noting.

Apparently, my arrival at Ilondola had already been known by local residents, as the priest who ran the program had spoken to a few elders about my possibly wanting to record some traditional material. Further, after we began working together, Evans Bwalya, had let the relevant families know that I was hoping to augment my knowledge of the two performers' lives. So it was Evans who arranged for me to visit the home of Stephen Chanda Chipalo's widow and her children. There were actually a few small houses in a compound that housed not only Mrs. Chipalo but also her daughters' families. I was received in her home and, having just changed into a better quality dress and *citenge*, Mrs. Chipalo sat on a bamboo mat (*butanda*) and chatted with me for a while, noting she'd been having problems with her eyes and that her legs were also troubling her. I promised to bring some simple eye drops I had in my room to see if they'd be helpful. I handed them a photo of a freeze frame of Mr. Chipalo's performance and a printed transcription of the story in its original Bemba-language form. After the usual polite but not entirely convincing compliments about the quality of my Bemba, I played both Mr. Chipalo's performance and that of Mr. Chakobe for the family. Almost all of them took to reacting to the performances as if they were in the audience; predicting lines before they were spoken, responding to what was being said, and laughing aloud at Mr. Chakobe's story. Then I asked some questions concerning Mr. Chipalo's background and recorded their answers on audiocassette.[118] I promised to return in a couple of days to take some photos then called it a day.

One interesting dimension that emerged was that Stephen Chipalo was thoroughly involved in the local Catholic Church. He held leadership positions in the church council and was an extremely devout and regular church-goer. His wife was, similarly, very active in the local women's league and other religious organizations. The sense I got from some of the priests who'd been at Ilondola for at least a decade was that Mr. Chipalo was very enthusiastic in his piety, in the sense that he was rather dogmatic in his approach to others and his interpretations of scripture. Similarly, Evans Bwalya, though very respectful of Mr. Chipalo's memory, felt that perhaps the tale he told was not as well-formed and focused as it might have been, and that the final explanation was somewhat forced and did not necessarily follow from the narrative's preceding details. While this does not detract from his original hospitable and cooperative response to my

---

118 Besides gathering relevant biographical information, I was left, in retrospect, with some conflicting information on Mr. Chipalo's age. While his family put his date of birth at 1926, they also said he died in 2001 at the age of 87. One or the other date/age does not add up, so for the purposes of this study I've set his birth date as the starting point and have marked his age at death in 2001 as 75.

request for a story, it is simply another dimension of his character and how it might have shaped that particular performance that is worth adding to other observations and interpretations of his efforts.

Mr. Chakobe's nephew, Mr. Jones Chibesa, the District Commissioner of Chinsali, lived in Chakobe village but had his office in town, some thirty or forty kilometers from Ilondola. After several near misses, I was able to briefly visit with Mr. Chibesa at his office in Chinsali. I gave him a photo of Mr. Chakobe and the text of his narrative and then he provided me with details of his uncle's life and accomplishments. As was the case with Stephen Chipalo's family, the focus was on simple information such as birth date, schooling and employment history, and date of death. Mr. Chibesa also spoke briefly about one of Mr. Chakobe's daughters, who'd married and moved to Botswana but, sadly, died of AIDS there. It seems her children had been adopted by a European missionary family, and the Zambian relatives were hoping to regain custody of them. He gave no indication of how this would eventually be resolved. After about twenty minutes, my companion, who had provided my ride to Chinsali, and I took our leave of Mr. Chibesa.

It is significant to note that Stephen Chanda Chipalo and Henry Chakobe were both school teachers and active in their churches. Both roles demand effective public speaking, often framed by traditional discourse in the form of proverbs or storytelling. This also meant that they had good proficiency in English as well as a good deal of higher education. The fact that neither ever chose to employ English in our interactions suggests their comfort with interacting with certain white visitors in the Bemba language and, thereby, maintaining a kind of easy distance or even control when it came to asking or answering questions. The stranger would have to be quite skilled in language in order to go much further than soliciting the stories, asking a few questions about the tales, offering basic greetings and conversation and, having little more to say, leaving.

Recording sessions among the Bemba, though in some ways different in each instance, had a number of common characteristics. All performers save one were elders, at least fifty some odd years old, and they were recorded in areas that were strongly influenced by the Catholic Church. Counting the performances at Chitimukulu's village, three of the four sessions included the singing of praise poetry, mostly *imishikakulo* and some *ngoma* forms. Elder practitioners of these genres included women as well as men. The knowledge of and ability to perform praise poetry seems, even in these small samples, rather widespread. One assertion I'd make here is that, compared to the four other groups I recorded, Bemba elders tended to more commonly learn and utilize these rather esoteric forms.[119] This is partly due to the fact that the areas where I recorded were near the *misumba* of major chiefs, Chitimukulu and Nkula. It also seems that historically, the praise forms were adapted and applied to various dimensions of Christian worship, even employed in parts of the Catholic Mass. At Ilondola, in particular, influences of the coming of Catholic missionaries in the early Twentieth Century seemed to be an ongoing and powerful local presence. The two narratives I collected there were at least partially shaped by Christian concerns, particularly the tale told by Mr. Chipalo, who quite literally tied it to Catholic theology and history by focusing on "the rock" that was the center of the story and an allegorical representation of the faith.

The most obvious assertion of gender politics took place in the session described in Chapter I, wherein women literally appropriated an event that began under male control. Some few hundred yards from the *musumba* of Chitimukulu, first one, then several women insinuated themselves into the performance of *ng'oma*, eventually pushing out all the men who'd been the focus of the recording session and asserting themselves in the form of drumming, song and dance, evoking imagery from several areas of their lives, including initiation [*cisungu*] songs. In a more understated, and perhaps more subversive, manner, the young mother Elizabeth examined the potential drawbacks of the polygamous marriage gone wrong. While not specifically identified as the youngest wife, Mweo is isolated, persecuted and eventually starved to death by her two co-wives. The taunts they threw at her, basically charging her with being lazy and worthless, are commonly directed at most junior wives, who are perceived as being the favorite and most pampered by the husband. The performer, clearly very young, with a newborn, nursing child, could easily be pointing to concerns that are familiar to her, even if she is not actually in a polygamous household. The other session involving women and men was the gathering at Fele's compound, where the competitive, sometimes tense, relationships between the sexes had been muted by age. The good natured taunting and sharing of wisdom and concerns for the

---

119 The only other praise poetry I encountered in the performances collected for this study was at the home of the Lunda elder and bard "Mano." Here, in an unusual example of access, the performer actually read praises from a notebook and interpreted them for me. Even when he moved to a set of praises that he simply presented orally from memory, he did not sing them as he would in a more formal occasion. This performance is detailed in Chapter V.

younger generation seemed not at all to be marked by gender as much as camaraderie. These shifting levels of gender interaction provide a spectrum of concerns that emerged in only a few performance sessions. They are nonetheless revealing in the social relationships they connote.

Overall, my recording sessions among the Bemba were marked by an unusual level of good-natured cooperation and engagement. The group of elders at Fele's village was particularly interested in sharing their thoughts and views of their immediate world, fashioning a set of overlapping observations that reinforced their views about age, wisdom, religion and their place in the order of things. While in many ways performing "their selves," this close-knit group was just as concerned to present a broader, more social snapshot of their beliefs and culture. At least for this small amount of time, a harmonious front was presented to the foreign visitor and, by extension of the video record, to the wider world.

IV. Bisa Storytelling: The Politics of Hunting, Beer-Drinks, and Elvis

> Then **three**, a constant visitor is very often the one who turns against you, your friend…
>
> …the one you like is the one who arrests you. Then **four**, a woman does not keep any secrets. You may have killed an animal in the bush, if a woman had seen it then she will reveal that secret. She will say, "He killed an animal." (Kabuswe C. Nabwalya, explaining a brief *mulumbe*, at Nabwalya)

In the 1988–89 academic year at the University of Zambia, I made two trips to Nabwalya in the Luangwa Valley. This region remains one of the largest wildlife preserves in Africa. The people who inhabit the center of the area, between the two parks, are Bisa, and they speak a language that is related to Bemba, though there are some fairly consistent sound shifts and many differences in usage. To accurately describe the conditions surrounding the recording of stories and my reception by the local residents, I need to very briefly explain the position of the Bisa in relation to Zambia's policies on game management and tourism.

The Bisa[120] have lived in this area, referred to as the Munyamadzi Corridor and situated basically between what are today the Luangwa North and Luangwa South game parks, for nearly two centuries. They have always hunted game for food and profit, and they also cultivate some

---

120 Most researchers refer to this group as the Valley Bisa in order to distinguish them from the larger group of Bisa living in the area south of Lake Bangweulu, in Northern Province. For the sake of brevity, I will simply designate the group living in the Munyamadzi Corridor as Bisa.

DOI: 10.11647/OBP.0033.04

subsistence crops, in particular sorghum. From the time of colonial rule throughout the independence era, officials have tried to preserve wildlife and manage the lands people shared with animals by employing varying policies. In the period immediately following Zambian independence, one commission recommended "relocating" the Bisa in order to insure the preservation of animals that had great economic potential for tourism and safari hunting.[121] This relocation was never carried out but it suggests the colonial government's prioritizing of animals over people at that time. The Bisa live in an area that is very difficult to reach by road, especially during the rainy season, and this isolation has in great part restricted the growth of their communication and transportation infrastructure. This has led to problems in the adequate development of local schools, clinics, retail shops, and postal services. In fact, this relative isolation has kept the Bisa somewhat out of the loop in terms of general socio-economic participation in Zambia's development.

While the problems of animals living near human habitats are not unique to the Bisa, they are perhaps one of the most obvious targets of government management and conservation programs. To simplify what are a number of competing policy visions, there are two basic schools of thought regarding the regulation of people and animals in such areas. The first harks back to colonial policies, which set out to preserve game and habitats under the structure of "indirect rule," requiring local chiefs to enforce anti-hunting laws and manage game areas, essentially criminalizing the taking of game that had been a practice long before the arrival of European rule. The other more recent, not entirely dissimilar, school of thought is the empowering of local people to preserve the flora and fauna in their areas by sharing in the profits to be had in the tourist and safari hunting industries. The reasoning behind this approach is that once they are made aware of the potential profits and gains in personal and communal spheres, local people would see the logic in giving up illegal hunting, cooperating with enforcement personnel, and turning to less destructive economic pursuits, such as farming and, perhaps, crafts manufacturing.

The problem of preserving animal populations is widespread in large game parks and preserves in east and southern Africa. There is a great deal of money to be made in tourism and licensed hunting, and the questions about what to do when people and animals compete for the same land are

---

121 See Marks 2005: introduction, also Marks and Gibson 1995.

long-standing ones. Due to several international economic developments, particularly the oil boom of the 1970s and 80s, the demand for elephant tusks and rhinoceros horns was fueled by the ability of potential buyers to pay lucrative prices, especially in parts of Asia. The dramatic drop in the numbers of these large mammals in east and central Africa was a major cause of concern for local governments and international conservationists. In the case of the Bisa, just before and after 1988–89, several initiatives were employed to try to control what the government defined as rampant illegal poaching. There ensued a complex set of political struggles at local, national and international levels. Two separately empowered groups were trying to install their own policies and procedures in the situation in the Munyamadzi Corridor. Each was backed by different agencies or entities, with funding for both initiatives coming from a combination of local and international sources.[122] While this is not the place to detail the complex of actors and issues pertaining to these conservation efforts, it is relevant to observe that the Bisa were directly in the middle of these initiatives and would find themselves having to mediate, fend off, or cooperate with official representatives and their policies in order to go about their daily lives.

For a long time before this period of dueling programs, government had established and maintained a steady presence in the Bisa area for the purpose of managing wildlife. Game scouts and guards circa 1988–89, more than earlier, kept up a high profile in order to curtail poaching. Less than several hours drive from Nabwalya, across the Luangwa River, are numerous game lodges that cater to a mainly foreign clientele. The revenue generated by tourism in the South Luangwa Park is substantial and the government sees the protection of wildlife, especially the endangered elephant and rhinoceros populations, as vital in the drive to increase this income. Safari hunters pay substantial license fees to be able to come to the area and shoot various types of big and smaller game. The situation is complicated not only by the historical hunting practices of the Bisa, but also by inconsistencies of enforcement policies, the shifts in approaches by the government, the fact that high-priced animals are often poached by well-equipped outsiders—in some cases, rumors and some actual instances suggest, by government officials—and the overall emotional responses to notions of game preservation and the needs of human beings.

---

122 See Gibson and Marks 1995; Gibson 1999; Marks 1999 and 2001.

Over time, there have simply not been enough sensible and logical incentives and rewards to keep Bisa hunters from plying their trade around Nabwalya. The reasons for this reside in great part in Bisa culture and traditions themselves. Hunting is more than an economic activity that provides meat and/or profit to individuals. It is a practice that is inextricably woven into the way Bisa society defines itself. Again simplifying a more complex set of relationships and dynamics, young Bisa men are linked matrilineally to older men, often uncles or "fathers", who help them to gain social status and even to carry out courtship and marital activities. These older men often teach others to hunt, supply them with hard to find guns—up until recently, of the muzzle-loading variety—and identify or set up the networks through which game meat is distributed within the lineage. As young hunters become successful and gain prestige and wealth, in the form of wives, land and admiration for their hunting prowess, they eventually become men of status and might even come to head up a section of a village or move out to establish their own small villages. These relationships are complicated by the role and status of the chief, in this case Chief Nabwalya, who on a larger scale warrants gifts of tribute and allegiance, which he then parcels out to others to enforce or initiate relationships of patronage and loyalty.[123] Moreover, for some decades in the 1960s to early 1980s, a good number of Bisa men established themselves in the society by migrating to other areas, often the copper mines, for wage labor and returning with financial resources to build a home and support themselves and their families. The declining economy of the 1970s, due in most part to the dramatic fall in international copper prices, meant that this avenue to success was less traveled, spurring recourse to local practices of hunting and strengthening lineage relationships.

When game management policies encountered Bisa life, even more complicated relationships ensued. During the days of colonial rule and the early independence period, when strict enforcement of game laws were in effect, Nabwalya remained so far off the beaten path that the occasional arrest and fining or imprisonment of local hunters had a minimal effect on what most people were doing. When, in the early 1980s, funding was increased for the two competing management schemes, with a concomitant infusion of larger numbers of game guards and scouts, the stakes were

---

123 Stuart Marks's *Large Mammals and a Brave People* details Bisa social structure and practice effectively and with a high degree of empathy for the complexities of the society and its relationship to governmental concerns of conservation and management of wildlife. See also Morris 1998 for another description of the complex relationship between humans, animals, farming and hunting in a neighboring society.

dramatically raised for Bisa hunters to pursue their activities. Where in the past, local game enforcement personnel had found paths of coexistence with villagers by only occasionally arresting offenders, sharing meat they legally cropped, and getting to know the locals, the new policies were more aggressive and provided clearer rewards for strict enforcement. In a culture where, from the colonial days on, a rather low key humanistic understanding of looking the other way and mediating things with a view towards peaceful coexistence was common, the harsher methods of enforcement would bring greater uncertainty to the lives of local people. One specific development around 1988 was the new policy of hiring local young men as wildlife scouts. These scouts, who knew and were known by resident Bisa, entailed a new kind of class who were empowered and emboldened to assert their influence in local affairs and at times challenge or subvert traditional sources of social order, such as elder men.

Needless to say, many Bisa are rather suspicious of strangers and tend to keep their distance even from the government officials they do know. Nabwalya is the largest of the Bisa villages in the area, and it is composed of small houses clustered in groups of four to ten and separated from neighboring compounds by at least two to three hundred feet. I first visited Nabwalya in October 1988, at the end of the dry season. At that time people were cutting tall grass and dried sorghum stalks before burning them in preparation for the coming rains. We arrived at the village, after a rather long, somewhat muddy (the first rain of the season had fallen the night before we came), drive over barren and difficult terrain. I was traveling with Stuart Marks, who had just returned to Zambia on a Fulbright award and who at that time had been conducting research in Nabwalya off and on for over twenty years. In our vehicle were two residents of Nabwalya, one a Rural Council postman and the other a judge at the local government court—whom we'd encountered at the game control barrier before descending the escarpment into the Luangwa Valley—and a young anthropologist on her first trip to Zambia. Our group was welcomed on the basis of our Bisa co-travelers and Stuart Marks, who was a well-known and clearly respected presence among the village leaders.

We spent the afternoon moving Stuart's gear into a newly finished government house, meant for an agricultural officer who had not yet appeared.[124] We set screens into the glass-less metal windowpanes, set up

---

124 Given its isolated location and paucity of amenities, it is not surprising that the government often had difficulties in filling positions in Nabwalya. It is also easy to see that strangers appearing in the area were commonly seen as seeking to exploit game or people.

a mosquito net in a bedroom, and basically organized the four rooms into a household/office. While this was going on, a young boy came to summon us to a meeting Chief Nabwalya and a village development committee were having with representatives of the provincial government. It is important to note that the government of President Kenneth David Kaunda was about to hold elections. At that time, Zambia was a one-party state (the United National Independence Party, or UNIP) with serious economic and political problems. Part of the reason for this visit was to remind people of the elections and their importance, especially the importance of voting for the president, who was running unopposed. Nabwalya had a year earlier made the international news for requiring emergency aid to stave off famine after overly heavy rains following a drought had combined to wipe out much of their staple sorghum crop. Government officials were sensitive to the negative national and international image perpetuated by such situations and were trying to work with local people to ensure a better harvest and more stable economic conditions. In fact, since the people of Nabwalya had not seen much progress and development under the current government, they certainly were ripe for feelings of disaffection and alienation. The person leading the government group was the Province's Member of the Central Committee, Mr. L.M. Ng'andu, who was also the Paramount Chief Chitimukulu of the Bemba people. After our presence was explained and we showed our identification, we were allowed to sit through the meeting. One issue that immediately came up was the language in which the talks were to be carried out. Though the Bisa constituents asked that Bemba be spoken, the government representatives insisted that the official language of the country, English, be the medium of discussion. This had the immediate effect of excluding some members of the committee from the conversation.

The village committee had many issues to raise with the provincial representatives. These included the problem that a new school building, to be constructed by local self-help labor, had received glass for its windows that was the wrong size, no recent graduates of the school had been accepted into secondary school, and there was concern over the quality of skills of local teachers. Further, the village had been granted a new vehicle by the World Wildlife Fund to assist with development projects, but this had basically been commandeered by the local game warden. A grinding mill, meant, again, for local self-help in pounding grains such as sorghum into flour, had been promised but never delivered. The list of issues presented by the Ward Chairman was mostly dismissed as district rather than provincial or national concerns. Very little attention was, therefore, given to these matters at the brief gathering.

After the meeting, one which left the Nabwalya committee frustrated and dispirited, feeling that they were having little input into the policies and decisions that affected their lives, we returned to Stuart's house to finish the move. Refusing the offer of hospitality of the local committee, the government group left before sunset to spend the night in the relative comfort of the quasi-legal game camp of a European working for a government development agency. The group had licenses to kill numerous types of game and was probably anxious to do just that in the evening or morning hours. That evening we were treated to some rice and buffalo meat supplied by local people, visited with the man who was then "Acting" Chief Nabwalya, then turned in by around 9 PM. The next day, after only a bit of commiserating with Stuart's friends and neighbors, and some time spent in the central part of the village, near the school and government offices, I left with our graduate student colleague and made the long drive out of the valley, up the Muchinga Escarpment, through Mpika and to Kasama, the capital of Northern Province.

I recorded stories during my next visit to Nabwalya, in mid-May of 1989. I traveled with my eight-year-old son Daniel and a woman friend whose husband worked for a Canadian Aid organization at Mpika. The rains had recently abated and the road to Nabwalya had not yet been used enough to mark a trail through the tall grass. It was a very difficult trip, taking us nearly sixteen hours, including at least one rather ill-fated wrong turn, to cover less than seventy miles. We arrived at Nabwalya after 10 PM and pitched our tent under the *nsaka* next to Stuart Marks's house. Stuart showed the signs of having been in the field for a long time without a break. He was thin, rather harried, and very sensitive to any discussions about his work or hunting. The pressure of living in the rather charged environment of mercurial government game guards and local friends and colleagues was clearly stressful. In Nabwalya, there were many levels of contestation, both internally and externally, regarding the livelihood of the Bisa, and it was plain to see how Stuart could find himself set in the middle of these conflicts, at least as an observer if not an outright advisor or participant.[125]

---

125 As noted in the first chapter of this study, the question of "capture" by the people with whom the researcher lives and works is an ongoing subtext of these interpersonal relationships. I will return to this concern in a broader discussion in the concluding chapter.

In some respects, this made my own efforts easier, since people seemed to find the recording of storytelling a rather innocuous pursuit compared to the more dramatic economic and cultural struggles involving hunting and game management. The morning after our arrival, Stuart and I spoke to a few of his friends and neighbors to arrange some recording opportunities. As we sat in Stuart's *nsaka*, a young man and an older man came to visit. The older man, Mr. Laudon Ndalazi, on hearing what it was I did, asked to tell a story. I was more than happy to comply and set up my recording equipment inside the *nsaka*. When he sat down, the camera framed him back-lit by the bright morning light, seeping over and between the unevenly-spaced sticks tied together to make a wall of the *nsaka*.

Mr. Ndalazi looked to be in his early sixties, with close-cut graying hair. He was average height and slim, with an engaging smile and knowing look that was reminiscent of the American Rock 'n' Roll pioneer Chuck Berry. The resemblance was enhanced by the short sleeved, collared knit shirt he was wearing. He wore dark brown trousers and on his left forearm he had a thin ivory bracelet with a carved braided pattern. Mr. Ndalazi sat on a very low slung wooden lounge chair, that caused his knees to come up nearly to his chest level, and he told a lot of his story with his elbows or forearms perched on his knees.

Bisa Storytelling 1 by Laudon Ndalazi*

Robert Cancel: It's alright *mukwai*, begin.

Laudon Ndalazi: My name is Laudon Ndalazi.

RC: Uhn humn.

LN: Then I will give you a little *mulumbe* and *nshimi*, bwana.

RC: Yes *mukwai*.

LN: There's the little *mulumbe*, a person kept a dog. He kept how many dog(s)? [Holds up one finger.]

RC: One.

LN: One. In the world there was great famine. Then that dog is the one that was catching animals for him, which he even used to leave for his children.

* To watch a video of this story follow this link: http://dx.doi.org/10.11647/OBP.0033.04/Bisa1

RC: Uh humn.

LN: Where he used to pass when going into the bush to hunt animals, there was one little old woman, a little old woman in the bush.[126] The little old woman had a hump on her back. Do you know a hump?

RC: Uhn humn. *Ng'ongo*, a pot.[127]

LN: Yes. She had a hump on her back. But he didn't give her anything whenever he killed an animal. Whenever he killed an animal he didn't give her anything. The little old woman was just observing. Whenever he killed an animal, he didn't give her anything. Then one day the little old woman thought of a plan. She said, "No, this person, it is too much, he is stingy. Now, today I will also come up with a plan so that we?...[128]we are of the same mind." Then he took the dog to go further. He went and found how many little animal(s)? [Holds up one finger.]

RC: One.

LN: One. Its name was *Kamunsulu*. The dog killed it. He had gone with his child. He gave it to his child to carry. He was going further. He went and found a duiker, *fya*! But that duiker went to pass just near?...near the green mamba, the dangerous snake...that dangerous snake so it was that little old woman who had?...who had turned into a green mamba.

RC: Oh?

LN: That little old woman he used to refuse to give her meat, so she turned into a mamba.

RC: A snake?

LN: Yes. The dog, when it came to pass, the animal passed, the dog was about to pass, paa! Right there, the dog died. And it [the mamba] even raised the?...the head. Then the person stood and said, "My child, the dog has done what? It has been caught by that...which is standing there." "What is

---

126 While the term *"kakote"* is not gender-marked, meaning literally "a little old person," my colleague D.C. Nkosha, who worked with me on this story's translation, felt that most hunchbacks in these kinds of stories were seen as women, so we went with this contextual choice.

127 I thought he was saying *nongo*, a clay pot. As the story went on, I finally understood what he was referring to, a *ng'ongo*, which was a "hump," as would be the case with a person who has a "hunchback."

128 Mr. Ndalazi enjoyed using a performance technique whereby he leaves a sentence unfinished for a moment, in an interrogative tone, as if expecting his audience to supply the end of the sentence or the proper word, then goes on to provide the information himself. I've marked this construction in the text by using a question mark followed by an ellipsis. If someone actually supplied the term, I include that as well, as in the more common question where a finger or fingers are held up to enumerate something at the same time the storyteller asks "How many?" (See Cancel 1989, pp. 66–67)

it?" He said, "No, it's a green mamba. Hurry up, let's return, it might bite us." And then they went back?...backwards.

RC: Uhn humn, to the pot?[129]

LN: Yes, going backwards. Then they went backwards for that old...that green mamba, that one...it returned home, that very little old woman, she went and changed again into a little old woman. And that sun did what?...it set. It set while they were there. They said, "Oh, we are going to sleep right here, you little old woman." There that little old woman knew to say, "It's I who've done that." She said, "Oh, you sleep." He even took that little animal they'd killed and gave it to the?...the little old woman. She cooked...*ubwali* and she gave them. She even showed them a **bedroom**[130], to this side. "No, you sleep this side, with the child." That's how they... they slept. However, the little old woman there, where she was sleeping in her **bedroom**, she thought of another plan. She took that very hump that...

RC: Uhm humn.

LN: Yes, she took the hump and went and put it onto the child while he was sleeping, humn! The child there, she went and put it on his back and it was humn! The child hurriedly rose, "I am burnt father! I am dead father!" His father looked, he said, "Oh, **sorry**. My child, you are deformed. Now what shall I do? This little old woman, if I say something she will kill me." Now, that person, then he thought, for his child to be cured of that hump...what did he think?

RC: Uhm. He had to plan.

LN: Yes, now what did he think?

RC: Oh...?

LN: Yes, it is alright *mukwai*. What did he think [of doing] in order to remove that hump from the back?

RC: Oh...I don't know.

Kabuswe C. Nabwalya [standing outside the *nsaka*]: No, I can't...

RC: It's difficult.

Kangwa Samson: **Ah that, I can't solve it, eh?**

RC: Un huh. So it's a *mulumbe*, isn't it?

LN: Yes, it's a *mulumbe*.

---

129 Looking at Mr. Ndalazi motioning to his back again, I'm assuming the "pot" is being placed onto someone's back. In fact, he's simply pointing backwards.
130 When the storyteller uses an English word in an otherwise Bisa language performance, I mark it in bold typeface.

IV. Bisa Storytelling: The Politics of Hunting, Beer-Drinks, and Elvis   133

RC: Oh! It's not a *lushimi*?

LN: Uh uhn. *Muulumbe*.

RC: Yah, it is just a *mulumbe*, really. It is very difficult. Can you explain?

LN: Ah?

RC: Can you explain it?

LN: Ah humn.

RC: Oh.

LN: Yes, as it is difficult for you like that. That person thought about it also. He said, "Me, if I speak to that little old woman and say, 'It is you who has given my child a hump,' uh uhn, it will be an offence." [He would be insulting her.]

RC: Uhm humn.

LN: "In fact, she could even kill us here." Then he woke up to look intently at the child, like that. He thought again, he said, "Uhn humn. You, my child, stop crying. This thing, don't think that it has...has any problem that can lead to your death, no. Now my child, we have wealth, riches, lots of it. All those friends of ours who have groceries, who are rich, those with cars, it is the hump they had looked for. Now, even us, we have good luck, we have found a hump, it has come to you. Even us, we are now going to sell it. From it we shall raise money to buy a car.

RC: Oh.

LN: Ahssh...The whole night, just like that, and the little old woman there was listening, there in the bedroom she...she was listening and said, "Oh no! I have given my friends wealth. So when they go they are going to sell it?" The little old woman pondered over it, she said, "Well, here things have gone wrong, my friends are going to sell it for?... (wealth)."[131] Then when it was morning, that person who had a child with a hump started off and said, "No *mukwai*, we are going. You received us very well. We are going, we have a job of selling this thing which is on the back of my child, this...hump." "Oh? You're going to sell it?" He said, "Yes, since we are now rich, it is finished." The little old woman said, "Uhn uhn, O.K." They went, those people, they reached quite far. The little old woman was greatly troubled. Then she started off to go to... to call those people. "You, people, come back." And these people said, "No, time is passing, we have a...a job of selling...the hump." She said, "No, first let's reason together." That's how she thought. She said the... little old woman said, "No, this hump...it is my hump. I said, 'Let me

---

131 The final words in this sentence are not clear, but he seems to refer to *icuma*, or wealth.

give it to the child, perhaps it is an illness,' but I have heard what you've said about it, it is true to say it's wealth. No, friends, give (it to) me." But this person also refused, he said, "No, I cannot give you this hump. We, we are going to sell it." Then the little old woman also said, "No, **please** friends, **please**. Let's, therefore, come and reason together. Me, I am bringing the hump, I will bring it right there, we go and sell it, we go and share even the money." She then took what? That little old woman, the hump on the back there, she got hold of it and put it on her back.

RC: Oh.

LN: Yes, until that man said, "Let's go my child!" And then they reached further, he said, "You see the plan I told you about. If I had said that, 'No, it is you who…who has bewitched my child,' the little old woman would have killed us." That's it, has it been understood?

RC: Thank you *mukwai*.

LN: Ehn?

RC: It's a job well done.

Laudon Ndalazi was a confident and animated performer, without being bombastic in any way.[132] His movements were fluid and economical. He had a kind of central point in his physical style, wherein he clasped his hands or held the wrist of one hand with the other in front of him, as he rested his elbows on his knees, when not using descriptive gestures. He often pointed with one hand or the other to spaces where action was taking place or to indicate areas where characters were planning to go or that they were describing. He kept referring to the hump by touching one or both hands to the rear of his shoulders, particularly when he demonstrated how the old woman removed it from her back and placed it onto the young boy. Then later he acted out her reaching over to the boy and taking the hump and returning it to her own back. One interesting set

---

132 Laudon Ndalazi had worked in Lusaka for over ten years as a cleaner for the Public Works Department, including time as a cleaner at State House. He was able to save enough money to build a house in Lusaka and, when he retired and moved back to the Nabwalya area, he rented it out. He was never known as an accomplished hunter but in 1962 had the misfortune of being caught using someone else's gun to kill what the Bisa term a "small" animal, an impala. He was arrested by game warden Phil Berry and did a bit of time in jail. Tragically, Mr. Ndalazi was murdered in 1997, allegedly by a close relative during an argument over money.

of gestures was employed to describe the poisonous snake the old woman turned into. Mr. Ndalazi held up one of his forearms, bent at the elbow with the fingers of his hand extended straight forward in a claw-like shape. This represented the snake's head, and he showed how it followed and struck at the hunter's dog to kill it. When both the old woman and the hunter were thinking about what course of action to follow next, Mr. Ndalazi would put a hand to his chin or the side of his jaw to indicate someone deep in thought.

When the point of the story reached the dilemma of how to cure the boy's condition, Mr. Ndalazi stopped and asked first me then, Stuart's friend and associate Kangwa Sampson, how the hunter should proceed. He sat forward in the chair, forearms on knees, and looked expectantly at one of us then the other, while smiling as if he held secret knowledge. When neither of us could offer a course of action, Mr. Ndalazi went on with the story, answering my request for an explanation by saying, "Yes, as it is difficult for you like that. That person thought about it also." When he ended the story, he leaned back contentedly, and received our praise for a story well told and cleverly explained.

Years after this session, Stuart Marks mentioned two things that emphasized the importance of performance context in any storytelling event. First, denying meat to the old woman was a powerful social statement of disconnection or estrangement, since the sharing of game meat is a crucial act of solidarity between relatives and allies. The fact that the hunter passed her place regularly on his way to and from the bush without offering her meat suggested an obvious and intentional slight. Second, and here is a good example of how knowing the area and people where you record narratives can be crucial, there apparently actually was an old woman in the village who was a relative of the chief and who was quite unpopular for having a combative disposition, never sharing and demanding things from her neighbors. She also happened to have a hunched back. Mr. Ndalazi was pretty clearly injecting this local dimension into his tale, something that can be a common practice in intimate or even public events.

After I replayed the audiocassette of this performance, Mr. Ndalazi wanted to tell another story, so I set up and began to tape again. He began slowly, saying he had a small *mulumbe* to impart, and held his left hand, elbow on knee, to the side of his forehead as he thought about what he wanted to say.

Bisa Storytelling 2
by Laudon Ndalazi*

Robert Cancel:	Let's begin *mukwai*.
Laudon Ndalazi:	Here is a little *mulumbe*, friend, this little one, Bwana.[133] A person had seven children, he bore seven children. Of the seven children, these two went to join the **army** to work. These other four were to travel with him, wherever you went even these four children set out. This other one was to sweep where you…if you soil yourself, yes, now he is sweeping that, yes. Then of the four children, this one, these other two are workers in the army, these other four were to travel with him, this other one was to wipe "dirt" from his father, yes. Now of these things, what was it Bwana?
RC:	Ee, I don't know.
LN:	Ask Mr. Marks.
RC:	Uhmmn?
LN:	You ask Mr. Marks, you ask Marks. Let him come and listen to this.
RC:	Ooh. Mr. Marks, Mr. Marks. Mr. Marks come here! [Stuart walks over from outside his house to the *nsaka*.]
Stuart Marks:	Yes?
RC:	Come. He's posed a *mulumbe*.
LN:	We've told a *mulumbe* to this one, this one's failed to explain what it means. I have said a person bore seven children. Of the seven children, two went and found a job in the army. These other four were to travel with him, where you go even the four children have to go. This other one was to wipe **dirt** wherever you sat. Which of these children would you choose as the truthful child? A trustworthy child?
SM:	**He's giving you a riddle, eh?**
RC:	Uh hunhm.
SM:	**Can you figure it out?**
RC:	**No.**

---

133 The term "Bwana" is most commonly employed by people old enough to have lived through the colonial era. Borrowed from Swahili, it was an honorific term used to address white authorities. The simplest gloss would be "Mr." or "Sir." Long after colonial rule, it remained in use by some elders in their interactions with white men.

* To watch a video of this story follow this link: http://dx.doi.org/10.11647/OBP.0033.04/Bisa2

SM: Do you know it?

RC: I don't know it.

SM: Me too, I've failed [to understand it].

LN: The child you would choose from these, these who have joined the army, and these you are traveling with they are four, and that one who is wiping "dirt"? Of these children which one is trustworthy?

SM: Let's hear *mukwai*, let's hear.

LN: Oh. Of the seven children, the truthful one, you know how a buffalo is, don't you? The buffalo, you know it?

RC: Yes, the buffalo.

LN: It has how many feet?

SM: Four.

LN: **Four** (folo). It sets out saying, "Let me drink water," all the four feet go there, all four.

RC: Oh, the feet.

LN: Yes, all the four feet go there. Then that tail, when the buffalo shits, what does it do? It wipes it. Then those two horns, if you…it has the urge to kill you, those will become army workers (soldiers). Now they are to kill you. Yes, that's it. Aahha. **Thank you.**

Audience: Good job.

As in the previous tale, Mr. Ndalazi is interested in testing his audience's perspicacity when it comes to solving dilemmas or conundrums. When he first sets out the situation for me, he speaks slowly and enumerates the various numbers of "children" on the fingers of his left hand, touching them with the fingers of his right as he describes each set. As is the case in riddles or metaphors, Mr. Ndalazi does not refer to the actual animal or its body parts but instead builds up a description, this wasn't really a "story," of what each individual or set of children did: two soldiers, four others who followed them, and "a sweeper." He acts out the four walking along as well as the sweeper, cleaning up behind the four. This last mime was enacted with his right hand reaching behind him and swatting back and forth behind his seated buttocks. As in the earlier performance, he leaned forward to ask me the answer and, when I said I did not know, he pointed to Stuart, who was nearby, and insisted I call him over to see if he could solve the conundrum. He then went through similar gestures to set out the problem again and, when neither of us even ventured a guess, he used his hands to set out the answer in the way he described the various parts of the buffalo's body. He framed the question of the puzzle in an awkward way, asking initially, "Now of these things, what was it Bwana?" Then he asked Stuart, "Which of these children would you choose as the truthful child? A trustworthy child?" The first question was most relevant to the conundrum's structure, though in the end, the answer he provided clarified what he was looking for from his audience. The question of choosing one of the three groupings over the other, ascertaining who was the most "trustworthy," seems not to belong directly to the question actually being posed. It served more as a kind of generic entry into the necessity to sort out the data and choose. In actuality, the question was linked to discerning the metaphorical—perhaps metonymical is the more appropriate trope—sum of the parts that added up to being a buffalo. The reference to children might have been an allusion to the way young people often entertain themselves with riddle competitions or stories. Again, Mr. Ndalazi seemed delighted with himself and sat back in his chair, saying "Thank you," in English. A young boy who sat next to me said to him, "Good job."

The overweening sense of this session was Mr. Ndalazi's desire to both show off and impart his knowledge. He performed *mulumbe* tales that set forth two different kinds of conundrums. The first was a rather involved narrative that focused on the clever ruse employed by the hunter to rid his child of the unsightly hump given him by the magical old woman. Asking his listeners for a solution to the problem was, unless they were familiar with that particular tale, pretty much rhetorical. It would have been almost impossible to "guess" the answer. The second performance was much less a narrative than an extended riddle, a bit like the classic posed by the Sphinx to Oedipus: what walks on four legs in the morning, two legs in the afternoon and three at night? In this case, the figuration involved a buffalo and some of its body parts. It may have been possible for a local audience to figure out the answer or to simply recognize the riddle as something that had been posed on other occasions. Stuart and I had not heard this one before and were impelled to ask Mr. Ndalazi to supply the answer. He clearly enjoyed his role as a teacher, or maybe just someone who had the chance to showcase his cleverness in a context he could control. It was also evident that the context of his two *mulumbe* was embedded in the local environment of hunting, social/familial relationships, especially those involved in sharing game meat, and the knowledge of animals and their characteristics.

We sat a bit longer, chatting, and eventually I set out for the primary school, where some of the students had been recruited to tell stories by one of their teachers, Mr. Elvis Kampamba. Elvis had ended up in our vehicle the evening before, volunteering to guide us to Nabwalya after encountering us while passing in another Land Rover owned by the Integrated Rural Development Project office at Mpika. Having someone who actually knew the road made the last six or seven miles of our trip much easier. We also had the opportunity to get to know a bit about Mr. Kampamba and his work as a schoolteacher in this rural, isolated venue. We walked to the somewhat dilapidated school building, which was scheduled for replacement by the proposed new structure discussed at the meeting I attended back in October, and set up a camera and a chair for the performers just outside the classroom. I recorded five young storytellers and then we were interrupted by rain. The rainfall was heavy enough to cause us to seek shelter in a section of the schoolhouse that did not leak, which turned out to be a bit of a challenge.

When the rain let up, we returned to Stuart's place. Stuart's colleague, Kangwa Samson, told me that he'd arranged something for the next day on the other side of the village. In the morning Kangwa guided me, my son Daniel, and our friend Marie to our destination. We walked along the Munyamadzi River and paused for a while to take some video of the crocodiles sunning themselves in the sand on the opposite bank and of the sizeable group of hippos entering and settling into the river. We eventually reached the section called "Chibale's Village," where Kangwa's mother lived and where a large group of men and some women, numbering around fifty, had gathered at a house to drink beer. The occasion was actually supposed to conclude the cooperative harvesting of a resident's sorghum farm, but the rains from the day before had made it impossible to properly gather the harvest. Since the beer drink had been arranged as payment for labor, and the beer had already been brewed, the group came together to consume its compensation before actually carrying out the work. When we arrived, a man was going around writing down the names of those who were there so that they could later be recalled to carry out the harvest. The groups gathered within and around a small *nsaka*, talking, laughing and drinking beer from at least one large clay pot. The beer was a kind of *katubi*, in this instance, a sorghum-based brew that was heated over a fire and, because of thick sediment that floats at the top, must be drunk through a straw poked down below the surface in order to sip the warm fluid underneath.

Kangwa did most of the talking when we arrived, and I set up my camera and gear in front of a house next to where the drinking was going on. A low, flat wooden stool served as the performers' perch, with open land forming the background of the camera's frame. A few men came by to talk to me, and I also contributed some money to keep the beer flowing at the party. Eventually, I got a volunteer to tell the first story, in front of an audience that seemed to be dividing its time between observing the performances and going next door for more beer.

George Mwampatisha[134] was in his mid thirties, he wore a heavy dark brown sweater, with the sleeves pushed up at the forearms. His trousers were dark gray with light tan square patches sewn over each knee. This informal dress style suggested that he, like most of the men at this gathering, had come dressed to work in the fields. Sitting on the low stool, with his knees just above waist level, Mr. Mwampatisha was not an overly demonstrative performer, taking on a rather serious mien and mostly employing subtle gestures as he began his story.

Bisa Storytelling 3
by George Mwampatisha*

GM: George Mwampatisha

Robert Cancel: Begin.

GM: There was a little thing. People lived… Listen thoroughly, children? Uhm hrghm. I am George Mwampatisha, listen attentively. People started off on a journey into the bush. A man and a woman. Then they walked into the bush to hunt animals.[135] They walked, they walked, they walked, they walked. They found nothing, there were no animals in sight. Aah! Right there, when they walked like that, when they passed through the bush, they walked, they walked. They were tired. And heavy rain came…very, very heavy rain. It rained heavily on them.[136] They were terribly soaked by the rain,

---

134 In this instance, Mr. Mwampatisha used a nickname. His real name is George Kalikeka. He has lived all his life in the Nabwalya area and had been the headman of Mukupa Village for ten years until around 2005. Mostly earning his living as a farmer, Mr. Kalikeka was never known as a hunter. Kangwa Samson estimated his age now as in his early sixties, which suggests he was in his mid forties when I recorded his performance.

135 The idea of a man and a woman hunting together in the bush can be mostly seen as a fabricated situation, since hunting is among the most strongly gender-marked activities in Bisa, and numerous other, Zambian societies.

136 In the repertoire of motifs and situations in Bemba-language tales, characters often find themselves driven by rain to seek some kind of shelter while traveling in the bush. Several Tabwa stories use this basic motif, while developing different plots. (Cancel 1989, pp. 125–128, 142–147)

* To watch a video of this story follow this link: http://dx.doi.org/10.11647/OBP.0033.04/Bisa3

now they felt very cold. They even became very tired.[137] Yaah! Then they saw a plume of smoke in the bush: futu, futu, futu, futu, futu... yaah! "What's that?" "Let's go there." When they arrived there they found people were seated. "Hello there *mukwai!*" "Come in. Who are you?" They said, "Hello, it's us." "What is the matter?" They said, "No *mukwai*, we went into the bush (to hunt) but animals are nowhere to be seen. Now we are feeling very cold, we are very tired.[138] Now we wanted to go to people in the village." Then they found lions seated in the bush.[139]

RC: How many lions?

GM: Two.

RC: Oh.

GM: And there was one cub.

RC: Uhn humn.

GM: Then right there now, certainly. They said, "Sit here." Then the lion responded and said, "Yah. It's very good. Yah! I have been agonizing about what to eat. Now food has come near." "Certainly, you man, it's good fortune that you've come here. Today you will see what I am going to do to you." Now as they sat, the man said (to himself), "Yah! Yes, this is truly a lion. It's very fierce. Now what am I going to do?" Then there arose something in the bush that said, "No, you, you... you should be very brave. They eat you and I also eat them. They eat you and I also eat them. They eat you and I also eat them." The lion said, "Oh. Is that so? My child, go. But because you are foolish do come back, because you are foolish do come back." The child (lion cub) left right away. He didn't come back. She sent another cub. She said, "Well, because you are foolish do come back", he also went. Then from there, that's how all of them rose and set off, running. Ubulubulubu! She said, "Yes, heh! Things are bad, yes!" That's how they went, those people. Yes, *mukwai*, yes. [Mr. Mwampatisha rises up as he ululates the ideophone and as he speaks the last words of the story he dances and turns in a circle before walking away, causing the audience to laugh loudly at the dramatic and abrupt ending of the performance.]

---

137   Combines Bisa and English to express extreme fatigue: "*Baanaka na* **over**."
138   Again, "*Twanaka na* **over**."
139   This development is not clearly explained, but it seems that the two hunters must have been speaking to "people" who were either obscured by all the smoke or somehow hidden by the small structure, since the residents are shown to actually be a family of lions.

George Mwampatisha began the performance with his hands clasped in front of him and his forearms on his knees. As he began he told the children in front and to his right to listen closely to the story. He might have initially been a bit nervous, as he gave his name a second time and told the children again to listen to him. When he began the narrative, he enumerated things on his left fingers, indicating them with his right, "People started off on a journey…a man and a woman…" He told a lot of the story using his left hand to indicate actions or resting his left hand on the side of his face as he described something. He'd also return to clasping his hands in front of him for relatively long sections of the narrative. Early on, when he uses an ideophone to describe the smoke rising from the shelter in the bush, he holds his left hand over his mouth to slightly distort the sound of "futu, futu…" Then he returns his forearms to his knees and grasps his right wrist with his left hand for a fairly long descriptive section, until the couple gets to the part of their explanation when they said "…we are very tired." He briefly spreads his hands to say "Then they found lions seated in the bush." Then there's another long period of speaking with his hands clasped. As each lion cub wanders away, Mr. Mwampatisha sweeps his right palm over his left to indicate movement and finality. After doing this several times, he narrates the final part of the story where in the confusion the humans rise up, ululating, turning in a circle and making their escape. He also walks off himself, saying, "That's how they went, those people. Yes *mukwai*, yes." The audience was clearly delighted by this last piece of dramaturgy and laughed and applauded the performance.

There seemed to be no great thematic point made in this tale. The man and woman who'd wandered in the bush only to find themselves among lions did not seem particularly resourceful and there seemed no other themes being played out in the encounter. Mr. Mwampatisha did not provide a lot of details to contextualize the narrative's plot development.[140] The couple, who are stranded in the bush and come upon a "village" of lions, seemed doomed until a voice begins to inform them that "They eat you but I also eat them." The voice is threatening enough to cause the lion

---

140 There is a more thoroughly detailed variant of this narrative told by a Bemba storyteller, Mr. Katongo Soolo, at Malole. (see Chapter III) In this one, a lion has been shadowing a man's actions in preparing a garden and, by implication, threatening to take over his farm and maybe even eat him. A Hornbill arrives to threaten the lion family, a boast which is clearly taken seriously, and the lions disappear in a manner similar to the one in Mr. Mwampatisha's story. On hearing this narrative, Kangwa Samson provided an alternate version, in English. See Postscript in this chapter.

adults to direct their cubs and, indeed, themselves, to surreptitiously but quickly leave the scene. At the point where the adult lions seemed poised to also disappear into the bush, the humans were able to jump up, making noise and dancing, and escape from the situation. The denouement of the narrative was rather vague, though Mr. Mwampatisha's dramatic flourish at the end was very pleasing to his audience. If a theme is to be identified, it is probably that the lions were frightened off by a terrible, boasting voice that confidently predicted it would devour them. In other versions of this tale, part of the point is to indicate that the voice frightening the lions belongs to a much smaller animal. The point seems to be that the lions were too easily intimidated by words alone. The overall context of encountering animals in the bush, as well as being unnecessarily put off simply by verbal threats, was an example of using everyday concerns as the backdrop to a narrative performance. Dangerous wild animals are much less common in other parts of rural Zambia than they are in the Luangwa Valley, and most likely lose their immediate connotations in the former environments.[141]

The next performer was a guitar player, identifying himself as "Johnny Walker,"[142] or, rather, some audience members supplied that name and he concurred with them. Mr. "Walker" was a relatively young man, probably in his mid twenties, who was dressed in a gray long sleeved collared knit shirt, with black and white horizontal stripes. He wore dark gray trousers with the cuffs rolled half way up his calves, again suggesting his readiness to help in the labor of harvesting sorghum. His guitar was most likely locally made, with a weathered rough-hewn neck and fret board, metal strings and an acoustic body with the top painted flat green. Mr. "Walker" played a rather long introduction, which inspired a man tending a fire just to his right and rear, to stand up and begin dancing in time to the music. An audience member encouraged the musician to sing. Instead, he stopped playing and gave the introductory formula to begin a story, "*Patile akantu, ine ...*" [There was a little thing, I...] but after five or six words he stopped and went back to playing. The man behind him continued dancing while someone behind me in the audience began to sing softly to the music.

---

141 In the concluding Chapter I will discuss the "realistic" contexts of narratives and how images and characters take on a wider, sometimes mythical, somewhat stock or fixed quality over time and distance.
142 Johnny Walker's actual name is John Kampatika, born around 1957. He was a farmer and, apparently, a good fisherman.

Another man in the audience told him not to sing. Soon thereafter, Johnny Walker stopped playing, stood and walked away.

At this point I was feeling particularly awkward, wondering if performers were simply going to put in a token effort then persist in cutting me off as they walked away from the camera. Eventually I would realize that the performers simply thought they were supposed to end their efforts, by getting up and walking away. Nevertheless, people were neither overly friendly nor particularly interested in talking to me about who I was and what it was I did. While not openly hostile, the reception was certainly ranging from lukewarm to indifferent. Eventually, the man who'd been recording everyone's names in a large notebook sat down to tell a story.

Lenox Paimolo[143] was still holding the pen in his hand as he told the narrative, having placed the notebook down on the ground.

Bisa Storytelling 4 by Lenox Paimolo*

Lenox Paimolo: There was a person. There were how many people? There were three. Of the three people, one was a grower of food, one was a hunter, one was one [who had] money. Three people. A **boyi** with money, a **boyi** [who was a] farmer, a **boyi** [who was a] hunter. These all set out to marry. When they went to marry, when they got there, then **number one** they asked if there were those who could be married. This was the farmer, with a hoe on his shoulder. When they got there they told them, "No, we have refused." Then the one with money, the one with money they accepted, [and] he married. The hunter, they refused him. Further on, they received the hunter of animals, and he married. The one with the hoe remained with his hoe. He just went, and went and went and went. He arrived here, they refused him. He arrived here, they refused him. He went elsewhere and that is where he married a woman. That woman he married, she lived very well. The hunter, where he was there, he

---

143 Lennox Paimolo still lives at Mukupa Village and was for a time a village headman. He had been working with a now-defunct company called "Leopard Ridge Safaris" as a "skinner." While he was never known as a hunter, he is an accomplished farmer. He was born around 1950.

* To watch a video of this story follow this link: http://dx.doi.org/10.11647/OBP.0033.04/Bisa4

IV. Bisa Storytelling: The Politics of Hunting, Beer-Drinks, and Elvis 145

was killing animals every day, *mpoo!* [gunshot] He cut it up, he cut it up, he cut it up then he took it [the meat] to the village, they would eat. And the one with money also used to wear very nice *citenge* cloth, suits [*masuti*], and very nice jackets [*majaketi*], but there was no profit [*polofeti*]. [Pauses for a moment to hand someone, mostly out of frame, the notebook and pen—probably to list more names for the future harvest work] But when you found the one with the hoe, who was farming [mimes drawing a hoe across the ground], he was hard working in cultivating food. Food in heaps, and heaps, and heaps; plenty.

Then there was famine in the country, a great famine. That hunger, the hunter had no food, no. The farmer…[pauses to remember correct character] that one with money, had no food. Food was with the one with the hoe, the cultivator, [again mimes hoeing] he is the only one who had food. From there, the hunter said, "**No**, meat is no longer appetizing, friends, we must go to the one with food, the one with the hoe." The one with money said, "We don't have food, what shall we do? Let's go and look for food." All these people headed to that one with food, the one with the hoe [again mimes hoeing]. Now the one who is superior is the farmer, the one with money [or] the hunter, is who? The one who is greatest is the one with the hoe, the one who farms [mimes hoeing]. Farming is the most important. If a person is cultivating he is honorable. He is a master. A person, if he spends time killing animals in the bush, he is doing nothing. A person, even if he has money in his pockets there, he is doing nothing. So, unless he holds a hoe to cultivate, to cultivate [mimes hoeing]…this is a superior person. He is the one we fear [respect]. These are the words we have in Mukupa at our place…[that]you are listening to.

Lenox Paimolo looked to be a man in his mid to late thirties, stockily built and with thin, trimmed mustache and goatee. He wore a short-sleeved grey, collared shirt, with the sleeves rolled up a bit over his biceps, and olive-colored trousers, rolled up to just below his knees, again, as with some of the other performers, indicating he had come dressed to work. He held a pen in his right hand as he told the story, and wore a baseball cap with a red brim, blue mesh top, and a white front piece that had the name "Randy" printed on it. On his left wrist, he had a metal-band watch.

Mr. Paimolo was a confident and animated performer. He had a strong voice and moved the story along quickly. One of his most common gestures was enumerating the three main characters, counting the fingers on his left hand with his right. He did this each time he compared the characters or asked the audience to decide which the most important figure of the three was. He mimed shooting a rifle, cutting up meat, and, particularly, hoeing. He kept his focus despite a steady din from the place where beer was being consumed and even among the people watching his efforts. Behind him, several boys walked into and out of the frame, trying to strike poses for the camera. Another man, smoking a cigarette and mostly following the story, left the frame to find a light for his cigarette, then returned to mime reactions to the tale's events and even applauded Mr. Paimolo at the end of the narrative.

His *mulumbe* struck an interesting chord in the context of Nabwalya's economic life. While cultivation is a constant of the village, hunting is its more glamorous and prestigious activity. Directly comparing farming with hunting and simply having money in your pocket is to get to a core concern, how to best maintain a level of food security in difficult times — the difficulties stemming from both natural impediments to growing crops and official impediments to hunting game. The farming emphasis also seemed relevant to the purpose of the gathering, and perhaps undergirded the obligation the beer drinking participants were being held to when it came time to bring in the delayed harvest. Overall, the sense of farming as a stable practice is the *mulumbe*'s main theme, a reminder that diversification was a crucial alternative to relying only on hunting for sustenance. Mr. Paimolo's theme might be somewhat contrived, since farming in the mid-Luangwa valley has always been difficult to carry out with any kind of regularity. Most good soil is found near the rivers, but these are subject to the twin plagues of flooding and drought. Further, the many animals in the area, often moving in the direction of the river for water, are always a threat to graze in people's gardens. As is the case with many narratives, links to actual practices or conditions may or may not be relevant to any particular tale, with symbolic or allegorical themes often taking precedence.

After a brief interlude that allowed me to videotape a bit of the beer drink and sample some for myself, the next performer, Mr. George Iyambe[144], who looked to be in his mid or late twenties, told a fairly long story, with a song in it and a good deal of audience participation. Mr. Iyambe sat on

---

144 While I initially recorded this performer's name as George Iyapa, Kangwa Samson specified that his name is George Iyambe, born in the Nabwalya area in 1957. In his youth he made a name for himself as a very good hunter. When the management/enforcement program known as ADMADE came to the area, he was hired as first a builder then promoted to the rank of a game scout. At the time of my conversation with Kangwa, Mr. Iyambe was a chief scout at a game camp.

a long log, with two colleagues on either side of him. One was the guitar-playing "Johnny Walker," and the other a stocky man wearing a thick sweater with sleeves pushed up over his elbows, the collar of his plaid shirt stuck out of the crewneck, and tan trousers with the cuffs rolled up over his calves. He also wore a pink "groundskeeper" cap. Mr. Iyambe wore a tan long sleeved collared knit shirt, with horizontal stripes, over another collared green cotton shirt. His trousers were dark green and someone handed him a baseball cap to wear during his performance. He fooled with the plastic fastener at the back of the cap while I was waiting for him to give his name before beginning. He placed the cap on his head as he started the story, but the fastener did not hold and the cap remained rather large and loose during his performance. This, along with the fact that he was missing his right upper front tooth, gave him a comical visage as he narrated the tale.

Bisa Storytelling 5
by George Iyambe

Robert Cancel: Let's begin. Give me your name.

Audience: See, let go of the walking stick slightly.

Audience: He says, "Your name!"

RC: He is about to come.

Audience: Mr. George…that's all.

RC: Begin, *mukwai*.

George Iyapa: My name is George Iyapa.

RC: Uhn humn.

GI: [says something like, "*Tabeni nkashina*," which, even with help, I could not later decipher, but might have something to do with his name, since *ishina* is the word for "name."]

RC: Oh. Begin.

GI: Then *mukwai*, a person had married. When he married a woman, but the woman he had married did not love him. The man himself loved the woman, but the woman herself didn't love her husband.

RC: No. She rejected him.

* To watch a video of this story follow this link: http://dx.doi.org/10.11647/OBP.0033.04/Bisa5

GI: She refused. Then as they continued living together, God blesses, He blessed them with a baby girl. The baby this woman bore was very beautiful. When his wife saw her she said, "Oh! See, now that we have a child, as for me, what's required here?" In the past people were not carrying their children in the ordinary cloths we see today. They used to kill animals. When they killed animals such as waterbuck, or impala, they skinned it, got the skin, and prepared it nicely, and they used it as a sling for carrying children. Then she said, "As far as I'm concerned, I don't want these other slings. I want a sling made from lion's skin."

RC: From the lion's skin?

GI: "That's what you should kill, my husband, so that our marriage may be strengthened, so that I carry our newborn baby in it." The man said, "Uhmm, my wife, that's an impossible demand. The lion, this lion is very fierce. It is not something you can just go out to catch, unless you have a gun."

RC: It is fierce.

GI: Then she said, "No, then our marriage will end." Then the husband said, "Well, that's alright then, so I'll go hunting." He took the muzzleloader. He pushed in how many balls of shot? [Holds up two fingers]

RC: Two.

GI: So, he even told his nephew, he said, "Let's go. We go and look...look for the lion. We should get its skin and use it to carry the baby."

Audience: The child.

GI: "Because with my wife, if I don't get the lion's skin as a sling, my marriage will end." They set out on a journey. They spent three days in the bush. On the fourth day they found a lion which was in the shrub. His nephew said, "Uncle, there's the lion, in the shrub." His uncle stared and said, "Ah...we must go back home, we've been away from home for too long. Now we must kill this lion." His uncle even started stalking it. He said, "But the lion had also seen them already."

Audience: That was the real problem.

GI: And you know he was even panicking, thinking to himself, "We should return home." He missed. Yes! Kulubulubulubulubulubu! He missed; the shot flew over the lion. The lion protested and said, "You want to demonstrate your shooting skills on me. I will outsmart you!" It devoured (him), bwa! It devoured (him), bwa! It even cut him into pieces. Only his little nephew remained. He was a very little boy of six years, he was quite small. He said, "Well, my uncle is dead. But the village we came from is very far away. What shall I do?" He got bits and pieces of his uncle's body, arranged them properly, and put the body somewhere.

He said, "Well, you know, I...now my in-law what has happened to my uncle. He is dead. The lion has killed him." He sang as if he was celebrating something. Now it was a celebration, that's what he sang. He sang a celebration now, a celebration. His nephew said,

> The Bisa women, yes.
> See what's happened. See what's happened.
> The Bisa women, yes.
> See what's happened. See what's happened.
> A different sling.
> See what's happened. See what's happened.
> One ends in the cruel jaws.
> See what's happened. See what's happened.
> Today uncle will not be seen.
> See what's happened. See what's happened.
> Today uncle will not be seen.
> See what's happened. See what's happened.

The young boy set out on his journey. He said, "This is the direction my uncle and I came from. I saw how I traveled with my uncle." He followed the traces, he struggled. Bam-bam-bam-bam-bam-bam-bam-bam-bam-bam. He slept, since they had traveled for three days. The boy slept in a big tree. The following day he set out.

> The Bisa women, yes.
> See what's happened. See what's happened.
> The Bisa women, yes.
> See what's happened. See what's happened.
> A different sling.
> See what's happened. See what's happened.
> One ends in the cruel jaws.
> See what's happened. See what's happened.
> Today uncle will not be seen.
> See what's happened. See what's happened.

Audience: Carry on!

GI: Then he reached the outskirts of the village. People heard and said, "Listen...there comes a court poet (bard)! There they come, those who had gone in the bush to look for a sling, the nephew is the one singing." That's what the people in the village said. "Aahg! Bwalya." He said, "There, listen, the child is weeping."

> The Bisa women, yes.
> See what's happened. See what's happened.
> The Bisa women, yes.
> See what's happened. See what's happened.

A different sling.
See what's happened. See what's happened.
One ends in the cruel jaws.
See what's happened. See what's happened.
Today uncle will not be seen.
See what's happened. See what's happened.

Distinguished friends, that's how he arrived at the village, abruptly! In narrating, he told people, "Well, my uncle has been killed by a lion." Then they asked people to gather. "What's the matter?" They said, "Let's go to the spot where your uncle died." They found that the lion had killed him. Then they said, "No, your in-law [the uncle's wife], although you are singing her this song, your in-law is not wise at all. She, too, will die right here." They took this woman, the transgressor of the law, and said, "If a man has no wealth, you insist that you want riches. That's bad!" They took that woman and killed her right there. This is the end of my **story**.

George Iyambe began the narrative with his elbows resting on his knees and arms crossed holding his biceps. He spoke in a loud voice, partly because the audience was a bit restive and rowdy, and emphasized his words by periodically jutting his head and shoulders forward. Early in the narrative he explained how in times past people carried babies around in slings made from animal hides, gesturing with both hands to emphasize how the skins were made and put onto mothers' backs. He also leaned forward when voicing the husband's argument against having to kill a lion to make a sling for the baby. In part, his performance posture was due to the long bill of the cap covering his eyes, so Mr. Iyambe had to lean forward and tilt his head up in order to make eye contact with the camera and his audience. Before the husband sets out on the hunt, Mr. Iyambe acts out loading the gun with ball and shot and tamping it down with a metal rod, using his left hand to hold the imaginary barrel and his right to repeatedly push down the load. He also used the formula of asking how many bullets and holding up two fingers, as I answered two. He then acted out a lot of the activity of going into the bush, spotting the lion, staring at it and aiming the gun. Within these activities, he touches the arm of "Johnny Walker," to his right, as if he were the hunter grabbing the young nephew's arm to say, "Ah…we must go back home…" When he acts out the lion disdainfully taunting the hunter before he kills him, he draws some laughter from the audience. He also combines a verb and ideophone ("Bwa!") to describe the lion killing the hunter, and acts this out by twice slapping the side of his left fist with his right palm, making as if to throw down the victim each time. He gestured emphatically to show the young boy escaping the lion and returning to recover what was left of his uncle. Then Mr. Iyambe crossed his arms over his thighs and leaned forward to sing the song. There was loud and enthusiastic singing of the chorus by the audience members and his two colleagues seated on either side of him. Near the end of the first rendition, a man and woman came behind them and danced to the song. He gesticulated broadly to describe the boy's movement over three days towards his village, then began to sing again, with the same level of response from his audience and the two dancing behind him. Before the next and final rendition of the song, George Iyambe broadly acted out the movement of the boy, pointing to the places he was going and portraying the reaction of people hearing his song in the village. During the singing of the song, he kept his forearms on his thighs and hands crossed at the wrists between his knees. He leaned so far forward that his hands were near his face, with knees up to his chin. He also moved his head and body rhythmically to the singing. The story's ending was spoken in an even louder voice and he jumped up and walked away at its conclusion, drawing loud applause and appreciative remarks from the audience.

Thematically, this performance clearly focuses on marital relationships and how these can be damaged by unreasonable expectations. The inclusion of a song marks the tale as a *lushimi*, one with a thematic explanation at the end. Mr. Iyambe takes time to detail the practice of making slings from animal hides to carry infants. He contextualizes this practice by reminding his audience that these days cloth is used for the same function. As in Mr. Mwampatisha's earlier story, a lion is encountered in the bush and, this time, the lion kills the human who has intruded in his realm. While the theme of an arrogant and unreasonable wife is at the forefront of the story's development, there is another important familial relationship developed here as well. The young nephew, who'd accompanied the hunter on the journey, would play a major role in moving the narrative to its just resolution. He returns to gather his uncle's remains, then finds his way back to the village while singing the incriminating song that alludes to what had transpired. Further, he is welcomed back by the people of the village, who then become the arbiters of justice when accounting for the hunter's death and his wife's part in it. The narrative role played by both the hunter and his nephew serves to move the story along to its conclusion but also, on a more realistic level, parallels actual matrilineal relationships between accomplished older hunters and their younger protegees, who are often maternal nephews.[145] This familial relationship in the end trumps the marital bond, with a clear misogynistic caution about women's unreasonable demands.

Mr. Paul Chandalube followed, with a story featuring Kalulu, the trickster hare.

Bisa Storytelling 6 by Paul Chandalube*

Robert Cancel:	Wait…we can begin. Give me your name.
PC:	Paul Chandalube.
RC:	O.K. Begin *mukwai*.
PC:	I am going to talk about the respect of animals, or how big the animals are. Who is the king of animals? Then it was Kalulu who said, "I am the king, *mukwai*."
RC:	Uhm humn.
PC:	Then there were animals such as the elephant, the buffalo, the zebra, all the animals. Hare was there, even Hippopotamus. They said, "We are the kings." The clever Kalulu spoke right there. He said, "Are you the king?" They said, "Yes." Hare said, "Well, all of you animals, would you say you are greater than I?" They said, "What insolence! This fellow, how can you ask whether or not we are greater than you when you are so small?" Kalulu said, "Well, you Elephant and Hippopotamus, can you defeat me in a tug-of-war contest?" They said, "What nerve! Try and you will see. We can pull you, draw you over the center line and even throw you away." He said, "O.K. It's alright. We can make a?…a rope. Let's go and strip bark-rope."

---

145 A similar situation plays out in the tale performed by Mr. Fermit Indita among the Bwile people, in Chapter VI. Here, the main character is aided by his nephew, a half-snake/half-human offspring of his sister's sexual relationship with a magical serpent. In this case, the nephew saves his uncle from his evil mother and also guides him to a new and prosperous village.

* To watch a video of this story follow this link: http://dx.doi.org/10.11647/OBP.0033.04/Bisa6

They went and stripped bark-rope and made a very long rope. He [Hare] said, "My Lord!" His honor the Elephant said, "Yes?" "Can you defeat me in a tug-of-war contest?" Elephant said, "Argh! You, Kalulu, you are so tiny." Kalulu said, "Let's go and try." He took the rope that was properly made, made a loop and fastened it around Elephant's neck. He pulled slightly and said, "Stand right here. I will come back again. I am also going to fasten the rope around my neck so that we can begin pulling." He went to Hippopotamus and said, "Hippopotamus!" "Yes?" Kalulu said, "Giant Hippo[146], can you defeat me in a tug-of-war contest?" Hippopotamus said, "Nnaah! You think, me…Kalulu, you think I can fail to do that?" Kalulu said, "O.K. Come here."

Then he [hippopotamus] came out [of the water]. Hare thought, "Let me do what, now?" He made another loop and fastened it around the hippopotamus' neck. He said, "O.K. I am also going to that side. Right when I pull, both of us should begin to pull." Then he went to a shrub somewhere there, got a big stick and hit the rope. Nku, nku. Yah! Elephant at the other end of the rope said, "**Damn it!** It's now time to pull each other." At the other end of the rope, where Hippopotamus was at the river, he said, "Kalulu said, 'Let's pull each other.' Mmpph!" "You have begun to pull each other *mukwai*." Kwe-kwe-kwe-kwe-kwe-kwe-kwe-kwe-kwe-kwe-kwe-kwe-kwe-kwe-kwe-kwe.

Elephant on the other side pulled hard. He pulled hard again. He said, "Well. Ahrgh! Auurgh!" Hippopotamus on the other side of the rope also pulled. "Ubruu urruuru!" They met at the center-line. Then Kalulu said, "You are the ones who said, 'We are the greatest.' I am the greatest of all the other animals." That's what Kalulu…that's what Kalulu said, "I am the greatest of all the other animals *mukwai*. All of you…you are very small. Have you seen the way you have treated each other?"

That's it *mukwai*. This is where I end. It is a short one [story].

Mr. Chandalube[147] was in his late early forties, wearing a white short sleeved collared shirt with thin gray lines in a grid pattern. He also

---

146 He uses a combination of Bisa and English, saying "Ci-Hippo."
147 Paul Chandalube was also known to people as "Mabale." He was born around 1945 and passed away in 2000. His death was attributed by some people to witchcraft, wielded by a specific young man. The suspected culprit was found guilty by a "witchfinder" (*mucapi*) of killing not only Mr. Chandalube but also other people. He was sentenced, not surprisingly, to work the farm of the witchfinder and pay a large sum of money. Chandalube was mostly a farmer in the area, as well as an occasional fisherman. He'd

wore light brown trousers. His clothes seemed newer and perhaps more expensive than those of the other performers. It's likely that he had not come to help with the harvesting of the crop. He had a rather deep voice and a serious, no-nonsense style of speaking. He began his narrative sitting straight up with his elbows on his thighs and left hand holding his right wrist. As he briefly identified animals that might vie for the title of the greatest or most powerful, he enumerated them on his left hand, using his right to touch each finger as he named them. He then bent low and touched the ground next to him with his right hand to indicate where Kalulu ranked in this hierarchy. He returned to holding his wrist as he spoke, until he acted out the initial interaction and challenge Kalulu makes to the larger animals. There's a bit of pointing at each other as they speak, then he used his left hand to act out Elephant and Hippo feigning grabbing Kalulu and tossing him to the side. He then mimes the making of a rope, and playing out the thick rope along the ground. Mr. Chandalube acts out the looping of the rope around the Elephant's neck by using his hands to indicate the shape of the noose and then moving them up to and behind his own head. Acting as Kalulu, he tells the Elephant to wait and gestures to how he's going to grab the end of the rope, which is out of sight. When he depicts the Hippo engaging the noose, he actually shapes it in front of him then acts out looping it around its neck while holding his hands out in front, as if he was placing it over the animal's head. Describing how Kalulu goes to a mid point between the competitors and bangs on the thick rope with a large stick, Mr. Chandalube points in front of him to show where the Elephant took up the challenge and began to pull, then points behind him to show where the Hippo was similarly engaged. Instead of acting out animals tugging on a rope, his description of the contest actually focused more on the long and loud ideophone, "Kwe-kwe-kwe..." whereby, elbow and forearm parallel to the ground, he rapidly moved his left hand, palm down, and forearm back and forth to indicate how the animals struggled to gain the advantage. When he ended by saying Kalulu had won, he again touches the ground with his right hand to emphasize the trickster's small stature. Paul Chandalube spoke more loudly and rapidly as he ended the performance, standing up and walking away as the others had done.

---

worked in Zimbabwe when he was a young man. From the time he came to Nabwalya he remained a farmer, supporting two wives.

This is a rather well known trickster narrative. I recorded a version that was very similar to this one when I visited the Lunda area later in the year.[148] Like many trickster stories, the plot revolves around using cleverness to defeat sheer size or strength. This particular performance, however, is at least partly shaped by the context of the narratives that came before it, so that the theme of animals and the bush again underlies the tale's machinations. The trickster hare, in this case, is like the hunter who must overcome large and dangerous animals. He is very similar to the clever hunter, in the session the day before, who had to find a way to get the evil but dangerous old woman to somehow remove the disfiguring hump from his son's body. He is like the clever nephew who chose to sing a falsely festive song to allude to the evil done his uncle by the wife. A central concern of this and other narratives I recorded treats the problems of greed and recklessness in a hostile environment. Mostly, animals are the danger here, but there is also the sense of potential danger from other, sometimes human and usually female, forces as well.

At this point, people were increasingly boisterous and obviously having a good time, but pretty much disinterested in the prospects of more performances. I thanked a few people nearby and let Kangwa know I was done. We said our good byes and walked back to Stuart's through another section of the village. Kangwa wanted me to see various things, like a house being built and sorghum drying on bamboo mats, etc. I photographed or shot video of some of these objects or practices as we paused at each location. We reached Stuart's place in time for some lunch.

Later that afternoon, I recorded three more stories at Stuart's *nsaka*: two from Kabuswe C. Nabwalya, the man who was working on a building project for Stuart and who had comprised part of the audience for Laudon Ndalazi's performances the day before, and a third from a young boy named Peter Chisanga Tembo, who was acting as a game-counter and assistant for Stuart.

I want to focus on only one of those stories, a brief *mulumbe*, told by Mr. Nabwalya.

---

148 See the performance by Mr. Moffat Mulenga, in the village of Kashiba, in the Lunda chapter of this study.

Bisa Storytelling 7
by Kabuswe C. Nabwalya*

Robert
Cancel: O.K.

Kabuswe C.
Nabwalya: My name is Kabuswe C. Nabwalya. I will present a small *mulumbe*. A person begat one child, and his wife died. The mother died. The child remained with its father.

Now as they lived, the father used to teach his child. He used to say, "My child, I am going to leave you on this earth but the world is very difficult.

One: You should marry a woman whose heart is as good as your mother's.

RC: Uh hmm.

KCN: And then **two**: Be careful in establishing familiarity with the government.

RC: Uh hmm.

KCN: **Three**: A constant visitor is very often the one who turns against you.

Four: A woman does not keep any secrets. This is how it was. Now [as for] what it meant…

RC: Uh hmn.

KCN: …it meant that **first**, you should marry a woman whose heart is as good as your mother's because he was an orphan.

RC: Uh hmm.

KCN: He needed to marry a woman whom he would get along with, and [they should] love each other even more than he and his mother loved each other.

RC: Oh.

KCN: Then **two**, be careful in establishing familiarity with the government because even if you are working for the government, if you commit not so serious an offence, as long as it is in government, you will be imprisoned.

RC: Uh hun.

KCN: Then **three**, a constant visitor is very often the one who turns against you, your friend…

* To watch a video of this story follow this link: http://dx.doi.org/10.11647/OBP.0033.04/Bisa7

RC: Oh.

KCN: ...the one you like, is the one who arrests you.

Then **four**, a woman does not keep any secrets. You may have killed an animal in the bush, if a woman had seen it then she will reveal that secret. She will say, "He killed an animal."

RC: Uh hah.

KCN: This is like a *mulumbe*, this is what it means.

RC: Yes *mukwai*. You've explained it well.

KCN: Yes *mukwai*.

RC: It's alright.

Mr. Nabwalya[149] was in his late twenties or early thirties, sitting back on a lounge chair slung with an animal hide to comfortably support his weight. He wore a green or khaki long sleeved cotton shirt, rolled up to his elbows and fastened with only one button below his chest, with the shirt tails knotted at his waist and a pair of light brown trousers. He'd been working on Stuart's *nsaka* both days we were in the village. Stuart later told me that Mr. Nabwalya was a son of the late chief and that he had somehow managed to visit Mpika and run up some bills in Stuart's name. The labor on the *nsaka* and some other chores around the place were his way of repaying the money. He told this brief narrative with minimal gestures, mostly resting his wrists or hands on his upper thighs. When he enumerated the four points of the *mulumbe*, he marked the first two by lifting his left index finger to signal first "one," then "two" of the points, but did not use his hands to signify the other two ideas. While explaining the answer, he alternated between subtly lifting one hand and the other to emphasize the father's commentary.

Looking over this very brief, allusive rather than specific *mulumbe*, it is notable that the social concerns set out by Mr. Nabwalya resonate with

---

149 Kabuswe C. Nabwalya is a son of the late chief, Moloson Kabuswe Nabwalya. He is also known as Petson Nabwalya. He left the village to join a company called "Tudor Conservation." Afterwards, when back in the village he farmed, and was known as a good hunter. He has recently suffered from some particularly bad luck. His wife was caught by a crocodile and maimed, but survived. Early in 2005, his daughter was taken away and killed by a crocodile. Around a week later, his sister was also taken and killed by a crocodile. He was, at the time I met with Kangwa Samson (2005), a "public scout," which is a rural version of what is known in other parts of the world as "neighborhood watch," looking out for and reporting any local illegal activities.

most of the narratives recorded in this village. Marrying a good woman is a concern, while at the same time he advises the audience not to trust women with secrets. This in part touches on the theme of Mr. Iyambe's story about the greedy wife. His other two points about distrusting the government and being suspicious of frequent visitors, even if they are ostensibly "friends," speaks to wider social concerns but also to the specific tensions of living in Nabwalya, at the center of the contestations between local cultural and economic imperatives and the efforts of government agencies to curtail the key activity of hunting. As mentioned earlier, one of the strategies taken by at least one agency was to appoint local young men as game scouts, thereby giving them a stake in enforcement of game laws. But these young men also became objects of distrust by local people, who were even more wary and secretive when it came to hunting activities. Hence the further relevance of points two and three in the *mulumbe*.

A few years after this visit to Nabwalya, I corresponded with Stuart Marks regarding my initial reading of barely suppressed hostility or discomfort and distance emanating from even the men who agreed to perform narratives for me. Stuart responded with a detailed letter that drew from both his memory and field notes. I quote one particularly salient passage:

> You are right about the stresses and strains of fieldwork. The isolation of the rainy season was coming to an abrupt halt and it was difficult to know what visitors each new day would bring. The previous week had brought two Land Rovers full of game guards and wildlife scouts to search for a "poacher's lair" that had been spotted near Nabwalya from Owens' aircraft.[150] The scouts had not gone far into the bush across the Munyamadzi River

---

150 At that time, Americans Mark and Delia Owens were living in North Luangwa Park and running their own operation to curtail poaching. They were a good example, if in some ways an extreme one, of conservation strategies based mainly on policing game areas by force. The Owens's methods, which at the time of my visit were being praised by many in the American diplomatic community, were to be seriously questioned later on when a now infamous incident involving the shooting of an unarmed poacher was broadcast internationally in an ABC television documentary, "Deadly Game: The Mark and Delia Owens Story," 1996. A more detailed critique of their approach and outcomes is written by Simon Ward (1997). For the Owens's point of view on their work in Zambia, see Owens 1993. The title suggests their "scientific" approach, which in some ways reads more like Rider Haggard than wildlife conservationists. Now back in the US, they run the Owens Foundation for Wildlife Conservation and also have a website that, among other things, emphasizes their efforts to develop the local economy of Zambians living in the vicinity of their operation in North Luangwa: www.owens-foundation.org. A 2010 *New Yorker* article by Jeffrey Goldberg revisits the Owens' time in Zambia and raises concerns surrounding their methods/tactics. (Goldberg 2010) The magazine published responses in the Owens' defense in the next issue.

and had not been very diligent in pursuing the "poachers," who in any case had already received word of the scouts' arrival. So the scouts had spent the rest of their time hanging around and harassing villagers. (personal correspondence)

This is only one example of the kinds of "visitors" who would drop in on Nabwalya's residents, mostly without warning. Almost all of the visitors had some relationship to game management agencies or conservation groups—or even just tourists or safari hunters hoping to observe an "authentic" rural village—who were usually more interested in animal than human welfare. Stuart even conjectured that the inordinate amount of time we'd spent videotaping the crocodiles and hippos in the river might have been seen by residents as yet another example of skewed priorities. It is therefore not surprising that people were not forthcoming with long and involved narrative performances, taking time out of their lives for relatively meager returns. This is an attitude that applies in most of the places I visited in the hope of recording performances, but it is manifestly most understandable and observable in a living situation as precarious as was the one in Nabwalya. Even the giving of their names by performers was a rather problematic choice, with "Johnny Walker" being the most obvious example of someone who did not want to be pinned down or identified later on, by me or more likely some representative of authority and game management. In general, people everywhere I went in rural Zambia may have been initially uncomfortable having me record their names on audio or videotape, but conditions were usually rather low key and after some explanation most performers accurately identified themselves.

It really was unusual in the places I've gathered oral traditions for there to be such an obvious overlap or literal parallel between the imaginary world of storytelling performances and the real life conditions of performers and their audience. Chief Nabwalya himself, Mr. Blackson Somo, had only recently been appointed, and even then under the tentative "Acting Chief" title, after a lengthy succession dispute, which led to even more instability and uncertainty in the village's socio-political relationships.[151] The position of chief in this polity was complicated by his interactions with outside agencies looking to provide material and economic opportunities

---

151 In 1984 Chief Nabwalya, Mr. Kabuswe Mbuluma, died after being in power for fifty-one years. This set off a long and complicated succession dispute. Mr. Blackson Somo emerged as the victor in the struggle, being appointed Acting Chief in 1988 and finally installed as chief in 1991.

to residents in order to offset profits previously made from hunting. The chief is often the main go-between in such negotiations and exchanges, and he is bound to spread the wealth to colleagues and others who will strengthen his social position. This sometimes means that not everyone in the community will share in this wealth, and this means that those who are not included in these benefits have little incentive to stop hunting. In any event, it is safe to conjecture that the performances I recorded and information I gathered were always passing through the filter of caution and suspicion that characterized the village's relationship to outsiders.

After this second day of collecting narratives, we settled in for the evening and, the next morning, led by Stuart and Kangwa we made a speedy return trip through the valley and up the escarpment to Mpika then Kasama. In an effort at reciprocity, I would then guide them to the village of Nsama, in the Tabwa area, where they consulted with local hunters about their beliefs and practices.

Postscript

Near the end of September 2005 I met Kangwa Samson at the government rest house in Mpika, Northern Province. Because I was traveling by public transportation, mostly buses, given the time and expense such a trip would entail it was not possible to make the long arduous journey to Nabwalya. Additionally, it was the hot season and the Valley was particularly inhospitable for travelers. I'd sent a letter to the Valley when I arrived in Zambia in late August, and hoped that Kangwa had received it so that we could meet. The first evening at the rest house, as I sat at a table in the lounge having a meal, there was a knock on the door and I answered it to find a very slim, bedraggled older man. I called the guesthouse's manager to greet the visitor then went back to my meal. The visitor was asking the manager about Dr. Cancel, and it was only then I realized that it was Kangwa Samson. Neither one of us had recognized the other, both having aged noticeably in the intervening sixteen years since we'd last seen one another.

We greeted each other warmly then he sat down to share my meal and catch me up on his journey. Kangwa was now headman of Mbuluma village some distance from Nabwalya and supported two wives and their nine children. One family lived with him and the other in a distant village. Mr. Samson brought greetings from Elvis Kampamba, who is now the headmaster at the primary school in Nabwalya. Kangwa had walked two and a half days through the scorching heat of the Valley, stopping at a village one night then simply sleeping in the bush the second night, to make our rendezvous. There'd been several years of drought which more or less decimated the crops and any grain and vegetable surplus in the area. Moreover, hunting enforcement was more stringent than ever and people mostly did not hunt with guns anymore. If anything, they set snares and pit traps to catch game, which was less noticeable to game management authorities. Elephants had, in fact, made a come back in the Valley. So much so that they were in some instances eating the meager attempts at growing crops by villagers and even beginning to destroy crucial sources of food by damaging mango and other fruit trees. He said that in the last five months two people had been killed by elephants. Kangwa claimed there was out and out famine in the Valley and promised food relief in the form of flour to make the staple starch *ubwali* had been slow in coming. By around 9 PM, we agreed to meet the next morning in my room in order to do some work, and Kangwa left to find a relative in town he planned to stay with.

At around 8:30 AM, Kangwa came by and we proceeded to watch the video record of Bisa performances on DVD. Our pattern, as it emerged, was to watch each performance, discuss possible themes of the stories, and, mostly, fill in biographical information on the storytellers. Most of this information has been worked into the footnotes of this chapter. Clearly, I am relying here on Kangwa Samson's knowledge and impressions, which is not the same thing as gathering similar information from the performers themselves or their families. However, in his years as a friend and research associate of Stuart Marks, and in the time I knew him back in 1988–89, Kangwa has proven to be very reliable in his impressions, observations, and gathering of data. Moreover, he had arranged and witnessed the original session, in his mother's section of Nabwalya, which is the central focus of this chapter, and knew most of the performers and audience members fairly well. Be that as it may, even in the few instances where I was able to speak directly to performers or their relatives, it's best to remember that biographical or autobiographical material is always passing through filters of time and/or intent.

When it came to evaluating the tale by George Mwampatisha [aka George Kalikeka], Kangwa Samson offered what he felt was a clearer, more common version of the story. In some ways, this story is actually quite different, but it retains the central section of the lion and his family being scared off by the threatening voice of a smaller animal. Kangwa chose to relate the story in English and I include it here for comparative purposes:

Bisa Storytelling, 8
by Mr. Kangwa Samson, 2005

Kangwa
Samson: There lived a lion in the bush, in a cave. One day a hunter with his son went out hunting looking for animals. Unfortunately, the heavy rain rained there, so they cau... they lost their way back home. They began wandering in the bush, looking for a shelter. But as they were going, they found a cave, where the lion was. So, they entered that place and found the lion there. So the lion was very happy, thinking that they have got meat to eat now, eh? Because they were starving by hunger. And the lion demanded to eat the...? Men, the son and father. Lucky enough there was a...a small rat, known as *mususungila*, with a long nose. And that, eh, rat was very kind to human beings. So the lion demanded to...wanted to eat the men. But that small rat was brave. It spoke loud words, saying, "Oh, you people, don't be afraid. If the lion eats you, I'm going to eat him also."

So, the family of the lion was afraid. The lion made a plan and ordered the first son to go out and bring some firewood. And he told him that, "If you are stupid, come back. But if you are clever, don't come back." So the son was aware, he knew what his father meant. When he went out, he never turned back. And the second one. And the third was the wah... wife. And the last one was the real, "he" lion, the male one. They left the place. The man and his son were left alone, safe.

Robert
Cancel: Because of the mouse.

KS: Yeah, because of that small rat.

This version of the narrative is certainly better developed when it comes to understanding how the lions were driven away. It also focuses specifically on the small rat, *mususungila*, which saved the humans. While not specified in Kangwa's discourse, similar versions of this tale specify that the smaller animal, in this case the rat, was hidden from sight and used a fearsome voice to address the lions. An audience would fill in these details from experience if they were not provided literally in the performance. As is the case in Mr. Mwampatisha's version, a main point is how bravado and trickery can at times overcome larger, more deadly adversaries. Moreover, this is a good example of how narratives can be shaped and reshaped depending on the intentions and focus of performers.

One main dimension of Kangwa Samson's observations on the video performances confirmed the cautious relationship between Nabwalya's residents and outsiders. This was the use of nick-names or even fabricated names by several of the performers. It is clear that despite my being introduced by Kangwa and supported by Stuart Marks, there was still a palpable level of distrust involved in the dynamics of that recording session. I was also struck by how many of the performers were not themselves known as hunters, even though many of their stories involved that central activity. This may be another example of how pervasive the practice is in the social context of the local society. Another dimension brought out by Kangwa's observations is one that pretty much came out of all my interactions with performers or their families and neighbors in 2005. This was a feeling of intense empathy bordering on nostalgia on my part. I'd spent nearly sixteen years looking at video and consulting notes and memories in order to reconstruct the performance events and had come to some tentative conclusions. Actually hearing about the performers and the details of the sessions answered some questions but mostly left even more gaps in my knowledge of these people and the paths of their lives.

After working till around lunch hour, we went into town where I sent some messages at an internet cafe—a very recent addition to Mpika's shops and businesses—including keeping Stuart Marks informed as to our progress and updating him on Kangwa's situation. We visited a couple of shops to have some cokes and bread. After I changed some dollars at the local bank, we returned to the rest house where we finished looking at the last two performances. Kangwa left to do some errands while I worked over the material I'd just gathered and tried to digest some of the new information. We met in late afternoon to wander around Mpika, speaking to a few people, buying some things for my bus trip the next day, and finally having dinner at a small restaurant on the edge of town. Just earlier that day, we discovered that we were actually born only a year apart. This unexpectedly made us age-mates and opened up our relationship in ways that hadn't existed before. All day long, our conversations were open and free-wheeling, touching on all kinds of topics from our families to government policies to the efficacy of witchcraft and the intricacies of hunting. Before parting for the night, I paid Kangwa the equivalent of a month's work at minimum wage in Zambia, which was around $40.

The next morning, he and a friend, a political representative of the Nabwalya constituency, met me at the guest house and escorted me to the post office, where I was to take the Post Bus to Lusaka. Kangwa planned to buy some supplies to bring back to the Valley then use the rest of his wages to keep the family in food until the next harvest. He intended to leave in the late afternoon, to avoid some of the heat of the day, for his long return walk home. We parted at around 9:30 AM and by 10:30 I was on my bus to Lusaka.

V. Telling Tales While Keeping Secrets: Two Lunda Storytelling Sessions

The collection of oral traditions is a process that usually combines simple electronic recording of living events with the more complicated elements of establishing relationships with the performers and their audience, negotiating the time, place and compensation for their efforts, and observing and noting information not readily obtained by videocamera or tape recorder. The process is rendered more difficult when the researcher is working with people, or in an area, that he or she does not know well. In this context and consistent with the overall format of this study, I want to consider two separate storytelling sessions I recorded in 1989, focusing on two kinds of observations. First, I will provide a detailed description of the performance context of the sessions, and then I will also look comparatively at the basic form, content and themes of the narratives. These two dimensions of description will lead to a consideration of what we can know about a specific set of performances and the possible intentions of the performers. As in earlier chapters, this analysis will detail the role played by the researcher in eliciting and paying for the performances.

The Lunda have ethnic ties over several regions of Zambia and the Democratic Republic of the Congo. This is mainly due to migration patterns and is partly the result of colonial boundary-drawing. I will focus only on the Lunda of the Luapula Province in Zambia. They live roughly in the area northwest of Mansa, the provincial capital, near the middle of the Luapula Valley to the small towns of Nchelenge and Kashikishi on the southern end of Lake Mweru in the north. The Lunda Senior Chief is Mwata Kazembe, and his village, Mwansbombwe, is located pretty much in the center of the region inhabited by his subjects.[152]

In 1988–89, my most direct contacts in the Lunda area consisted of relationships with two Zambian graduate students (Mr. Anthony Kafimbwa and Mr. Samuel Ng'andwe) and their families. Both students were conducting field projects in oral traditions for their MA degrees from the Department of Literature and Languages at the University of Zambia. As a visiting lecturer, I was doing a minimal amount of advising on these projects. On a January swing through the area, my son Michael and I traveled with Mr. Kafimbwa as far as his uncle's home at Kashikishi, where he was hoping to develop contacts to do a project on the praise singing of one of Kazembe's bards/advisors. We dropped him off there on our way to Kaputa District to visit old friends and conduct a bit of research among the Tabwa people.[153] On our way home, we accompanied Mr. Kafimbwa to the village of Mbereshi, where he visited a Lunda bard who treated us to an example of playing the *mondo*, or talking drum. The bard, Mano—an honorific title, meaning literally "(Mr.) Wisdom"—agreed to work with Kafimbwa on his project, and also agreed to sponsor me on my next trip through his village to record stories. On our way to Mansa, we stopped near the village of Kashiba to contact Mr. Ng'andwe, who was recording local oral narratives. We located his sister, Ms. Chishimba, at Mofwe Investments Bar—an extraordinary establishment that at the time, which was during ongoing national shortages of basic foods and goods, was well-stocked with Zambian and Congolese beer and served various types of food as well—where she worked as a waitress. She guided us to Kashiba, where Mr. Ng'andwe greeted us and said he'd arrange for some storytellers to work with me when I returned later in the academic year. We did not

---

152 There is a lot of scholarship on Lunda history, and even broader scholarship on the larger group that migrated into Zambia with the Lunda, the Bemba people. Among the best sources of Lunda history, with an extensive bibliography, is Cunnison's work, as listed below. His best-known and most detailed monograph is *The Luapula Peoples of Northern Rhodesia* (1959). Several well-known studies on Bemba culture and history provide details of their earlier migration and political structure. Most convenient, as far as having an extensive bibliography and developing a detailed history from oral and written sources, is A. Roberts 1973. There is, of course, more recent scholarship on these people and areas, notably Gordon 2006, but the earlier works provide a thorough grounding in culture, history and politics from the time of the migrations into Zambia.

153 On this trip, for example, I recorded the narratives from Mr. Chipioka Patrick that I discuss in the Tabwa chapter of this study.

stay long, as it was clouding up and we needed to drive at least another hour to reach Mansa before dark.

Kashiba/Mkomba

On the last day of May, 1989, my family and I drove from Mansa to Kashiba and again located Mr. Ng'andwe's sister at Mofwe Investments. She agreed to help us set up in the village after lunch. We drove, with Mofwe's manager, Mr. Chola, further north to the town of Mwense, which was the district capital and had a government rest house, where we checked in. We drove back to Kashiba and, guided by Ms. Chishimba, we located Mr. Moffat Mulenga in Mkomba, a section of the larger Kashiba village, who was known for his storytelling; in particular his tales about Kalulu the trickster hare. Explanations were proffered, noting that I was a lecturer at the University of Zambia, working with Samuel Ng'andwe, and I wanted to collect narratives to preserve them at the University's library for future generations to appreciate. Mr. Mulenga, a soft-spoken, rather shy man, wanted to fix some sort of compensation, so I arbitrarily offered to pay twenty kwacha (at that time, a bit less than four dollars) for three stories. He agreed to the deal and we moved to the front of a nearby home, whose owner brought out two wooden chairs for Mr. Mulenga and me. After a few minutes setting up the tripod and camera, we began the session. I'd estimate there were around twenty-five people in the audience. Most of them were children, seated or standing around Mr. Mulenga, with a few adolescents standing near him within the camera frame, and a few adults as well. Moffat Mulenga was probably in his mid fifties, and was nearly six feet tall and very slim. He wore a gray v-neck sweater, that seemed a few sizes too large, since the sleeves reached down to the knuckles of his hands, with a white shirt whose collar was folded out over the sweater's neck, and a pair of tan trousers that were rolled midway up his calves, with holes worn at both knees. It's clear that these were clothes he wore when working at some task, perhaps cultivating his garden or fishing.[154]

---

[154] On a return visit to Mkomba, I learned a bit more about Moffat Mulenga. He was born in 1930, which meant he was just over fifty-eight years old when I taped his performance in 1989. He'd lived his whole life in the area, farming and fishing, as many men did. More commonly known as Bashi Mwenya ("Father of Mwenya") he had eight children and, by the time of my visit in 2005, many grandchildren. He passed away in 1993 at age sixty-three.

Lunda Storytelling 1 and 2 by Moffat Mulenga*

Moffat
Mulenga: So then Kalulu went to Mr. Elephant to say, "Grandfather, could we engage in a tug-of-war?" The elephant said, "Ala? You're just a youngster right there you've claimed, it's me you'll pull?" He said, "Yes, it's I who could pull you." "You?" He said, "Yes." He said, "Fine." He went and slept, that Kalulu, and that elephant, he went and slept. In the morning, Kalulu set out in the morning to go to his uncle there. "How are you my uncle, Mr. Elephant?" He said, "You've come?" He said, "Yes." Little Kalulu had a large rope and he tied it around his (Elephant's) neck. He said, "Now, thus I'll go here, I'll go and I'll pull you. When you feel me tug you like this then begin pulling." He said, "Oh." He went far unfurling the rope; he went far unfurling the rope, going and arriving at the dambo (flood plain).

He found Mr. Hippopotamus. [Hippos live near water, so the dambo was a natural place to find one.] That Mr. Hippopotamus said, "Uncle, why have you come down to the dambo?" He said, "Yes, *mukwai*. I want to pull against you." "Oh, pull against you, can you pull me out of my place?" He said, "Yes, I can pull you, you'd come here to the bush." He said, "Fine, no problem." Ah, he tied him with the rope as he'd tied the elephant. So there he said, "Uncle, here I'm going to the rise, when I tug you then we can begin to pull." He said, "Ooh, that's fine."

So little Kalulu set out, he went, he went. So then he arrived at the middle of the rope and grasped and shook it there, at the one at the dambo, and he began to shake it towards that one who was in the bush. So there! So he jumped down, he went and sat there. So when the elephant returned the pressure, his friend pulled from the dambo over there. He said, "And what is it that pulls me towards that dambo? This Kalulu is the one who's pulling me towards the dambo?" So over there, this was the one who started all this. And that elephant, hmmn, they went on for a long time. Now they were tired. "Ala! So Kalulu's the one we've been pulling against? That very one who's so small? That's where we're pulling...it's that [one] that has me panting? Fine, we'll see." They shook their heads.

Again, he (Kalulu) went and shook it. Again he laughed. Now what to do, to run away, what did he do? He ran away. Over there the elephant came, he followed the rope, he said, [he] wanted to know if it was Kalulu pulling against him. And that hippopotamus there, he too came following the rope, to come and see if it's Kalulu pulling against him. Then over

---

* To watch a video of this story follow this link: http://dx.doi.org/10.11647/OBP.0033.05/Lunda1

there, when they came and met this way, he said, "Ala! So it's you I've been pulling against?" He said, "Yes." "And where's Kalulu?" He said, "No *mukwai*, that one's not here. We didn't know it was that one, who did this thing to us?" He said, "Yes." "Aah." That one's done. [Referring to the narrative itself.][155]

******

I'm starting this *mulumbe*. It's that again, Kalulu himself built a very large house. So when he built the house, he said, "All the animals in the bush come to my place for a party." So th...the animals agreed. They agreed. So then some of them laughed hard, "Yes, yes, Kalulu, at your house?" He said, "Yes." The animals were very merry. Now then "What ni...ni... night shall we come?" He said, "No, tomorrow so that I'll go arrange things. All the animals who are in the bush come here." He had built a very large house. "Fine, tomorrow?" He said, "Tomorrow come to the house." So just all the animals, their wives prepared pots of beer. [He addressed the following question to me: "Do you understand? Speak up *mukwai*." I didn't catch this, so I did not answer his question.]

So what happened there? When all those animals gathered there, they went to...they...they...they all sat there filling the house to capacity. Then he told them, "Friends, there's no place to pee, there's no place to shit. If I catch you (doing this) you'll die?" He said, "Yes *mukwai*, grandfather, we understand." "Yes *mukwai*, grandfather we understand." So now, the animals in the house went to sleep. So now they slept, they slept, they slept, they slept. So now ten o'clock at night arrived, now he began to smear fermented millet [basis for millet beer, *katubi*, which looks like faeces] on the anus, on the anus, smearing the fermented millet on the anus, on the anus. So now there, when one woke up he said...because he soiled himself, "Oh my!" He said, "Oh my, I've shit." He said, "Oh my, we will die, oh my, we'll die." He said, "Have you shit, grandfather?" He said, "I've shit, truly." Just like that, he who woke up said, "Oh my, and me too I've shit." One over there said, "And me too!" He said, "Ala!" He said, "And what about you, the great elephant?" He said, "Ala! I've shit, I'm no longer great." So they just sat there speechless. So now over there, no *mukwai*, this had affected every one, just like that. It was the same thing, then, when the morning came. Little Kalulu said, "Let me go and see people [that] are in the house." All of them ran away, now finding just some, these are the ones he beat hard. All who remained ran away. Now this *mulumbe* is...is finished.

Robert
Cancel: That's good...

---

155 This is a common Kalulu tale and is widely spread in other parts of Africa. Owomoyela summarizes the same tale with the Turtle as trickster for the Yoruba people and other West African groups (2004, p. 476). See also La Pin 1980, p. 336. A version of the tale is discussed in the previous chapter, as told by a Bisa storyteller, Mr. Paul Chandalube.

When Mr. Mulenga began his performance, it was apparent that he was a bit nervous. His hands were pressed together between his thighs, and he spoke softly and slowly. However, in a very short time, he became more animated. In fact, he proved to be a skilled performer, using his voice, gestures and acting skills to flesh out the narrative. He focused on the size and strength of the adversaries, providing their respective verbal responses to first Kalulu's challenge then their surprise at the difficulty of the contest. As the tug-of-war went on, Mr. Mulenga's pace and rhythm of speech and gestures became more rapid, using both miming of physical actions and stylized gestures—such as tamping down his palm over the fist of his other hand to indicate the initial setting of the contest and securing the ropes around each participant—to bring the narrative to life. The audience seemed engaged with the story, with a few children chuckling at some of the images. But the performance was also rather brief, quickly moving to resolution and ending with Mr. Mulenga saying "That one's done."

With barely a pause, he moved on to the second narrative, saying "Now I'll begin another *mulumbe*." This performance revealed more of Moffat Mulenga's skills as a storyteller. The scatological elements of the tale were inherently funny for his mostly young audience. Many of the children delighted in the imagery of Kalulu spreading fermented grain (*fipote*) on the animals' anuses. Further, Mr. Mulenga took maximum advantage of portraying the various humiliated and despairing animals as they awoke to the signs of their apparent transgression. He acted out their reactions by holding his left hand to his buttock, as if trying to stem the flow of something that had already happened, and holding his right hand to the right side of his head and face, as if lamenting what had occurred and fearing what was to come. "*Mawe!* ("Oh my!") I've shit!"…"*Mawe*, we will die, oh my, we'll die." As another animal woke to find he too had violated the warning, Mr. Mulenga grabbed his right buttock with his right hand, again suggesting astonishment and a building panic. Not only the children, but several adults and adolescents began to chuckle at the developing scene. After several depictions of animals discovering their humiliation, Mulenga closed the story, almost anti-climactically, by describing how most of the animals ran away when Kalulu returned and took revenge on the remaining partygoers.

At this point, I asked Mr. Mulenga to wait a bit. Mostly, I was trying to keep him from simply appending another quick story to the two he'd already told. I was then able to playback the audio of the tales and have everyone, especially Moffat Mulenga, hear what he sounded like. This technique had in the past proven effective in having performers evaluate their earlier efforts and gear up for future recording sessions. While I can't really guess what Mr. Mulenga's reactions were, he did begin to tell a longer, more nuanced story. This third Kalulu tale focused on how Kalulu tricks all the animals into killing their mothers.

Lunda Storytelling 3 by Moffat Mulenga*

Moffat Mulenga: There was a person, just like this. It was Kalulu himself. Kalulu over there gathered together all the animals. He said, "Friends, let us kill our mothers." "Ala! Kill our mothers?" He said, "Yes, and I myself will kill my mother." No, all the animals laughed, "Yes, let's kill our mothers. Let's kill our mothers. And you, Mr. Kalulu, you'll kill (her)?" He said, "Again, I'll kill my mother. As for me, I'll kill my mother." So all those animals began to kill their mothers, began bringing the blood to Kalulu, because he'd been lying, saying, "I've killed my mother." So then he who killed brought blood to Kalulu. He who killed brought blood to Kalulu. Just like that.

But one (Kalulu) played a trick; he took his mother and put her in a cave and closed it up. So all his friends finished killing their mothers. So now that one went out. So that one said, "As for me, friends, I'm going to kill my mother, If there's not... I will come show you the blood, that's what I will come to show you." He said, "Oh, fine." He went and spun around. "You stone, what is it? You stone, what is it?" He knocked at his mother's place. That Kalulu closed it up. He went to the *mulombwa*, the large *mulombwa* tree. He picked its sap, he picked, he picked. Then he smeared himself with that same blood—because it was like blood—then he went to his friends who'd killed their mothers. So, he cried falsely, "Mother, I've killed my mother, no it's very sad." Now seeing that, his friends said, "Really, he's already killed his mother, yes. He's covered in blood and rolling in the dust [an act of mourning], he's covered and rolling in the dust. So it's a bad thing to kill our mothers, how will we eat?"

So now he... he'd do this, when he went, he went and opened the stone. His mother made him *ubwali*, he ate, he closed it up. He'd go again to the *mulombwa* tree and smear himself [with the red sap], smear himself to return to his friends. They knew him, he said, "He went to mourn this mother he killed." Then he'd go to eat at his healthy mother's (place).

* To watch a video of this story follow this link: http://dx.doi.org/10.11647/OBP.0033.05/Lunda3

So then one day, he did the same as usual, he was going. Now the tortoise followed him, he said, "Ala! Did he really kill his mother?" He went and she just cooked *ubwali* for him, she just cooked for him. So when Kalulu arrived here, tortoise also arrived. "Ala! Friend!" So now he stretched out his hands (beseeching him), "My friend, ala! I did not kill my mother. Don't go reveal the lie to those over there. I'll just die, I'll die. If you just go say, 'No, that one, so it's a lie he's told us, his mother is right there!' I'll just die, they'll just kill me.'" He said, "No, grandfather, again it's me who saw you." So, "You will eat, you'll be full. Let me open up my mother's (hiding place)." So, "Mother, mother, mother." So, he got the large rock, he opened up. So *mukwai*, (there was) a portion of *ubwali* and chicken. They just prepared a large chicken leg, they gave it to him. So with what was left, they began to eat. They ate, they ate, they ate. So they ate that leg, tortoise put it in his shell. He hid it. Then he said he finished. So, he hid it.

So now there, he [Kalulu] went there, he went and rolled and smeared himself, he rolled and smeared himself completely. So they went like that. So that tortoise, he went. So there Kalulu stayed and smeared himself in the same way he'd done. So he [the tortoise] went to pay his respects to Mr. Elephant. "Hmmm. So, that one just lied to us, he didn't kill his mother." He said, "Ala! That was no lie, you are lying." He said, "This is what's left of the chicken we ate." He said, "You, what a surprise. So how do you know so much?" So now they slept. Early in the morning they went with the elephant. They sharpened sticks, sharpening, sharpening. No, they just arrived, she said — again she didn't recognize them — she said, "My child has come." "Mother open up, mother open up." They came and got the door, one said, "Let me open up." They came and drove the sticks in here (at the base of her skull), po, po, po. No, they squeezed in. No, she died right there. They got the rock, they closed up, then they went.

So Kalulu who carried... hadn't been there to his mother's that day. In the morning he went there to find her. "Mother open this up. Mother open this up. Mother open up. Aah!? Where's my mother? Can you come open up? Yaa! Mother, they've killed you. Tortoise, it's the tortoise that caused this. Yangu! Father! Poor me, what'll I do? Mother, poor me, ee! It's tortoise. What can I do? There's no recourse here. So now, I can just wander aimlessly. What my friends did was not good. So I didn't kill my mother." So then his friend was the one who lied. So now Kalulu went wandering aimlessly. And the *mulumbe* is finished.

This last narrative was literally twice as long as either of the earlier two. In part, this was due to the way he developed the repeated actions of Kalulu going to visit his mother in the cave. The first visit was fairly detailed, and the second condensed the description, while the third included the appearance of the Tortoise. Mr. Mulenga, as in the first tales but not so frantically, detailed Kalulu's several dramatic efforts, as he falsely lamented his mother's death, smeared himself with fake blood and recounted an action he never performed. This degree of duplicity, so common in the trickster's repertoire, has a kind of inborn power to elicit laughter from an audience. Coupled with Mr. Mulenga's histrionics and the inherent scatological humor of the imagery, the events make for satisfying entertainment. But the tale also differed from the earlier ones because it portrayed one of the instances where Kalulu's cleverness is bested by the even more inventive Tortoise. Though Kalulu tries to make a pact with the Tortoise, like hare himself is prone to do, the Tortoise proceeds to immediately break the agreement. As if allowing for a form of revenge built up over the previous two stories, Mr. Mulenga's narrative portrays the other animals tricking and killing Kalulu's mother. At the end of this tale, Kalulu is forced to flee and wander aimlessly [ciyeyeye] in some world away from the animals he'd deceived.

While the performance mostly elicited laughter when depicting Kalulu's feigned over-wrought lamentations, the second half of the story where Kalulu is bested brings the other narratives full-circle and adds another dimension of meaning and breadth to the range of tales featuring the trickster hare. Moreover, the narrative's plot intersects with another cluster of stories that feature the killing of the elders in a village or society. These usually have to do with the importance of elders when it comes to preserving and applying wisdom in the society and how the arrogance of youth or power can take that source of knowledge for granted.[156]

Before further discussion of the three Kalulu stories Mr. Mulenga performed, I will first describe the efforts of the second performer, Mr. Idon Pandwe, who owned the house in front of which the session took place. Mr. Pandwe took some interest in Mr. Mulenga's performance and, moreover, he'd been perusing sections of my soft-bound doctoral dissertation that I often brandished by way of introduction to potential storytellers. Mr. Pandwe spoke

---

156 See Cancel 1989, pp. 43–45 for an example of this kind of story told among the Tabwa as well as references to versions/variants in other neighboring traditions. The narrative themes focusing on the importance of elders and the challenges that come from precocious adolescents are discussed above in the chapters on Tabwa and Bemba performances.

English very well, to the point of introducing his performance in English, as I answered in Bemba:

Lunda Storytelling 4 by Idon Pandwe*

Idon
Pandwe: **I've got three stories.**

Robert
Cancel: Uhhmm. Begin.

IP: **Can I speak all at once?**

RC: If you'd like.

IP: **O.K.**

People lived in a very large country. In one village was a chief who ruled the village. And that chief brought a proclamation, saying, "I don't want old people in my country, only young men and young women, alone, because elders go bald and have white hair and they don't dress well and are dirty. So I only want young men and young women who will have elegance in my village." So all the people killed their parents. Now there was one person, that one didn't kill his parent. He went and hid him in the bush in an ant hill, that's where he hid him. So, whenever he went for a walk, he brought *ubwali* and water to wash and drink, and all the things (he needed).

As the days go by, that chief had a small *nsaka* where he sat and ate his food. So then, one day that chief was in the *nsaka*. In the rear was a large snake. **A big snake**, a very large snake, entered. So it came and wound itself around the chief's neck. It wound, it wound, around and round [English borrowing, "**roundi, roundi**"], it wound and wound. It came and wound its neck and head around the chief's head. That chief (cried out), "I'm dying, ee! I'm dying, ee!" And what did people do when they came? No *mukwai*, the snake was just flicking its little tongue. Not even one person could come near, no. All of them were afraid.

Now that person who hid his father in the bush, then he ran quickly to the bush, to go and speak to his father, he said, "We here are in trouble." "What is it?" He said, "A snake's wrapped itself around the chief's neck, now we don't know what to do." So his father answered, "Let the chief die, he has no wisdom. The elders know what to do. So, now you go and catch a small rat. Tie it up with bark rope, the little rat. When you go and arrive near where the chief is, that's when the

---

* To hear a recording of this story follow this link: http://dx.doi.org/10.11647/OBP.0033.05/Lunda4

rat will jump around, and the snake will go and unwind itself from the chief's neck." And truly, that young man carried a small rat, he tied it with bark rope, and arrived there. He placed it near where the chief lay. The large snake looked [at it]. It looked. It said, "What's that little thing jumping around? What'll I do? Let me catch it." When it said it would catch it, it unwound a bit [from the chief's neck]. It said, "Let me grab it." Again, it began, the snake unwound a bit. "Let me grab it." Again, it began, the snake unwound a bit. Finally that snake, it unwound itself, so that they killed it.

Now the chief asked him, "What of this wisdom, where did it come from?" He said, "No, I will not tell you the source, I just thought of it myself." He refused [to believe him], he said, "No, I just don't know where you got this wisdom, just speak up, just speak up." So that young man spoke, he said, "I, this wisdom, I hid my father in the bush, and it's he who told me this wisdom." He said, "So go and bring him to me." So when that young man went and got his father, the chief gave him the country, and told him, "As from today I will not revile elders in my village." So, it's this that was said now, "Where there are elders, they will provide a shield so that nobody is burned. Where there are elders, there are fewer cases of misconduct." The *mulumbe* is finished.

Mr. Pandwe was probably in his early fifties and well dressed; collared white shirt with a pen clipped to his pocket, clean and pressed tan trousers with a new-looking black leather belt, and polished black shoes.[157] When he began his performance he did something that was quite unusual, at least in my experience of sitting in an audience during story-performances. He held my bound dissertation on his lap with both hands and proceeded to hold on to the volume for all three of his narratives. From a stylistic point of view, he was curtailing virtually all the hand and arm gestures that comprise the repertoire of most performers. This meant that he'd convey the stories mostly with vocal skills and some rather subtle movements of his head, shoulders and upper body.

---

157 Again, during my 2005 visit to Mkomba, I met some of Idon Pandwe's relatives and found out that he'd died in 2004, at the age of sixty-seven. His style of dress and use of English suggested that he was a bit wealthier and perhaps better educated than his neighbor. In fact, he'd spent a good deal of his life working as a heavy machinery operator on Zambia's Copperbelt. He came to live in the village after retiring and did a bit of farming and a good deal of fishing. He had a much smaller family than did Moffat Mulenga, and they seemed materially better off than Mr. Mulenga's.

I mistakenly left the lens cap on the video camera for Mr. Pandwe's first narrative, so it's hard to discuss any but his vocal performance techniques. The narrative obviously echoes the preceding one, where Kalulu convinced all the other animals to kill their mothers. In this tale, a chief orders all elders to be killed because "I don't want old people in my country, only young men and young women, alone, because elders go bald and what's left is white hair and they don't dress well and are dirty." Given the unexpected opportunity to have only a verbal record of this narrative-performance, a few qualities of Mr. Pandwe's verbal technique were even more apparent. First, as already mentioned, he tried to establish an English language conduit between him and me as the collector of the narratives. He began the session by asking me questions in English. Then in the telling of the story itself, he qualified the Bemba word for a large snake, *icisoka*, "Big snake." At around the same point in the tale, he described how the snake wound itself around the chief's neck by combining Bemba and English verbs, "...*capomba, capomba*, **roundi, roundi**," "...it wound round, it wound round, **round, round**..." Second, Mr. Pandwe enunciated the language of his narratives very clearly and at a moderate, rather than slow or fast, pace. This made the story very easy to follow, particularly for me, and elucidated the various details and nuances quite clearly.

His second performance actually relates a narrative that is examined earlier in this study.[158]

Lunda Storytelling 5 by Idon Pandwe*

Idon
Pandwe: There was a little thing, all the animals lived in the bush, they lived in a very large area. Now, Lion also lived in a hut with his wife and children. Now one day Kalulu carried bark to bring to the lion so that he could make bark cloth for him. When he arrived there he found the lion and his wife had gone to the bush. He found only the children were there, that's all. Now Kalulu asked the lion's child, "And where did your father and mother go to?" The children answered, "They've gone to the bush to do a little work." That lio...Kalulu said, "You come and tell your father that this bark I've brought, he must make me a bark cloth garment, because your father is my nephew. I'm his uncle. If he doesn't make the bark cloth he will be like the

---

158 See the two versions of this tale performed by Mr. Stanley Kalumba in the Tabwa area and discussed in Chapter III. It is worthwhile noting how each performer externalizes and shapes the familiar images of the tale.

* To watch a video of this story follow this link: http://dx.doi.org/10.11647/OBP.0033.05/Lunda5

bushbuck with a year to live. And he won't be living here." Kalulu returned. The lions returned from the farm, and the cubs came to report the situation, "Father, your uncle came here but we didn't know him. He's even the one who left this bark and said, 'He must make bark cloth. If he refuses to make it, he won't be living here. He'll be like the bushbuck with a year to live.'"

Now the lion thought, "As for me, here in the bush, it's I alone who am the most powerful, there's no one greater than me. Now who is this uncle? Fine, let me go make the cloth, I'll see my uncle because when he comes to get the cloth, that's when I'll come see him." And in fact that lion pounded that bark cloth, and he sewed it, he put it down by a tree. Then one day Kalulu again came. He came and found the lions were not there, they'd gone to the bush. So he saw the bark cloth garment was on top of a large tree. He asked the children, "You children, and today your father is not here?" He said, "No he's not here." He said, "When he comes you tell him truly, I found the cloth he sewed, he pounded and sewed it. Now I thank him very much. When he comes tell him that his uncle has taken it. So I'll take it, I'm going, thanks very much." When the lions returned from the bush, they came to find the bark cloth was not there. He asked the children, "What about the cloth?" He said, "It was your uncle, he came and got it." "My uncle?" He said, "Yes." "Now this same uncle, how will I know him? So let me make a proclamation, I'll gather together all the animals. If I gather all the animals, that…that animal that comes wearing the bark cloth that I made, that's how I'll know him, he says, he's my uncle."

So Kalulu [Lion] made a proclamation, "Every one gather, all the animals come gather, all animals, so that not one remains." So *mukwai*, that little Kalulu said (to himself), "You, we've been summoned to the palace, that's the place they call us to." He took that bark cloth and wore it. "You know at that time the cloth was seen as a **suit** [English borrowing], if you're wearing it, you're even showing off." So *mukwai*, Kalulu went, Kalulu went, he found the bushbuck. The bushbuck wore rags. Then he questioned him, he said, "You bushbuck, where are you going?" He said, "Over here, they've called us to the lion's palace, that's where I'm going." He said, "But how can you go with rags like this? So since you are my elder, I'll give you the barkcloth. And since I'm your junior, I'll wear the rags. Let's go change." So they switched and switched. Kalulu took the bark cloth, he gave it to Bushbuck. Bushbuck took the rags, he gave them to Kalulu.

When they arrived at the palace there, no *mukwai*, all the kinds of animals were gathered. Now the lion, as he looked at all those animals, he saw his bark cloth was on the bushbuck, that's where it was. He said, "Ala! So Bushbuck is my uncle? This very one who's a useless person. Today he will see." So then that lion began (to explain) the case, "That's why I called you, my people. I received bark here, and I didn't know the one who brought it, he said he was my uncle. So I pounded the bark cloth and sewed it together. And when he came to take it I wasn't around. That's why I gathered you together, so that I could know my uncle. So my uncle is the bushbuck. He's the one who's wearing my bark cloth garment. So, you bushbuck, you're my uncle? Grab him, we'll kill him." No, so they…little Kalulu himself leaped up and choked him round his neck. When he spoke, saying, "No *mukwai*, it's Kalulu!" He said, "Shut up, a slave dies with words in his mouth." No, that bushbuck, he was killed. This is a situation with many people, they do something then blame their friend, their friend is the one who dies. The *mulumbe* is finished.

Again, what stands out in Mr. Pandwe's performance style is his almost total reliance on verbal dramatic techniques. He enjoys speaking in a high pitched voice as he provides dialogue for various characters. His steady delivery of narration often punctuates the end of sentences or scenes by raising the intonation level of his voice. This pattern is one of several rhythmic elements that provide a vibrant verbal structure to the narrative. He noticeably quickens the pace of his narration when Bushbuck is grabbed and beaten by the animals. Several children laugh at this image of Bushbuck's desperate attempts to be heard and Kalulu's speedy retort, using the proverb about slaves dying with words in their mouths. He even laughs a bit himself, considering the absurdity of the situation. While Mr. Pandwe does not consistently elicit the easy laughter, or expectation of laughter, that Mr. Mulenga established, his storytelling is solid in its exposition, clear in its various plot developments, and effective in drawing audience involvement. Mr. Pandwe includes two of the proverbs found in Stanley Kalumba's Tabwa versions of the story, the warning about the bushbuck with a year to live and the truism of a slave dying with words in his mouth. The sayings seem linked to the preserved and transmitted images of the narrative. However, he also adds an explanatory note at the end, observing how people often blame their friends for things they themselves have done. This extends the connotations of the tales told by Mr. Kalumba in a different though obviously related way. There is a quotidian concern in Idon Pandwe's explanation, about people blaming others for their own misdeeds, while Stanley Kalumba evokes a broader message about the potentially subversive power of cleverness and loquaciousness.

Lunda Storytelling 6 by Idon Pandwe*

Idon Pandwe: **Another?**

Robert Cancel: If you'd like.

IP: Hhmm?

* To watch a video of this story follow this link: http://dx.doi.org/10.11647/OBP.0033.05/Lunda6

RC: Yes.

IP: There remains one more *mulumbe*, it's the same Kalulu himself. Kalulu set out to marry. When he arrived there to marry, he got married. He lived with his wife. So the rainy season arrived. He went and requested a plot from his in-laws. That plot he asked for, his mother-in-law showed it to him; she showed him a very large plot. Then that little Kalulu, *mukwai*, he got a hoe. He hoed, hoed, hoed, hoed, hoed, hoed, hoed, hoed, hoed, hoed. He finished a very large garden. He planted a large crop: groundnuts [peanuts], ground peas, maize, cassava and all the things that remained (to be grown).

Mukwai, those things, the month these things ripened, Kalulu's mother-in-law and father-in-law began to harvest the groundnuts. As you know, those groundnuts when they're digging them up, that's when they eat them. When she harvested the groundnuts Kalulu's, mother-in-law, she did not cook them, saying she'd take them to the in-laws, not to the one who worked the garden. Only they would eat them. Now that Kalulu looked in expectation that the groundnuts will come, no, the groundnuts will [not] come, no. "So what will I do? Those groundnuts I grew, my mother-in-law is just eating without giving me some! No, really I'll formulate a plan of ensuring that I eat groundnuts also." So as days went by, Little Kalulu went to the bushbuck. He went there and said, "Friend, listen to me, my in-laws are refusing me the groundnuts I grew. Now, I want to make believe I'm sick. When I feign illness then you're the one who'll come diagnose me. When you come to diagnose me you also know the way things are." He said, "No, I understand my friend. I've got it, my colleague. I'll come to diagnose you. You just go and feign illness."

So little Kalulu returned. He began the next evening to pretend to be sick. "I'm dying, ee, I'm dying, ee, I'm dying, ee!" His wife started a fire. He began warming himself, he covered himself with a blanket, all pretense. He warmed himself and groaned heavily. "What is it?" So his wife went to her mother and said, "Ala! My husband is ill and hasn't slept today." "What is it?" No, the mother-in-law came, which is when Kalulu acted even sicker, feigning illness almost to the point of dying. That's when that father-in-law began to speak, "No, my in-law has just been bewitched by someone in the village. There have been so many years and..." Then that little Kalulu said, "You, my wife, go to my friend Bushbuck, so that he comes and finds medicine. I'm going to die." Very early, that little Kalulu...Kalulu's wife went to Bushbuck's over there, she arrived, she said, "Ala! Your friend there, Mr. Bushbuck, Mr. Kalulu is very ill. I've come to get you." "He's sick?" She said, "Yes." "So, that's what I noticed, these days he didn't visit me. So he's sick? I'll be right there, I'll come to find him medicine."

No, little...little Bushbuck went and dug some medicine/herbs, he carried them, he took them to Kalulu. When he gathered together the mother-in-law and father-in-law and everyone, and gave them medicine, he said, "This medicine, you grind the remains of an animal, when you grind these remains then add [them] to the groundnuts as you roast them. When you [put] these remains in the groundnuts, then you give them to Kalulu he'll begin to eat. So the special ingredient is groundnuts." So, this was the plan little Kalulu devised just so that he could eat his in-law's groundnuts. So now his mother-in-law went and got those groundnuts. She roasted them with the remains of an animal, she put [them] in with them. She mixed them and roasted them with salt and what have you. So she gave them to little Kalulu, he began to eat. Then he said to himself, "Are not these things I'm eating those they had denied me?" So, he ate slowly, slowly. Tomorrow at sunrise, "How did you awaken today, father?" He said, "No, *mukwai*, today, today I'm awakening feeling better. However, when roasting groundnuts today, put in more groundnuts. Ensure that there are more groundnuts." So, the mother-in-law opened the granary for more groundnuts, saying, "No, that's good father, he's getting better, so groundnuts are the medicine." She took out groundnuts, she roasted them, she roasted them. She took them to him, he ate, he ate, he ate, he ate. Tomorrow, like this, very early, he began to feel good, he said, "No *mukwai*, now I'll be fine as long as today they roast a dish full of groundnuts…" Then she went and got all the groundnuts from the granary. She roasted them, she roasted the dish to the brim. Little Kalulu ate, he ate, he ate, he ate. So he got better, that little Kalulu got better. So, that's how Little Kalulu ate his in-law's groundnuts. **This is the end of the stories.**

Mr. Pandwe ended the narrative as he began it, using English to affirm that "This is the end of the stories." In terms of performance style and overall framing of the story and his own persona, Mr. Pandwe was quite different from Moffat Mulenga. However there are other elements that link his efforts to those of Mr. Mulenga. Looking at this narrative in the context of the five that have come before it, there is an interesting reiteration of Kalulu's cleverness, but in this tale Bushbuck is his ally, not his dupe. Here, too, Kalulu is shown overcoming a built-in potential inequity of custom, the duties of labor a newly-wed owes his in-laws. The theme is a serious one that is handled with humor and hyperbole in the framework of a trickster tale. Five of the first six tales told at this session featured Kalulu as the main character. In all of them he exhibited degrees of cleverness and resourcefulness that characterize the trickster throughout Africa. Moreover, there is a range of thematic dimensions that emerges in the context of the five tales. In Mr. Mulenga's three stories, Kalulu seems to simply want to antagonize and humiliate other animals, as he tricks Elephant into a tug-of-war with Hippo, fools animals into believing they've defecated in his new home, and convinces the animals to kill their mothers. Similarly, Mr. Pandwe's rendition of the hare includes Kalulu tricking Lion into making him a bark cloth garment and then gets the bushbuck unjustly killed. Both Mulenga and Pandwe also produce narratives where Kalulu has the tables turned on him, first by Tortoise who discovers the secret of Kalulu hiding his mother and contrives to have her killed, and, at least temporarily, by his in-laws who demand he follow the tenets of newly-weds in the matrilineal system. This web of narratives is also entwined with the only non-trickster story, where unadulterated wisdom, rather than self-serving guile, is celebrated in the person of the elder. In this latter tale, part of the basic plot of Mr. Mulenga's third Kalulu story is recycled, featuring only humans and pointing at the potential abuses of chiefly power and the counter force of elders' wisdom. In contrast to Mr. Mulenga's performances, Mr. Pandwe ended two of his stories with the didactic explanations that often characterize the *mulumbe* genre.

Further, based on how they were dressed and how they handled their performances, at least subtle differences in class were evident between Moffat Mulenga and Idon Pandwe. Mr. Pandwe had been thumbing through a copy of my dissertation, suggesting his level of literacy, then held the volume in both hands like some sort of literary talisman while he told his stories, thereby, atypically, privileging voice over physical gesture in the performance of the tales. It may well have been that his understanding of what the session meant was very different from Mr. Mulenga's. Certainly, Mr. Pandwe's slower paced narration, attention to detail, and explanatory conclusions suggest that he was making sure I was clear on the meanings of his tales. He was most likely aware that the narratives were being recorded for posterity, and less concerned with the monetary transaction.[159]

---

159 I've made this a recurring assertion in this project. It speaks to the notion of performers seeing beyond an immediate situation to something broader, perhaps more oriented towards the preservation of the event and the individual for future appreciation. A telling incident took place in 2005 when I stayed a night at a guest house in the Luapula town of Kashikishi. It was my second time there, following up on my 2003 trip, and the first time I'd met the owner of the place, as I sat outside on a chair drinking a beer at around 7 PM. He was originally from the Democratic Republic of the Congo, and had come to Zambia with enough money to start some businesses and build and run this rather pleasant place. His English was not overly good, so we spoke in a combination of Bemba and French. My notebook details part of this encounter: "He was fixated on my book;

When Mr. Pandwe finished his performance, the audience had grown to probably fifty people. After I played back the last narrative, we all sat around looking at each other, with a few people trying to goad others onto the wooden chair to take a turn at performance. Finally, a woman, perhaps in her mid forties, named Luva Kombe took a seat in order to tell a story. Ms. Kombe was of average height and slim build. She had close-cropped hair and, somewhat unusual in women her age, did not wear a headscarf. Her violet dress only showed from the waist up, since she also wore a long, patterned *citenge* wrapped around her lower body and knotted above her hips. Unfortunately, somehow the video camera malfunctioned—or, more likely, I malfunctioned—and it was not turned on for the first minute or so of Ms. Kombe's performance. However, the tale was a good one and I choose to discuss it here even in its slightly truncated form.

The first words caught on video are describing the interaction of an older co-wife and her aggressive younger co-wife. At this point, Ms. Kombe is laughing uncomfortably, somewhat nervous about being videotaped. As she expresses her nervousness, she is admonished by women in the audience not to laugh and to tell the story properly. She quickly recovers and continues.

Lunda Storytelling 7 by Luva Kombe*

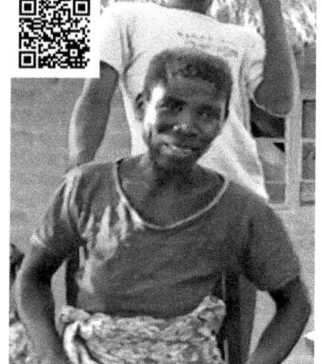

[Beginning of the story, a minute or two, is lost]

…now there…there they slighted that elder (wife), there she went to whom?…to the junior wife.

Audience:	Don't laugh. [Addressed to people noting Ms. Kombe's initial discomfort]
Luva Kombe:	That's where they went, right there to the junior wife. That's where they lived. That's where they lived. That's where they lived. That's

---

skimming parts and asking a lot of questions. Finally he wanted to know how he could get into the new book. He said he's read a lot of books but never met anyone who'd actually written one. He says he's going to write down a really good *mulumbe* to send me. He wanted to know if I wanted stories of animals or humans and I said either was fine." I never received anything from him and, ironically, had he given me his name I'd have been able to provide at least a little of the notoriety he was seeking.

* To watch a video of this story follow this link: http://dx.doi.org/10.11647/OBP.0033.05/Lunda7

where they lived. Now the elder said, "Why do they despise me? Let me go ask my husband." He said, "Go back where you came, I just despise you, that's all." She went to her friend [co-wife], and she ridiculed her, she just ridiculed her. She said, "You, ala! I have taken your husband." She said, "No, no problem, let me just go live [alone], like that." She just lived alone, that elder wife, she just lived. That elder wife died. Now when she died, they buried her. Now when they buried her, it ended there. He [her husband] went to her family, they said, "No, we will give you a replacement wife, it is not difficult." So they performed the rite, they gave him a substitute wife. He even stuck to the new wife. Now that wife he stuck to...Ala! [Pauses as if she's forgotten something in the story, some audience members giggle.] Lale! No, I've forgotten— that new wife, they stuck to, now even to live, they lived there.[160] That one had even died. So then, over there he even forgot that one he'd been given as a substitute wife, he left her. Now he did [this], he the husband said, he's the one who said, "What about that garden you haven't been weeding?" She said, "Ala! No, I'll weed it sometime." He said, "No, go and weed it, it's a very large garden. Don't neglect it."

Now that companion, the one who remained, when she went off to the bush, she went and looked at the garden, all weeds, her desire was lacking [for that task]. She just went to the graveyard to go and fight with the one who was despised. That's where she went to pick a fight. She found her, "Tuu! Come out, let's fight! Come out, let's fight." And that companion said, "Friend, I left your husband. Why do you come following me to fight with me here at the grave?" She said, "No, my husband still keeps coming here to your grave." Now she said, "Ala! No, he's your husband entirely, they even gave him a substitute. Now why do you keep coming here to fight with me at my grave?" She said, "No, my husband's coming here." Now there, that's it. She summoned these companions in the graveyard. Then, they all just rose, *tupu*! They said, "You, you left her husband long ago, so why does she keep following you here? Let's team up and teach her a lesson." So they joined in the attack, they took her to the village. Now she began, her companions began a song. [To the audience: "Will you help me?" "Yes."] She began:

> Ridicule, ridicule, mother.
> Ridicule, ridicule, mother.

---

160 Ms. Kombe seems to first indicate that the family of the dead wife has provided a new wife and performed a rite to absolve the husband of any hand in his spouse's death. Then she realizes that it's important that the husband be alone with his younger wife, so that she can continue to harass his first wife, even in death.

>   Your jealousy causes you to fight [What sort of jealousy is this?]
>   Ridicule, ridicule, mother.
>   It causes you to fight those already dead.
>   Ridicule, ridicule, mother.
>   Residents of this neighborhood are not here.
>   Ridicule, ridicule, mother.
>   So they can come watch their friend.
>   Ridicule, ridicule, mother.

Audience: They escorted you…They escorted you…"

LK: "They escorted her to what? … they escorted her near where? … near to the village. They said, "You dog, what sort of fighting is this? And yesterday you came to fight, and the day before. Is this the way your friends fight? They don't fight this way, no. You end up fighting with what? … with a ghost. You fight because of jealousy. Go away, **come on**, go to the village." She returned to the village. They teamed up against her.

Now she arrived in the village with dust and grass all over her. Her husband asked, "My wife, is that how they go to the bush? You've gone there since sunrise, and now you return in the afternoon. No, I refuse to allow you to go to that difficult place." She said, "No, I go to weed and I'm almost done." He said, "No, and what of all this dust?" "No." He relented. He relented. Now another day, she again went. She looked at the garden. She looked at it carefully. Carefully, carefully, carefully. "I won't weed, no." This young woman was very persistent. "And even today, my husband may have come by here. He didn't go to the what? … to the dambo [marsh], no. It's right here he's passed, to the grave yard." She went to the graveyard there. Now she went to find her friends and they were surprised. They hid themselves, they hid, they hid, they hid, they hid. She said, "This person, now as she comes today, her jealousy which has not been witnessed by all her friends. How can you come to fight over a man so often, and every day? Today we will go escort her to? … to the village, so that she's disgraced, because her jealousy is too much." Now uhmn! … they waited, this one hid himself, this one hid. Now she knocked on the tomb… she wouldn't go to weed [the garden], her heart was not in it, she just went to fight over her husband. She knocked on the tomb, *tuu*! "Just come out, let's fight. Let's fight." Her companion refused, she said, "I won't come out. I left your husband long ago; long ago I left that husband for you. Now why do you keep coming to fight with me, I left your husband to you. Me, I died long ago, but you keep following me. My friend, I beg you, I refuse. Today I won't come out." She said, "Ala! Just come out. Let's fight." Ahh!

Before she realized it, her friend came out. "Oo, so you are strong? Because I left your husband long ago, now you keep coming back to fight with me everyday. Now today, let me come and we'll confront each other." She said ... she spat [performer spits on the ground]. She spit on the ground. She spit. "You, it's you...it's you, you want to fight me, you won't beat me, you won't punch me. You won't beat me, no." And that one said, "Friend, here where I have come, there are many rushes [used for whips], where you come from there are no rushes." She said, "No, let's just confront each other, if you want, I have these whips." "You don't come to garden. You just follow me. I've left your husband."

So right there, they went at each other, they went at each other, they fought, they went at each other, they fought. So the...the companion, yes ... that companion... those companions now descended on her, now the companions said, "Really, you go escort her to the village so that her jealousy can end." No, hmn! Now they rolled her on the ground, they rolled her, they rolled her, they rolled her. It was like this: her companion beat her, this other one beat her, this one beat her, this one beat her until she grew tired. When she was exhausted, they forced her to the village. "There!" Those companions of hers were pushing her along, and she jumped on to her back. Before she realized it, she was struggling. "Leave me alone. Leave me alone." She said, "It's me you keep following. You are a strong person. You come here to fight. Why do you come out from the village where the living are? Why do you always follow me? So, she tried to shake her off, she tried to shake her off...as if...her friends just followed, pushing her, pushing her. Finally, they arrived at the village, at the side of the village. They started to sing.

> Ridicule, ridicule, mother. Ridicule, ridicule, mother.
> Your jealousy causes you to fight. [What kind of jealousy is this?]
> Ridicule, ridicule, mother.
> It causes you to fight those already dead.
> Ridicule, ridicule, mother.
> Residents of this neighborhood are not here.
> Ridicule, ridicule, mother.
> So they can come watch her friend.
> Ridicule, ridicule, mother.

And in the village of Sofia, now the chief said, "Alaale! Alaale! Isn't this the woman they married there, this one? It's this one who's come. No, I'm surprised. Listen to her co-wife." "This one, that's why this one comes to the garden, so that she'll go fight." "Her husband has told her to stay." [The husband said,] "As you see, me I was widowed and was given a substitute woman, I was given [one]. 'You should just go weeding in the garden.' But she did this, when she went there, she returned to the grave yard to go fight that one who remained there, her co-wife…she didn't mind me, no. She's always going to fight, all the time. So that's why today, it's all beyond me." Now the chief said, "I've never seen this in the land, this kind of jealousy. Of all here in the land, where there is jealousy, the **"number one"** is this one. Now what will you do to … to get her off your back?" As for the husband, he said, "Alaale! I thought, 'Maybe she's where? … she goes to weed the garden.' But you go fighting your friend, who you go to fight with every day, every day, and she's even died. And I've been cleansed, they cleansed me and gave me a substitute wife. You are obsessed, young woman. Ahh, today you're going to see." So, now there, what did they do? The chief came. He said, "This is very difficult." "Chief, what will you do?" He said, "No, this person, let's plead with these who are dead." So the chief began to plead, he begged, he begged, he begged. "What to do?" He said, "Perform some rituals." They performed rites, they performed, they performed. "Go back, she won't return again to come and fight. This person is obsessed." So they pacified her [the dead wife]. What did they do? They pacified her. And what did she do? She went away.

Now the husband said, "How come? This is the one I first married long ago, then you kept fighting with her until she died. You are cast out." That's where they drove her out, *mukwai*, cast her out and threw her belongings after her, throwing her belongings after her. She went to her family. Now the husband remained a bachelor. That's where I've finished *mukwai*. [Ms. Kombe then quickly stands up and walks away but is brought back by the audience's demand that she "Sit down!" I think the intention was to be sure she held her place at the center of attention to receive proper acknowledgement of her efforts.]

Ms. Kombe's performance differed from the earlier two storytellers' efforts. First, she was more dramatically engaged in the tale's events, using broader and exaggerated gestures and verbal description. Further, she provided dialogue for the story's principal characters in a very engaged manner, illustrating the loud and aggressive nature of the young wife and the more righteous character of the older wife. When she keeps referring to how the husband asks the younger wife to go weed the garden, Ms. Kombe is also suggesting that this woman is not only combative but lazy and/or negligent of her wifely duties. Structurally, the story revolved around the repeated visits to the graveyard and the song that the ghosts sang about the young woman.[161] Ms. Kombe actually pauses before singing the song the first time

---

161 A Tabwa narrative with a different plot but a similar repeated scene of ghosts singing

in order to ask the audience if they are prepared to help her sing. When they answer affirmatively, she goes on to lead them in the song, where they repeat the chorus and she fills in the one-line verses. Through the lyrics, there is a commentary on the young co-wife's improper, even extreme behavior. Generically, then, this narrative is closer to what the Lunda and other Bemba-speaking groups call a *lushimi*, generally connoting a tale with at least one song in it and often not containing the literal didactic elements of tales called *mulumbe*. Obviously, didacticism is not absent from this tale, since the final images depict the discussion and action taken by the society to correct the problems brought on by the jealous young wife's actions.

The narrative is thematically more complex than the earlier stories. It does have a relationship to Mr. Pandwe's last narrative about Kalulu being bound to provide labor for his in-laws. In this tale, the problem revolves around marital relations, especially as they pertain to a polygamous household, where the co-wives do not get along. Clearly, a woman willing to drive her co-wife out of the marriage then continue to fight with her after the older woman dies, is carrying rivalry to unwarranted extremes. The fact that the situation must be remedied by the village performing special rites to appease the angry ghosts suggests the serious nature of this kind of jealousy and marital dissonance. It is also obvious that Ms. Kombe is of the age of someone who may, in fact, be an elder co-wife in a polygamous home. Though I had no proof, or even any inkling, that this was the case, Ms. Kombe's narrative is still all the more effective for having been performed by a woman who is at least aware of these possible conflicts.[162]

It is notable that a story about jealous co-wives was told by the young Bemba mother Elizabeth at Malole (Chapter III) from a different view point. The three co-wives who resurrect their husband are portrayed as initially harmonious until two plot against the other. While it is not specified, the targeted wife was most likely the youngest, since there were accusations of laziness and not helping the others. From the point of view of Elizabeth, then, the more difficult position in a polygamous household is that of the youngest wife, clearly inverting the situation decried by Ms. Kombe.

---

a song to arrogant and combative wives is included in my 1989 monograph. A similar thematic point emerged, whereby ghosts imparted both wisdom and justice regarding improper domestic behavior (Cancel 1989, pp. 45–48).

162 Of the four performers I taped at Mkomba in 1989, Ms. Kombe, Bana Luka [Mother of Luka], was the only one still living in 2005. Born in 1936, at the time of our recording session she was fifty-three years old. She had indeed been the elder of two co-wives and managed, it seems, to outlive her husband.

On a broader level, questions about women performing in public before a mixed audience are raised by Ms. Kombe's efforts. While the women performing in the Bemba contexts examined earlier were elders and among a small mixed group of age-mates, Luva Kombe stepped into a situation where men had been performing and setting the tone of themes and discourse before a large group. She exhibited nervousness when she began, and was encouraged by other women to calm down and do a good job. When she finished the story, Ms. Kombe quickly jumped up to vacate the seat where the previous performers had been sitting, only to be instructed, again by other women, to remain in place. Generally, women tell stories most commonly in the more intimate settings around the hearth in the evenings, populated by small groups of children and relatives or when gathered with other women doing chores or relaxing. The choice to speak out in the form of a narrative about the potential inequities of polygamy, in the form of a fictional narrative, had wider resonances than simply one performance session. Due in large part to the nature of how sessions were organized and carried out, most of the performances documented in this study did not allow for women to break into male-centered events. The potential for tension and the expression of these tensions is suggested by Ms. Kombe's performance, as well as the session discussed earlier at Chitimukulu's village, wherein women insisted on performing *their* songs and taking over the playing of drums from the men.

While not a central part of this study, it is important to acknowledge that the groups recorded were matrilineal in most respects, though no less patriarchal when it comes to gender politics and overt expressions of power. That older men and women seem to get on comfortably in friendly and cooperative ways does not suggest that this is the case for all neighbors and for men and women of younger, more competitive age groups. Feminist scholars of folklore and cultural expressions make it clear that women perform themselves in complex ways within patriarchal societies and within the frames of creative activities. Among Bemba-speaking societies, the gender divide is complicated by the fact that women undergo formal initiation into adulthood while men do not. Instruction and solidarity are imparted by elder women in various symbolic activities within these rites.[163]

---

[163] Women's initiation in the north of Zambia is most famously detailed in Audrey Richards' landmark study of Bemba rites, *Chisungu* (1988). Meagan Vaughan also provides an important contemporary contextualization of Richards' work on gender

Further, communal norms are always shifting when it comes to actual familial and social positions held by men and women. Mostly speaking of western societies, Patricia Sawin asks, "[i]n what ways might a woman's performance challenge male privilege or hegemonic structures that support male dominance?" (2002, p. 41)[164] While Ms. Kombe and Elizabeth depict situations in which it is the women who break the norms of harmony, the deeper connotations have to do with a polygamous system that is often fraught with tension and the potential for discord.

After Ms. Kombe's performance, the audience had grown in size to seventy or eighty people. My young sons were becoming real objects of interest to a good number of children, and the noise level of the gathering was making it hard to be heard, particularly for the last performer, Ms. Daria Mwape.[165] We decided to leave after settling the compensation of the storytellers. It was difficult to try to justify to the two women, who had each told one story, that they were receiving half of what the men received—five, versus ten kwacha. However, they eventually seemed to accept that the original agreement was three stories for ten kwacha and that this was why the men were paid more. Obviously, pondering such matters in retrospect, it's continually embarrassing to consider how little compensation I actually paid out in comparison to what the performers provided me. What I've done historically, especially working with Tabwa performers who I visit more than once, is to bring monetary or material gifts when I return, but this was not the case in the brief contact I had with most of the performers in this study. My family and I returned to Mwense to spend the night at the rest house and start out again the next morning for the large village of Mbereshi.

---

in the 1930s (1992). Corbeil contributes a detailed pictorial volume on the symbolic emblems/art works used in the *chisungu* rites (1982).

164 Sawin lists three possibilities: "First, a female performer might persuasively depict or enact an image of women at odds with the society's naturalized vision of 'woman's role.'" (p. 41); Second, the female performer might take on a role or perform a genre conventionally reserved for men, thus claiming for a woman a role that confers prestige and controls ritual knowledge." (p. 41) "The third possible threat...explores the emotional dimension of the performer/audience relationship. A successful performance *moves* the audience." (p. 42)

165 In fact, the noise level drowned out around 40% of Ms. Mwape's words on the video and audio tapes. I've chosen to omit her story from this study because of the difficulty in trying to transcribe and translate it. On my return visit in 2005, I found out that Daria Mwape was the wife of Moffat Mulenga, Bana Mwenya.

Postscript

I returned to Kashiba in October 2005, taking a minibus from Mansa, where I was staying with friends. Getting off near the local shops, I showed around photos of the performers until someone recognized Idon Pandwe and directed me about a mile back down the road to the village of Mkomba. I dropped by the home of the village headman, who was not home, but one of the men sitting at the *nsaka*, Mr. Lawrence Chita, guided me across the street to the home of Moffat Mulenga, aka Bashi Mwenya. There were several homes in the compound and there were a lot of children and adolescents in the immediate area. At least two adolescent women bore a striking resemblance to their father, Mr. Mulenga. After I explained who I was, a few people remembered my earlier visit. We walked across to an area shaded by a tree and I set up the DVD player on a chair someone provided. Within minutes there were thirty or forty people, mostly children, watching the playback of the performances. Word also spread around that I was asking about the families of Mr. Pandwe and Ms. Kombe, and their relatives also came around. I showed the photos and transcripts of the narratives and, with the help of Mr. Chita, managed to identify then speak to the sons of Mr. Mulenga and Ms. Kombe and a daughter of Mr. Pandwe. They filled me in on some details of their parents' lives, mostly consisting of birth years, employment history, and year of death. Of the three, Ms. Kombe was still alive. Known as Bana Luka ("Mother of Luka"), Ms. Kombe was suffering from some sort of mental illness, wherein she was quite withdrawn, not often aware of things going on around her, and had virtually no reaction to my visit, other than, perhaps, fear and discomfort at all the activity around the event. She'd had six children and some of them still lived near her home. Clearly, Ms. Kombe was being cared for by at least two of them.

After around two hours, I took some photos of the families. If it were possible to judge by the number of people who posed for the pictures, I'd say that Mr. Mulenga had a lot of his relatives still living in the village, Ms. Kombe's was second in number, and Mr. Pandwe's third. I collected names and addresses of where to send the photos, then pushed on, with Mr. Chita, back to the headman's compound, where I took a few more pictures, then walked back to the shops for something cold to drink before a bus for Mansa arrived at the stop.

In retrospect, most of my impressions regarding the performers at that 1989 session seemed accurate. Mr. Pandwe was better educated, well-traveled and wealthier than Mr. Mulenga. Ms. Kombe had indeed been a first wife in a polygamous marriage. Like most of my return visits on this 2005 tour, my inquiries simply elicited more questions than answers, as the few meager dates and biographical bits really did little to explain a life or verify intent when it came to the stories performed. As in most of the other instances, my sixteen years of observation of moments frozen in time were butting against a larger and more complex reality.

Mbereshi

The next day, leaving the rest house at Mwense, we hoped to find some kind of lodging at the Mabel Shore Girls Secondary School. The headmistress of the school, Mrs. P. Ngalande, was kind enough to allow us to stay in a room in her home. I visited Mano that afternoon and we agreed to meet in the morning, when he would gather together a few of his friends for a recording session. The rest of the late afternoon was spent trying to track down diesel fuel for my Land Rover, since there was a shortage in the region and we were trying at all locations to keep topping up the tank. We spent the evening with Mrs. Ngalande, then I set out a little before eight in the morning, along with the school's bursar Mr. Kapampa, to record the session at Mano's, whose full name is Chipolobwe Madya Misenga.

When we arrived, no one had yet come, so we sat in Mano's *nsaka* and chatted for around a half-hour until his colleagues showed up. Mano proceeded to discuss his health and some problems he was having with his eyes. I promised to come by later and give him a small bottle of eye drops I had. Eventually, two elder men and a woman arrived and we set up some chairs and stools outside of the *nsaka*, where the sun was much warmer than sitting in the shade.

After we took turns explaining what I was doing, the woman, named Emeliya Muleya, began by performing a *lushimi* that contained a song. The context of this session was very different from the conditions of the previous day at Kashiba. We comprised an audience of about six people, sitting quietly at Mano's homestead, with only the noise of a few chickens filling the background. Ms. Muleya was probably in her late sixties or early seventies, with graying close-cropped hair, and a sturdy though not overweight build. She wore a sleeveless white blouse, with horizontal red stripes along its lower half, and had a blue and white tie-dyed patterned *citenge* around her waist and legs. On her left wrist and forearm she wore five simple plastic bracelets of various colors.

Lunda Storytelling 8 by Emeliya Muleya*

Robert Cancel:	Your name?
EM:	Emeliya Muleya.
RC:	OK. You can begin *mukwai*.
EM:	Yes. There was a little thing, *mukwai*. People lived like this in a country. There was a child of a common man; her name was Rose. Her father was a hunter. They went into the bush. They walked and walked and walked; they walked and walked. She became pregnant. She begot two children, twins, a boy and a girl. When she gave birth to two children, they grew up. When they grew up the boy said, "Father, Mother, I want to marry." They answered, "Where?" He said, "I myself, I know." They answered, "You know?" He said, "Yes."

He went to the house, entered and shut the door. As he shut himself inside the house, his father said, "Where has this boy gone? Well, I don't know." Then his sister said, "Well, he is sleeping and he has shut the door." They called him, "You, let's go and eat *ubwali*." He answered, "I do not want to." Uhmn! His mother prepared *ubwali*. She took it to him. He said, "Who are you?" "I am your mother," she answered. He began,

"I want Rose 'of the crocodile clan' [lit. 'spouse of the crocodile']...

My voice is off-key? [To audience]

Audience:	That's fine.
EM:	Oh yes, 'of the crocodile clan'. Off key, yes the tune is off key. I want Rose of the crocodile clan. Oh yes, of the crocodile clan. The one my mother gave me, Of the crocodile clan.

* To watch a video of this story follow this link: http://dx.doi.org/10.11647/OBP.0033.05/Lunda8

>Oh yes, of the crocodile clan.
>When we went to dig cassava tubers,
>Of the crocodile clan,
>Oh yes, of the crocodile clan.
>She is the desired one,
>Of the crocodile clan.
>Oh yes, of the crocodile clan.

>He has refused. He wants Rose. Whoever came, he refused, he wanted Rose. Rose arrived with her *ubwali*. Knock, knock! "Who are you?" he asked. "I am Rose," she replied. He opened the door. The stubborn lad ate *ubwali*. It went on like that. And here ends the story.

Ms. Muleya had a very relaxed, casual style of performing. Her hands were mostly in her lap, with the left hand loosely set on her right wrist. The few times she gestured, she raised one or both of her hands slightly off her lap in order to illustrate some kind of movement or situation. Her most emphatic gesture was the stylized sign of tapping the side of her right fist with the palm of her left hand to indicate the young man had firmly closed the door behind him when he entered the house. When she began her song, Ms. Muleya sang the first verse then paused to ask the audience and me if she could sing, and I answered yes, "Uh hmm." She sang softly and unhurriedly, and used only one rendition of the song, which is unusual for most performances. Songs are commonly repeated at least once in order to set up a relationship or establish a certain kind of repetition of action, motive or situation that will be broken when a significant conclusion is reached. When Rose arrives with food for the protagonist, and he eats, Ms. Muleya simply states, "And it went on that way," and ends the story by lightly putting her hands together in the common gesture of finality that often marks a performance's conclusion.

The theme of this narrative was not particularly clear. It seems the initial young woman Rose travels with her father and becomes pregnant. Without any reference to marriage or any other characters, there is at least the implication of incest. When twins are born to Rose and grow up, it seems the son will only marry a woman named Rose. This might, again, connote incest or, if there is a less deviant theme implied, that the son is very selective and chooses to marry someone who is as good or as beautiful as his own mother. The resolution of the problem is reached when he finally chooses to eat the *ubwali* brought by the "Rose" of his desires which also seems to be his mother. The song refers to Rose as being of the crocodile clan, which is the royal lineage of the Bemba but not the Lunda. There seems a lot in the narrative that goes unsaid, and Ms. Muleya seemed in no hurry to provide an explanation. Formally, the initial scenes of the mother getting pregnant after traveling in the bush is being compared with the son's refusal of any woman other than Rose. The tale may, in fact, have been an unstated or unasked conundrum narrative, but the mystery remained unremarked. This disinclination towards interpretation or clarification would continue in her next story.

I played back the video of the performance for all to see. Ms. Muleya at first did not notice the video images on the small screen of the monitor, but then saw herself telling the story and seemed a bit surprised and uncomfortable. The men in the audience suggested she tell another story, but she seemed hesitant, even unwilling to do so. When they eventually prevailed, they also tried to coach her before she began: "To look well, and the voice…because you have to look well in the photographs, you should sit properly without shaking, and empty your voice." I think this last bit of advice was meant to have her speak clearly, but her answer was, "I have no voice." Ms. Muleya seemed to be saying she did not have much to say or offer, but she then began the story.

Lunda Storytelling 9 by Emeliya Muleya*

Robert Cancel:	Give me your name.
Audience:	To look well, and the voice…because you have to look well on the photographs, you should sit properly without shaking, and empty your voice.
Emeliya Muleya:	I have no voice.
Audience:	Begin, will you?
EM:	The people, one was in, say, Kawambwa and the other one was here. He had made a very big garden. After making his garden, pigs used to eat his crop. One day he found that the sweet potatoes had been eaten by the pigs. It is not the ordinary pigs at all, it is human being-like pigs which ate the sweet potatoes. Now, there were only how many potatoes? [Holds up one finger.]
RC:	One.

* To watch a video of this story follow this link: http://dx.doi.org/10.11647/OBP.0033.05/Lunda9

EM:	One. It was the only one left. He arrived. "What about this potato? Who has dug it up? I will see him." He even sat in the *cifumbe* shrub, that's where he sat. As he sat in the *cifumbe* shrub like that, he had put aside his calabash of water. He stayed and stayed there until sunset. This man had thought, as he thought, he arrived at the *nsaka*, left his parcel and went away. He went to his house and stayed and stayed. He returned. He found that nobody had eaten that sweet potato. Then he spoke, he said, "Hmmn! My friends! I left the sweet potato here but nobody ate it!" Then he left the *nsaka*, and he did not want to remain in that village at all. He left and he went to make another garden in a different place. He grew all sorts of crops. Surprisingly, as people passed by they used to dig potatoes. When he found that potato again, he sat in the *cifumbe* shrub. He waited and waited, but nobody showed up. He went. He even found people sitting in the *nsaka*. He left his potato there and went to his house and stayed. He stayed...
Audience:	You should speak up [raise your voice].
EM:	...stayed and stayed!!! [says this last word very loudly] He stayed and stayed. He returned to the *nsaka*. When he returned to the *nsaka*, what was he told? You elderly ones? [To the audience] I have even ended my story.
Audience:	Explain what it means.
EM:	Should I explain? I will explain later. When he returned to the *nsaka*, he found the potato had been eaten. After they had eaten it he said, "My friends, you like me." This is how it was, *mukwai*.
RC:	It is all right *mukwai*.

At this point, I simply replayed the story for all to see and there was little discussion of the tale's meaning. This seemed puzzling at the time, but as with the first performance, I assumed I'd missed some details that would be revealed when I worked on the material. If anything, the story's meaning is less obvious to me now. It can be conjectured that the farmer's crops and his relationships with his neighbors was the thematic focus of the narrative. There seemed to be a lesson about sharing, hospitality, and community that was linked to both the way the last sweet potato was not taken and the way people in the man's *nsaka* ate that last potato in the end. The man's reaction to this, "My friends, you like me," suggests that he understood that people would only take his food if he could afford it, but not eat his last bit of sustenance. Yet, the protagonist seemed to feel that a true friend would, indeed, take and eat his last potato. In any event, after her brief explanatory epilogue, Ms. Muleya had nothing else to say on the subject, and neither did her audience.

The second person to perform was a man named Peter Bwalya. Mr. Bwalya was probably in his late fifties or early sixties, and had a thick-set build. He wore a rumpled, chocolate-brown collared shirt, with the sleeves rolled up on his thick forearms, and pea-green trousers. He had a deep voice and an easy manner of speaking. The only sign of nervousness was that he initially began the story holding his chin with his left hand, in a contemplative manner, as if trying to remember the details of the narrative.

Lunda Storytelling 10 by Peter Bwalya*

Robert Cancel:		You begin *mukwai*. Give me your name.
PB:		Peter Bwalya.
RC:		OK.
PB:		A *mulumbe*. There was one village where people lived. The chief had begotten a female child. Then this female child grew up. Then this girl was abducted. After she had been abducted, the chief made an announcement. "Friends, my daughter has been abducted. What shall we do?" And then four persons stood up. There was a hunter and a thief. And there was… even the one who repaired boats and the…the…they…the one who was in charge of the boat engine. All together, four. Then when they set out like that, they went to look for that person [the chief's daughter]. They found that person where she had been taken. The thief stole that woman and put her in the boat. They set out. That demon which had abducted the girl said, "Ah! The woman has been taken." It set out and followed those people. That hunter also said, "This is now my turn to show my expertise." He killed that beast, and they even took that woman across the river, that's where she was taken. Among these four persons, who married that woman? We can interpret that the one who married that woman among those four persons is her father. He is the one who married that woman.
RC:		How?

---

* To watch a video of this story follow this link: http://dx.doi.org/10.11647/OBP.0033.05/Lunda10

Audience: [Ms. Muleya wonders about who married whom, and Mano supplies the thought, "Because all of them had failed..." and Mr. Bwalya seems to echo that remark.]

PB: Because all of them had failed. They had found it difficult.

RC: Is it a *mulumbe*?

PB: It is a *mulumbe*, yes. This is where I end *mukwai*. This is the only one I know.

RC: Oh.

Audience: [Ms. Muleya] Bring a song...

It was, in fact, a very brief story, told in the style of a conundrum, wherein a chief's daughter is kidnapped by a demon and four men set out to bring her back. When audience members seem to call for an interpretation of the conclusion, Mr. Bwalya echoes the opinion offered by Mr. Mano, that the four had failed and that's why the chief married the girl. When I asked Mr. Bwalya if this was a *mulumbe*, he said that it was and claimed, in a good-humored and mildly embarrassed way, that it was the only one he knew. He stood up to signal he'd finished his performance.

As in the preceding narrative, it is difficult to draw a clear thematic conclusion from this performance. A couple of elements of the tale add to this uncertainty. First, there was not a lot of detail provided for the actions of the story. It is not clear why the demon kidnapped the chief's daughter. It is not clear what each of the potential rescuers did to save the girl. Second, even the characters themselves are not well delineated. Usually in this kind of conundrum story, the rescuers each have a notable skill that will be used to complete their mission.[166] While the hunter and thief are clearly drawn, Mr. Bwalya hesitated while enumerating the

---

166 In the Bemba narrative told by Elizabeth, the three co-wives each had a certain skill that was used to bring their husband back to life. It would not be difficult to rework this tale into a conundrum narrative, asking at the end which wife had the most important skill or, if the plot was slightly reworked, which of the women deserved to marry the man. In the brief Tabwa conundrum told by Cipioka Patrick, the question centered on the meaning of how a man could marry a woman, have the fetus grow in the mother-in-law's womb, then have his own mother give birth to the baby. Laudon Ndalazi poses the conundrum about the parts of the buffalo in the Bisa village of Nabwalya. Also at Nabwalya, Lenox Paimolo sets three men's skills against one another and explains that the farmer was "superior." Similarly, Kabuswe Nabwalya in his Bisa *mulumbe*, focuses on four points of advice a father provides his son, then explains what each one means.

other two rescuers. He even asks himself if he can remember the others, finally listing two rather vague characters: someone who was the boat's "engineer" and someone who repaired boats. So, audience expectations as to what each character will contribute to the mission are not clearly set up. Third, in the action of the story, the rescue is only vaguely described, with the thief and hunter contributing their skills in a forthright manner, but the two other characters do not emerge in well-defined images. Finally, it is not clear why the chief marries his daughter, just as it is not clear, in the explanation, why it was interpreted that the rescuers had failed. It is notable that the incest theme carries over from Ms. Muleya's first story. In some respects, it may be easiest to see the narrative as one in a larger corpus of stories that the audience had heard before, and they were simply supplying the details from their memories of earlier versions of the tale. In any event, if the theme was clear in a wider context of narratives, it was neither explained nor pursued in a way that would have helped me understand its meaning.

The next performer was Mano, and he had prepared a selection of royal praises to Chief Kazembe, along with explanations of each.

Lunda Storytelling 11 by Chipolobwe Mwadya Misenga [Mano]*

Robert Cancel: Your name?

Chipolobwe Mwadya Misenga: I am "Wisdom is obtained from people, not wisdom from oneself." This means, as for me, I should be led by my friends out there. One should not say, "I have my own wisdom." This is my praise name; it is not the name I was given at birth. My birth name, the name of my ancestors whose royal chieftainship I have inherited here in Mbereshi, is Chipolobwe Mwadya Misenga. These are the praises we use to praise ourselves or to praise Mwata Kazembe when he is at a meeting or among people.

Number one: *Sensele* [a kind of elephant grass] the grass which farmers fail to conquer. This means that Mwata Kazembe does not have any challenger. Is that clear?

RC: Uh huhn.

* To watch a video of this story follow this link: http://dx.doi.org/10.11647/OBP.0033.05/Lunda11

CM: **Number two**: We praise Mwata thus, "One may die in one's wanderings but one cannot sprout." This means even if Chief Mwata Kazembe dies in the bush, he cannot blossom or flourish like a flower [he can't rise again, living] just as the Chief who dies in his own village can't gain his life. Even a common person cannot gain his life, whether he dies in the bush or in the village. He who dies in the bush will be just as dead as the one who dies in the village. He will not blossom like a flower at all. The same thing applies to the one who dies in Europe and he or she who dies in Africa; it is the same death. Is it clear?

RC: Yes *mukwai*.

CM: **Number three**: Wagtail, the great one, the bird that is covered with plumes, child of John, he who will be victimized for the splendor of his plume which his father John gave him. This means Chief Mwata Kazembe will die as His Royal Highness because he is on the throne of chieftainship left by his father. Is that clear?

RC: Uh huhm. I see.

CM: **Number four**: Large head which has filled the palace of Mwansabombwe. This means Mwata Kazembe is the over all ruler of the whole respectable, rich Lunda kingdom.

Number five: The mischievous moth [*sumbalala*] brought trouble upon the innocent ones. This means wickedness leads to death.

RC: Uh huhn.

CM: Is it clear? The mischievous moth brought trouble upon the innocent ones. Wickedness brings death or trouble, you bring trouble upon elders. *Sumbalala* is an insect, a small animal, it brings trouble upon larger species of its kind. This is clear, isn't it?

Audience: Yes, *mukwai*.

CM: **Number six**: The beast that withdraws its claws in its hiding place. This means when the leopard is in a tree its sharp nails are withdrawn, but when it sees a human being, it pushes out the sharp nails and attacks him or her. This is the same way a human being behaves. He/She doesn't reveal the anger or bitterness that may be in his or her heart.

Number seven: The double-tongued one before the crowds will betray you. Two persons could be discussing certain matters but when such matters become known to the public, one of these two persons betrays his or her friend; his/her friend gets into trouble and ends in prison while he himself/she herself escapes the noose though both of them committed the offence. This is the meaning

	of "the double-tongued one before the crowds will betray you." In front of the crowd he/she betrays his/her friend; he/she refuses to testify in his/her favor. We are teaching now, eh? [Referring to me.]
Audience:	I am learning something from…
CM:	**Number eight**: Pay homage and be endeared. These are the people who are called "informers" in English. They work towards making their friends lose employment. The two of them could be employed in one company, one of them goes to their boss and says, "My friend has gone to such and such a place, he has gone to such and such a place," until his friend is dismissed from employment. This is treachery!

Eh, eight…uh, nine.

Number nine: He/She who looks small is as heavy as a stone. Someone may look simple but deep in his/her heart, he/she is a dignified person. This is as it is with Kazembe. Kazembe, especially the current one, looks small but nobody can challenge him.

I finished with what number? |
| Audience: | Nine. |
| RC: | You've arrived at ten. |
| CM: | **Number ten**: Elders used to say, "People make up the world, without people it is a wilderness." This is to say it is the people who rule the world. If there are no people for the chief to rule over, then he is presiding over a desert. That is why they say, "People make up the world, without people it is a wilderness.

[pauses for a minute as he looks through his notebook]

Number eleven: Giant hawk who went to plead with god to kill him. Through mischievous deeds one can bring death upon oneself. This is what we mean when we say, "Giant hawk who went to plead with god to kill him." We are talking about mischievous acts.

Number twelve: Wisdom is obtained from people…that's what I said earlier on. One cannot pretend to be "all-knowing" at all. One should be assisted by one's friends [in making important decisions]. This is where I end. |
| RC: | You have done a good job. |

I was immediately struck by several elements of Mano's performance. First, he was an imposing figure, somewhere around his late sixties or early seventies, standing nearly six feet three inches tall, and quite slim. For the occasion, he'd dressed in the ceremonial regalia of Lunda nobles: a cloth headdress [frilled cloth in four stripes colored red, white, green and blue] sitting high on the back of his head, a dark green/brown suit jacket, a pressed collared shirt with rust colored vertical stripes, and a light-colored waist wrap that went from his hips to his ankles, worn over his trousers.[167] He also wore round steel-framed eyeglasses, which gave him a decidedly scholarly look. This impression was underscored when he began to recite the praises by reading them from a sheet of paper where he had written them out. The genres of oral praises—sometimes called *ngoma* [drum poetry] or *imishikakulo* [praise poetry] or, as Mano refers to them here, *malumbo* [which is a generic term for praise names or poetry]—usually involves singing and, often, some kind of instrumentation. Some months earlier, Mano had demonstrated a version of the art form by playing the talking drum, *mondo,* for us. So it seemed rather anomalous when he opted to simply read the texts instead of using the oral memory postulated by scholars such as Albert Lord and Walter Ong, who at times even claimed this kind of memory and performance does not co-exist with written literacy.[168] He even used English language numbers to identify each praise, "Number one," "Number two," etc. Mano elaborated on each praise without further consulting the text, which suggested that he was spontaneously explicating the material. The language of the praises was difficult to follow, at times archaic,[169] but even the explanations were a bit dense for me to take in at that point, though when he'd periodically ask me if I understood his points, not wanting to interrupt the flow of this discussion and, admittedly, not wanting to seem more ignorant than I actually was, I'd usually answer yes. He recited twelve praises along with their explanations.

After we listened to and watched the playback, Mano opted to recite a praise and eulogy for "Mwata Kazembe **number four**, Keleka Msosi Kanyembo **number two**."

Lunda Storytelling 12
by Chipolobwe Mwadya Misenga [Mano]*

Robert
Cancel: All right, you can begin.

Chipolobwe
Mwadya Misenga: What?

Audience: He says you can begin.

---

167 For a broader discussion of Lunda royalty and customs, see Cunnison 1959. See, also, Cancel 2006.
168 See Lord 1960 and Ong 1982.
169 Sometimes the language draws on forms of the Luba language or what Chiwale and Chinyanta refer to as "Lubanized Bemba." (1989)

* To watch a video of this story follow this link: http://dx.doi.org/10.11647/OBP.0033.05/Lunda12

CM:	This is a eulogy for Mwata Kazembe **number four**, Keleka Msosi, Kanyembo **number two**. Mother of Chibangu the ancient one who outlives the rest, Kashekele passed away. You are the one who has assumed leadership. Great one, you are the remnant of the ancient Royal Highness. The sovereign ruler who is as firmly planted as a banana tree. The strong one, you walk over the weak ones and subdue even those who resist your firm control. You are Keleka Msosi, Keleka the chief, we long to be protected, we have suffered a lot. You are the supplier of our daily needs, you even take care of the destitute. You have even overcome foreign influence. You conquer territory after territory. You cannot be defeated. You, son of Ilunga, the one who is one of the founding fathers of this chieftainship.

Although he consulted a hard-bound notebook to make sure of the exact name of the deceased chief, Mano proceeded to recite the entire string of praise epithets without looking at the text. The language of the praises was quite allusive, taking many angles and paths to create laudatory images. As with most praises, numerous tropes in the form of allusions, metaphors, similes and comparisons were employed. He finished by referring to the late Kazembe as "You, son of Ilunga, the one who is one of the founding fathers of this chieftainship." This last reference links him to one of the early chiefs who led the Lunda migration to the Luapula region and who are still recognized as a vital part of the history of the region and the ruling lineage.

The last performer of the morning was Mr. Paolo Kaoma.

Lunda Storytelling 13
by Paolo Kaoma*

Robert Cancel:	Give me your name and begin.
Audience:	The name.
PK:	Paolo Kaoma.
RC:	You can begin.
PK:	The *mulumbe* states that the world is cruel. The dictum [that] the world is cruel has become our…our common saying, we the Bemba [-speaking] people. Many don't know what we mean when we say the world is

---

* To watch a video of this story follow this link: http://dx.doi.org/10.11647/OBP.0033.05/Lunda13

cruel. There were people who lived like this, some in Kawambwa others in Kazembe. Then someone died and the relatives said, "We shall not bury this person here. We shall take his body. They took the corpse and mid-way on their journey they stopped to rest. And then a woman also...that woman who was pregnant, left Mbereshi to go there [probably to Kawambwa]. Mid-way on her journey she met those people who were carrying a corpse. That woman stopped briefly to mourn that dead person. When these people lifted the corpse so that they could continue their journey, this woman also started off. The child in the woman's womb told that one who was in the womb, [rather] the corpse told the child in the woman's womb, "When you are born, don't speak. You should be a dumb child so that you see how cruel the world is." That pregnant woman left. Those who were carrying the corpse went to bury it. I think she just stayed two days. She gave birth. That child lived and started making sounds that babies make, "Ng'a, ng'a." When he began sitting unaided, he still couldn't say "Daddy." "Ah! What's the problem? This child is dumb." They tried traditional Bemba medicine, but it didn't work.

He started crawling, but was still unable to speak. He started walking, but was still dumb. When he reached the age of four – five, his friends started taking him to the surrounding bushes and dambos [wetlands] to set bird and rat traps. They set rat traps, they set some traps in places where birds liked resting. The dumb child's trap caught a bird, but the other boys got his and took it home. They reported that they were the ones who killed it. The dumb boy, hmm, he remained silent. They lived like that. They stopped setting bird traps and began going far into the bush to set animal traps [using ropes]. The dumb boy's trap caught an animal. The other children who were able to speak got that animal from the dumb child's rope. They took it home and reported that they were the ones who killed it. His mother beat him and entreated him not to go into the bush, but he continued going with his friends.

Then they resolved to stop using ropes to trap animals because, so they argued, they were only able to kill small animals such as duikers. Therefore, they began digging game pits right in the bush. They made fences [barriers] and left openings where they dug game pits. When they went back they found an animal had fallen into the dumb child's [*Chibulu's*] game pit. The other children got it.

RC:	Which...which animal?
Audience:	What kind of animal?
PK:	The roan antelope.
RC:	Oh.

PK: They took it home and ate [it]. They went back the following day and found the bushbuck had fallen into Chibulu's game pit. The ones who were able to speak took it home and ate [it]. Chibulu was again beaten by his mother but he did not stop going with his friends. It went on like that. They continued killing animals. The following day, they killed the roan...the eland in Chibulu's game pit. They got it. They killed animals, many animals like that. Now the child of the chief, like Chief Mano or Mwata Kazembe, the child of the chief said, "Let me go and fetch firewood from the bush." Those game pits, you know they used to cover them up with soil don't you? Now as she went *"pwa"*...the chief's daughter fell into the game pit and died. She didn't return home at all up to sunset. People began looking for her. They discovered that she had fallen into the game pit. They exclaimed, "Ah! You...you people of this village, who has dug these game pits?" Others said, "It is these boys and Chibulu." These people took the boys there. The boys said, "It is Chibulu. It is Chibulu's game pit that has killed this animal. He is the one who has killed this person."

They took this person [the chief's dead daughter]. They said, "Call Chibulu's mother." They got her and made her sit in the center [of the crowd] just like this, and said, "You too will die today. Bring a sword." Chibulu still remained silent. Some people went to get the sword from the house so that they could kill his mother. As he sat there, he said, "Hmm. Certainly I was told that the world is cruel." "Friends, Chibulu has spoken!" "Well, *mukwai*, let me explain," he said. "When we began trapping birds, my friends used to steal my birds. When we switched to trapping animals using ropes, my friends who are able to speak began stealing my animals. I was physically disadvantaged because I was unable to speak. And now, in that place where we dug game pits, I have been killing all the animals people eat in this village. My friends don't kill anything. Then this chief's daughter who is dead, the game pit she fell into was dug by this boy." "What a surprise! He has spoken! Chibulu! Chibulu has spoken! Chibulu has spoken!" Chibulu continued, "So let's go to the place where we dug game pits so that I show the owners to prove what I am talking about." The whole group left for the bush.

Chibulu began, "Whose game pit is this?" One boy said, "It's mine." "What about this one?" One boy said, "It is yours." "What about this one?" Another said, "It's for this one." "And this one?" "It's for this one." "What about the game pit the chief's daughter fell into and died?" Someone said, "It's this one." People even started going back to the village. "Your Royal Highness, Chief, this is what happened, this is what happened, this is what happened.

The game pit your daughter fell into and died belongs to...it is for this one. It is the game pit in which your daughter died."

This is the origin of the *mulumbe* [linked to the] saying that the world, therefore, the world is cruel.

Mr. Kaoma seemed to be in his late fifties or early sixties, medium height and slim. He had very short, graying hair, a mustache and a small "patch" of beard under his lower lip. Mr. Kaoma wore a gray sport coat, slightly rumpled white collared shirt, and blue/green trousers. Most of the time he spoke he would occasionally move a crumpled red handkerchief from one hand to the other. His overall bearing was not so much grave as serious, a no-nonsense attitude. Mr. Kaoma told the lengthiest tale of the session, beginning by saying, "This *mulumbe* states that the world is cruel. The dictum [that] the world is cruel has become our...our common saying, we the Bemba [-speaking] people. Many don't know what we mean when we say the world is cruel."[170]

Mr. Kaoma's rather restrained gestures, framed his story, which was told at a slow, deliberate pace. His hands mostly remained in his lap, while occasionally pointing with one arm or the other in the direction of action or indicating where characters were located or were moving to. He fixed me and the other members of the audience with a serious countenance and even as he acted out some moments of high excitement, such as when people discovered that Chibulu could talk, he remained restrained and deliberate. Overall, Mr. Kaoma kept control of the various details of the story and similarly kept his focus on elaborating on the saying with which he began the performance. Of the other three narratives, this one most successfully foregrounded and gave depth to the events and theme of the tale. The fatalistic saying was well-illustrated by the ill-treatment of the seemingly mute and passive hero. It was a saying that was passed on, in an inversion of the usual expression, from the grave to the cradle, from a dead person to a baby not yet born. The image involving the death of the chief's daughter in a game pit is found in numerous other narratives I've recorded among the neighboring Tabwa people.[171]

After a bit of commiserating, I paid Mano around twenty kwacha, who in turn would distribute the money to his friends, and the session broke

---

170 A Tabwa storyteller, Mr. Datson Kaselekela, performed a tale that similarly explored a saying that pointed to the darker side of humanity, "A human is evil in this world." The phrase recurred throughout the narrative, as the various characters illustrated the truth of this claim (Cancel 1989, pp. 149–153).
171 See Cancel 1989, pp. 129–158.

up. I drove the session's participants to a PTA meeting at the local primary school, stopped at the hospital to buy some diesel—arranged by a British doctor we'd met the night before—and returned to Mabel Shore to gather up my family, bid Mrs. Ngalande farewell, and set out for Kashikishi and, later that day, Puta.

The performances by these four elders formed a range of thematic concerns and dramaturgical strategies. Ms. Muleya's two tales focused on two kinds of human relationships, marriage and community/friendship, respectively. The details were sparse, and she offered a sketchy explanation of the second story, about the man who grew the sweet potatoes. Both narratives contained images that seemed quite allusive, perhaps related to other versions that had broader, more detailed exposition in the telling. The performer also used food as important images in both tales. While Ms. Muleya displayed relaxed and confident performance skills, she was not interested in revealing the meaning of either tale, providing only minimal explication. Mr. Bwalya's performance, truncated and rather vague, seemed more the result of nervousness or uneven storytelling proficiency. The evidence suggests that he simply had not worked out the details of the tale in his mind before or during his performance. Yet this narrative is probably the most intriguing of the four, mostly due to the strange ending and interpretation, particularly the notion that the chief would marry his own daughter. There is at least a remnant of a theme found in other narratives in the broader traditional context whereby a father, sometimes a chief, cannot bring himself to give his beautiful daughter to a suitor and therefore sets seemingly impossible tasks as conditions of courtship. Similarly, Ms. Muleya's tale of the young man who refused to eat and secluded himself in his mother's house suggests another kind of extreme when it comes to courtship.

Mano was actually working in a vein opposite to that of the storytellers who preceded him. He was taking what are intended to be esoteric compositions and explaining them to me. He clearly felt it important to impart this knowledge and to exhibit his own depth of understanding of the praises. Lunda praises are actually unusually well-documented and explained in several published works. This links into a wider tradition, written and oral, of Lunda history and the documentation of the first Lunda chiefs' arrival and ongoing prevalence in the Luapula area.[172] Similarly,

---

172 Lunda praise songs have been collected, annotated and published by Mr. Chileya J. Chiwale. See, for example, Chiwale 1989. Lunda ethnography and history was

Mr. Kaoma's entire tale focused on the explanation of an old truism, "the world is cruel" [literally, "the country/land is difficult" (*icalo caayafya*)]. Paolo Kaoma made sure that the pessimistic sentiment was established at the beginning of the narrative and emphasized it by describing the difficult life of Chibulu, repeating the saying through the mouth of Chibulu, and finally underscored it by literally linking the notion to the explanation of the story.

The performances in this session, therefore, pulled in two different directions, but like the elephant and hippo in the well-known trickster tale, the overall effect was a kind of balance or stasis between mystery or deep allusion, and a didactic and emphatic turn towards detailed explication. In some ways, we can see the earlier session at Kashiba in the same way, with Mr. Mulenga simply spinning trickster tales as fast as he could in order to get it over with and get paid, and Mr. Pandwe trying to fulfill the promise of the *mulumbe* form by detailing and explaining his narratives for the edification of his immediate audience and me in particular. Ms. Kombe was similarly looking to explore the theme of the difficulties of a polygamous household when principles of respect and cooperation are not upheld.

Part of what we can conclude in considering these sessions is that each performer, indeed each session, had his, her, or its own characteristics. How these emerged, or perhaps were withheld, in performance is part of what is continually being negotiated and created in any living enactment. In both sessions, I have to take the credit or blame, or maybe both, for initiating the events. The overall focus of this project is to describe how this complex relationship plays out in any one instance.

Postscript

Although I'd returned to the Lunda area several times since my initial 1989 visit, I never had the opportunity to follow up on my earlier recorded data. Instead, I began a long project of attending and videotaping the annual

---

seminally compiled and published by Ian Cunnison in the late 1940s and 1950s. There is also the impressive Bemba-language historical text compiled by Mwata Kazembe XIV Chinyanta Nankula, a team of Lunda elders and a "White Father" Catholic priest named Labrecque in the late 1930s and 1940s, Kazembe XIV Chinyanta Nankula and Labreque 1951. This was published in Bemba and later translated by Ian Cunnison under the title of "History on the Luapula"(Cunnison 1951). Macola develops a through discussion of the historical and social circumstances behind this influencial text (2001).

Lunda kingship festival known as the Mutomboko. (Cancel 2004, 2006) In the course of my visits, I usually ran into Mano, who was playing his role as both a respected Lunda elder and the court bard who invariably used a string of praises to introduce the Lunda king, Mwata Kazembe, on the last day of the festival, right before the Mwata performed the culminating Mutomboko dance. When the then current Mwata passed away in 1998, Mano was implicated in an intense succession dispute and within a year or two had been more or less demoted by the new Lunda king.[173] He moved his compound to a small village between Mbereshi and Mwansabombwe, the royal capital.

When I arrived at Mbereshi in 2005, I asked about finding information on the earlier performers at the guest house I was staying at. The caretaker directed me to the section of the village where Mano had been headman and suggested I speak to an elder who'd lived there for many years, Mr. Job Kachingwe. As I asked around to locate the proper house, a young man named Daniel Chiwele volunteered to steer me to the right place. On hearing of what I was looking for and perusing the photos and transcription texts I carried, Mr. Kachingwe invited me to sit in his home as we watched the DVD of the performances from both Mkomba and Mbereshi.

Mr. Kachingwe, consulting with four young men who sat with us in the house, claimed that Emeliya Muleya was still alive the last time they'd heard of her, and had moved to the Democratic Republic of the Congo. No one could offer an accurate estimate of her age other than she was very old. They also estimated that Peter Bwalya, who still lived nearby, had been born in 1931 and had done a stint in the British colonial army. They described him as a tin smith and all-round handyman. They noted that Mano, Chipolobwe Mwandya Misenga, had originally come to Mbereshi from Congo, where he'd been previously dispatched by an earlier Kazembe, Paulo Kanyembo. Paolo Kaoma was a builder and carpenter who'd also worked as a cook, and had lived and worked for a brief time on the Copperbelt. He'd passed away in 1997. Finally, Mr. Kachingwe agreed to interpret Ms. Muleya's story about the protagonist and his sweet potatoes. Basically, he said the man was using what appeared to be his last potato as a test to identify the people who were truly his friends, and this was the case in the final location where they did not hesitate to eat the potato. I thanked Job Kachingwe, paid him around $5 (K20,000), took some photos

---

173 See stories depicting an attempted "palace coup" in the *Times of Zambia* and the Zambian *Daily Mail* after the 1998 succession of the new Kazembe.

all around, left him with Ms. Muleya's and Mr. Kaoma's photos and texts to pass on to their families, then walked with Daniel Chiwele the short distance to Mr. Bwalya's home.

We found him sitting on a low stool on his verandah, with a young boy who was one of his children. He'd gone gray and was considerably slimmer. Gauging by the birth date I'd just written down, I'd estimate his age at around the early seventies. After a bit of explanation, he remembered my visit, if only in vague terms. I gave him a photo of his performance and the transcription, then showed him the DVD, and he did not have a lot to add to what was already there. He confirmed that he was mostly a *panga fyela* [blacksmith] and had moved to Mbereshi in 1977, the year he'd married. He and his wife had eleven children, of whom six were still alive. He posed for a couple of photos with his son and I promised to send them to him.

Mr. Chiwele and I took our leave and, on the way to his compound for another photo session, we passed the home of Imelda Kapambwe, Chipolobwe Mwadya Misenga's daughter. Like her father, she was tall, though more broadly built. After some explanation, I gave her the photograph I'd taken of Mano in 1989, along with the texts of his praises and poetry. She said he'd been born in 1914 at Mwansabombwe and in 1981 he became headman Mano at Mbereshi. He'd previously been a school teacher, a clerk and businessman at Kawambwa, some twenty or so miles away. Ms. Kapambwe also seemed to be saying he'd briefly served as chief, or more probably a regent, when the former Kazembe died in 1998. She confirmed that he was living in a subsection of Mwansabombwe, near a stream, around five miles from Mbereshi. I gave Ms. Kapambwe a couple of dollars, photographed her with her young daughter, sitting with a woman neighbor, and wrote down the address where to send them. We then crossed the road and I took some pictures of Mr. Chiwele and his family and gave him around $2 (K10,000) to compensate him for his time. In the end, due to time constraints, the inconvenient location of his new compound, and, I have to admit, the awkward situation of visiting Mr. Misenga in what was more or less a place of exile and diminished status, I did not make the effort to visit him when I left the next morning.

VI. Stories on Demand: A Performance Session Among the Bwile

Ubushiku bwaluba umukote, ne cimbwi cinye mfwi.
 [The day an old person gets lost[in the bush], you will find white hairs in the hyena's dung.]

The discursive style of this study leans toward a combination of description, reflexive commentary, published scholarly data, consultation with colleagues and cautious analysis. In this chapter I will combine the description of how I arranged the session with my personal travel to and brief stay in the village of Chief Puta. I will also provide some of the Chief's background, details of our longer term interactions, some historical context for the Bwile people, and whatever else seems relevant for the consideration of the following performance session. More so than in earlier chapters, I will focus on description of specific techniques used by performers to shape their tales. As in the other chapters, a postscript will provide additional information and context gathered in October 2005.

The Bwile are a numerically small ethnic group living at the northern-most point of the Luapula Province, touching Zambia's border with the Democratic Republic of the Congo and bounded to the west by Lake Mweru.[174] Like most of the people living along the lakeshore, the Bwile's main economic activity is fishing and they also grow several

---

[174] For several hundred years, the peoples of the Luapula Valley and the eastern shore of Lake Mweru have come under varying degrees of Lunda hegemony. This history has been documented in numerous studies, most of them by the colonial era scholar Ian G. Cunnison (1959). The Bwile themselves are more specifically situated in the history of the region in Musambachime 1976, and 1981.

DOI: 10.11647/OBP.0033.06

crops. Seasonally, many of them also process and sell salt that is found in several areas where hot springs bubble to the surface. Chief Puta's village is located just south of Chiengi, a district "sub-boma" [which since the time of this recording session has been given full district status] that was historically one of the earliest sites of British administration in the area.[175] In addition to a few administrative offices, the site also contains a government rest house. On June 3rd 1989, after reporting to the officials at the government offices, our family moved into a room at the Chiengi rest house. My wife and I had fond memories of the place that, in 1976, had been impressively kept up and was very comfortable when we'd first stayed there. By 1989, the water pump no longer worked, the generator wasn't operating, the formerly white walls inside and out had been covered with either dark blue or bright green enamel paint, and rats scurried across the rafters of the ceiling's crawl space for a good part of the night. However, the place was still situated on one of the loveliest spots in Zambia, overlooking Lake Mweru, the DRC, and the lake's northern shore that curved towards the Zambian border. Early administrators had named that shoreline "Livingstone's Bowl," since it is the spot where the famous explorer landed when crossing back from the Congo on his last journey in Africa. In a matter of weeks, debilitated by fever and often delirious, he would die in June 1873 south-east of what is now the provincial capital, Mansa, among the Bisa people [who are related to but not in the same location as the Bisa in the Luangwa Valley] in the village of Chitambo.[176]

The next morning, Saturday, I drove out to see Chief Puta, who I'd first met in 1985. At that time, his young wife was running a small business out of his compound, selling Simba beer, brewed in what was then Zaire, to bars and individuals. My traveling companion and I had the opportunity to spend time with the chief, purchase a crate of beer, and overall establish an initial relationship at court. His home, or *musumba*, was set near the lake and had a large courtyard and strong wooden pole fence around it. In 1989, he remembered me and had received my photos

---

175 Chiengi is well documented in the records of the early district notebooks. One of the earliest government officials at this boma was a fascinating and rather tragic character named A. Blair Watson. After his time at Chiengi, he led an expedition to remove the, by then weakened, forces of Msiri (Mushili) from Kilwa Island on Lake Mweru. (A. Watson 1957, pp. 70–74) Soon thereafter, Watson would die mysteriously, apparently by his own hand.
176 See Livingstone 1874.

from 1985 as well as a recent letter asking to record stories at his place. We chatted for a while and arranged to meet at the local school at around 2 PM. Driving back to the rest house, I bought some provisions for lunch and we settled in to walk along the lake and relax until it was time to eat and then to go to the primary school. Accompanied by Mr. Banda, from the Office of the President[177] and my son Daniel, I drove to the school, unloaded my gear, and sat with the chief and some of his colleagues. After a short time, I was asked to speak to the group, which by now consisted of some 30 or 35 men, a few boys, and a good number of people leaning into the open windows of the classroom. I explained my status as a lecturer/researcher at the University of Zambia, my background of recording stories among the Tabwa, and my current project and desire to record stories from other groups. Then Mr. Banda, as sometimes happens when people are not used to hearing my poorly accented Bemba, basically repeated what I'd said so that the participants were clear on what was going on. While I slipped outside to gather my equipment from the verandah, the group discussed the situation and its meaning. Some of the men felt I should stay until Monday, when a better-organized session could be put together. I explained that I was due at Kaputa on Monday, and everyone seemed ready to leave without performing any narratives. However, after I played for them a video sample from my Friday session at Mbereshi, they decided to give it a try.

Chief Puta began the session by telling a brief history of the Bwile area. Puta is an unusual example of longevity in local rulers.[178] He apparently succeeded to the title while still a young man, in the 1930s. At the time of our recording session, he was in his mid 70s, but still quite vigorous and sharp.

---

177 "The Office of the President" had, for many Zambians, become synonymous with the term "secret police" by 1989. While I had never really had any unpleasant run-ins with members of this bureau, they were the entity most commonly associated with political surveillance and rooting out subversive elements among the citizenry. In my last visit to Chiengi, in 1985, my companion and I aroused the suspicions of the OP officer by simply showing up in such a remote place, near the Zairean border, for what must have seemed the flimsy reason of being on "holiday" and wanting to visit the chief. Mr. Banda, in 1989, was polite though also cautious in respect to my scholarly intentions. He simply accompanied me on my trip to record narrative performances, at one point being kind enough to clarify my request and requirements to the gathering of elders and headmen.

178 Chief Puta Kasoma was born in 1914 and took power in 1937. He died at the age of eighty-five. He had worked a bit on the Copperbelt as a businessman before succeeding his uncle, Chief Puta Chongo. Among the ritual specialists he brought to his court to help control attacks by crocodiles and lions, was a well-known practitioner named Chipongola.

Bwile Storytelling 1 by Chief Puta*

Chief Puta: We the Bwile, when they came here to this country, our origin, where the Bwile came from, is known as Kumwimba Kasongo. We were Mpweto, Chisabi, Kasama, Lambwe Chomba. They are the ones we came with from Kabwile. We were on the other side of…of Nkumwimba. Our original home is Nkumwimba Kasongo. Then the Kola [stream] went across the river, cutting it in half, on the other side were the Bwile of Kasongo Mwimba. Then on this side, the Lunda were there. The Lunda would go from their place to harass the Bwile where they were. They would burn their houses. So then they ran away from there; we ran away saying that the place was no good, our friends were too much [trouble].

So we came, as we came, arriving at…at Bwile, there was a stream known as Kabwile…a swamp with water lilies. That same place is where we settled. Then they told us that…[it was] the spirits that said that "This place you've arrived at is called Kabwile." That's where we settled. At Kabwile, right where we settled, we saw it was a nice place.

Ntinda Nchelenge…Nchelenge of Chitutu, the one sent by Chief Nkuba [for he (Ntinda) was the overseer of this place], as far as Kabwile there, including Lambwe. As for him [Ntinda], he was living at Chitutu. That is where he lived. Ntinda was Nkuba's *kapitao* [a borrowed word for "captain," or second in command]. When he found us staying at Kabwile, he fell in love with Queen Mwanto Ikolo, Puta's sister. After their marriage, he said he would take her with him, because he was a hunter, with dogs. He was piling up elephants in the bush, where he piled up elephants. Then when they gave him permission, the elders gave him permission, Mpweto and Puta agreed, saying, "It is alright to go with the queen so that she can know your place." So after taking her, they arrived there at Chitutu. There Ntinda killed lions. He would kill lions and crocodiles and pythons and monitor lizards. They were eating them. Then when he got there, he was a hunter with dogs, he killed a dog. The queen was newly pregnant. The queen was pregnant by Ntinda Nchelenge of Chitutu, the one who was sent as kapitao by Nkuba. When they cooked for the queen, they cut it up, they cut it up. They cooked for the queen. When the queen ate, she did not feel well at all, because we do not eat lions, we do not eat pythons, we do not eat crocodiles. So there, after the queen had eaten she started to get sick. When she got sick, she aborted her pregnancy. When she lost the pregnancy, they set off with her husband

---

* To watch a video of this story follow this link: http://dx.doi.org/10.11647/OBP.0033.06/Bwile1

Ntinda. "Because you are so sick, let us go, I'll take you to the elders." Then he found Mpweto, Puta, Kasama and Chisabi. Then they told him that, "You have a case to answer. You served the queen that which she doesn't eat. You fed her lions, you fed her leopards, and you fed her crocodiles, including pythons and monitor lizards. This queen does not eat these [things]. And dog, we do not eat dogs. You see now the sort of problem you have brought? This is a real problem. You have brought a case." He said, they told him that, "You are going to compensate us."

He gave them ivory. He piled ivory on top of elephants for the chiefs. "That elephant, I will give you elephants." They refused, saying, "No, you will have to give us something bigger, you've brought a serious offense to our place." They set off together, he began to give them the country, giving Kasama, Chisabi and Pweto up to Lunchinda, and Puta here this land up to…what's it called…to Kalobwa…up to the Kalungwishi [River], not to Kalobwa. Up to the Kalungwishi. When they got to the Kalungwishi, that's where Puta's land ended. On this side was Mofwe, in Mukupa, here we arrived as far as Mukupa in the Mofwe. Then he acquitted himself. Nkuba gave him his approval, saying "You have done well, to have done something of this sort. We have freed ourselves of this kind of problem with the Bwile."

This is how we came to live here. Mpweto remained at Kansa. The boundary was at Luncinda. This side was mine, stretching as far as the Kalungwishi. That's how we have lived. This is the history of the Bwile people.

Dressed in a dark green, short-sleeved "safari suit" with a light green t-shirt underneath, Chief Puta sat in a chair at the front of the classroom, with the blackboard and one of his advisors behind him. Like many men who have, or aspire to, a significant occupation or standing, Chief Puta had a ballpoint pen protruding from his shirt pocket, indicating his literacy. The advisor stood, overseeing the performance, and basically seemed to be keeping watch over the chief. The narrative is, like many histories, a migration story—naming important chiefs, leaders and locations—of how the Bwile people came to live in their current location. As most storytellers do, Puta used gestures such as pointing to either side to indicate where events occurred. Space and territory were established by these gestures so as to give form and substance to the main events of the account. For example, when he says "The Lunda would go from their place…" he points to his left with his left hand and then uses his right hand to point right as he continues "to harass the Bwile where they were." He continues pointing right as he elaborates, "They would burn their houses. So then they ran away saying that the place was no good, our friends were too much [trouble]." Employing the usual dynamics of storytelling, Chief Puta's words and gestures create a rhythm of sound and movement to both frame and flesh out the performance.

One interesting counterpoint of the pointing and moving between several locations is that there are long moments when he held his hands on his knees or in his lap. This stasis seemed linked to elements of the story that described times of stability, either social harmony or physically staying in one place. For example, when Puta is describing events concerning the ancestor Ntinda, he keeps both hands on his knees while saying, "That is where he lived. Ntinda was Nkuba's *kapitao*. When he found us staying at Kabwile, he fell in love with Queen Mwanto Ikolo, Puta's sister." A bit later on, Puta again describes events by either keeping his hands on his knees or raising them both up at the same time to gesture in a kind of parallel or balanced manner: "When they cooked for the queen, they cut it up. They cooked for the queen. When the queen ate, she did not feel well at all, because we do not eat lions, we do not eat pythons, we do not eat crocodiles. So there, after the queen had eaten she started getting sick. When she got sick she aborted her pregnancy."

When Ntinda is confronted by the Bwile elders in the story, Chief Puta again keeps his hands on his knees or simply uses his left hand to subtly enumerate the kinds of food that Mwanta Ikolo was given to eat by her husband. "You have a case to answer. You served the queen that which she does not eat. You fed her lions, you fed her leopards, and you fed her crocodiles, including pythons and monitor lizards. This queen does not eat these [things]. And dog, we do not eat dogs. Now you see the sort of problem you have brought? This is a real problem. You have brought a case." He then uses his left hand to emphasize his next words, "You are going to compensate us." This negotiation results in the Bwile receiving the land on which they now live as compensation. Chief Puta ends the story by putting his hands on his knees and saying, "That's how we have lived. This is the history of the Bwile people." At these final words, he leans back and exhales a deep breath, indicating the end of the narrative. All in attendance applauded his efforts.

We replayed the audio recording of his words, and he seemed pleased enough to augment his remarks with a description of how the Bwile make their living and some of the things they've historically produced, such as salt.

Bwile Storytelling 2
by Chief Puta*

Chief Puta: We have salt at Katete, where our people process it. There at Ifuna at Kalembwe ['s area] is a salt pan where they make salt, and [also] here at Katete. And we live with people who are very good at making salt.

We also have men, and they too have nets and boats. They go on the lake, killing fish. Then the fish they catch, they take to the Copperbelt,[179] to go and feed those at the Copperbelt. That's where they go to sell them.

Long ago, crocodiles infested this lake. Those crocodiles were many and daring, it was incredible how...all the people they killed—those casting nets and those bathing—they grabbed. However, because of my concern, when I saw my people suffering in this manner, I invited those wise people who came. They came and protected my people from being caught.

Then again on the land lions suddenly appeared. Those lions too were taking people. They would come right into the middle of the village and catch people. [For] them too, I brought in wise people so that we...we would improve, make [things] better, to chase off the lions, to send them far away. Even the crocodiles have gone far away.

That's why now my people at this time live in peace.

This historical and cultural description was performed in a similar style as the previous narrative. The main difference is that Chief Puta was recalling events he'd seen and participated in. After he described two crucial economic activities, salt-making and fishing, he then talked about how dangerous wild animals came to plague his constituents. Things became so dire that he himself decided to consult experts and have them come to eradicate the problems. He is quite vague about whom the "wise people" were and what they did, but it's clear he was referring to ritual specialists who were able to prescribe the correct rites and activities to protect people from the crocodiles and lions.[180] This brief exposition also served, in its

---

179 As noted in earlier chapters, the Copperbelt is the region in north central Zambia that borders on the DRC where the nation's mineral wealth is concentrated, with many mines and dense urban populations. Historically, this has been a ready market for all manner of goods, particularly fish coming from many areas.

180 While details of these rites go unspoken, also unspoken is the widely held belief that attacks by crocodiles and lions on humans are, depending on their circumstances, not always the product of natural events. If people are attacked in or near their villages or

* To watch a video of this story follow this link: http://dx.doi.org/10.11647/OBP.0033.06/Bwile2

juxtaposition, to insert Chief Puta into the historical/mythological events he'd been earlier describing. The audience was once again pleased with his efforts and supported him with applause.

After the chief's performance, an elder, perhaps in his early sixties, named Fermit Indita, told a moderately long story of a brother, a sister and her evil serpent husband.[181]

Bwile Storytelling 3 by Fermit Indita*

Fermit Indita: There was a little thing. A chief ruled people in the country. So then the chief had decreed, "Whoever gives birth to a baby girl will be killed." Truly, one gave birth to a girl. His advisors went and confirmed that a baby girl was born. Truly, her brother went to see where his mother gave birth to his sister. He ran away with her, carrying her on his back. He went to the middle of the bush, with a pot and a spoon. Arriving at a marshy area, he cooked for the baby. A bird came to the middle of the bush. It came and found the young man cooking for his sister. It said, "How are you?" He said, "*Mukwai*, at the court of Puta they forbade giving birth to girl children. 'Who ever has a girl we will kill.' That's why I've abducted my sister." The bird said to him, saying, "Get on my back, along with your pot." Truly, that bird went up. It went into the middle of the wilderness, going far, going. It went and found houses there that were well-constructed and beautiful, and a large lake just like Mweru. Indeed he put...put him down, that bird. It led him away, saying, "Let's go so that I show you the house where you will raise your sister." It showed him the house. It had twelve rooms. He arrived; he opened this one [and] showed him. He opened this one [and] showed him. He finished. How many rooms remained? Only one. He said,

---

in apparently safe places, that is, away from the usual hunting grounds of predators, then there is a suspicion of malevolent human intervention. The intervention can take several forms, from sorcerers directing crocodiles or lions to attack specific people, to killing people in a way that resembles attacks by these predators, or even transforming themselves into these deadly animals. (See Cancel 1986, p. 99, for a brief survey on scholarly literature on "lion-men" or "leopard-men," also a more extensive treatment in A.F. Roberts 1986; and, for a more detailed discussion of this phenomenon as framed in the discourse of "sorcery," see West 2008.)

181 Information gathered in 2005, claims that Mr. Indita's actual name is Feremu Chisongo Chilindi. He was known as a good, successful fisherman. He was physically impeded by a leg that was described as "not so straight," and he had a large family. He passed away in 1989 at around sixty years of age.

* To watch a video of this story follow this link: http://dx.doi.org/10.11647/OBP.0033.06/Bwile3

"This one you should never enter." He said, "Yes *mukwai*." "All the plants, and the bicycles, automobiles, whatever, are yours. The boats in Mweru are yours." That bird went away, it [finally] told him, "I will be visiting you."

They lived, they lived, they lived. That young girl grew up. He just took care of her. He just took care of her. She developed breasts. Eventually she came of age. So *mukwai*, her brother then set off, saying, "I am going fishing." So his sister who remained there opened all the rooms. Then she looked, "And what of this one they forbade to us?" Truly, she entered. She opened the door, it closed itself. Again, she opened another one, it closed itself. She went and found a large snake with twelve heads. It said to her, "Come in, do not run away." Truly, that young woman entered. So *mukwai*, all the things that men and women know about, she did. [Some laughter by men in audience.] She returned and opened [the doors], and she went outside.

Her brother, where he was fishing, returned. His eyes saw nothing unusual. Truly, his sister just continued going right over there. So eventually she would tell her brother, "I don't feel like eating fish, I feel nauseous." "What is it?" he would ask. "No, it's just nausea." "Fine." Eventually, her brother saw that she was pregnant. "Ala! You, my sister, where did this pregnancy come from?" She said, "I don't know where it came from. They just wished it on me." He said, "Really?" Finally, she gave birth. It had a spot here, here it was a snake, with a human head, but with a spot here. The day he was born the child said, "How are you uncle?" greeting the uncle. "How are you uncle?" "Ala! He was born today and he's come to greet me? Fine, no problem."

So that sister of his, now here with the husband, it was just like a marriage. She would go there every day. Now that sister of his spoke, "You, my husband, we should kill my brother." But that little nephew of his spoke. He said, "My uncle! They are planning to kill you," [he said] when he had gone fishing with his uncle. "Really?" He said, "Yes." "Alright." They came back. The next day they went again. Then his brother-in-law said, "I will follow him to the lake, that's where I'll kill him." Indeed, the snake uncoiled itself. That little nephew of his again said, "Uncle, let us make twelve machetes." Truly, his uncle agreed. They made twelve machetes. When they made those twelve, they took them out to the lake. And his uncle...his brother-in-law followed along to the lake, in order now to kill his brother-in-law, and they arrived in a steamboat. Truly, his young nephew dr...he dreamed. He said, "Uncle, father is coming. Let's get ready, because he's in a steamboat, and he's opened the windows." He said, "Father is coming." Truly, he thought and said, "Uncle." He said, "Yes?" "Father, there he comes, see him in the rainbow?" Then he said, "Uncle, you go to sleep, I'll kill father." The snake arrived right there, saying to himself, "Perhaps I'll now strike my brother-in-law." He [the nephew] cut off its head as it rose to strike. He cut off all the heads, until the twelve were finished.

So he roused his uncle. And that large snake got itself inside. Now the uncle... that little nephew said, "Uncle, bring the steamboat for me to drive. Let's go." He drove the steamboat. He drove the steamboat fast, arriving at the shore. When he arrived at the shore, he said, "Uncle, I'm going to kill my mother because she...you are the one who cared for her. She now turns around trying to kill you. I will kill her." Truly, they took that snake and put it at the crossroads. He went into the bedroom and killed his mother.

He pondered. He said, "I tell you, uncle, I know where they brought you from. Let's go, I know the place. We will cross the middle of [Lake] Mweru." Truly they embarked with his uncle. He drove the steamboat fast, arriving at the harbor. "Uncle, you go across to your village. But I, I will remain in the steamboat. Go and move everyone, we will take them to nice houses." Truly, they arrived. So then, he said, "Uncle, there where you are going, do not tell people that you have a nephew with a spot on his neck. Don't you dare." Truly, that uncle disembarked and arrived at that village. So then the people saw him. "Yangu! The one who left! Yangu! The one who ran away! The one who escaped! The one who escaped!" So they gathered around him, so then he began to make his explanation. "Listen, listen, listen!" "Really?" He said, "Yes. I came to take you so that we will go where we have been living."

Truly, all the families squeezed into the steamboat and they...they set off. No one was allowed to sit where the nephew was, not a person. Just the uncle and the nephew sat together. They went driving the steamboat at full speed, arriving at the destination. He told them that, "If you find anything in the path, don't spit. Just keep going." Truly, they arrived. On getting there, they were shown those very beautiful houses.

Mukwai, this *kashimi* is over.

Mr. Indita seemed a shy and friendly man, judging from his mildly flustered smile and initial hesitancy in performance. He was dressed in a light tan jacket, something like a three quarter-length raincoat, a white buttoned shirt with the collar out over the jacket's collar, and faded blue jeans. The sleeves of the jacket were pushed around six inches up his forearms from his hands, and he wore a thin ivory bracelet on his left wrist. He began speaking with both hands together, between his knees. This compact posture looked as if it was an attempt to steady his initial nervousness. To emphasize the first few lines of the story, Mr. Indita rhythmically raised his hand up and down a few times. When he came to the point where he said, "His advisors went and confirmed that a baby girl was born…" he pointed to his left into the distance to indicate where the men went to find the baby. He gestures left again when saying, "Truly, her brother went to see where his mother gave birth…" When he says, "He ran away with her, carrying her on his back" he mimes gathering belongings together from the ground then uses his two hands, in fists, to gesture, up and down, indicating the brother placed his sister on his back. Like Chief Puta, he often used his gestures to set the physical space of the narrative's events. In this case, when indicating the brother and sister "went to the middle of the bush," Mr. Indita points with his left hand almost directly behind his head, looking almost like a military salute.

As the story unfolded, Mr. Indita became more demonstrative with his gestures, acting out the parts of the various characters. He was particularly adept at slightly altering his voice for each character and also depicting certain actions, like the half-snake, half-human nephew humbly clapping his hands to greet his uncle, the narrative's main character. This scene elicits a bit of laughter from the all-male audience. There was even louder laughter earlier, when Mr. Indita describes the young woman's interaction with the twelve-headed snake by saying, "So *mukwai*, all the things that men and women know about, she did." Mr. Indita indicates what happened by putting his palms together near his left shoulder then sweeping them to his right, the top right hand sliding off the left in a gesture of finality, as if saying "That was it." The audience also laughed when the sister says to her naïve brother, "'I don't feel like eating fish, I feel nauseous.' 'What is it?' he would ask. 'No, it's just nausea.'" The implication that she was pregnant was not lost on the men listening to the tale. As often happens in narratives with rather fantastic events and relationships, Mr. Indita kept his narration rather understated, the effect being that there seemed nothing all that unusual about what was going on. He also—perhaps it was a characteristic of his performance style, since he did not seem nervous after getting into the story—almost never raised his eyes to look at the audience or the video camera.

It is clear that Mr. Indita's histrionics are closely tied to the story's various actions and characterizations. He uses numerous techniques of gesture or mime to create the various images of the tale. The description of the bird telling the brother and sister to enjoy all he has given them but not to go into the twelfth room is framed by some elaborate gesturing. The bird says, "All the plants, and the bicycles, automobiles, whatever, are yours." The performer looks to his left while saying this and uses his left hand and arm in sweeping gestures, stabbing a finger to indicate each thing he enumerates. He raises his voice as he ticks off the good things to be had there. He pauses briefly after saying, "whatever…"

puts his hands back in his lap and says in an emphatic voice, "*Fyobe*" [All (are yours)]. As he follows this by saying, "The boats in [Lake] Mweru...are yours," Mr. Indita uses both hands to indicate the enormity of the lake by twice sweeping them from below his chest outward. When he described how the young girl and her brother lived in that place after the magical bird left them there, he said "They lived, they lived, they lived" and clapped his hands quietly three times to punctuate each phrase and to indicate and emphasize the passage of time. Similarly, when Mr. Indita said, "He just took care of her. He just took care of her," he clapped his hands twice.

The story was shaped and moved along by the smooth, efficient and descriptive interaction between voice, physical gesture and mime, and the intricate elements of the plot as it unfolded. On one level, the tale's theme had to do with ingratitude on the part of the sister, who not only disobeyed the bird's warning about opening the twelfth door but also spurred her snake-husband to try to kill the brother who had saved her life.[182] The magical nephew, possessing traits from both human and animal realms, shows the proper respect for his uncle and uses his fantastic powers to save the story's protagonist, kill both the serpent and the treacherous sister, then, finally, move the original village across the great lake to the newer, more prosperous habitat. The protagonist's relationship to his nephew reflects the strong familial link between nephews and maternal uncles, referred to as "father" in a structural kinship sense. This relationship, at least in the narrative, supersedes the one between the nephew and his biological parents. The tale also establishes a link between the compassionate brother and the magical bird that assists him and his sister in moving to the magical house. Further, the bird's helpful nature and wondrous powers are echoed in the heroic nephew, a composite of animal and human. The narrative's main character is essentially a type of passive hero, whose goodness brings him aid from

---

182 In my collection of Tabwa narratives, there are tales that contain elements or motifs of this story. In one tale, recorded in 1983 from Mr. Wilson Katai, a brother and sister living alone are divided by the brother's violent ingratitude for the sister's unrelenting care and affection. As she wanders, at one point, wounded and scorned from human society, a magical fish appears from the river and transports her to a new place, where a large and prosperous village is conjured for her to rule. In another, longer narrative, a helpful demon aids the hero on his quest by employing a magical "steamer" a train that can transport them very rapidly from one place to another (on this latter narrative, see Cancel 1988–89, pp. 85–109). A similar version of this tale can be found in Mbele 1999, pp. 66–74.

other magical characters, leading him and his society into a positive transformation. While he breaks the chief's interdiction about killing girl infants, he obeys the warnings of the magical bird about the forbidden room and of his nephew about not telling others about the spot he has on his body. For exhibiting these positive traits, the protagonist not only prospers individually, but the village is physically moved to a new place of positive transformation.[183]

While more can be thematically discerned from this tale's imagery and character interactions, it also has a notable relationship to the two earlier historical narratives by Chief Puta. For one thing, Mr. Indita specifies that the initial interdiction against bearing female babies is given by the unnamed chief. Moreover, the place where all this occurs is identified by the heroic brother when he tells the bird that these things happened at Puta's seat of power [*musumba*]. Ironically, the draconian edict is proven to be correct, when the sister marries a twelve-headed snake and turns against her brother. In the end, the magical nephew moves the people of the chiefdom to a more prosperous and beautiful country, thereby validating the deserving nature of both the chief and his subjects. In several ways, the tale mythically replicates Chief Puta's "historical" version of how the Bwile came to be where they are. In his tale, the breaking of serious food prohibitions by the new in-law Ntinda, causing his Bwile wife to abort her pregnancy, leads to the compensation of large amounts of ivory and, most importantly, the expanses of territory that constitute the Bwile's land. In Mr. Indita's tale, an errant young woman ignores an interdiction, improperly marries a magical snake and bears a half-human, half-animal child. However, this impropriety eventually leads to the magical nephew instigating the move to a new and more prosperous territory. In the fictional story, the hero obeys the nephew's various instructions and the interdiction not to tell the people about him and, finally, the people arriving in the new land obey the interdiction not to spit if they find something in the path. The comparison of proper and improper behavior underscores the tale's themes.

After Mr. Indita's well-received performance, Mr. Fred Kafankwa told a lengthy tale.

---

183 For a more detailed discussion of the "passive hero," see Cancel 1989, pp. 200–205.

Bwile Storytelling 4 by Fred Kafankwa*

Fred Kafankwa: There was a little thing, there was a person. His name was Mupita [One who carries on one side]. This person lived in the bush. In the bush he used to dig game pits. But in the pits he used to…at dawn, he would go to check his pits, to see if an animal had fallen in. In the pit, if he found an animal there, he would lift it and take it to make into relish [meat or fish] to eat in the bush where he was. He would be returning to the village like that, he would kill, in the bush, leaving his hut, dry the meat and then return to the village. But one day, that friend, there was a person who was walking in the bush. He passed by a pit. [indistinct word] He found Mupita Kumo. "Mupita Kumo, how are you doing here, friend?" "Well friend, it is just like this." "Relish[184] is a problem [i.e. scarce]." He took some food that he had and gave him. That person went back to the village.

Three days passed, [and] into the pit of the young man Mupita a lion had fallen.[185] Mupita, when it dawned, said, "I will not go to the pit. For many days I've been killing tiny animals, which are not good. Today I will rest perhaps for three days, I won't go there." He rested three days and the lion was in the pit. After it spent three days there, it felt hungry and it lost weight. On the third day, when Mupita went, the person went there in the morning; he went and looked into the pit. He saw there was a lion. He felt so frightened that he wanted to run. He went, but the thing had seen him. It called to him, saying, "You, grandfather, I beg you, don't be frightened of me, take me out. I am your brother. I am your relation, me, myself." But that person, as a human being, felt frightened to see this, saying, "No, you grandfather, you are difficult, if I take you out I will carry that which I can't throw away. Me, I can see that you have lost a lot of weight; I will be relish to you. You would eat me. No, I can't do it." But he pleaded a lot, he pleaded for a long time. The person cut a log, saying, "If after doing this you eat me, there I will be found, I am a man." He cut a log and threw it in there where the lion was. The lion climbed out. When he came out he said, "Grandfather, well done." No, he fell down and rolled. "I have never seen a chief like you. If it weren't for you I would have rotted in the pit. Grandfather, you are honorable and

---

184 "Relish" is a common English gloss for the Bemba word *"umunani,"* a meal's main course of meat, fish or vegetable, usually cooked in a sauce. When people are saying that food is scarce or times are tough, they'll often say something like *"takuli munani,"* "there is no relish."

185 In my collection of Tabwa narratives, there is a set of stories that contain similar images. (see Cancel 1989. In particular, NP14, pp. 136–139)

* To watch a video of this story follow this link: http://dx.doi.org/10.11647/OBP.0033.06/Bwile4

you have pity. But what I very much want from you is for you to tell me your name. Your name, what is your name?" "I am One-who-carries -on-one-side. What will make me carryon two sides is you, lion." "You are Carry-on-one-side?" "Yes." "O.K. I have heard grandfather. So you can go back to the village. If you hear me calling, 'Mupiita Kumo, Mupiita Kumo! Mupiita Kumo!' ['One who carries on one side, One who carries on one side'] [Audience laughs at the falsetto, powerful repetition of Mupita's name.] you should know that he [Lion] has slaughtered, my friend wants me."

And true enough, when one day passed, he tried to listen to what his friend had told him, he was not called at all. The following day, he heard "Mupiita Kumo!" His roar went "Ooooh." "My friend is calling me. You, my friend, are the one who carries, who will be difficult if he comes…" [Audience laughs at this image of Mupita's trepidation.] "Mupiita Kumo! Mupiita Kumo!" "Maama." He said, "Yes." "I'm going to the bush to get relish." He took his spear alone, and took it and went…[indistinct]…where he was coming from. "You man, you have come, you stay there…Ooh, you have come?" "Yes." He found he had killed four buffaloes. "Boy, this little relish, you can eat it." [Mupita claps in thanks] "My friend, truly you have done well." [Mr. Kafankwa uses hands and arms to indicate Mupita throwing carcasses over his right shoulder to carry all of them home.] He took all the carcasses and speared them on one side, behind, without putting them on the other side. He walked away to the village, he carried [them] and went… The lion looked as Mupita Kumo just went. "That Mupita Kumo, to just go there taking all those animals as big as buffaloes and pierce them on one side without putting [them] on this side!?" [Suggesting that it is insulting that Mupita does not carry the very heavy gift over both shoulders.] [Audience laughs at Lion's consternation, expressed in a falsetto voice.] So he went away annoyed. He [Mupita] went and arrived at the village. They [the people] ate. The following day, he [the lion] was annoyed and said, "Now I will follow, 'Mupiita Kumo, Mupiita Kumo, Mupiita Kumo!'" When he went there and found four elands, he pierced this side. "Aagh!," the Lion said, "No, I can't have a friendship with a person like this. Tomorrow and tomorrow I will not rest until I kill him." No, he [Mupita] was annoyed, "My friend, he can't even rest when I have not even finished drying the meat." "Mupiita Kumo! Mupiita Kumo!" He found he had knocked down many elephants right there. He pierced them at the back, not at the front. [Performer uses hands to indicate how Mupita carried the animals and also to suggest how he began walking.] As the person started going, he [the lion] also went and hid in a bush. As he was hiding there, the person was going, going. No, he was piercing here, to the front, to the front that is where he was piercing the animals. [Imitates sticking spear down into animals to pick them up.] He was not piercing them in the back, no, he was piercing them in the front. So as he was going there, the Lion said, "Now this time has passed." He said, "Wuuu! I have caught [you]." He knocked himself down on the side that was remaining [i.e. the other side]. He impaled himself on the spear from behind. On this side there are animals and he himself was pierced on this side. He [Mupita] said, "You have brought me an evil omen. Since my birth from my mother's womb I have never carried [anything] on two sides. Now it is you who have done this, eh? It's you who've made me carry [on two sides]. That's what I told you, I said that I am One-who-carries-on-one-side, it is you who would make me carry on two sides, it's you Lion. No, you see now I am carrying on two sides." He started singing a song, he said,

> You just provoked me...[pauses to remember words of song]
> ... you just provoked me...
> he said...ah!...he said [trying to remember lyrics]
> I felt pity for you, you just provoked me, myself.
> You just provoked me.
> I felt pity for you, you just provoked me, myself.
> You just provoked me.

When Lion realized that, he said, [Pointing behind himself as if indicating where Lion was in relation to Mupita.] "Truly, my friend I beg you, I beg you." [Claps to indicate Lion's submissive, pleading attitude.] So, his friend said, "O.K., you can remain." He removed it [the spear] from him. When he removed it from him, he forgave him, "No, boy, don't worry, [Claps again] don't do this."

Two days passed, awaiting the wound from the spear to heal. He called again, "Mupiita Kumo. Mupiita Kumo. Mupiita Kumo!" Again he called with great force. He found six buffaloes. He pierced them right there. "Aagh! No, this person he's placing them one on the other." Like that the week passed. There followed five days, and he was killing for him like this. But on the sixth day, he again became annoyed. "No, no, this person can't be carrying animals in front as if he is ridiculing me who kills them. And these claws are painful and my arms are overworked in catching things, as if he is belittling me. Today he must die." Again he went ahead as if he were going to kill an animal. When he went ahead he hid. Just as he was about to pass, he pounced, "Wuuu." Onto the spear, kwa!!. He [Mupita] told him, "Again you brought me an evil omen. I am One-who-carries-on-one-side. What will make me carry on two sides is you. You see, now I have carried on two sides today."

Robert
Cancel: Wait *mukwai*. [Pause while video cassette is changed] Continue speaking.

FK: He sang a song:

> You just provoked me, myself.
> You just provoked me, myself.
> You just provoked me, myself.
> You just provoked me.

So at the village, he went and carried [the meat] himself [Mupita]. And the Lion that, that is where the enmity between people and the lion came from. People hunt lions, [and] lions kill people. It started with Mupita Kumo and the lion.

Fred Kafankwa was the youngest of the session's performers.[186] He was probably around forty years old, solidly built with a rather rounded paunch that suggested relatively good living. He was dressed in a long sleeved collared shirt, made of some kind of synthetic, bronze colored fabric that had a bit of a sheen to it. He wore light blue dress trousers and, like some of the other performers, had a ball pen visibly displayed, but clipped into the space between his top two buttons, due, I imagine, to the fact that the shirt had no pockets. Mr. Kafankwa sat at an angle to the camera, facing a bit to its right. He began the performance with his hands folded loosely in his lap, indicating location and action mostly with his head, either looking in the appropriate direction or tilting/nodding at various points in the narrative. His voice was clear and strong, and he often used a falsetto voices to portray agitation or anger in the story's characters.

Mr. Kafankwa set up his narrative by keeping his gestures minimal and subdued for most of the story. He mainly used his hands and arms to indicate when the story's hero, Mupita, speared the dead animals and carried them over his right shoulder. As the narrative's action picked up, so did his use of gesture. This is particularly evident when the lion hides in a bush looking to pounce on Mupita. Mr. Kafankwa uses both hands to indicate the position of the lion in the bush and Mupita's path as he's walking. When the lion jumps out at him, indicated verbally by the lion's cry "Wuu!," the performer shoots both hands up and wide, as if he's diving ahead. In a much calmer, confident manner, Mupita exclaims, with his hands spread low and palms up, that he's never seen such a thing. This causes laughter among audience members. He also gestures behind him, indicating how the lion's been impaled and stuck on the spear until Mupita frees him. When Mupita begins his song, Mr. Kafankwa is casting around, trying to recall the lyrics. He places his hands in his lap, palms up and fingers curled, and tries to establish a kind of rhythm, looking almost as if he's hoeing, moving hands down and back towards his waist, as he remembers the song. For the remainder of the narrative, the performer is quite animated, indicating most actions by the characters with some sort of mime or gesture. The audience members, including many of the young

---

186 Information gleaned in 2005 specified that Mr. Kafankwa was a farmer who had moved to the area from far away. He had died while still in his fifties, but no one could remember the year he passed away.

children looking in through the school house windows, clearly appreciated the humor and, at times, absurdity of the story.

The theme of the narrative, which given the inclusion of a song is technically a *lushimi*, is difficult to specify. On the one hand, it is like many other tales wherein someone whose life is saved turns against the person who rescues him or her, not unlike the ungrateful sister of the previous tale. Certainly the lion is guilty of ingratitude several times, as Mupita first extricates him from the pit and later on removes the spear that had impaled him. There is also a kind of arrogance displayed by Mupita, if not consciously, whereby he keeps carrying the large, heavy game carcasses with one arm and on only one shoulder. This causes the lion to feel it's being mocked. Mupita carrying "on two sides" is also a rather vague allusion, since it is not clearly stated why this distresses Mupita. It seems to be based on the power exhibited by someone who can carry such large loads over one, instead of the normal two, shoulders. In any event, this jealousy and boasting is given as the etiological reason for the enmity between humans and lions.

Mr. Kafankwa's performance was followed by that of Mr. Timothy Kachela.

Bwile Storytelling 5 by Timothy Kachela*

Timothy Kachela: There was a little person. The little person had how many children? Four. All girls. So three were having children and one was not. Now as that one went by, went through life, she would say, "God did not do well by me, because I've been unable to conceive a child." She said, "He is very bad." She just complained.

So she went to the bush. She heard an axe chopping, po, po. That's where she went. So she went and arrived and found [people] were gathering honey. So she arrived, "You, my brothers, give me some of your beeswax. So they fetched some of that beeswax and gave it to her. She said, "Truly, I'll collect some firewood, and I'll return to the village." She arrived at a place where she was collecting firewood, carrying the wax.

As soon as she got to the village she put it in the clay water pot. She put it in an empty one without water. As she went about her life, she

* To watch a video of this story follow this link: http://dx.doi.org/10.11647/OBP.0033.06/Bwile5

went on, in that pot is where the wax remained. So one day, she went and looked in there. There emerged a child who was all white, a girl. "I have a child!" She took her out from the pot, she put her aside. "God the savior you've given me a baby, God the almighty. I thank you very much, God the almighty." So they lived with the child. And we men, we do not miss much. The child was being admired. She developed breasts. She reached puberty. They said she was ready to marry. So when they sent a spokesman to negotiate with her mother, the mother said, "No, me, my child does not walk in the sun. Again, she does not open doors. I can't allow my daughter to marry anyone. As far as I'm concerned, this child is simply meant to stay by me, the mother." He said, "This one we will marry, she is such a radiant one."

So that was the end of the discussion. So the mother agreed. The brideprice was paid, they betrothed her. Then after the engagement, they wed. After the wedding, the groom was told by his mother-in-law, she said, "You, father, this child, the person you insisted on marrying, this one should not begin to touch doors. I beg you very much; you alone, when the sun rises you must open [the door]." "Yes *mukwai*, I understand." "Even closing the door, you should close it yourself, because you yourself have loved my daughter of your own free will."

So there at that place after each night's sleep, she [the girl's mother] would take warm water to her son-in-law to bathe. He got up and opened the door, and bathed and bathed. He finished. Each time, the wife remained in the house, that's where she would remain.

So now as the mother-in-law acted in this way, the son-in-law said, "Why is it that this woman can't open or close doors? I will see. I will see for myself." Now then at that place when night came they slept. Now the mother-in-law, when she heard the cockcrow, she started to heat water for her son-in-law to bathe. So when that water was hot, she carried it. Going to the door, nku-nku-nku. The son-in-law kept still. Nku-nku-nku. Now the daughter finally said,

> You mother, I have heard you, me, the beeswax.
> You mother, I have heard you, me, the beeswax.
> The snoring man is still sleeping, me, the beeswax.
> The snoring man is not yet awake, me, the beeswax.
> Open for me man, so that I can go see mother, me, the beeswax.

So he lay still on the mat. He said, "I will see for myself today." "You do not begin to touch the door, don't dare, my child, just sit still on the mat." Nku-nku-nku. The son-in-law did not move at all.

> You mother, I have heard you, me, the beeswax.
> You mother, I have heard you, me, the beeswax.
> The snoring man is still sleeping, me, the beeswax.
> The snoring man is not yet awake, me, the beeswax.
> Open for me man, so that I can go see mother, me, the beeswax.

So finally the daughter got up. She touched and froze onto the door. At that very moment she touched the door, she began to melt. "My child, don't touch the door."

> You mother, I have heard you, me, the beeswax.
> You mother, I have heard you, me, the beeswax.
> The snoring man is still sleeping, me, the beeswax.
> The snoring man is not yet awake, me, the beeswax.
> Open for me man, so that I can go see mother, me, the beeswax.

To no avail. Now she melted this far, here, that's how far she got. Even the upper body had begun to melt. "Yah, this son-in-law will kill my daughter. Now what kind of sleep is this?" Nku-nku. "You father, get up and open up." No, that one did not move. The daughter said,

> You mother, I have heard you, me, the beeswax.
> You mother, I have heard you, me, the beeswax.
> The snoring man is still sleeping, me, the beewsax.
> The snoring man is not yet awake, me, the beeswax.
> Open for me man, so that I can go see mother, me, the beeswax.

So now the wax went this far, this is as far as it got. She [the mother] said, "No, this is very sad news." Nku-nku-nku.

> You mother, I have heard you, me, the beeswax.
> You mother, I have heard you, me, the beeswax.
> The snoring man is still sleeping, me, the beeswax.
> The snoring man is not yet awake, me, the beeswax.
> Open for me man, so that I can see mother, me, the beeswax.

No, now she melted all the way to the ground. Then she was quickly beaten down because of the tragedy of opening [the door]. Then when the mother-in-law picked up a stick, trying to hit him, he escaped and ran away. He went and went. There remained only a large puddle [of wax] right there.

Mr. Kachela was probably in his early sixties, slim with a few streaks of gray in his hair.[187] Like Mr. Indita, he had one of his upper front teeth missing, which became evident when he smiled. He wore a light green, weathered shirt that seemed several sizes too large. Neither sleeve was buttoned and the wide cloth around his wrists flapped as he gestured during the performance, making him seem even slimmer than he was. As we began the recording, some audience members encouraged him to fasten

---

187 Mr. Kachela was born around 1920, making him about sixty-nine years old when he performed this tale. He was born close by, in the Tabwa area, and grew up in the Bwile village of Shebele. He mostly made his living from farming and passed away in 1991, near the age of seventy-one.

the second from the top button of his shirt, which he did, with slightly embarrassed good humor.

Like the performers before him, Mr. Kachela used a set of gestures and mimes to give the story spatial dimension and to rhythmically punctuate the pacing of the verbal narrative. He began with his right hand holding his left bicep as he touched his chin and face with the index finger of his left hand. At the point in the tale when the woman encountered the people gathering honey, Mr. Kachela crossed his arms. The crossed arm position would center the set of gestures for most of the performance, with his body at times leaning in one direction or another, and his head indicating a similar direction or activity. When the woman receives the beeswax, he cupped his hands to mime her taking up the gift. As specific actions were described, Mr. Kachela used one hand or the other, at times both, to mime or indicate activity. He usually returned to his crossed-arms posture after such gestures. He used both hands to mime the mother removing the newborn child from the pot where she had put the beeswax. Both hands are again used to suggest the rounded shape of the young girl's breasts, "She developed breasts." His arms crossed again as he continued, "She reached puberty."

As the tale went on, Mr. Kachela gestured more frequently and emphatically. He also altered his voice when speaking as different characters. When he describes how the mother asked the new husband to respect her wishes, Mr. Kachela bent lower and clapped his hands in supplication, saying, "I beg you very much, you alone, when the sun rises you must open [the door]." While describing the habitual pattern of the mother warming water and delivering it for the husband's bath each morning, the performer rhythmically emphasizes his verbal pacing in the way he moves his hands. Beginning with his hands pressed together between his knees, Mr. Kachela said, "So there at that place after each night's sleep, she [the girl's mother]..." He continued by using his left hand to gesture at and indicate a place to his left, "...would take warm water to her son-in-law to bathe." With his right hand, Mr. Kachela mimed the son-in-law opening the door, "He got up and opened the door..." Then the storyteller used his left hand to move left to right, and his right hand took up where the left stopped and indicated the area where the bath water was placed, "...and bathed and bathed." Mr. Kachela drew his hands together at chest height, "He finished." Finally, he points down to his right to show where the wife stayed without moving, "Each time, the wife remained in the house. That's where she would remain."

Still returning to the crossed-arm position between gestures, Timothy Kachela moves the story to its central set of actions, the young wife's song that ends each line with the chorus "me, the beeswax." Preceding each rendition of the song, the performer mimes the mother knocking at the door, "Nku-nku-nku." As he leads the first four renditions of the song, Mr. Kachela keeps his arms crossed, uncrossing them to gesture or mime the actions that follow. When he sings the last repetition of the song, he holds his hands together in his lap. At song's end, he raises both hands over his head and swings them down to the ground in front of him, suggesting how the magical girl "melted all the way to the ground." When he ends the narrative, Mr. Kachela moves his hands from lying in his lap by flopping them down, palms-up on either side to indicate the finality of the tale's events.

While this *lushimi* may seem to have a somewhat tragic theme, wherein the barren woman miraculously receives a child originating in beeswax, the audience and performer were not particularly moved to sadness. There was a good deal of laughter elicited at various points of the story. For instance, when Mr. Kachela described the girl maturing, saying "And we men, we do not miss much. The child was being admired," the audience chuckled at the notion of a beautiful young girl drawing the attention of older men. They laughed louder when the young husband decides to find out what his mother-in-law was hiding by not opening the door himself, "I will see for myself today." Each time the young wife's song ended and the performer described how far her melting had progressed, the all male audience laughed, until they laughed hardest and longest after the song's fourth repetition, when Mr. Kachela indicated the girl had melted all the way up to her armpits, "...this is as far as it got." At this point he pauses, while he and everyone else chortles at the imagery. The narrative finally ends amidst more laughter and applause. Where, in most narratives, broken interdictions usually end badly for the person who breaks them, the husband who went back on his pledge to always open the door for his new wife managed to simply run away, escaping the angry mother-in-law's outraged but ineffectual attack.

As in two of the previous narratives, Timothy Kachela's story is about a marital relationship and the breaking of an important interdiction. This tale focuses on the mother-in-law and her ties to the magical daughter who was born of the beeswax. Clearly, Mr. Kachela and his audience were less concerned by the fragile circumstances of the new wife than they were in having the husband investigate the odd nature of the relationship. While the new husband is not necessarily evil, he does break his agreement with his mother-in-law in order to discover the secret of the wife who seems incapable of carrying out ordinary marital duties. The humor with which the tale is received strongly suggests a lampooning of the pampering of a newly wedded wife by her mother, possibly connoting real tensions between in-laws. In actuality, at least traditionally, it is the husband who is usually obliged to live near and provide labor or service to his new in-laws at the start of a marriage.[188] Like the interdiction of the chief who ordered newborn girls to be killed, the mother-in-law imposes what seems to the new husband an unjust condition of marriage. Like the other narratives, this one emphasizes a decidedly male point of view regarding theme and plot development.

Mr. Samson Kapongwe was the last performer at this session. He seemed, aside from Chief Puta, the eldest man to tell a story.[189] He wore blue-gray trousers, a white long-sleeved shirt with the cuffs rolled up to just below his elbows, a white knit buttoned vest, with dark maroon trim and a checked pattern, and what looked a bit like a worn, white golf hat with the back brim turned up. On his left wrist, he wore both a watch and a thin ivory bracelet. His relaxed manner, facial features, and style of dress, particularly his hat, reminded me a bit of a Zambian embodiment of the famous American entertainer Bing Crosby.

Bwile Storytelling 6
by Samson Kapongwe*

Samson Kapongwe: There was a person, among people living in the middle of...of the bush. So then as they lived in the middle of the bush there, then they walked, they walked. Then they found, they found smoke rising. It was rising over there. So then he said, "So let us go there." But, when they went there to the huts, there was one person when he went there, a man. Because he was a hunter, then he found a woman. Then going and arriving, he said, "Odi, odi." She said, "Come in. Who are you?" He said, "It's me, a person." So...uhmn..."A human, is that all, without a name?" He said,

---

188   See Kalulu story told by Idon Pandwe in Chapter V, where Kalulu is being cheated of his ground nuts crop by his greedy in-laws.
189   According to information gathered in 2005, Mr. Kapongwe was born in 1908 and died in 1994, at the age of eighty-six.

* To watch a video of this story follow this link: http://dx.doi.org/10.11647/OBP.0033.06/Bwile6

"I am Kaly...Kalyaneka [I eat alone]." "You, you are Kalyaweka [you eat alone]?" He said, "Yes." "So where have you come from?" "I was just in the middle of the bush, where I am hunting. I'm a hunter." "Yes. So what have you come for?" "Me, because I'm a bachelor, I want, since I have found you, I want to marry you." Then she said to him, "Would you follow the rules which I have?" He said, "Yes, I can follow them." She said, "No, you, my father, go away." He said, "No, I won't go away. In fact, I'm Kalyaneka." "No, because you are Kalyaweka. No, then you must go." "No, it's just like that, I have to marry you."

So now then, that lady agreed. Then they...they lived, they lived. So, they had a child. So, they just lived on. This child grew. He was the first one. So, again, they just lived and lived. They just lived. Again they had another one, the second. Again that one grew. They just lived, again they had another one. Now they were three. Again, they just lived, just like that they were four, **folo**. So, now again they just lived on, they were **faifi**. Then they just lived, there were **sixi**.

Then he said, "You, woman, now among all these children we have produced, these, me, I have a method which I can give the children so that they are respected." Then she said, "No, just ask the children." So he asked this child, the first born. Then he said to him, saying, "You, my child, listen. I have respect, I have witchcraft which you can move with, any difficulty you can overcome [it]." So he said, "No, me I am a Christian, I would not want that." "You refuse?" He said, "Yes." He said, "Listen, my wife, this child of mine, what I want to give him he has refused." She said, "He himself does not want it." He spoke to another...this one...he who...one who followed again [the first]. And that one answered in the same way [when] he said, "You, my child, I want to give you what can give you respect. When you travel [with this] people will fear you." And that one said, "No." And that one refused. Again he went to another child. Again he said, "You, my child, I want to give you, listen, this respect." And that one refused. "You, my wife, so the children, what I am asking them now, that I give them respect. I could give them dignity. I am a hunter, I do all things, but the children are refusing." She said, "Ala, let me ask them." Again, he asked another who came after. Now there were four. No, and that one again refused, he said, "No, I, I am a Christian, you can't give me something like this. No father." "You refuse?" He said, "Yes." He said to his wife, again, she said the same thing, she said, "Ala, it's me, even if I ask them, can I enter into their hearts?" So, again he went and asked the one who followed, the youngest child. So that one remaining, he asked, he said, "You, my child, listen, I want to give you respect that...that even when people see you, no, it would be fine." That one refused. So then that one who remained there, the smallest child who was like this friend of ours [Note: I can't tell who he's referring to, though the circumstances of the performance session, suggests he was alluding to me], so, saying, "Listen, my child, listen my child, listen." He said, "Yes. You can give that to me." He agreed. So, "You agree?" He said, "Yes." So then he did to him that very magic. He bestowed [it] on him, bestowed him, bestowed him.

So then they set out on a journey. They went. They were walking. He said, "We're going to Mporokoso." So, as they went on the trip, that child, they reached half way, thirst for water gripped him, his throat became dry. Then he saw people bringing water from within the bush, where they went to draw water from far away. And the water in the water holes was dried up. Now he said, "Father, can I ask for water?" He said, "Yes, ask." So he said, "My mother, I want water." She said, "Ala! We are carrying water on our heads as if we were slaves. Where we went to draw water, it's very far, you too can go there." He said, "Yangwe! Father, now that magic you gave me, I'm going to bewitch them." "No, my child, it's not that, no." "Ah, so you've just given me a useless thing. You told me that the magic was mine, [that which] you now gave me. When they do not give me water, my throat is dry, [and] you are stopping me. I'm going to bewitch them." "Ala! No, be patient." He calmed him down. So they went, they went, they went. They found old millet fields. Others were digging cassava in the same way and they stacked it up. Then he said, "I'm going to ask for cassava, the hunger is strong." But when he went, he said, "My mother, give me cassava." She said, "Bring money." As you know, long ago money was difficult to find, so then they just went on their journey. They had nothing, no. That made him there again say to his father, he said, "Father, they refused me cassava, I'm going to bewitch them." He said, "No, my child, be patient." He said, "So then you've given me something useless. So the hunger should be just like this? You stopped me when I was thirsty there, you stopped me here." He said, "No, be patient my friend."

So they went, they just went on that journey. They went far. When they arrived, when it was just evening, they arrived in a village. All along they had walked through old millet fields and grass. As the sun went down, that's when they entered the village. They found an argument between relatives. Siblings were arguing. They said, "Unless I didn't see the hoes [before you]? [i.e. "I wasn't born first."]" He said, "No, we didn't see each other, I was not born with you." He said, "Listen my child, you who want to bewitch, want them to bewitch you." He said, "You must be joking. You try there so that we see." There those called, when he tried. "So then you intended that you will show [me]." So, these...these very ones, again, who kept talking, became quiet, both became quiet. That's where that thing says, "The day an old person gets lost, [said in unison with those in audience, who recite the second half of the proverb. This occurs each time the proverb is spoken.] you will find white hairs in the hyena's dung. The day an old person gets lost, you will find white hairs in the hyena's dung. The day an old person gets lost, you will find white hairs in the hyena's dung."

So that is the source of the *mulumbe* that says, "The day an old person gets lost, you will find white hairs in the hyena's dung." It is there where those who were talking now, is the one who sets out with magic and he bewitched that one, he died.

This narrative was the last of the afternoon and was well received by the audience. Mr. Kapongwe, like the performers before him, used a mostly subtle set of gestures and mime to tell the story. He kept his hands, palms together, in his lap for most of the performance. He often used his head or bent slightly at the waist to emphasize points or to simply move rhythmically with his words at various times. He often looked left or right when approximating a conversation between characters. Early in the narrative, he mostly used his right hand to provide significant information, especially subtly enumerating the six children as they were born. He moved between Bwile and English, as many people do, in his enumeration: "wanu" (1), "babili" (2), "batatu" (3), "folo" (4), "faifi" (5), and "sixi" (6).

When he depicted the attempts by the father to entice a child to take up sorcery, Mr. Kapongwe created a sense of space and action in a clearly discernable way. He looked down and to his right when talking to a child. He emphasized the great power the magic would bring by using his right hand in a sweeping gesture, from left to right, "…I have witchcraft which you can move with, any difficulty you can overcome [it]." When he spoke to his wife, usually to complain about the unresponsiveness of the children, he looked to his left. At one point, after several refusals, Mr. Kapongwe mimes the main character's frustration by using both hands in a helpless gesture, raising them outward from his lap then dipping them downward, "Tch! Agh! Ala! I'm asking them [with no response]!"

When, finally, the protagonist and his youngest son set out on the journey, Mr. Kapongwe's frequency and complexity of gestures and mime increases. He generally sets most of the action of the people they encounter to his left. He mimes the son being thirsty, after being refused water, by speaking the son's dialogue while also pointing to his throat. Similarly, when refused food and complaining about it, the son touches his stomach to indicate hunger. At both occasions, the audience laughs at the ingenuousness of the son, who keeps asking his father if he should use magic against those who refused him. The laughter was partly due to the implicit understanding that the boy did not comprehend the nature of such power, and he also naively had no real conception of what he was getting himself into. Mr. Kapongwe verbally gave form to the son's confusion and anger, in the way he spoke his dialogue. The father's responses were uniformly quieter and calmer, assuring the son that he would understand eventually.

As the narrative wound down to its somewhat macabre conclusion, the proverb took center stage, obviously eliciting strong responses from the audience. Like most proverbs, this one had two parts. Mr. Kapongwe uttering the first part spurred the audience's response of providing the second part: "*Ubushiku bwaluba umukote...ne cimbwi cinye mfwi.*" [The day an old person gets lost...you will find white hairs in the hyena's dung.] When Mr. Kapongwe first pronounces the proverb, the audience response is a bit slow and quiet. He then repeats the proverb two times, each time more quickly, and the audience responds immediately and loudly. Mr. Kapongwe ends the story by saying, "So, to end the *mulumbe*, he said, 'The day an old person gets lost, you will find white hairs in the hyena's dung.' It is there where those who were talking now is the one who sets out with magic and he bewitched that one, he died." The audience responds with supportive applause and obvious delight in the overall performance.

While this proverb is not an uncommon one, I have, even consulting with some Zambian friends and colleagues, not been able to definitively mine its complete meaning. The most common interpretation stresses that the proverb was employed to suggest coincidence. This would imply that if an elder loses his or her way in the bush and white hairs are found in the hyena's droppings, there would not necessarily be a direct connection; the deduction or supposition that the hyena ate the elder is not the same as absolute proof. The danger in such a situation would be jumping to the wrong conclusion. Another interpretation, that I am tempted to embrace because it seems relevant to the contents of the narrative, is that an elder rarely gets lost in the bush, knowing the paths to walk on and those to avoid. If that person does not show up, then something has gone seriously wrong, as is evidenced by the hyena's dung. The sad or tragic deduction thereby indicates some kind of unexpected event or reversal of fortune. This interpretation would suggest the mysterious nature of the father, the gullibility of the son, and the overall danger of fooling with powerful and dangerous forces. The rather allusive last scene where the father and son come across two apparent siblings arguing is not clearly rendered and adds to the mysterious nature of the uses of magic and its human practitioners. There is an ultimately sinister quality to the encounter and it does not end well for the ambitious youngest child. In any event, the narrative thematically seems to serve as a cautionary tale about the unstable and potentially fatal nature of practicing or embracing witchcraft. This theme is further textured by the knowledge that the tale's main character is also a hunter, someone who commonly employs forms of *muti* [medicines, charms, ritual acts] to ensure both protection in the wild and success in the hunt. Information provided to me by two Bwile elders in 2005 also added a very salient dimension to both the narrative and the performance context, specifying that among other occupations Mr. Kapongwe was also a practicing "witchfinder" (*mucapi*).

After playing back this last narrative, the gathering pretty much broke up. The session had run over two hours and afterwards I took photos of the group, and explained that I'd visit the chief the next day. Though clearly somewhat fatigued, people seemed gratified by the quality of the performances and I had the overall sense that they felt they'd fulfilled Chief Puta's request. I paid the previously negotiated compensation—around ten or twelve dollars—to the Chief, who, ostensibly, would parcel out the money to the performers. I packed up the gear and, accompanied by Daniel and Mr. Banda, drove back to Chiengi and the rest house.

Even though I had no opportunity to discuss it further with the participants, an overall evaluation of the session can be put forward. Certainly the frame of the event was the Chief's summons and the stature of those in attendance. The performers and audience were clearly elders or men of some status. This was evident in their being summoned and also in the way they carried themselves during the session. Most of them wore thin ivory bracelets, often denoting an elevated social status. After Chief Puta set the tone with his brief historical narratives, the performances explored some related and some broader themes. Mr. Indita's tale focuses mostly on the ingratitude of a sister and the loyalty of a half-human nephew. In a matrilineal society, the alliance, through "marriage," between the sister and the twelve-headed snake, yields a magical son who has the special link that nephews have to their mother's brother. Moreover, this relationship supersedes the brother-sister link. In fact, at least in this story, it also supersedes the son-parents link, and leads to the formation of a new, more prosperous resituating of the society. This fictional tale parallels the earlier historical narrative of the founding of the Bwile territory.

Mr. Kachela's story of the girl made from beeswax brings up another unusual form of birth. The barren woman is embittered by her condition and consistently complains about how God has ignored her pleas. She will soon change her tune when the magical daughter is born of the beeswax gestating in a clay pot. The image of a product of nature, and the cultural practice of gathering honey, coming to life inside a womb-like artifact, is a powerful, evocative one. Yet, the unnatural source of the birth, and the mother's unreasonable expectations that the girl must not marry, then later on that she avoid ordinary domestic duties, will turn out to render these circumstances unacceptable to the society. This is not surprising, given the gender of all the performers and their audience. As in Mr. Indita's tale, women are potential sources of problems and instability, and men must be wary of their machinations.

Fred Kafankwa's story of Mupita and the lion stands out from all the others in the sense that it does not seem to jibe with the themes of women and/or male power. Rather, the narrative focuses on the prodigious nature of the hunter and the origin of humans' antagonistic relationship with lions. There is, however, the sense of ingratitude on the part of the lion, echoing the sister's ingratitude in Mr. Indita's narrative. Further, the rather deadpan humor of Mupita casually carting off what seems to be thousands of pounds of game meat with one arm creates a sense of hyperbole that also underscores the power of certain heroic figures. Overall, the performance seemed to be among the most entertaining of the narratives, if audience reaction is to be an accurate barometer.

Finally, partly returning to earlier themes, Mr. Kapongwe's narrative is about another odd or unnatural marriage. In this case, the husband is the dangerous element in the story. As in Mr. Kafankwa's narrative, the protagonist is a powerful "hunter." His mysterious origins in the bush and his suspicious name, "I eat alone," casts doubt on his suitability as a husband as well as his very identity as a human being. Yet, the tale is more about power than marital relationships. By bringing in the dimension of witchcraft, the performer sets the tale on a serious level of contention. In Chief Puta's second historical narrative, he told how he had brought in specialists to rid the lakeshore of its troublesome crocodiles and lions. He did not specify the actions these "specialists" took. In a way, this overlooking of details glosses over the kinds of protective practices that probably included forms of preventive magic. In Mr. Kapongwe's story, sorcery will be countered by Christian beliefs that will, in the long run, save the siblings who refuse their father's overtures. This kind of parable about competing systems of belief or spirituality lends the overall session a broader depth of thematic exploration that is underscored by ambivalence over the efficacy of magic, and its broader relationship to social power. The proverb that ends the story seems both an enigmatic and appropriate way to close the session.

Though the performers each had their own styles of putting a story across, they created thematically related narratives. Moreover, they seemed to compete with one another in telling the most valued or appreciated story. The overall themes mostly framed an assertion of male power, linked to a matrilineal system of descent and inheritance. Power, as it pertained to this session, was most obviously displayed by Chief Puta, who within a matter of a few hours on a Saturday afternoon, summoned a large group of notables and led them in performing a series of engaging tales. Obviously, compensation for these efforts was another spur to action, as this was part of my initial remarks to the gathering and, earlier, to the Chief.

We stopped at the *musumba* on Sunday morning, and found Chief Puta in a nicely cut grey suit. We took photos of him and his family, and for most of these he changed into what looked to be a black academic, or perhaps a legal, gown over his suit. He also wore an ornate cap I'd never seen before. I assume it was a new addition to his regalia. Before we took our leave, I gave him a small gift of cash and he presented us with a chicken—always an appreciated addition when one is traveling and has only meager food resources.

Postscript

In October 2005 I returned to the village of Puta, on Lake Mweru. After spending the night at a recently constructed guest house, I walked to the *musumba* of Chief Puta, who had succeeded the man I knew and recorded in 1989. I had been following the activities of the current chief in the Zambian newspapers for a year or two. He has been very active in the newly reconstituted "Council of Chiefs," which is a group consisting of the traditional heads of Zambia's largest ethnic polities. Chief Puta has spoken out more than once on the slow pace of development in his constituency as well as about real or perceived slights to his and other chiefs' positions by the national government. The Chief's activist stance on raising the level of investment and infrastructure in his area ran parallel to the proactive work of the district's dynamic Member of Parliament, who relentlessly pushed for this somewhat isolated corner of the country to get its share of the national pie. While a main bone of contention, the poor quality of the road that ran from the town of Kashikishi, on Lake Mweru to Puta had not been addressed by the government, it was clear to me that there'd been substantial development in the Chief's village since my last visit. Village houses had been generally upgraded with paint, freshly thatched roofs, carefully tended yards, and well-kept, very straight dirt streets divided the homes into a neat neighborhood grid of households or compounds. Chief

Puta had moved into the large, impressive home of his predecessor, and this too had been upgraded and fenced with newer materials.

Inside the *musumba*, the chief greeted me politely but in a reserved manner. He seemed to be in his early forties, compactly built, with a shaved head. His English was very good, so we opted to use it in most of our discussion. He watched the various performances on DVD and then told me that the information provided by his predecessor on Bwile history was not entirely accurate or complete. He told me to come back in the afternoon so that he could enlist the assistance of some of his elder advisors in responding to the material and providing accurate biographical information on the performers.

In the afternoon, joined by Mr. T.D. Koti, a former MP from the area, and Mr. Ferry Chansa, a local headman, we once again viewed the video material from the 1989 session. Chief Puta charged Mr. Koti with updating or correcting several issues raised by his predecessor, and I then proceeded to record his comments on audiocassette.

Bwile Storytelling 7 by Mr. T.D. Koti, 2005

Robert
Cancel: Begin *mukwai*.

T.D. Koti: When we came from Kasongo wa Kumwimba, we were not called Babwile, no. We were called Baluba Kati. Our chief was Kasongo wa Kumwimba. Abaluba Kati. When we arrived at Kaansa, at a small river, at a tributary called Kaansa, that is where we settled. And our friends the Lunda were on the other side. They began going behind our backs and would burn our houses, burn our livestock, grab our livestock. Then we said, "What shall we do?" That is when we decided to fashion sculptures, made from carvings, which we erected to look like soldiers. They erected [here], they erected there. The men praised the leader we were with on the trek, saying, "Mpweto, the crowd-erector. He has excreted troops. He has [multiplied] troops. He has increased the number of troops in our group. He has increased the number of troops."

And now when the fighting was over, we got rid of those Lunda, to defeat them. Then the Lunda came back as if they were just passing by, ostensibly to come and see the area where we fought, only to find that there were no troops. There were sculptures. They were still standing. Then they said, "These people, so it was a hoax."

	Hence the group came to be the Bwile. They started referring to us as Babwile because there a trick had succeeded. [At this point Mr. Koti switches to English (marked in bold type)—I assume it was an attempt to be sure I understood the main point of the story] **[It was a] trick to defeat those Lunda people, yes. We made some... some carve[ing]s of...in the form of soldiers...**
RC:	Uh hmn.
TDK:	**Yes, with their bows and arrows. Pretending. Now the Lunda people ran away.** They ran away, saying, "We are dying. Those [people] are too many." When all there was were mere carvings that had been erected. Erected here and erected there. [They were] saying, "We are dying."
	That is how we defeated those Lunda. We then crossed over. Crossed on the other side [of the river]. The Lunda also went over there further down where they originated from. We crossed the Lualaba River [coming back]. Coming across the river. The Lunda, too, ran away, settling where they are today. As for us, the boundary of our domain continued as far as the Kalungwishi [River] [to the south]. That's as far as our boundary went. As time went by, it [the boundary] somehow returned to the Kalobwa [River]. That is where it is today.

Mr. Koti's brief narrative was focused on augmenting the historical overview provided by the elder Chief Puta in the 1989 recording session. He provides some important details such as the successful turning away of the attack of the numerically superior and historically more militant Lunda people. More specifically, by carving statues that looked like warriors, the Bwile were able to deceive their attackers into believing their defense force was much larger than it actually was. This claim is significant in part because the Lunda of the Luapula area are the best known and largest group in the region, with a longstanding written historical and cultural presence in scholarship. Defeating such a powerful enemy is thus a clear assertion of Bwile prowess and significance. The claim also leads to the etiological importance of the word *bwile* itself, which Mr. Koti claims means "trick."[190] While he was narrating the account, Chief Puta was obviously concerned that this information be recorded and preserved

---

190 The *White Father– English Dictionary* has several definitions for the word, including "2. a string trick played by children..."; "3. mystery, unaccountable thing; enigma, riddle, puzzle..."; and "4. a small net which pulls the trigger of a trap..."

as an important dimension of the polity's history. He was so intent on this goal that he immediately began to emphasize these details to me after I turned off the recorder. After about a minute or two, I suggested that he make his case more forcefully and indelibly by allowing me to record his explanation.

Bwile Storytelling 8
by Chief Puta, 2005

Chief Puta: When Ntinda Munchelenge offended [the Bwile] by feeding the [Bwile] princess meat from animals with claws, which we did not eat, such as monitor lizard, crocodile…

Audience: Pythons.

CP: Pythons, snakes. That's how when he brought the princess to the Bwile elders, those who came included: Mpweto, Puta, Kasama and Chisabi. They told Ntinda that "Actually, this matter you have brought [before us] is very serious; is a very big one. And so we do not know even what to do to you." So, what do you call him, Ntinda went back to his family to Mununga at Chititu, to Chief Nkuba. When they sat down he said, "I would like to compensate you for the case concerning the princess, whom I impregnated. Whose constant sickness, due to what we made her eat, what she used to eat is forbidden to consume at…at the Bwile where she comes from, no. So this is a very serious matter facing us."

So they told him that, "OK. You take those elephant tusks. Take elephant tusks as compensation." So Ntinda took elephant tusks, lots of them, and brought them there to the Bwile, the Bwile chiefs, saying it should settle the matter. The chiefs refused to accept [them], saying "What you did was too serious and it was worth more than tusks." He went back and they sat again. "What shall we do? They have refused. They keep saying that it is a very serious offense that you committed. So now how shall we vindicate ourselves?" Then they said, "So what happens is this: Let us give them part of our domain." So they partitioned their domain. Up to the Kalungwishi River from the Lualaba, up to the Kalungwishi. He said, "This territory belongs to me, the Bwile. We have given it to them as compensation."

So when they saw this they said, "Yes, now you've appeased us. Because you have paid, we accept." That's how they accepted.

	Our land, of the Bwile, went as far as the Kalungwishi. And the Shila, they're from the Kalungwishi, going there where they share a boundary with the Lunda. Very far away there, on the other side are the Lunda, the entire [Lake] Mweru area. Because this territory belongs to Nkuba of Lubemba, that Ntinda was like the captain of...what's his name, of Nkuba, who was overseeing the land on the other side. In addition, he was a hunter, hunting with dogs. He would wander about in their area, wandering about. It is during his wanderings that he came across the princess [in question]. He liked her when he saw her. He said that, "This one is suitable for me to marry. They allowed him to take her. That is when he fed her such things. This is the reason for the case I have just explained. They made him pay accordingly. Then here to the Lualaba, reaching as far as the Kalungwishi.
	Now as days went by it...
Audience:	Aah.
CP:	He was Lambwe Mutumpa. He was nicknamed "The foolish one" because he gave up the land. This is where the name "Mutumpa" came to be. He what do you call it...at the Shila people, he committed adultery with a princess there.
Audience:	At the Shila, there.
CP:	At the Shila there. So they said [to the Bwile], "We too will penalize you for this one's misbehavior, you Bwile." So they apportioned part of our land. This time they took land from the Kalungwishi River up to the Kalobwa River. Now this became our boundary. Our portion that extended as far as the...what do you call it, the Kalungwishi, it now became theirs, up to today. As for us, our territory extends as far as the Kalobwa River, because of what transpired.

Chief Puta not only felt it important to have his counselors recount the battle with the Lunda and the trickery that ensued, he himself essentially repeated what had been said in 1989 by his predecessor then added a bit about Mutumpa's indiscretion that led to ceding part of the Bwile territory.[191] Clearly, there was a desire to put his stamp on the kind of

---

191 He asserts an etiological relationship between Mutumpa's indiscretion and the actual Bemba/Bwile word for a stupid person, *mutumpa* [root word: *-tumpa*].

information I had recorded then and now (2005) in order to emphasize his role as ruler and owner of his polity's history.

After our session with Chief Puta, Mr. Koti and Mr. Chansa accompanied me to a small church building across from the *musumba* so that they could watch the other performances and provide information on the storytellers and, in a few cases, the tales' themes. We finished our meeting in the late afternoon and I compensated them for their time and walked back to the rest house to spend one more night in Puta before traveling on to Kaputa the next morning.

VII. Conclusions: Lessons from Frozen Moments

A fieldworker cannot but take events out of context and people out of their lives. The injustice of shaping other people's lives around a research budget and university calendar is only vaguely implied in this short discussion. Zambians are not monolingual, nor do they have to fit into the neat categories that the researcher needs to think with, in order to turn noise into signal. Whether one is rural or urban, localist or cosmopolitan, one is always creating meaning. This involves the endoginisation of foreign culture and the modification of existing order. That is why Zambian English, or Catholicism, football, rock music or the family are different from the ideal types. (Sichone 2001, p. 377)

The slippage between immediate and non-immediate subjectivities is particularly striking in storytelling. Every story is Janus-faced: while one aspect is turned outward toward a world that is shared, another is turned inward, answering more immediate individual needs. Indeed, stories reconcile and make 'ego-sytonic'… the multiple and frequently discrepant truths that every society, as well as every individual, contains within it. So too with myths. Though said to be primordial and immutable, every recitation of the myth shows evidence of present concerns and changing circumstances. (Jackson 2006, p. 294)

The most significant dimension of the preceding chapters is the strong emphasis on contextualization of performance events and acknowledging the relative paucity of data that was arrayed in this effort. I have focused, no doubt *ad nauseum*, on the main sources of information in what was mostly a set of brief encounters as consisting of the video record, field notes, published scholarship, consultation with Zambian scholars and a brief return to most of the recording sites. Moreover, the interdisciplinary nature of this study has kept it from comfortably alighting onto one or another clearly established scholarly field. I want to frame these concluding remarks with the notion of "capture" when it applies to a scholar and the people he or she studies, a reiteration of my concerns about the inherent complexity of these efforts, and a summary of overlapping themes in the tales that suggests there are many commonalities between these societies when it comes to their narrative-performance practices. In this latter regard, I focus on the contributions of the performers represented here and identify some stable elements of the oral tradition as they were utilized and embodied by individuals.

In 1988–89, as now, there was a long standing legacy of colonial rule and its numerous structures. By this, I do not mean to imply that the legacy of struggle and awareness of the oppressive realities of colonialism still predominate in Zambia. I think the details and themes of that struggle are in many ways seen as information in history books or part of the national mythology by many young Zambians, the majority today being under thirty years old. Concerns of current and recent governments and policies, of immediate economic conditions and opportunities, are foremost in contemporary media such as newspapers, broadcasting and popular culture. However, among many colonial conditions that flowed into the independence era and still persist was the complicated relationship of people moving to and from urban areas and the various networks of family and economics that inevitably kept many of them linked to rural areas. The network includes crucial concerns such as rural land ownership, or allocation, and fealty to extended family, clan and kingship entities— which is another way to frame the concept of ethnicity. So even my basic effort to record and compare the oral narrative performances of five "ethnic groups" is by its nature open to contestation and debate as to what actual differences exist among these people. As stated earlier, for some people ethnic assertion has undergone shifting periods of relevance and action during and after colonial rule. Moreover, the cases of men, not commonly women, who worked in cities and returned to homes in rural areas, are not particularly uniform in how they were able to either maintain or restart the links to family and land that would make for a smooth return.[192] In 1988–89 some of the elders I recorded had substantial cosmopolitan

---

192 Sichone 2006, pp. 375–376 gives a brief but significant explanation of the Bemba term *ukuikusha*, which is negatively applied by neighbors to some returning urban workers who, in their estimation, exhibit arrogant or inappropriately ambitious behavior. In the post-1990 era of structural adjustment and economic liberalization of the Zambian economy, urban/rural migration has taken on even more complexity and urgency, as noted in quantitative detail by Mulenga and van Campenhout 2008.

experience and had put in enough employment time to earn adequate retirement benefits, as opposed to the conditions of the post-liberalization era of Zambia's economy that took place a few years later. While these men were comfortable with my presence and project, there still existed among many a distrust of European strangers, both as a legacy of colonial rule and the post-independence visits of foreign researchers, aid workers and commercial representatives. This was compounded by various levels of distrust of the national government, as difficult economic times and the death throes of the one-party state were being played out. Without living in an area long enough for people to feel comfortable with my presence, in order to establish interactions that in some ways suggested my willingness to be captured by local interests, four of the five groups I recorded maintained a distance that was often difficult to bridge.[193]

Another critical dimension of complexity in accurately presenting and interpreting these performances is the language of storytelling itself. Some of the significant differences between the five groups whose performances are documented above reside in local usage of what is a widespread Bemba language, rife with dialects and tropes that at times differ dramatically in their application or usage.[194] Moreover, the traditional context may be part of the repertoires of all these groups, but tales and their constituent elements accrue varied local meanings the more they are told, repeated, altered and discussed. When proverbs, songs, praises and other examples of deeper levels of the language are employed, the complexity involved in understanding or interpreting increases. As long as I've worked with oral traditions in general, and with these performances in particular, I have been uncomfortable definitively interpreting a story's meaning, while also acknowledging the many compromises necessitated in the translation of Bemba-related languages into English. When it comes to language

---

193 The notion of "capture" is complicated by many factors. Most commonly, it means the simple building of relationships and obligations between researcher and local residents that leads to mutual favors. In some cases this results in real and long-lasting friendships. The classic local contribution of some researchers is simply possession of a vehicle and the provision of transportation of neighbors and/or their goods. Similarly, access to hard-to-find goods and the ability to purchase and give them as gifts or compensation is another way that researchers establish themselves within a community. Even these simple material interactions are complicated by who develops ties to the researcher and how others see this access. A thornier situation can emerge when the researcher writes up his or her findings and how he or she portrays the host community.
194 Kashoki's work on "town Bemba" (1972) is but a single example of the ways the language adapts, grows and contracts in the living environment. See also Spitulnik 1998.

as the center of interpretation of storytelling, the inclusion in this study of an audio-visual record reveals the absolute necessity of examining the extra-linguistic performance elements of physical and contextual dimensions. This certainly expands the field of possible data originally imagined in any kind of "ethnography of communication." When we add the consideration of formal aesthetics of composition to the mix—elements of repetition, shaping and detailing of images and recurring motifs, genres, etc. — we only raise the level of complexity in this enterprise.

The content and themes of the narratives and songs collected herein range from relatively clear and obvious to rather esoteric to veiled and mysterious, at least as far as my efforts are concerned. How particular characters, actions or images are rendered in a single performance relies strongly on what came before in the experience of a storyteller and his or her audience.Intertextuality and genre are key elements here, but there is also a degree of depth of meaning that resides at the core of the traditional context, the place where ordinary tale or song meets deeper structures and meanings of mythology and didacticism. These deeper structures go beyond the storytelling activities to tie in to social practice and even more esoteric discursive and physical manifestations in the areas of hunting, farming, fishing, rites of passage, healing, and defensive or aggressive assertions of power in the spectrum that constitutes traditional religious beliefs as well as Christian beliefs. Many of these socio-cultural dimensions have been represented in the performances in this collection. While we can fairly easily discern some of these themes in the tales examined, the actual associations made by audiences to the more allusive levels of performances remain difficult to ascertain. For example, when the group of elders at Malole is making small talk while a performer tries to get over a coughing spell, they jokingly compare the coughs to the sounds made by both the roan antelope and the bushbuck. A rather deep form of rural knowledge is being casually exhibited here that has ties to hunting and other important activities.[195] If these elders share what seems a common knowledge, does the same knowledge exist for younger performers and audiences or performers with little direct experience of this side of rural life? Do the animals portrayed in tales carry realistic connotations for all audiences or are these associations linked in a deeper web of knowledge that might be tied to origins of the

---

195 Responding to this specific incident in the Bemba performance session, Stuart Marks provided a list of animals and their traits that he'd elicited over his many years studying Bisa cultural and hunting practices. (personal communication)

tales and relationships that define particular societies? Can these be seen as symbolic representations, in action and characters, of crucial religious beliefs that make for both individual and social definitions? Are, as A. F. Roberts puts it when referring, at least in part, to elements of Tabwa myths in the DRC, "animals good to think with"?[196] Every narrative has roots not only in other tales but in an aesthetic and representational system.[197] It is tempting for scholars to piece together these numerous tales in relational ways, revealing, or some might argue constructing, these complex systems of thought and representation; finding one's way through what Turner called a "forest of symbols", as Lévi-Strauss did for the Americas and de Heusch did for Central Africa.[198] As we consider the numerous narratives in this project, some small sense of these links will emerge, but in so many ways the ultimate analysis of the discourses recorded in these performances requires much more data and a particularly strong knowledge of the local cultures. Assertive interpretations based on incomplete or superficial data only risk instances of essentialism. Moreover, story performance, myth and the wider verbal arts are only part of larger signifying or meaning-making systems found in these societies. Among those systems are plastic arts, religion, architecture, medicine, and economic practices such as fishing, farming and hunting and elements of urban and cosmopolitan labor. These interpretive efforts should ideally be carried out by Zambian scholars and their local collaborators.

The subtitle of this study, "theory, method, practice and other necessary fictions," is intentionally ironic in that it expresses the need for scholarly frames of reference while also noting their inevitably provisional nature. So we choose our discourses of and approaches to collection and analysis in specific terms and note their inadequacies and the often tenuous nature of this endeavor. When working with the performance events, we again acknowledge that most of what can be gleaned is what the storytellers at those moments chose to share with the camera and their audiences.

---

196 See A. F. Roberts 1997.
197 Jackson notes that "myths frequently become fragmented and pared down in the course of migration, surviving only as folktales, with their original cosmological, metaphysical and natural oppositions reduced to parochial homilies." (2006, p. 197) While I do not believe that there is such a facile relationship between the genres of myth and folktale, his point about the depth of meaning and allusive potential of performed narratives is valuable.
198 We could add to Turner's *"Forest"* (1967) and Lévi-Strauss's *"Mythologiques"* volumes (1969, for example), and de Heusch's (1982) work, the earlier efforts of Griaule to piece together Dogon cosmology in the words and tales of Ogotemmeli (1965).

How much of this was a way to engage or capture me as researcher/chronicler and how much was basically a way of appeasing my requests by expending the least amount of energy and creativity possible is something we can carefully examine but only, in the end, speculate about. However, as in all fieldwork, patterns and themes do emerge and elements of the performances and performers exhibit similarities and differences that are instructive. We can then begin the summation of this project by considering these patterns and what they mean when it comes to the efforts to capture, versus the desire to simply appease, the researcher in performance.

Like Jackson, I have tended in this study to "emphasise storytelling over stories—the social process rather than the product of narrative activity" (2006, p. 18). I have also, however, kept the tales themselves in close focus, since these are indeed the products created by the storytellers. Looking at the contexts of performance, I've been raising the question of how the individual performs the self in public, making as Arendt says "the private public." (1958)

This concept, too, is complicated by what Jackson calls an "existential imperative" (2006, p. 30) for individuals to feel empowered by transforming their worlds through performance, if even in small personal ways. For me, this means not only constructing and performing narratives to share with others but also choosing not to tell stories at all, or refusing to interpret or explain the stories that are told. This is a broad range of responses to my simple request for tales. It applies to my attempts to glean ideas and assertions from performers and their willingness to either provide the material or resist the request.

Performance can obviously take many forms in any culture and even when narrowed down to storytelling the activity is a complex one. Schechner rightly asserts that "[b]ecause performances are usually subjective, liminal, dangerous, and duplicitous they are often hedged in with conventions and frames: ways of making the places, the participants, and the events somewhat safe." (2003, p. xix) Each context of narrative-performance is different and exhibits varying manifestations of risk or uncertainty. Indeed, skilled storytellers can employ these conditions to their own ends, shaping tales that touch their audiences in different ways, to elicit various effects. This is why any consideration of narratives and their performers need to frame the context of their transmission. There is not only a thematic focus for most tales but also a desired impression or interaction that performers strive for while working with what is both familiar and uncertain during any instance of storytelling.

Stanley Kalumba, in the Tabwa region, more than once tried to explain the meaning of tales or their components to me. He understood that my project was in part the preservation of narratives and their meanings and he felt this to be an important endeavor. While his efforts were not always successful, his intention was to bring me and by extension my readers to a clearer vision of the culture. Similarly, the Bemba elders who gathered at Fele's home in Malole felt there were certain themes that needed to be explored, shared and preserved in the tales and ruminations they provided me and my recording equipment. When the current Chief Puta saw that the history narrated by his predecessor was somehow inaccurate, meaning that it did not conform to **his** vision of the Bwile past, he first had his advisors present a more detailed, nuanced version of a segment of the account, then he too provided an even sharper focus on what needed emphasis. Moreover, while the Lunda storyteller Moffat Mulenga sped through his stories about Kalulu, his neighbor Idon Pandwe performed detailed narratives that were thematically clear and interspersed with English words or phrases to both reach a wider audience and demonstrate his own competence in that language. These are all instances where performers sought to capture me, or rather my recording and interpretive efforts, for their own purposes. Since these assertions also involved engaging audiences of their peers, their use of storytelling techniques and the vital interactions that constitute living performance made the narrators' creative visions a shared experience. Moreover, common themes, story content and performance styles suggested many cultural similarities across all five ethnic groups.

In the highly charged environment of Nabwalya, Bisa narrators at the most public of my recording sessions in that village tended to keep their stories brief and, at times, cryptic. Even though both a researcher of long-standing in the community and a local resident had supported or sanctioned my efforts, the general distrust of strangers and the specific reaction to a recent visit by government game-enforcement personnel mitigated against open or unfettered cooperation with me. The propensity of performers to simply get up and leave when they finished suggested a grudging willingness to supply cultural material as well as an overall disinterest in providing depth or interpretation of their stories. Only one performer, Lenox Paimolo, seemed interested in clearly emphasizing a theme or point of view, and this had to do with the efficacy of farming as an economic endeavor over hunting or simple wealth. He made his thematic points through the vehicle of a conundrum story, where three suitors for a beautiful woman would be compared and only one found to be worthy. It is further notable that Mr. Paimolo chose to emphasize this theme on the occasion of what was meant to be the harvesting of a sorghum crop by a group of neighbors. While the other narratives, indeed, had identifiable themes, none were explained at the end of the performances. In contrast, under very different recording conditions, Laudon Ndalazi in fact challenges his very small audience of three or four people to work out the puzzles he'd set. His obvious goal was to reveal his own mastery of the ideas and details that shaped the narratives' themes. It may well be, as was the case with both Idon Pandwe and Stanley Kalumba, that Mr. Ndalazi's experience working in an urban area led him to interact with me in familiar and proactive ways that encouraged recording and sharing with a wider reading or viewing audience.

If gendered difference was minimized by the group of Bemba elders who seemed to work easily and cooperatively in developing certain common themes, this was not the case in several sessions among the Bisa and Bwile. At least three or more tales told by Bisa men warned about the disruptive and selfish nature of women. Laudon Ndalazi described an evil hunchbacked old woman who directed her resentment at a father and son. George Iyambe told of a greedy wife who put her husband's life in jeopardy by demanding the skin of a lion to make a sling to carry their baby. The dead husband's nephew both laments and accuses in his song lyric, "The Bisa woman, yes. See what's happened. See what's happened. One ends in the cruel jaws." Kabuswe C. Nabwalya warns that "A woman does not keep secrets." Among the all-male group of Bwile storytellers, Fermit Ndita depicted an ungrateful woman who, after being saved by her brother, instructs her serpent husband to kill his in-law, while her half-human son acts to save his uncle. Timothy Kachela, and his audience, show little compassion for the woman who miraculously conceived her daughter from a pot of beeswax, humorously supporting the son-in-law's breaking of a marital agreement and having his new wife inexorably melt into a puddle of wax. While only one of these tales was performed before a mixed audience of men and women, at least one cluster of themes in the traditional contexts of these locales and sessions clearly took a misogynistic stance.[199]

---

[199] Mills 2001 makes a convincing point that misogyny in stories told by men is not necessarily a fixed attitude or stance, showing the example of the same performer taking inverted views of women's agency and intentions in two different performances.

If polygamy is at one angle seen as an imposition of patriarchy, then the Bemba tale performed by Elizabeth, of the jealous co-wives that cause their family's destruction, and Luva Kombe's Lunda story of the aggressive and destructive young woman who hounds her elder co-wife into the grave and beyond can be seen as questioning this cultural practice. Moreover, if polygamy itself is less the target than the ways in which the ideal can go unrealized in actuality, the performers are laying out their cases for not only their immediate audiences but especially for the camera of a visiting stranger who, although a man, is in many ways exempt from the local strictures between men and women. The narratives are complementary, told from the inverted viewpoints sympathetic to younger and older co-wives, respectively. In the case of Elizabeth, her performance was in front of a group of women, Mr. Dismas Kampamba, and me. Her theme centered on the jealousy or pettiness of the two wives who, at least by the order they were presented, seemed to be seniors of the third, Mweo, or "Life". Women in the audience guided Elizabeth's efforts by telling her to speak up. In this atmosphere, she emphasized the importance of a co-operative and supportive household in ensuring a successful family atmosphere, where disharmony literally leads to death. With women in the majority at this performance, showing their cooperation by singing along to the narrative's main song, Elizabeth found a receptive audience. In contrast, Luva Kombe stepped into what had been a male-dominated session in order to assert her presence and shape her narrative themes. When she initially falters in her presentation and some audience members respond by laughing at her efforts, other women supportively intercede to demand they cease and give Ms. Kombe a chance. Her thematic emphasis is again the pettiness and jealousy that can poison a polygamous household, but this time the target is a younger co-wife who baits and challenges her elder. In the face of a large audience, with men and women of all ages present, Luva Kombe overcame what would have been a natural stage fright to present her story and make her thematic points.

Themes of generational conflict emerge from several narrative-performances, on both sides of the divide. The Tabwa storyteller Chipioka Patrick makes a detailed and amusing case for the efficacy of youth in the adventures of his protagonist Biti Mupalume. The point-of-view of the *balumendo* in local and related societies is clearly set out and manages to destabilize the overall rule of elders and tradition in the face of youthful assertion. The Lunda performer Fermit Ndita portrays a youthful serpent-nephew who turns aside the treachery of his mother and father in order to both save his uncle and bring a new order to his society. On the other side of the equation, among the Lunda, Idon Pandwe depicts the foolhardy chief who mandates the killing of all elders in his jurisdiction, then has to cope with trying to unwind a deadly snake from his neck. He is saved only by the wisdom of the old man who has been hidden by his son. Stitching together a series of narratives and discussions, a group of Bemba elders lament the loss of the authority of parents over the younger generation. One tale focuses on the doomed young roan antelope who "lacks ears" when it comes to his father's advice. Another oration decries the many instances of young women bearing children out of wedlock or simply rejecting the wisdom of tradition wholesale in favor of embracing a kind of shallow modernity. Each of these performances makes an effective case for the generational stance they favor.

The figure of Kalulu, the trickster hare, emerged in performances among four of the five groups recorded. While a deeper consideration of what the trickster is and does in this culture region would be the subject of a full length study, it is worth noting how he is deployed in some of the performances presented above. There are three versions of the tale that depicts Kalulu first fooling Lion into making him a bark cloth garment then placing the blame on Bushbuck, resulting in the antelope's death. The core details of the narrative are consistent in all three stories, but the degree of detailing, repetition of interactions, specifics of events, and explanatory comments vary enough to reveal the efforts to shape individual visions by the performers, Stanley Kalumba and Idon Pandwe. Thematically, while each version had a slightly different shading, Kalulu's dual propensities, to bring down and deceive the arrogant and powerful as well as take advantage of the dimwitted and innocent, come across quite clearly. In these tales he shows absolutely no distinction between the weak and powerful as targets he chooses to exploit for his own gains. This situation can be contrasted with two versions of a narrative where Kalulu simply takes advantage of two of the most powerful animals in his world, Elephant and Hippopotamus, as performed by the Lungu storyteller Moffat Mulenga and by Paul Chandalube among the Bisa. By challenging them to a tug-of-war, Kalulu exemplifies a core trickster trait, using the power and arrogance of his adversaries against them, as cleverness trumps brute strength. In two other stories, by Moffat Mulenga and the Bemba performer Henry Chakobe, Kalulu first succeeds in fooling his targeted dupes, but then is eventually found out and either forced to leave the community to "wander aimlessly" or actually dies as a result of his trickery. After Kalulu tricks his fellow animals into killing their own mothers, he hides his in a cave, where she regularly provides him with large meals, until Tortoise uncovers his deception and reveals it to the others. Hare is consequently driven from his habitat. In Henry Chakobe's narrative, Kalulu first succeeds in fooling his usual dupe Bushbuck into climbing a tree and throwing down delicious fruit. The tables are turned, however, when the antelope finally acts on his suspicions and steals the hare's skin, causing him to painfully dry to death. Finally, the trickster plays two similar roles, one central and the other peripheral, when he treats themes of obvious social concern. In Idon Pandwe's story of how Kalulu fools his in-laws into sharing the ground nuts he'd helped them grow through traditional marriage obligations, there is an exploration of the potential for abuse involved in an important social duty. Bemba performer Peter Mutale told the story of the young roan antelope who ignored his parents' warning and was eaten by lions. Here, in a rather minor role, Kalulu performs the task of physically cutting off the roan's ears to demonstrate how he'd refused to heed the good advice of his elders.

In these and other performances, Kalulu plays varied but well known roles. As is the case with many tricksters, his reputation precedes him and makes for certain expectations among audiences. Moreover, and this is a particularly important characteristic in this region, the trickster is not only protean by nature, that is he can take on disguises or any number of personalities in his deceptive repertoire, but he also plays a versatile role in the thematic shaping of tales. He is useful beyond his obvious humorous and entertaining side because of the many ways he can intervene in a narrative as at times a source of social disruption and shaking up the system and, at other times, a moral guide or restorer of order when harmony has been fractured by other characters. When considering whether a universal definition or application of the figure of trickster is possible or desirable, Beidelman provocatively suggests that, "we abandon the term and renew analysis from the concerns manifest within each particular society considered." (1980, p. 38) I raise the point, in this context, to note that the Kalulu figure among these Bemba-speaking groups does not at all times exemplify certain trickster characteristics mandated by earlier studies.[200]

---

200 These studies are numerous but certainly Radin 1956, including the essays by Jung and Kerenyi is a highly influential study. Babcock-Abrahams 1975 contributed a broadly referenced and detailed consideration of these multifaceted figures in many cultures

Finally, the notion of capture is inextricably tied to the notion of power as it relates to the interactions and relationships between researchers and their subjects. In this respect, though specific details and perspectives will surely vary, in the long run these conditions prevail for both foreign and local researchers. Capture, if we are doing what we should be doing, is inevitable. The real question is the degree of "capture" and how we continually negotiate these relationships. We have to educate ourselves in the local politics and dynamics that mark virtually everything we do in the field. Where do our associates and friends fit into the overall social network of the places where we work? Is it possible to balance these associations with other relationships, so that we maintain an overall balance of how we are seen locally? If we keep too much of an "objective distance" from the people we work with, there is a danger of never establishing trust and reciprocal relationships. If we allow our ties to become too strong, we develop obligations that approach those of actual family members. In some cases the former works best and in others the latter could be advantageous to our collection efforts. There is also the very familiar case of finding a degree of security and satisfaction in the close ties that indeed link us to certain friends and their families.

In the end, the process comes down to a matter of professional and personal integrity, when it applies to both collecting and representing these verbal arts. There is first the responsibility of carefully explaining our intentions to the people we ask to contribute to our projects. Second is the question of intellectual property and how we can best uphold these performer's rights while also disseminating their efforts in our writing. While it is the rare scholarly monograph that actually spurs financial gains for its author, in the instances when this actually happens, there is a clear responsibility to somehow share these profits with the artists who feature in these texts. As in most social interactions, we build relationships of obligation and reciprocity and these links remain an ongoing responsibility to be maintained and honored at least on some

---

before turning specifically to the Winnebago's trickster, Wakdjunkaga. Pelton's (1980) specifically African purview is salient because he clearly focuses on "divine" tricksters that exist in some kind of mythology or cosmology, often seen as a "gods" themselves, and this contrasts with the mostly secular and "realistic" nature of eastern and southern African figures such as Kalulu or Sungura. For an interesting rethinking of a character that scholars have historically considered to be a trickster figure, see Wessels 2008 on the /Xam mythological being /Kaggen, the Mantis.

basic human and humanistic level. In a larger frame, researchers develop relationships with their host institutions and their host nations, and these also comprise an ongoing set of interactions and negotiations. In sum, "capture" works both ways and must inevitably figure in the fundamental equations of our research and scholarship.

Works Cited

Achebe, Chinua. *Things Fall Apart*. Greenwich, CT: Fawcett Books, 1959.

Anderson, Benedict R. *Imagined Communities: Reflections on the Origin and Spread of Nationalism*. London and New York: Verso, 1991.

Arendt, Hannah. *The Human Condition*. Chicago: University of Chicago Press, 1958.

Ashcroft, Bill, Gareth Griffiths and Helen Tiffin. *The Empire Writes Back: Theory and Practice in Post-Colonial Literature*. London and New York: Routledge, 1989.

Babcock-Abrahams, Barbara. "'A Tolerated Margin of Mess': The Trickster and His Tales Reconsidered." *Journal of the Folklore Institute*, 11/3 (March, 1975), pp. 147–186.

Barber, Karin and P.F. de Moraes Farias, eds. *Discourse and Its Disguises: The Interpretation of African Oral Texts*. Birmingham University African Studies Series 1. Birmingham, UK: Centre of West African Studies, University of Birmingham, 1989.

Bauman, Richard. *A World of Others' Words: Cross-Cultural Perspectives on Intertextuality*. Malden, MA: Blackwell Publishing, 2004.

—. *Story, Performance and Event: Contextual Studies of Oral Narrative*. Cambridge: Cambridge University Press, 1986.

—. *Verbal Art as Performance*. Prospect Heights, IL: Waveland, 1977.

Beidelman, T. O. "The Moral Imagination of the Kaguru: Some Thoughts on Tricksters, Translation and Comparative Analysis." *American Ethnologist*, 7/1 (February, 1980), pp. 27–42.

Ben-Amos, Dan. "Introduction: Folklore in African Society." In Bernth Lindfors, ed. *Forms of Folklore in Africa: Narrative, Poetic, Gnomic, Dramatic*. Austin: University of Texas Press, 1977, pp. 1–36.

Briggs, Charles L. and Richard Bauman. "Genre, Intertextuality, and Social Power." *Journal of Linguistic Anthropology*, 2/2 (1992), pp. 131–172.

Burawoy, Michael. "Revisits: An Outline of a Theory of Reflexive Ethnography." *American Sociological Review*, 68 (October, 2003), pp. 645–679.

Butler, Judith. *Gender Trouble: Feminism and the Subversion of Identity*. New York: Routledge, 1990.

—. *Bodies That Matter: On the Discursive Limits of "Sex."* New York: Routledge, 1993.

Callaway, Henry. *Nursery Tales, Traditions, and Histories of the Zulu*. (1868) Reprint, Westport, CT: Negro Universities Press, 1970.

Cancel, Robert. "Broadcasting Oral Traditions: The 'Logic' of Narrative Variants – The Problem of 'Message.'" *African Studies Review* (Special Humanities Issue), 29/1 (1986), pp. 60–70.

—. "Three African Oral Narrative Versions: Text, Tradition and Performance." *The American Journal of Semiotics*, 6/1 (1988–89), pp. 85–109.

—. "Asserting/Inventing Traditions on the Luapula: The Lunda Mutomboko Festival." *African Arts*, 39/3 (2006), pp. 12–25 and 93.

—. "Festivals: Mutomboko Festival of the Lunda." In Philip M. Peek and Kwesi Yankah, eds. *African Folklore: An Encyclopedia*. London and New York: Routledge, 2004, pp. 123–125.

—. *'Inshimi' Structure and Theme: The Tabwa Oral Narrative Tradition*. PhD dissertation, University of Wisconsin, Madison, 1981.

—. *Allegorical Speculation in an Oral Society: The Tabwa Narrative Tradition*. Series in Modern Philology 122. Berkeley: University of California Press, 1989.

Carpentier, Alejo. *Los pasos perdidos*. Madrid: Alianza, 1999.

Chinyanta, Munona and Chileya J. Chiwale. *Mutomboko Ceremony and the Lunda-Kazembe Dynasty*. Lusaka: Kenneth Kaunda Foundation, 1989.

Chipungu, Samuel N., ed. *Guardians in Their Time: Experiences of Zambians Under Colonial Rule, 1890–1964*. London and Basingstoke: Macmillan, 1992.

Clifford, James and George E. Marcus, eds. *Writing Culture: The Poetics and Politics of Ethnography*. Berkeley, Los Angeles, London: Univesity of California Press, 1986.

Clifford, James. "Power and Dialogue in Ethnography: Marcel Griaule's Initiation." In George W. Stocking, ed. *Observers Observed: Essays on Ethnographic Fieldwork*. Madison, WI: University of Wisconsin Press, 1983, pp. 121–156.

Colson, Elizabeth and Thayer Scudder. *For Prayer and Profit: The Ritual, Economic, and Social Importance of Beer in Gwembe District, Zambia, 1950–1982*. Stanford: Stanford University Press, 1988.

—. *The Social Consequences of Resettlement*. Manchester: Manchester University Press, 1971.

—. *Marriage and the Family Among the Plateau Tonga*. Manchester: Manchester University Press, 1958.

Comaroff, Jean and John Comaroff. *Of Revelation and Revolution: Christianity, Colonialism, and Consciousness in South Africa*. Chicago and London: University of Chicago Press, 1991.

Corbeil, J.J. *Mbusa: Sacred Emblems of the Bemba*. London: Ethnographica, 1982.

Cosentino, Donald. *Defiant Maids and Stubborn Farmers: Tradition and Invention in Mende Story Performance*. Cambridge: Cambridge University Press, 1982.

Crehan, Kate. *The Fractured Community: Landscapes of Power and Gender in Rural Zambia*. Berkeley: University of California Press, 1997.

Creider, Cher A. "Interlanguage Comparisons in the Study of the Interactional Use of Gesture: Progress and Prospects." *Semiotica*, 62/1–2 (1986), pp. 147–163.

—. "Towards a Description of East African Gestures." *Sign Language Studies*, 14 (1997), pp. 1–20.

Cunnison, Ian G. *The Luapula Peoples of Northern Rhodesia: Custom and History in Tribal Politics*. Manchester: Manchester University Press, 1959.

—. translator and annotator. *Historical Traditions of the Eastern Lunda: A Translation of Ifikolwe Fyandi na Bantu Bandi by Mwata Kazembe XIV Chinyanta Nankula and Fr. E. Labrecque*. Rhodes-Livingstone Communications 23. Central Bantu Historical Texts II. Lusaka: The Rhodes-Livingstone Institute and Manchester University Press, 1961.

Deng, Francis Mading. *The Dinka of the Sudan*. New York: Holt, Rinehart and Winston, 1972.

Dégh, Linda. *Narratives in Society: A Performer-Centered Study of Narration*. Helsinki: Academia Scientiarum Fennica, 1995.

Derrida, Jacques. "Structure, Sign, and Play in the Discourse of the Human Sciences." In Jacques Derrida. *Writing and Difference*. Chicago: Unversity of Chicago Press, 1978, pp. 351–370.

Diouf, Mamadou. "Engagning Postcolonial Cultures: African Youth and Public Space." *African Studies Review*, 26/2 (September, 2003), pp. 1–12.

Doke, Clement M. *Lamba Folk-Lore*. (1927) Reprint, Millwood, NY: Kraus Reprint, 1976.

Dwyer, Kevin. *Moroccan Dialogues: Anthropology in Question*. Baltimore: Johns Hopkins University Press, 1982.

Eastman, Carol M. and Yahya Ali Omar. "Swahili Gestures: Comments (*vielezi*) and Exclamations (*viingizi*)." *Studies in African Linguistics*, 48/2 (1985), pp. 321–332.

Fabian, Johannes. "Review Symposium" on Harry West's *Ethnographic Sorcery*. *African Studies Review*, 51/3 (2008), pp. 135–38.

Finnegan, Ruth. *Oral Literature in Africa*. Cambridge: Open Book Publishers, 2012.

—. *The Oral and Beyond: Doing Things with Words in Africa*. Oxford, Chicago and Pietermaritzburg: J. Currey, University of Chicago Press, and University of KwaZulu-Natal Press, 2007.

—. "Oral Literature: Issues of Definition and Terminology." In Philip M. Peek and Kwesi Yankah, eds. *African Folklore: An Encyclopedia*. London and New York: Routledge, 2004, pp. 310–313.

—. *Oral Traditions and the Verbal Arts: A Guide to Research Practices*. London and New York: Routledge, 1992.

Freehling, Joel and Stuart A. Marks. "A Century of Change in the Central Luangwa Valley of Zambia." In E.J. Milner-Gulland and Ruth Mace, eds. *Conservation of Biological Resources*. Oxford: Blackwell Science, 1998, pp. 261–278.

Frost, Mary. *'Inshimi' and 'Imilumbe': Structural Expectations in Bemba Oral Imaginative Performances*. PhD dissertation, University of Wisconsin, Madison, 1978.

Garvey, Brian. *Bembaland Church: Religious and Social Change in South Central Africa 1891 to 1964*. Leiden: Brill, 1994.

Geertz, Clifford. "Thinking as a Moral Act: Ethical Dimensions of Anthropological Fieldwork in the New States." *Antioch Review*, 28 (1968), pp. 139–158.

—. "Deep Play: Notes on the Balinese Cock Fight." In Clifford Geertz, ed. *The Interpretation of Cultures*. New York: Basic Books, 1973, pp. 412–454.

Gibson, Clark C. "Killing Animals with Guns and Ballots: The Political Economy of Zambian Wildlife Policy, 1972–1982." *Environmental History Review*, 19/1, (Spring, 1995), pp. 49–75.

—. "Bureaucrats and the Environment in Africa." *Comparative Politics*, 31/3 (1999) pp. 273–294.

—. *Politicians and Poachers: The Political Economy of Wildlife Policy in Africa (Political Economy of Institutions and Decisions)*. Cambridge: Cambridge University Press, 1999.

—. and Stuart A. Marks. "Transforming Rural Hunters into Conservationists: An Assessment of Community-Based Wildlife Management." *World Development*, 23/6 (1995), pp. 941–958.

Goffman, Erving. *Frame Analysis*. New York: Harper and Row, 1974.

Goldberg, Jeffrey. "The Hunted." *The New Yorker*, (April 5, 2010), pp. 42–63.

Gordon, David M. "Rebellion or Massacre: The UNIP – Lumpa Conflict Revisited." In Jan-Bart Gewald, Marja Hinfelaar, and Giacomo Macola, eds. *One Zambia, Many Histories: Towards a History of Post-colonial Zambia*. Leiden and Boston: Brill, 2008, pp. 45–76.

—. *Nachituti's Gift: Economy, Society, and Environment in Central Africa*. Madison, WI: University of Wisconsin Press, 2006.

Griaule, Marcel. *Conversations with Ogotemmeli: An Introduction to Dogon Religious Ideas*. London: Oxford University Press, 1965.

Hall, Richard Seymour. *The High Price of Principles: Kaunda and the White South*. New York: Africana Publishing Corporation, 1970.

Haring, Lee. "Performing for the Interviewer: A Study of the Structure of Context." *Southern Folklore Quarterly*, 36 (1972), pp. 365–72.

—. *Malagasy Tale Index*. F.F. Communications, 231. Helsinki: Academia Scientiarum Fennica, 1982.

Herskovits, Melville J. and Frances S. Herskovits. *Dahomean Narrative: A Cross-Cultural Analysis*. Evanston, IL: Northwestern University Press, 1985.

Heusch, Luc de. *The Drunken King, or, the Origin of the State*. Translated and annotated by Roy Willis. Bloomington: Indiana University Press, 1982.

Huggan, Graham. "Anthropologists and Other Frauds." *Comparative Literature*, 46/2, (1994), pp. 113–29.

Hymes, Dell H. "Breakthrough Into Performance." In Dan Ben-Amos and Kenneth S. Goldstein, eds. *Folklore: Performance and Communication*. The Hague: Mouton, 1975, pp. 11–74.

—. *Ethnography, Linguistics and Narrative Inequality: Toward an Understanding of Voice*. London: Taylor and Francis, 1996.

—. *Foundations of Social Linguistics: An Ethnographic Approach*. Philadelphia: University of Pennsylvania Press, 1974.

—. "The Ethnography of Communication." *American Anthropologist*, 66 (1964), pp. 6–56.

Jackson, Michael. *The Politics of Storytelling: Violence, Transgression and Intersubjectivity*. Copenhagen: Museum Tusculanum Press, University of Copenhagen, 2006.

—. *Minima Ethnographica: Intersubjectivity and the Anthropological Project.* Chicago and London: University of Chicago Press, 1998.

—. *Paths Toward a Clearing: Radical Empiricism and Ethnographic Inquiry.* Bloomington: Indiana University Press, 1989.

—. *Allegories of the Wilderness: Ethics and Ambiguity in Kuranko Narratives.* Bloomington: Indiana University Press, 1982.

—. *Barawa and the Ways Birds Fly in the Sky.* Washington, D.C.: Smithsonian Institution Press, 1986.

—. *Existential Anthropology: Events, Exigencies and Effects.* New York and Oxford: Berghahn Books, 2005.

—. *In Sierra Leone.* Durham: Duke University Press, 2004.

Joubert, Annekie. *The Power of Performance: Linking Past and Present in Hananwa and Lobedu Oral Literature.* Berlin and New York: Mouton de Gruyter, 2004.

Kapchan, Deborah. "Performance." In Burt Feintuch, ed. *Eight Words for the Study of Expressive Culture.* Champaign/Urbana: University of Illinois Press, 2003, pp. 121–145.

Kashoki, Mubanga E. "Town Bemba: A Sketch of Its Main Characteristics." *African Social Research*, 13 (1972), pp. 161–186.

Kaunda, Kenneth D. *Zambia Shall Be Free: An Autobiography.* New York: Praeger, 1963.

Kenyatta, Jomo. *Facing Mount Kenya: The Tribal Life of the Gikuyu.* With an Introduction by Bronislaw Malinowski. London: Martin Secker & Warsurg, Ltd., 1938. Reprint, New York: Random House, 1965.

Kingsley, Judith. *Pre-colonial Society and Economy in a Bisa Chiefdom of Northern Zambia.* PhD dissertation, University of Michigan, 1980.

Klassen, Doreen Helen. *'You Can't Have Silence with Your Palms Up': Ideophones, Gesture and Iconicity in Zimbabwean Shona Women's ngano (Storysong) Performance.* PhD dissertation, Indiana University, 1999.

—. "Gestures in African Oral Narrative." In Philip M. Peek and Kwesi Yankah, eds. *African Folklore: An Encyclopedia.* London and New York: Routledge, 2004, pp. 149–151.

La Pin, Deirdre. "Tale and Trickster in Yoruba Verbal Art." *Research in African Literatures*, 11/3 (Fall, 1980), pp. 328–341.

Labov, William. *Language in the Inner City: Studies in Black English Vernacular.* Philadelphia: University of Pennsylvania Press, 1972.

Landau, Paul S. *The Realm of the Word: Language, Gender, and Christianity in a Southern African Kingdom.* London: J. Currey, 1995.

Lévi-Strauss, Claude. *The Raw and the Cooked.* Translated by John and Doreen Weightman. New York: Harper and Row, 1969.

Lightfoot, Cynthia. *The Culture of Adolescent Risk-Taking.* New York and London: The Guilford Press, 1997.

Lindfors, Bernth. *Forms of Folklore in Africa: Narrative, Poetic, Gnomic, Dramatic.* Austin: University of Texas Press, 1977.

Livingstone, David. *The Last Journals of David Livingstone*, H. Waller, ed. London: John Murray, 1874.

Lord, Albert. *The Singer of Tales*. Cambridge, MA: Harvard University Press, 1960.

Lukhero, M.B. *Ngoni Nc'wala Ceremony*. Lusaka: NECZAM, 1993.

Macola, Giacomo. "Literate Ethnohistory in Colonial Zambia: The Case of '*Ifikolwe Fyandi na Bantu Bandi*'." *History in Africa*, 28 (2001), pp. 187–201.

Magel, Emil. *Folktales of the Gambia*. Pueblo, CO: Passegiata Press, 1984.

Magubane, Bernard M. *African Sociology: Towards a Critical Perspective*. Asmara: Africa World Press, 2000.

Malinowski, Bronislaw. *A Diary in the Strict Sense of the Term*. New York: Harcourt, Brace & World, Inc., 1967.

Mapoma, I. Mwesa. '*Ingomba*': *The Royal Musicians of the Bemba People of Luapula Province in Zambia*. MA thesis, University of California, Los Angeles, 1974.

Marks, Stuart A. "Wildlife is Our Main Resource, Poverty and Hunger Our Biggest Problem: The Legacy of a Zambian Community-Based Wildlife Program." In B. Child and M. Lymann, eds. *Natural Resources as Community Assets: Lessons from Two Continents*. Madison, WI, and Washington: The Sand County Foundation and the Aspen Institute, 2004, pp. 181–209.

—. "Profile and Process: Subsistence Hunters in a Zambian Community." *Africa*, 41/1 (1979), pp. 53–68.

—. "The Bisa of Zambia's Luangwa Valley." In Robert Hitchcock and Alan Osborn, eds. *Endangered Peoples of Africa and the Middle East*. Westport, CT: Greenwood Publishing Group, 2000, pp. 64–78.

—. *On the Ground and in the Villages: A Cacophony of Voices Assessing a "Community-based" Wildlife Program After 18 Years*. Zambia: Mipashi Associates, 2008.

—. *Large Mammals and a Brave People: Subsistence Hunters in Zambia*. New Edition with a new introduction and afterword by the author. New Brunswick, NJ: Transaction Publishers, 2005.

—. *The Imperial Lion: Human Dimensions of Wildlife Management in Central Africa*. Boulder, CO: Westview Press, 1984.

Mbele, Joseph. *Matengo Folktales*. Bryn Mawr, PA: Buy Books on the Web.com, 1999.

McKenzie, Jon. "Genre Trouble: (The) Butler Did It." In Peggy Phelan and Jill Lane, eds. *The Ends of Performance*. New York and London: New York University Press, 1998, pp. 217–235.

Mills, Margaret. "The Gender of the Trick: Female Tricksters and Male Narrators." *Asian Folklore Studies*, 60 (2001), pp. 237–258.

Miner, William. "Body Rituals Among the Nacerima." *American Anthropologist* 58/3, (June,1956), pp. 503–507.

Molteno, Robert. "Hidden Sources of Subversion." In Ellen Ray, William Schaap, Karl Van Meter, and Louis Wolf, eds. *Dirty Work 2: The CIA in Africa*. Secaucus, NJ: Lyle Stuart, 1979, pp. 94–111.

Moore, Henrietta L. and Megan Vaughan. *Cutting Down Trees: Gender, Nutrition, and Agricultural Change in the Northern Province of Zambia 1890–1990*. Portsmouth, NH: Heinemann, 1994.

Morris, Brian. *The Power of Animals: An Ethnography*. Oxford, New York: Berg, 1998.

Mulenga, Shula and Bjorn Van Campenhout. "Decomposing Poverty Changes in Zambia: Growth, Inequality and Population Dynamics." *African Development Review/Review Africaine de Developpment*, 20/2 (September, 2008), pp. 273–283.

Musambachime, Mwelwa C. *Development and Growth of the Fishing Industry in Mweru-Luapula 1920–1964*. PhD Dissertation, University of Wisconsin, Madison, 1981.

—. *Changing Roles: The History of the Development and Disintegration of Nkuba's Shila State to 1740*. MA thesis, University of Wisconsin, Madison, 1976.

Mwata Kazembe XIV Chinyanta Nankula and Fr. E. Labrecque. *Ifikolwe Fyandi na Bantu Bandi [My Ancestors and My People]*. London: Macmillan and Publications Bureau, Lusaka, 1958.

Ngugi wa Thiong'o. *Homecoming: Essays on African and Caribbean Literature and Politics*. London, Ibadan and Nairobi: Heinemann Educational Books, 1972.

Nsugbe, P.O. *Ohaffia: A Matrilineal Ibo People*. Oxford: Oxford University Press, 1972.

Ocholla-Ayayo, A.B.C. *Traditional Ideology and Ethics Among the Southern Luo*. Uppsala, Sweden: The Nordic Africa Institute, 1976.

Ochs, Elinor and Lisa Capps. "Narrating the Self." *Annual Review of Anthropology*, 25 (1996), pp. 19–43.

Oger, Louis. "Where a Scattered Flock Gathered," Ilondola, 1934–1984: A Catholic Mission in a Protestant Area, (Free Church of Scotland) Chinsali District (Zambia). Ndola, Zambia: The Missionaries of Africa, 1991.

Okpewho, Isidore. *Myth in Africa*. Cambridge: Cambridge University Press, 1983.

—. "Towards a Faithful Record: On Transcribing and Translating the Oral Narrative Performance." In Isidore Okpewho, ed. *The Oral Performance in Africa*. Ibadan: Spectrum Books, 1990.

—. *African Oral Literature: Backgrounds, Character and Continuity*. Bloomington: Indiana University Press, 1992.

—. *The Epic in Africa: Toward a Poetics of the Oral Performance*. New York: Columbia University Press, 1979.

—. "Rethinking Myth." *African Literature Today*, 11 (1980), pp. 171–175.

Olofson, Harold. "Hausa Language about Gestures." *Anthropological Linguistics*, 16 (1974), pp. 25–39.

Ong, Walter. *Orality and Literacy: The Technologizing of the Word*. New York: Methuen, 1982.

Ouologuem, Yambo. *Bound to Violence*. Translated by Ralph Manheim. London: Heinemann Educational Books, 1973.

Owens, Mark James and Cordelia Dykes Owens. *The Eye of the Elephant: An Epic Adventure in the African Wilderness*. New York: Mariner Books, 1993.

Owomoyela, Oyekan. *Yoruba Trickster Tales*. Lincoln and London: University of Nebraska Press, 1997.

—. "Tricksters in African Folklore." In Philip M. Peek and Kwesi Yankah, *African Folkore: An Encyclopedia*. London and New York: Routledge, 2004, pp. 476–477.

Pelton, Robert D. *The Trickster in West Africa: A Study of Mythic Irony and Sacred Delight*. Berkeley, Los Angeles and London: University of California Press, 1980.

Pottier, Johan. *Migrants No More: Settlement and Survival in Mambwe Villages, Zambia*. Bloomington: Indiana University Press, 1989.

Price, Richard and Sally Price. *Two Evenings in Saramaka*. Chicago and London: University of Chicago Press, 1991.

Propp, Vladimir. *Morphology of the Folktale*. Translated by Laurence Scott. Austin: University of Texas Press, 1968.

Rabinow, Paul, *Reflections on Fieldwork in Morocco*. Berkeley, Los Angeles and London: University of California Press, 1977.

Radin, Paul. *The Trickster: A Study in American Indian Mythology. With Commentaries by Karl Karényi and C.G. Jung*. New York: Philosophical Library, 1956.

Richards, Audrey I. *Chisungu: A Girls' Initiation Ceremony among the Bemba of Zambia*. Introduction by Jean La Fontaine. London and New York: Routledge, 1988.

—. *Land, Labour and Diet: An Economic Study of the Bemba Tribe*. London: Oxford University Press, 1939.

Roberts, Allen F. *Animals in African Art: From the Familiar to the Marvelous*. New York: Prestel, 1997.

—. "Difficult Decisions and Perilous Acts: Producing Potent Histories with the Tabwa Boiling Water Oracle." In J. Permbertion III, ed. *Insight and Artistry: A Crosscultural Study of Divination in Central and West Africa*. Washington: Smithsonian Institute Press, 2000, pp. 83–98.

—. "'Like a Roaring Lion': Late 19th Century Tabwa Terrorism." In Donald Crummey, ed. *Banditry, Rebellion and Social Protest in Africa*. Portsmouth, NH: Heinemann Books, 1986, pp. 65–86.

—. *Heroic Beasts, Beastly Heroes: Principles of Cosmology and Chiefship Among the Lakeside BaTabwa of Zaire*. PhD dissertation, University of Chicago, 1980.

—. "'Fishers of Men': Religion and Political Economy Among Colonized Tabwa." *Africa*, 54/2 (1984), pp. 49–70.

—. "Anarchy, Abjection and Absurdity: A Case of Metaphoric Medicine Among the Tabwa of Zaire." In L. Romanucci-Ross, D. Moerman and L. Tancredi, eds. *The Anthropology of Medicine: From Theory to Method*. 3rd edition. New York and Amherst: Bergin for Praeger Scientific, 1996. pp. 224–239.

Roberts, Andrew D. *A History of the Bemba: Political Growth and Change in Northeastern Zambia before 1900*. London: Longmans, 1973.

—. *The Lumpa Church of Alice Lenshina*. Lusaka: Oxford University Press, 1972.

Rose, Tricia. *Black Noise: Rap and Black Culture in Contemporary America*. Hanover, NH: University Press of New England, 1994.

Sawin, Patricia E. "Performance at the Nexus of Gender, Power and Desire: Reconsidering Bauman's Verbal Art from the Perspective of Gendered Subjectivity as Performance." *Journal of American Folklore*, 115/455 (2002), pp. 28–61.

Schapera, Isaac. *The Tswana*. London: International African Institute, 1953.

Schechner, Richard. *Performance Theory*. London and New York: Routledge, 2003.

Scheub, Harold. "Translation of Oral Narrative-performance to the Written Word." *Yearbook of Comparative and General Literature*, 20 (1971), pp. 28–36.

—. *The Xhosa Ntsomi*. Oxford: Oxford University Press, 1975.

Schumaker, Lyn. *Africanizing Anthropology: Fieldwork, Networks, and the Making of Cultural Knowledge in Central Africa*. Durham and London: Duke University Press, 2001.

Scollon, Ronald and Suzanne B. K. Scollon, *Linguistic Convergence: An Ethnography of Speaking at Ft. Chipewyan, Alberta*. New York: Academic Press, 1979.

Seitel, Peter. *See So That We May See: Performances and Interpretations of Traditional Tales from Tanzania*. Bloomington: Indiana University Press, 1980.

Shuman, Amy. *Other People's Stories: Entitlement Claims and the Critique of Empathy*. Urbana and Chicago: University of Illinois Press, 2005.

—. *Storytelling Rights: The Uses of Oral and Written Texts by Urban Adolescents*. Cambridge: Cambridge University Press, 1986.

Sichone, Owen. "Review of 'Expectations of Modernity'." *Journal of Southern African Studies* (Special Issue on Fertility in Southern Africa), 27/2 (June, 2001), pp. 369–379.

Snow, David A. and Calvin Morrill, "Reflections on Anthropology's Ethnographic Crisis of Faith" *Contemporary Sociology*, 22/1 (1993), pp. 8–11.

Spitulnik, Debra. "The Language of the City: Town Bemba as Urban Hybridity." *Journal of Linguistic Anthropology*, 8/2 (1998), pp. 30–59.

Stocking, George W. Jr., ed. *Observers Observed: Essays on Ethnographic Fieldwork*. Madison, WI: University of Wisconsin Press, 1983.

Stoller, Paul. *Fusion of the Worlds: An Ethnography of Possession among the Songhay of Niger*. Chicago and London: University of Chicago Press, 1989.

Tannen, Deborah, ed. *Spoken and Written Language: Exploring Orality and Literacy*. Norwood, NJ: ABLEX Publishing, 1982.

Tedlock, Dennis. "Interpretation, Participation, and the Role of Narrative in Dialogical Anthropology." In Dennis Tedlock and Bruce Mannheim, eds. *The Dialogic Emergence of Culture*. Urbana and Chicago: University of Illinois Press, 1995, pp. 253–288.

—. "Toward an Oral Poetics." *New Literary History*, 8/3 (1977), pp. 507–520.

Theal, George McCall. *Kaffir Folk-lore*. Reprint, Westport, CT: Negro Universities Press, 1970.

Thompson, Stith. "Myth and Folktales." In Thomas Sebeok, ed. *Myth: A Symposium*. Bloomington: University of Indiana Press, 1958, pp. 104–110.

Titon, Jeff Todd. "Text." In Bruce Feintuch, ed. *Eight Words for the Study of Expressive Culture*. Champaign/Urbana: University of Illinois Press, 2003, pp. 69–98.

Turner, Victor W. *The Forest of Symbols: Aspects of Ndembu Ritual*. Ithaca, NY: Cornell University Press, 1967.

Vail, Leroy and Landeg White. *Power and the Praise Poem in Southern Africa*. Charlottesville: University Press of Virginia, 1992.

—, ed. *The Creation of Tribalism in Southern Africa*. London and Berkeley: J. Currey and University of California Press, 1989.

van Binsbergen, Wim M.J. *Religious Change in Africa: Exploratory Studies*. London and Boston: Kegan Paul International, 1981.

van Meijl, Toon. "The Critical Ethnographer as Trickster." *Anthropological Forum*, 15/3 (November, 2005), pp. 235–245.

Vansina, Jan. *De la tradition orale*. Tervuren: Musée Royal de l'Afrique Central, 1961.

—. *Kingdoms of the Savanna*. Madison, WI: University of Wisconsin Press, 1966.

—. *Oral History as Tradition*. Madison, WI: University of Wisconsin Press, 1985.

Vaughan, Meagan. "Anthropology and History: Audrey Richards and the Representation of Gender Relations in Northern Rhodesia." *African Studies Seminar Paper*, 309 (1992).

Ward, Simon. "The End of Fortress Conservation?" *The Southern Africa Trumpet*, 2 (June, 1997).

Watson, A. Blair. "The Occupation of Kilwa Island." *Northern Rhodesia Journal*, 3 (1957), pp. 70–74.

Watson, William. *Tribal Cohesion in a Money Economy: A Study of the Mambwe People of Zambia*. Manchester: Manchester University Press, 1958.

Webber, Sabra J. *Romancing the Real: Folklore and Ethnographic Representation in North Africa*. Philadelphia: University of Pennsylvania Press, 1991.

Wendt, Albert. *Flying-Fox in a Freedom Tree and Other Stories*. Honolulu: University of Hawaii Press, 1999.

Wessels, Michael. "The Universal and the Local: the Trickster and the /Xam Narratives." *English in Africa*, 35/2 (October, 2008), pp. 7–35.

West, Harry G. *Ethnographic Sorcery*. Chicago and London: University of Chicago Press, 2007.

White Father's Bemba – English Dictionary. Society of the Missionary [sic] for Africa, Zambia. Ndola, Zambia: Mission Press, 1991.

Wilson, Michael. *Performance and Practice: Oral Narrative Traditions Among Teenagers in Britain and Ireland*. Aldershot, UK: Ashgate Publishing Limited, 1997.

Yai, Olabiyi Babalola. "The Path is Open: The Legacy of Melville and Frances Herskovits in African Oral Narrative Analysis." *Research in African Literatures*, 30/2 (Summer, 1999), pp. 1–16.

Index

Achebe, Chinua 8
Anderson, Benedict 28
Arendt, Hannah 252

Babcock-Abrahams, Barbara 257
Banda, Mr. 213, 238
Barber, Karin and Farais, P.F. de Moraes 41, 42
Bauman, Richard 14, 36, 55, 80, 87, 106
Bemba 11, 18, 19, 26, 43, 47, 50, 55, 75-122, 140, 142, 166, 173, 181, 188, 197, 201, 206, 224, 244, 248, 249, 250
  language 9, 16, 18, 25, 26, 27, 35, 56, 85, 106, 123, 176, 188, 249, 257
  people 16, 17, 23, 26, 65, 75, 93, 102, 105, 120, 187, 193, 253, 256
Ben-Amos, Dan 39
Bisa 17, 23, 25, 26, 27, 30, 56, 60, 73, 100, 123-164, 169, 197, 212, 250, 253, 254, 256
Botswana 95
Briggs, Charles 80, 106
Burawoy, Michael 6
Butler, Judith 37-38
Bwalya, Evans ix, 118-119
Bwalya, Peter (storyteller) 196-198
Bwile 23, 26, 27, 30, 100, 152, 211-246, 253, 254

Callaway, Henry 79
cantefable 80
Carpentier, Alejo 24
Chakobe, Henry (storyteller) 55, 56, 111, 114-120, 256, 257
Chama, Elizabeth (storyteller) 84-87
Chandalube, Paul (storyteller) 152-155, 169, 256

Chansa, Ferry 241
Chilengwe, Chola 44
Chinsali 72, 109, 116, 120
Chipalo, Stephen Chanda (storyteller) 56, 110-113, 117-121
Chipungu, Samuel N. 9
Chitimukulu, Paramount Chief 9, 17, 22, 23, 62-64, 76, 85, 96, 102, 120, 128, 188
Chitompwe, Bernard 19-20
Chiwale, Chleya J. 8-9, 206
Chola, Rabbon ix, 60
Clifford, James 3, 4, 7, 25, 40
Colson, Elizabeth and Scudder, Thayer 25
Comaroff, Jean and Comaroff, John 87
Corbeil, J.J. 189
Cosentino, Donald 42
Crehan, Kate 26
Creider, Cher A. 41
Cunnison, Ian 8, 27, 166, 200, 206, 207, 211

Dark Benediction. *See* Miller
decontextualization 87
Dégh, Linda 33
de Heusch, Luc 251
Democratic Republic of the Congo 26, 43, 165, 208, 211, 212, 217, 251
Deng, Francis Mading 9
Derrida, Jacques 42
Diouf, Mamadou 59, 70
Doke, Clement M. 65, 66, 100
Dupont, Bishop 86
Dwyer, Kevin 15

Eastman, Carol M. and Omar, Yahya Ali 41

Elizabeth (storyteIlller) 80-84, 86, 121, 187, 197, 255
ethnographic
  authority 1, 2, 42, 71
  deal-making 33
  liberalism 3
existentialism 5, 37

Fabian, Johannes 2
Fele (Stephen Komakoma) ix, 76-77, 84, 85-86, 87-88, 90-92, 93, 97, 102-108, 121-122
Finnegan, Ruth 80
folklore 2, 31, 39, 41, 188

Garvey, Brian 87
Geertz, Clifford 3, 4, 6, 7, 14, 30, 35
Genelot, Michel 110
Gluckman, Max 10
Goffman, Erving 36
Gordon, David 57, 110, 166
Griaule, Marcel 3, 4, 25, 40, 251

Hall, Richard 110
Haring, Lee 33, 39, 55
Herskovits, Melville J. and Herskovits, Frances S. 40
hikayat 35
Huggan, Graham 24
Humanism 104, 105
Hymes, Dell 14, 36

Ilondola 23, 56, 109, 118, 121
Indita, Fermit (storyteller) 152, 218-223, 254
ing'omba 20
Institute for African Studies 9, 10, 11
intersubjectivity 6, 10, 35
ishingilili 19
Iyambe, George (storyteller) 146, 147-152, 158, 254

Jackson, Michael 1, 4, 5, 6, 14, 24, 25, 42, 60, 247, 251, 252
Joubert, Annekie 34

Kachela, Timothy (storyteller) 228-233, 254
Kachingwe, Job 208
Kafankwa, Fred (storyteller) 224-228
Kafimbwa, Anthony 166
Kalulu, the trickster hare 47, 50, 54, 55, 89, 92, 102, 112, 113, 114, 117, 152, 154, 167, 168, 169, 170, 171, 172, 176, 178, 179, 187, 233, 253, 256, 257, 258
Kalumba, Stanley (storyteller) 31, 40, 42-43, 44-50, 53, 54, 55, 57, 58, 70, 71, 178
Kalunga, S.M. 76
Kampamba, Dismas 77, 107, 255
Kampamba, Elvis 138, 160
Kangwa, Densa (storyteller) 93-95, 107-109
Kaoma, Paola (storyteller) 202-207, 208
Kapchan, Deborah 34, 37, 54
Kapongwe, Samson (storyteller) 233-239
Kaputa
  Chief 12
  District 57, 166
  District, capital 43
  Village 44, 47, 62, 65
Kasama 13, 17, 20, 23, 57, 62, 76, 107, 129, 160, 214, 243
Kashiba Village 155, 166, 167, 190, 207
Kashoki, Mubanga 249
katubi 18, 139, 169
Kaunda, Kenneth David 22, 28, 70, 104, 110, 128
Kawambwa 194, 202, 203, 209
Kazembe, Mwata
  Chinyanta, Nankula XIV 206
  Munona Chinyanta XVIII 9
Kelibian 36
Kenyatta, Jomo 3, 8
kgotla 95
Klassen, Doreen Helen 41
Kola, origin place of Bemba-speaking polities 27, 214
Kombe, Luva (storyteller) 182-191, 255
Koti, T.D. (storyteller) 241-243
Kuranko 4, 5

Labov, William 14, 53, 54
Lake Mweru 57, 166, 211, 212, 240
Lake Mweru Wantipa 57, 58, 71
Lamba
  people 65, 66
  stories 65, 79, 100
Landau, Paul 95
La Pin, Dierdre 169
Lebrecque, Edouard 9
Lenshina, Alice 110

Lèvi-Strauss, Claude 6, 251
Lightfoot, Cynthia 67
Lindfors, Bernth 39
Livingstone, David 66, 212
Lord, Albert 201
Luangwa, game park 27, 123, 125, 127, 143, 146, 158, 212
Luapula 8, 16, 23, 27, 28, 57, 165, 166, 181, 202, 206, 207, 211, 242
Luba 26, 27, 76, 85, 103, 201
Lubwa, mission 87, 110
Lukhero, Matshakaza Blackson 1, 9
Lumpa Church 110
Lunda 8, 17, 24, 26, 27, 28, 30, 55, 65, 77, 101, 107, 121, 155, 165-210, 211, 214, 215, 241, 242, 244, 253, 255

Macolak, Giacomo 207
Magel, Emil 44
Magubane, Bernard M. 9
Malawi 50
Malinowski, Bronislaw 2, 3, 4, 6, 8, 10
Malole Village 13, 17, 20, 75, 76, 99, 100, 102, 106, 107, 113, 116, 142, 187, 250
Mapoma, I. Mwesa x, 19
märchenstock 40
Marks, Stuart A. 25, 73, 126, 127, 135, 158, 161, 163, 250
Mbele, Joseph 222
Mbereshi 77, 166, 189, 191, 198, 202, 208, 209, 213
McKenzie, Jon 37, 38
Meijl, Toon van 54
Misenga, Chipolobwe Mwadya (Mano) (storyteller) 198-202, 205-206
Molteno, Robert 11
mondo 166, 201
Moore, Henrietta and Vaughan, Megan 11
Morris, Brian 126
Movement for Multiparty Democracy 28
Mpika 110, 118, 129, 139, 157, 160, 163
Mporokoso 57, 62, 66, 69, 103, 235
Mukupa Katandula ix, xi, 12, 44, 58-60, 65, 70, 71-72, 140, 145, 215
Mulenga, Moffat (storyteller) 155, 160-174, 175, 180, 181, 189, 190, 191, 253, 256
Mulenga, Shula and van Campenhout, Bjorn 248

Muleya, Emeliya (storyteller) 101, 191, 192-196, 206 208
mulumbe 50, 68, 77, 88, 90, 111, 112, 113, 116, 123, 130, 132, 135, 136, 138, 146, 155, 156, 157, 169, 170, 172, 175, 178, 179, 181, 187, 196, 197, 202, 204, 205, 207, 235, 237
Mununga 57, 243
Munyamadzi Corridor 123
Musambachime, Mwelwa C. x
Mutale, Peter (storyteller) 88, 108, 113, 117, 257
Mutomboko (kingship festival) 9, 28, 207
Mwamba, Chief 76, 86, 103
Mwampatisha, George (storyteller) 100, 140-144, 161, 162
Mwansabombwe 199, 208, 209
Mwenya, Falace 60-61, 72

Nabwalya 6, 25, 101, 123
Nabwalya, Kabuswe C. (storyteller) 123, 155, 156-160, 161, 254
Nc'wala (kingship rite) 9
Ndalazi, Laudon (storyteller) 56, 130-138, 155, 197, 254
Négritude 8
Ngalande, P. 191, 206
Ng'andu, L.M. 17, 76, 128
Ng'andwe, Samuel 9, 166-167
Ngoni (people) 9, 87, 103-104
Ngugi wa Thiong'o 3, 4
Nkula, Chief 23, 76, 87, 103, 109, 110, 116, 118, 121
Northern Province, Zambia xi, 11, 13, 26, 47, 72, 75, 76, 109, 123, 129, 160
Nsama 12, 44, 53, 58, 66, 160
nshimi 27, 88, 130
  lushimi, singular 75, 80, 88, 133, 151, 187, 191, 228, 232
Nsugbe, Philip O. 9
Nyerere, Julius 105

Ocholla-Ayayo, A.B.C. 9
Ochs, Elinor and Capps, Lisa 36
Office of the President 213
Oger, Louis 109
Okpewho, Isidore 26, 38, 40
Olofson, Harold 41
Ong, Walter 201
oral text 41, 42, 87. *See also* verbal text

Ouologuem, Yambo 7, 8, 24
Paimolo, Lenox (storyteller) 144-147, 197, 253
Pandwe, Idon (storyteller) 173, 174-182, 187, 190, 253, 256, 257
Patrick, Chipioka (storyteller) 61-63, 64, 65-73, 166, 197, 255
Pelton, Robert D. 258
performance context 2, 16, 21, 36, 38, 40, 41, 54, 55, 66, 135, 165, 238
performance studies 2, 36, 41
Pottier, Johan 11
Price, Richard and Sally 34
Puta, Chief 9, 23, 102, 206, 211-213, 221, 223, 233, 238, 239, 240-241, 242, 253
  storyteller 214-218, 243-245

Rabinow, Paul 11
Radcliffe-Brown, A.R. 10
Radin, Paul 257
recontextualization 6, 11, 87
reflexivity, reflexive methodology 4, 6, 16, 25, 34, 35, 42, 211
Rhodes-Livingstone Institute 9, 10
Richards, Audrey 10, 11, 76, 188, 270
Roberts, Allen F. 43, 218, 251
Roberts, Andrew D. 27, 66, 76, 87, 110, 166
Rose, Tricia 67

Samson, Kangwa (storyteller) 101, 132, 139, 140, 142, 146, 157, 160, 162-164
Sawin, Patricia 189
Schechner, Richard 21, 36, 37, 252
Scheub, Harold E. 39, 40
Schumaker, Lyn 1
Scollon, Ronald and Scollon, Suzanne B.K. 14
Sédar Senghor, Leopold 8
Seitel, Peter 40
sensele 19
Shapera, Isaac 95
Shila 244
Shuman, Amy 14, 67
Sichone, Owen 9, 56, 247, 248
Sierra Leone 4, 42, 60

Snow, David A. and Morrill, Calvin 34
Soolo, Katongo (storyteller) 75, 95, 96-102, 142
Spitulnik, Debra 249
St. Francis Secondary School 13, 17, 76, 109
Stocking, Jr., George W. 4
Stoller, Paul 25
Sungura, East African trickster 50, 258
Swahili 50, 136

Tabwa 1, 3, 11, 12, 13, 14, 16, 22, 26, 27, 30, 31-74, 79, 80, 88, 95, 100, 140, 160, 166, 173, 176, 178, 186, 189, 197, 205, 213, 222, 224, 230, 251, 253, 255
Tannen, Deborah 14
Tedlock, Dennis 15, 40
Theal, George McCall 80
Thompson, Stith 39
Titon, Jeff Todd 15, 31, 34, 35
traditional context 30, 36, 40, 41, 52, 53, 65, 100, 206, 249, 250, 254
Tunisia 35
Turner, Victor W. 37, 251

Ujamaa 105
United National Independence Party (UNIP) 128

Vansina, Jan 38, 270
verbal text 40, 41. See also oral text

Watson, A. Blair 212
Watson, William 11, 56, 270
Webber, Sabra J. 35
Wessels, Michael 258, 270
West, Harry G. 24, 54, 56, 218
White Fathers order
  (now "Missionaries of Africa") 12, 86, 206, 270
Wilson, Godfrey 10
Wilson, Michael 67, 270

Yai, Olabiyi 31, 41
Yuba, Ng'ongo (also Kangwa Kabunda) 19, 20, 23, 102

This book does not end here...

At Open Book Publishers, we are changing the nature of the traditional academic book. The title you have just read will not be left on a library shelf, but will be accessed online by hundreds of readers each month across the globe. We make all our books free to read online so that students, researchers and members of the public who can't afford a printed edition can still have access to the same ideas as you. Our digital publishing model also allows us to produce online supplementary material, including extra chapters, reviews, links and other digital resources. Find *Storytelling in Northern Zambia* on our website to access its online extras. Please check this page regularly for ongoing updates, and join the conversation by leaving your own comments:

http://www.openbookpublishers.com/isbn/9781909254596

If you enjoyed this book, and feel that research like this should be available to all readers, regardless of their income, please think about donating to us. Our company is run entirely by academics, and our publishing decisions are based on intellectual merit and public value rather than on commercial viability. We do not operate for profit and all donations, as with all other revenue we generate, will be used to finance new Open Access publications. For further information about what we do, how to donate to OBP, additional digital material related to our titles or to order our books, please visit our website: www.openbookpublishers.com

The World Oral Literature Project is an urgent global initiative to document and disseminate endangered oral literatures before they disappear without record. Our website houses collections of recordings of oral literature, free-to-download publications of documentation theory and practice, and links to resources and funding for oral tradition fieldwork and archiving: www.oralliterature.org

In partnership with Open Book Publishers, the World Oral Literature Project has launched a book series on oral literature. The series preserves and promotes the oral literatures of indigenous people by publishing materials on endangered traditions in innovative ways.

www.ingramcontent.com/pod-product-compliance
Ingram Content Group UK Ltd.
Pitfield, Milton Keynes, MK11 3LW, UK
UKHW021317180426
11947UKWH00015B/1285